THE BEATLES'

—THE LONG & WINDING ROAD—
A HISTORY OF THE BEATLES ON RECORD

Neville Stannard

Edited by John Tobler

 AVON
PUBLISHERS OF BARD, CAMELOT, DISCUS AND FLARE BOOKS

AVON BOOKS
A division of
The Hearst Corporation
1790 Broadway
New York, New York 10019

Copyright © 1982 by Neville Stannard
Published by arrangement with Virgin Books
Library of Congress Catalog Card Number: 83-45915
ISBN: 0-380-85704-9

First Avon Printing, February 1984

AVON TRADEMARK REG. U. S. PAT. OFF. AND IN
OTHER COUNTRIES, MARCA REGISTRADA, HECHO EN
U. S. A.

Printed in the U. S. A.

DON 10 9 8 7 6 5 4 3 2 1

CONTENTS

See 'Beatles Box Single Collection', page 119.

The following music papers were researched for recording information and record sales:
New Musical Express
Melody Maker
Disc
Record Mirror
Sounds

The following record sales charts were used for chart positions and statistics:
New Musical Express (British Beatles records)
Billboard (American Beatles records)
Music Week/British Market Research Bureau/BBC (other artists' hits and British Beatles records)

Apple Records,
ATV Music,
Autofidelity Enterprises (UK) Ltd.,
Billboard Ltd.,
Capitol Records Inc.,
Charly Records Ltd.,
EMI Records (for Harvest, Music For Pleasure &
Parlophone)
Everest Records UK Ltd.,
Goughsound Ltd.,
K-tel International (UK) Ltd.,
Mobile Fidelity Sound Lab.,
New Musical Express,
Northern Songs Ltd.,
Phonogram,
Pickwick International Inc.,
Polydor Records Ltd.,
PRT Ltd.,
Silhouette Music,
World Records Ltd.

Chart information © Music Week/BBC/Gallup

The author wishes to express his gratitude to the
following: Phil & Cally, Brian Southall, James Devereux,
Herbert A. Belkin, Ron Winter, Denise Jerome, Peter
Wilkinson, Robin Taylor, Jean Luc Young, Len Leonards,
Christopher L. Robinson, Colin Tyler, Ron Braddick,
Simon Dormer and George L. Allen.

PREFACE

The reaction to the first edition of this book was so positive that it quickly became obvious that an updated and corrected version would be desirable, both to reflect the continuing story of The Beatles as the third decade of Beatles records begins, and to clarify or otherwise correct errors of omission and commission which unfortunately crept into the first edition. My own role in this edition has scarcely been more than in the original — Neville has provided the overwhelming majority of the facts, and I have assisted where possible in clarification and correction. Both Neville and I hope that this edition will prove even more satisfying than its predecessor, and would like to offer grateful thanks to the following for making our task simpler and more pleasant: Robert Devereux, John Brown, Catherine Ledger, Catherine Cardwell and John Sibley.

John Tobler
May 1983

PREFACE TO THE FIRST EDITION

The first time I ever saw (or heard of) The Beatles was when they appeared on *Thank Your Lucky Stars* singing *Please Please Me*, long before I became truly interested in music. My two elder sisters used to buy records during the late Fifties and early Sixties, and I can thus remember many early hits by artists like Cliff Richard, Tommy Steele, Elvis Presley, The Shadows, etc. During my Secondary Modern school days, I enjoyed all of the "pop" groups of the Sixties, The Beatles were always my favourite group. It wasn't until I started working in 1967, that I was able to buy records, and my first purchase was *Peak-a-boo* by the New Vaudeville Band. Then in February, 1967, I bought my first Beatles' record, *Penny Lane/Strawberry Fields Forever* (which must be the greatest single ever produced), since which time I have been an ardent Beatles' fan, collecting every record they have released in Britain as a group and as soloists.

There have been many discographies published dealing with the Beatles' records, but I have been waiting for many years for one to be published that would tell me everything I could want to know about each Beatles' record and song; who wrote each song, why, how and when each song was written; how, when and where each song was recorded; how many copies has each record sold and how well each did in the charts? I found a great many of the answers to these questions, but they were all in different books and publications, so about five years ago I decided that I would compile a discography on The Beatles' records, that would answer as many of the above questions as possible. I originally compiled the book in about 1973, but later started to re-write it, getting halfway through and giving up. At the beginning of 1977 I started to re-write it again, changing the format and updating as many of the entries as possible, and at the beginning of 1978, I again changed the format and updated a few entries, and added the appendices. Although the factual content of the book is far from complete, I feel that it is the most informative and complete Beatles discography ever compiled.

Neville Stannard
January 1982

The Beatles as nature intended.

"Get Back" is the Beatles new single. It's the first Beatles record which is as live as can be, in this electronic age.

There's no electronic watchamacallit.

"Get Back" is a pure spring-time rock number.

On the other side there's an equally live number called "Don't let me down".

Paul's got this to say about Get Back… "we were sitting in the studio and we made it up out of thin air…we started to write words there and then…

when we finished it, we recorded it at Apple Studios and made it into a song to roller-coast by".

P.S. John adds, It's John playing the fab live guitar solo.

And now John on Don't let me down. John says don't let me down about "Don't let me down".

In "Get Back" and "Don't let me down", you'll find the Beatles, as nature intended.

Get Back/Don't let me down (Parlophone 5777)

 **EMI /Apple Records**

BRITISH SECTION

The main part of this book is divided into two sections, the British Section (pp. 11—**123**) and the American Section (pp. **125—170**). In the British Section, I have listed all records in chronological order giving each, except compilation albums, a "Record Number" (which is on the left at the start of each entry). Below the record title is the catalogue number with the date of release, and where a song reappears on other records, the song number receives a suffix letter, i.e. a song's first reappearance is indicated by suffix letter "a", its second by "b", etc. Therefore the first appearance of a song is indicated by its song number without a suffix.

Each entry is laid out as follows: the first part deals with the record's chart achievements and sales. The second part deals with recording details and any sleeve design notes and other information relating to the record. Each song is then dealt with separately, with the "A" side song (or songs for EP's and albums taken in same order as on the record) appearing first, followed by the "B" side. Any details concerning recordings of songs by other artists come at the end of the entry for that particular song.

Following the song title, the timing for each song is given in brackets; these are my own timings and therefore may not be exact. Where a song reappears, the reference for the original entry is given.

In this section I have only dealt with records released on the Parlophone and Apple labels, and not with other recordings.

1a **LOVE ME DO** *(2.21)* (RED LABEL) **P.S. I LOVE YOU** *(1.59)*	

R 4949—October 5, 1962

The Beatles' first single entered the charts on October 24 at No. 27, and immediately dropped out, thus being in the Top 30 for one week only. After American release in April 1964, the single achieved a million global sales and sold 100,000 in Britain.

1 **LOVE ME DO** (first version)

Paul played truant from school to write this song with John, who contributed the middle eight, while Paul wrote the greater portion.

This first version of the song was recorded on Tuesday, September 4, 1962, at the group's first Parlophone session at EMI's No. 2 studio in their St John's Wood studio complex. The Beatles spent most of the day rehearsing six numbers, with *Love Me Do* and *P.S. I Love You* being recorded in the evening. Seventeen takes were needed before George Martin was satisfied with *Love Me Do*, and he also decided that, as he was uncertain of Ringo's ability as a drummer, he would bring in a session drummer, Andy White, for the second recording session on September 11, a week later. At this session, *Love Me Do* was re-recorded with White on drums and Ringo playing tambourine, while *P.S. I Love You* was also re-recorded with White drumming and with Ringo on maracas.

The earlier, September 4, recording of *Love Me Do* was initially released as the Beatles first Parlophone single, with a red label, but following the inclusion of the September 11 recording of the song on the *Please Please Me* album, this later version replaced the earlier one as a single and was released on the black Parlophone label. (See following record and also page 000 for re-entry details of *Love Me Do*.)

The two versions are of slightly differing lengths, the most significant audible difference being the addition of tambourine, courtesy of the demoted Beatle drummer, on the second version. Paul and John share lead vocals with George as backing singer and John plays harmonica. The recording was made on single track tape, and therefore no true stereo version of the song exists.

2 **P.S. I LOVE YOU**

Written mainly by Paul but with John assisting with some of the lyrics. Paul sings lead, with John and George supplying background vocals. Andy White plays drums, with Ringo playing maracas. (See *Love Me Do* for full story.)

1b **LOVE ME DO** *(2.18)* (BLACK LABEL) **P.S. I LOVE YOU** *(1.59)*	

R 4949—approx. April 1963

This is the second pressing of the *Love Me Do* single, which was introduced following the decision to include the second (September 11) recording of *Love Me Do* on the *Please Please Me* album. The two pressings, although having the same catalogue number, have different coloured labels, the first being red with silver lettering and the second having a black background but with re-styled silver lettering. The "B" side of both singles is the same version of *P.S. I Love You*.

10 **LOVE ME DO** (second version)

(See *Love Me Do* first version above.)

2 **P.S. I LOVE YOU**

2 **PLEASE PLEASE ME** *(1.58)* **ASK ME WHY** *(2.22)*	

R 4983—January 11, 1963

The second single from The Beatles entered the charts on January 30, 1963 at No. 17, and went to No. 1 three weeks later on February 22. It was at No. 1 for two weeks, in the Top 10 for eight weeks and the Top 30 for eleven weeks. It sold 310,000 in Britain, thus receiving a Silver Disc, and with American sales of a million, world sales amount to over 1.5 million. It should be noted that, in some charts, this single failed to reach No. 1, peaking at No. 2.

This single, as with *Love Me Do*, was initially released on the red Parlophone label, but was later replaced by the more common black label.

3 **PLEASE PLEASE ME**

Written by John, who sings lead with Paul and George joining him for harmony. The song was recorded on November 26, 1962, and was originally considered and nearly used as the "B" side of *Love Me Do*. During the *Love Me Do* recording session, the group played *Please Please Me* for consideration as its "B" side to George Martin, but he was unhappy with the song's arrangement, and suggested doing another song instead, which would leave *Please Please Me* for a later date, when he hoped they could improve on it.

Please Please Me also reached the Top 30 in 1974, when David Cassidy's version entered the charts at No. 25 on July 30, remaining in the list for four weeks and peaking at No. 18. Cassidy scored nine British hits between April 1972 and the end of 1975, including chart toppers with *How Can I Be Sure* and *Daydreamer/The Puppy Song*, while he also made the chart with five other hits between 1971 and 1973 as the featured singer of The Partridge Family. The "Family" were created to star in a television series, in which the "heart-throb" lead part of Keith Partridge was played by David Cassidy.

4   ASK ME WHY

Written by John and Paul. Lead vocal by John, with Paul and George providing harmony. Recorded on November 26, 1962.

3   PLEASE PLEASE ME

PCS 3042—March 22, 1963

The Beatles' first LP entered the Top 10 album charts on March 27 at No. 9, and after seven weeks in the charts, on May 8, rose to No. 1, where it stayed for twenty nine weeks. It stayed in the Top 10 charts for sixty three weeks, selling 175,000 by August 13 (its eighteenth week in the charts), 250,000 by October 11 (twenty-sixth week). The album eventually sold over 500,000 in Britain, and holds the record for the longest continuous stay at No. 1 in the *NME* album charts.

Its American counterpart, *Introducing The Beatles* sold over a million, thus the combined world sales of the two albums are well over 1,500,000.

The cover photograph was taken by Angus McBean on the staircase of EMI House, Manchester Square, London. Paul had designed a cover for the album, calling it *Off The Beatle Track*, but this was obviously discarded, although the title was used later by George Martin for his album of orchestrated Beatles hits.

The new songs for the album were recorded on February 11, 1963, taking sixteen hours to record, and costing £400. On all tracks George plays lead guitar, John rhythm guitar, Paul bass and Ringo drums.

A SIDE

5   I SAW HER STANDING THERE *(2.50)*

Written by Paul, who sings lead backed by John. This was the "B" side of *I Want To Hold Your Hand* in America, and also appeared on *The Beatles' No. 1* EP in Britain. It was recorded as a single by Duffy Power with the Graham Bond Quartet and released on April 26, 1963, on the Parlophone label, although it was not a hit.

A later live recording of *I Saw Her Standing There* by The Elton John Band, featuring John Lennon and The Muscle Shoals Horns, was the "B" side of Elton's *Philadelphia Freedom* single, released March 1, 1975. It entered the Top 30 on March 19 at No. 19, and rose to No. 12, staying in the charts for seven weeks. This version was recorded on November 28, 1974, at Madison Square Garden, New York.

After John Lennon's death in December 1980, DJM Records were given permission by EMI to release all three tracks recorded at the Madison Square Garden concert by Elton John and John Lennon. The tracks were released as an EP, with *I Saw Her Standing There* on the "A" side, backed with *Whatever Gets You Thru The Night* and *Lucy In The Sky With Diamonds*. As a result of Lennon's murder, his appearance with Elton John became his last live performance.

The EP was released by DJM Records on March 13, 1981, in a picture sleeve, showing two previously unpublished photographs from the concert. The record made a one week appearance in the *NME* Top 30 at No. 24 on April 24, 1981.

6   MISERY (1.46)
Written mainly by John, with Paul's help, for Helen Shapiro, with whom The Beatles were touring at the time. Lead vocals are by John and Paul. This also appears on the British EP *The Beatles No. 1* and on the American EP release *The Beatles*, which was priced as a single. John and Paul also gave the song to Kenny Lynch, who released his version as a single on March 22, 1963 on HMV, but failed to make the charts.

7   ANNA (GO TO HIM) (2.52)
Lead vocal by John with Paul and George providing harmony. Originally recorded by its composer, Arthur Alexander, and released as a single on September 17, 1962 on the Dot label.

8   CHAINS (2.22)
Lead vocal by George — with Paul and John helping on backing vocals. Both this song and *Anna (Go To Him)* appear on the British EP *The Beatles No. 1* and the American EP *The Beatles*.

The song was written by husband and wife songwriting team Gerry Goffin and Carole King (who are now divorced). During the early 1960s, Gerry and Carole were one of several famous songwriting teams operating from the famous Brill Building, which can be found at 1819 Broadway, New York City. Among the other teams in the building were Barry Mann and Cynthia Weil, Jeff Barry and Ellie Greenwich, and a number of other writers including Howard Greenfield, Carole Bayer Sager and Neil Diamond. Goffin and King wrote dozens of hit songs, among the best known being *Up On The Roof* (recorded by The Drifters, and a Top 5 hit), *Will You Love Me Tomorrow* (The Shirelles, and a chart topper), and other Top 10 items including *Just Once In My Life* (The Righteous Brothers), *Don't Bring Me Down* (The Animals) and *One Fine Day* (The Chiffons). Also, during this period, Carole King recorded *It Might As Well Rain Until September*, a Top 3 hit in 1962 on both sides of the Atlantic on the Dimension label. The same label was also the one on which the original version of *Chains*, by The Cookies, was released, on October 2, 1962. This version reached the Top 20 in America for three weeks, peaking at No. 17.

After Carole King was divorced from Gerry Goffin, she embarked on a solo career, the highlight of which was her 1971 LP *Tapestry*, one of the top selling albums of all time, having sold more than ten million copies worldwide.

9   BOYS (2.22)
Solo lead vocal from Ringo with the others providing harmony.

Written by Luther Dixon and Wes Farrell, *Boys* was originally recorded by The Shirelles as the "B" side of their third million selling single, *Will You Love Me Tomorrow*, which was released on November 7, 1960 and was a No. 1 hit for two weeks in America in 1961, during a Top 20 residency of eleven weeks, getting to No. 3.

4a   ASK ME WHY (2.22)
(See *Please Please Me* single.)

3a   PLEASE PLEASE ME (1.58)
(See *Please Please Me* single.)

B SIDE
10a LOVE ME DO (2.18)
The second version of *Love Me Do*, with Andy White on drums. (See *Love Me Do* for full story.)

2a   P.S. I LOVE YOU (1.59)
(See *Love Me Do* single.)

11   BABY IT'S YOU (2.36)
John on lead vocals with Paul and George harmonising.

Another Shirelles single, written by Mack David, Burt Bacharach and Barney Williams, and released in America on December 4, 1961 on the Scepter label, where it reached No. 8 in the American charts, remaining in the Top 20 for nine weeks. The Shirelles had four million selling singles; three in 1960 — *Dedicated To The One I Love, Tonight's The Night* and *Will You Love Me Tomorrow*, and one in 1962 — *Soldier Boy*.

12   DO YOU WANT TO KNOW A SECRET (1.54)
Written by John, who got the idea for the song from a Walt Disney film, which he thinks was either *Cinderella* or *Fantasia*, for George to sing. Paul and John help out with the backing vocals. Brian Epstein allegedly offered this song to Shane Fenton (later to be known as Alvin Stardust) as an inducement to join his stable of artists at NEMS Enterprises.

Billy J. Kramer and The Dakotas' version of this song was released as a single in Britain on April 26, 1963, backed by another Lennon and McCartney number, *I'll Be On My Way* (written by Paul), which was never recorded by The Beatles. It entered the Top 30 on May 1 at No. 22, rising to No. 1, where it remained for two weeks, on

May 29, during a stay in the Top 30 of thirteen weeks. In America the single was released on June 10, 1963 on the Liberty label, but did not make the charts.

(See Appendix 1 for Billy J. Kramer's other Lennon and McCartney hits.)

13 A TASTE OF HONEY (1.59)
Double tracked lead vocal by Paul. Written by Ric Marlow and Bobby Scott for the 1960 play A Taste Of Honey.

The first recording of the song, by The Victor Feldman Quartet, was released on June 4, 1962, while another instrumental version became a minor hit for Martin Denny after it was released on June 18, 1962. The first vocal version was released by Lenny Welch on September 17, 1962.

14 THERE'S A PLACE (1.47)
Written by John who shares the vocals with Paul.

15 TWIST AND SHOUT (2.31)
This was the last number to be recorded for the Please Please Me album, and was cut because George Martin needed one more song to complete the album. Although The Beatles were very tired after a long day's recording, and John had almost lost his voice, they chose this song, written by Bert Berns, using an alias of "Medley/Russell", as a closer, and reputedly recorded it in one take, with John rasping out a very fine vocal, even though his throat was very sore.

This song had been the first Top 20 hit for the Isley Brothers (Ronald, Rudolph and O'Kelly) in America, getting to No. 17, and staying in the Top 20 for four weeks. It was released on May 7, 1962, and was the Isley's second million selling single, their first being Shout in 1959, and their third It's Your Thing in 1969.

Twist And Shout was also recorded a few months later by Brian Poole and The Tremeloes, who released it as a single in Britain on June 28, 1963. It became a major hit, reaching No. 4 during a chart stay of eleven weeks which began on July 3, 1963. It has been suggested that the Poole version (on Decca) might not have been a hit had The Beatles released their version in single form, and it is ironic that when both The Beatles and Poole and his group auditioned for Decca Records, The Beatles were judged less promising than Poole and The Tremeloes.

4 FROM ME TO YOU (1.54) THANK YOU GIRL (1.59)

R 5015—April 11, 1963

The third single by The Beatles entered the charts one week after release at No. 6, and went to No. 1 a week later, where it remained for five further weeks. It was in the Top 10 for twelve weeks and the Top 30 for sixteen weeks, and sold over 250,000 in Britain. After American release in 1964, global sales reached over one million.

16 FROM ME TO YOU
John and Paul were inspired to write this number by the New Musical Express letters column "From You To Us", and they wrote it on a coach journey between York and Shrewsbury during the Helen Shapiro tour on February 28, 1963. The song nearly wasn't recorded, as they felt it was too bluesy, but after recording it on March 4, 1963, with George Martin scoring it for harmonica, played by John, they decided it was satisfactory. John and Paul share the lead vocals and are supported by George's harmony singing.

17 THANK YOU GIRL
Also written by John and Paul, who share lead vocals. John plays the harmonica.

5 TWIST AND SHOUT

GEP 8882—July 12, 1963

The Beatles' first EP release comprised four tracks from their No. 1 album Please Please Me, which, at the time of the EP's release, had been at No. 1 for ten weeks. The EP entered the charts on July 17 at No. 13 and reached its highest position of No. 4 on August 7. It was at No. 4 for two weeks and in the Top 10 for six weeks, and was also the first EP to enter the NME Top 10 — up to 1967 it was the highest placing achieved by an EP in the singles chart. (The previous highest position attained by an EP was No. 11 reached by Elvis Presley's Follow That Dream in 1962.) By August 13, the EP had sold 250,000 in Britain, and by November the total was over 400,000. The EP initially stayed in the Top 30 for ten weeks, dropping out after September 18, but eight weeks later on November

20, it re-entered at No. 29, rising to No. 12 and staying in the Top 30 for a further ten weeks, making a total of twenty weeks in the Top 30. For eighteen weeks it was the highest placed EP in the charts. The EP was the fourth biggest seller of 1963, the top three being singles: *She Loves You* (1,300,000) and *I Want To Hold Your Hand* (1,250,000), both also by The Beatles, of course, plus *Glad All Over* by The Dave Clark Five (800,000). It was No. 1 in the EP charts for twenty-one weeks, remaining in the charts for a full year. The EP eventually sold 650,000, making it the biggest selling EP in Britain up to 1963, and had exceeded 800,000 by 1981.

A SIDE

15a **TWIST AND SHOUT** *(2.31)*
13a **A TASTE OF HONEY** *(1.59)*

B SIDE

12a **DO YOU WANT TO KNOW A SECRET** *(1.54)*
14a **THERE'S A PLACE** *(1.48)*

(For all above titles see *Please Please Me* LP.)

During the first six months of 1963, there were 2.5 million records sold by Liverpool groups with just seven titles: two singles (Please Please Me and From Me To You), one EP (Twist And Shout) and one LP (Please Please Me) by The Beatles; two singles (How Do You Do It and I Like It) by Gerry and The Pacemakers and one single (Do You Want To Know A Secret) by Billy J. Kramer and The Dakotas. All seven records were produced by George Martin.

6	**SHE LOVES YOU** *(2.18)*
	I'LL GET YOU *(2.02)*

R 5055—August 23, 1963

With advance sales of 235,000 by August 14, and 500,000 immediately before release, *She Loves You* entered the charts at No. 2 on August 28, one week after release. By September 3 it had sold 500,000, and was No. 1 the following day, where it stayed for four weeks. By October 11, after seven weeks in the Top 10, it had sold 750,000 copies. Having dropped from the No. 1 position for seven weeks, on November 20 it returned to the top spot for two more weeks, and by November 27 had sold 1,050,000. By the end of the

year, it had sold 1,300,000, making it the top selling single in Britain for 1963. By January 1964, sales had reached 1.5 million, and the figure now stands at about 1,600,000. Up to December 1977, *She Loves You* was the top selling single in Britain (with *I Want To Hold Your Hand* a close second with over 1,500,000), but lost that title in 1978 to *Mull Of Kintyre*, recorded by Wings, which initially sold 1,667,000 copies and was later to top two million, making it the best-selling and fastest selling single of all time in Great Britain.

She Loves You was in the Top 10 for twenty one weeks, and in the Top 30 for twenty four weeks. It sold three million in America and total world sales were estimated at over five million.

18   **SHE LOVES YOU**
Composed jointly by John and Paul while touring in a coach in Yorkshire. The song was recorded on July 1, 1963 and features John and Paul singing lead with George joining in for harmony.

On January 30, 1981, EMI released Peter Sellers' version of *She Loves You*, recorded at the same session as *A Hard Day's Night* and *Help*, which he released as a single in 1965 (see *A Hard Day's Night*). The single, titled *The*

Unreleased She Loves You, came out on Parlophone, and includes two versions of the song, the first subtitled "inspired by Dr. Strangelove" and narrated by Sellers as two German scientists, and the second subtitled "inspired by Phil McCafferty — The Irish Dentist" and narrated by Sellers as two Irishmen. The vocal only tapes of the recording were rediscovered by George Martin in his private collection. Martin produced the original Peter Sellers spoof of *A Hard Day's Night*, and after adding some music and cleaning up the *She Loves You* tapes, he played them to Paul McCartney, who was very keen to have them released. Unfortunately, this belated follow up to Sellers' 1965 "Beatle" hit did not make the charts.

19   **I'LL GET YOU**
Another joint effect from John and Paul, both vocally and in terms of composition, with John supplying the backing harmonica. Recorded on July 1, 1963.

7	THE BEATLES' HITS

GEP 8880—September 6, 1963

The Beatles' second EP contained

their first three hits and one single "B" side, and entered the Top 30 on November 6 at No 30, eventually rising to No. 17 for one week. It was in the Top 30 for eight weeks and was the highest placed EP in the charts of November 6.

The cover photograph was taken by Angus McBean, who also supplied the shots for the *Please Please Me* LP and the following EP *The Beatles (No. 1)*. Tony Barrow supplied sleeve notes for not only this EP but also for the *Twist And Shout* and *The Beatles (No. 1)* EPs and the first three albums.

A SIDE
16a **FROM ME TO YOU** *(1.54)*
17a **THANK YOU GIRL** *(1.59)*

B SIDE
3b **PLEASE PLEASE ME** *(1.58)*
10b **LOVE ME DO** *(2.18)*
(For all above titles see respective singles.)

8   THE BEATLES (No. 1.)

GEP 8883—November 1, 1963

Another four tracks were lifted from the chart topping *Please Please Me* album to make this EP, which entered the Top 30 at No. 27 on November 13, with the album still at No. 1. It dropped out and re-entered the Top 30 three times and stayed in the Top 30 for six weeks, reaching its highest position of No. 24 on November 20.

A SIDE
5a **I SAW HER STANDING THERE** *(2.50)*
6a **MISERY** *(1.46)*

B SIDE
7a **ANNA (GO TO HIM)** *(2.52)*
8a **CHAINS** *(2.22)*
(For all above titles see *Please Please Me* LP.)

In less than a year, The Beatles sold approximately seven million records (singles, EPs and albums) in Britain alone.

On November 18, 1963, The Beatles received two Silver Discs (representing sales of 250,000) for their Please Please Me and With The Beatles albums. The With The Beatles award was actually made prior to the album's release, as it had accumulated advance orders of 300,000. At the same time, George Martin presented the group with miniature Silver Discs for the Twist And Shout EP, which had sold over 400,000.

9   WITH THE BEATLES

PCS 3045—November 22, 1963

With The Beatles entered the Top 10 album chart on November 27 at No. 1 and, at the same time, entered the Top 30 at No. 15. It took over the No. 1 position held by the *Please Please Me* album, and stayed there for twenty one weeks, completing the longest continuous stay at No. 1 by any artist, group or soundtrack album — fifty weeks (i.e. twenty nine weeks by *Please Please Me* and twenty one weeks by *With The Beatles*). In its second week in the Top 30, the album rose to No. 11, making it the highest placed LP in the singles chart, beating the previous record held by Frank Sinatra. It stayed in the Top 30 for seven weeks, and in the album charts for forty weeks.

The album had advance orders of 270,000 two weeks before release, and by November 27, six days after release, it had sold 530,000. By January 17, 1964, sales amounted to 885,000, and by the end of 1964, the total was 980,000. The "magic" million was reached by September 1965, making this the first British album to sell a million copies in Britain. The only other album to sell a million in Britain before *With The Beatles* was the soundtrack of the American film *South Pacific*, which was released in Britain in 1958, and sold a million by November 1963, six years after release. *With The Beatles* achieved the same goal in less than two years.

The American equivalent to this album, *Meet The Beatles*, has sold over five million, making the combined global sales of the two albums close to 6.5 million. Thus it remains one of the biggest selling British LPs (along with *Sgt. Pepper* and *Abbey Road*, which have both sold over 10 million).

The entire *With The Beatles* LP was recorded on July 15, 1963, and on all tracks, George plays lead guitar, John rhythm guitar, Paul bass guitar and Ringo drums.

A SIDE

20 IT WON'T BE LONG (2.09)
Written by John, who takes lead vocal with Paul and George singing harmony.

21 ALL I'VE GOT TO DO (1.59)
Written by John, who again takes lead vocal, backed by Paul.

22 ALL MY LOVING (2.04)
Paul wrote *All My Loving* whilst shaving one morning, and sings lead, with John and George providing vocal backing.

23 DON'T BOTHER ME (2.24)
Two theories exist concerning the circumstances in which George wrote this, his first song. The first account has George in bed in a Bournemouth hotel during a tour. The rigours of touring had resulted in his needing to rest, and to overcome the boredom produced by his feeling run down, he decided to attempt to write a song. After some experimentation with his guitar, the tune for *Don't Bother Me* began to appear. The second theory is recounted by Bill Harry, erstwhile editor of the Liverpool music paper *Mersey Beat*. George had previously written the purely instrumental *Cry For A Shadow*, and Harry saw no reason why he should not write something else, particularly because, unlike most other groups of the era, The Beatles had demonstrated their ability to write much of their own material. Harry pestered George on this subject to the point where the latter began to cringe every time the two met, finally becoming so irritated that he determined to silence Harry by doing as he was urged. The title *Don't Bother Me* had been the phrase George used in his attempt to evade Harry's well-meaning urgings.

George sings a double tracked solo vocal. Paul plays claves, John tambourine and Ringo a loose skinned Arabian bongo.

24 LITTLE CHILD (1.43)
Written by John and Paul, who also share vocals. Paul plays piano while John supplies the mouth organ.

25 TILL THERE WAS YOU (2.10)
Paul takes solo vocal, while John and George switch to acoustic guitars with Ringo on bongos. Paul is on bass guitar as usual.

Till There Was You was written by Meredith Willson for the 1957 musical "The Music Man", where it was sung by Robert Preston and Barbara Cook, who made the first recording of the song for "The Music Man" (Original Broadway Cast) LP. Anita Bryant (who also had major hits with *Paper Roses* and *In My Little Corner Of The World* in 1960) sold a million copies of her version, also by 1960.

26 PLEASE MR. POSTMAN (2.30)
John is double tracked on lead vocals, with Paul and George supplying backing.

Please Mr. Postman was The Marvellettes first single and hit in America, the start of a string of hit singles including *Playboy, Don't Mess Around With Bill*, and *When You're Young And In Love*. The song was written by the Tamla-Motown writing team of Brian Holland, Robert Bateman and Berry Gordy (Tamla Records' President), and the single was released on August 7, 1961. It entered the American Top 20 on November 6, and reached No. 1 for one week on December 11, 1961, remaining in the Top 20 for eleven weeks and selling a million.

The song entered the singles chart for a second time when The Carpenters released their version towards the end of 1974, when it topped the charts in both Britain and America. It stayed in the Top 30 for nine weeks in Britain, and the American Top 20 for eight weeks, where it was The Carpenter's fourteenth Top 20 single, and their tenth British hit.

B SIDE

27 ROLL OVER BEETHOVEN (2.42)
George takes double tracked solo vocal while all four Beatles add hand claps.

Roll Over Beethoven, a Chuck Berry classic, was released by Berry on May 14, 1956 on the Chess label. Although only reaching No. 29 in the American charts, it has sold a global million over the years.

The Electric Light Orchestra scored a hit with their partially orchestrated version of the song in 1973, when it was in the British Top 20 for five weeks, its highest position being No. 6.

28 HOLD ME TIGHT (2.28)
Written by John and Paul, but mainly Paul, who takes lead vocal backed by John and George.

29 YOU REALLY GOT A HOLD ON ME (2.58)
John and George supply the lead vocal, with Paul helping out on the choruses. The piano was added by their producer, George Martin.

You Really Got A Hold On Me was the second million selling single by The Miracles and was written by William "Smokey" Robinson, the group's lead singer. It was released on November 19, 1962 on Tamla, entering the US Top 20 charts on January 26, 1963, and reaching No. 8, during a seven week residency in the Top 20. Their first million selling single *Shop Around*, was the first of a string of hits which includes: *Mickey's Monkey* (million seller 1963); *Ooh Baby Baby* (1965); *Tracks Of My Tears* (million seller 1965); *My Girl Has Gone* (1965) and *Going To A Go Go* (million seller 1966). As Smokey Robinson and The Miracles, the hits continued with *I Second That Emotion* (million seller 1967); *If You Can Wait* (1968); *Don't Cry* (1969) and *Tears Of A Clown* (million seller 1970), which topped both British and American charts.

30 I WANNA BE YOUR MAN (1.56)
Written by Paul, with John helping him to finish it. Ringo takes the vocal spotlight, with the others helping out on harmony and backing vocals. John plays the Hammond organ.

This number became The Rolling Stones' first Top 10 hit when it was released on November 1, 1963 in Britain and on February 17, 1964 in America. It entered the UK Top 30 on November 6 at No. 30, rose to No. 9, its highest position, on January 15, 1964, and was in the Top 30 for thirteen weeks.

The story behind The Stones' version is an interesting one. At the end of 1963, The Stones were still playing around London, where one of their regular gigs was a residency on Sunday afternoons at Ken Colyer's Studio 51. The imminent success of his group was causing Andrew Oldham some problems, and while hanging around Jermyn Street one afternoon, he bumped into John and Paul. He informed his ex-employers of his difficulty in obtaining recording material for his group, upon which John and Paul casually mentioned that they happened to have a spare unrecorded song with them. The three then went along to Studio 51, where John and Paul sang the first verse and chorus using The Stones' instruments, but informing them that the song was not finished. The Stones liked what they heard, so John and Paul said that the song would be completed shortly and disappeared into another room. When they reappeared a few minutes later, they were asked if they had forgotten something, but replied, "Thank you, no — we've just finished the middle eight and last verse". John and Paul ran through the song a couple of times and The Stones accepted it, and after a couple of weeks recorded it at Kingsway Studios with Eric Easton producing.

After *I Wanna Be Your Man*, The Stones went on to become the second biggest group of the Sixties, with such hits as *It's All Over Now, Little Red Rooster, The Last Time, Satisfaction, Get Off My Cloud, Paint It Black, Jumping Jack Flash* and *Honky Tonk Woman*, which all reached No. 1.

This song made its second appearance in the charts in August 1979, giving UK band The Rezillos a minor hit for a single week. Before breaking up at the end of the 1970s, The Rezillos scored three hit singles in Britain, although only their debut hit, *Top Of The Pops*, reached the Top 30 in 1978.

31 DEVIL IN HER HEART *(2.22)*
George on lead vocal with John and Paul on harmony. Ringo plays the maracas.

Devil In Her Heart was written by Richard B. Drapkin, and recorded by The Donays for single release on August 6, 1962 on the Brent label, but was not a Top 20 hit.

32 NOT A SECOND TIME *(2.03)*
Written by John who is double tracked on the vocals. George Martin plays piano.

Extract from *The Times* written by their music critic, William Mann, in an article entitled "What Songs The Beatles Sang":

"...But harmonic interest is typical of their quicker songs too, and one gets the impression that they think simultaneously of harmony and melody, so firmly are the major tonic sevenths and ninths built into their tunes, and the flat submediant key switches, so natural is the Aeolian cadence at the end of 'Not A Second Time' (the chord progression which ends Mahler's 'Song Of The Earth')..."

33 MONEY (THAT'S WHAT I WANT) *(2.46)*
John sings lead with Paul and George backing. George Martin supplies piano.

Money, written by Janie Bradford and Berry Gordy, was originally a hit for Barrett Strong in 1960, when it reached No. 23 in the American charts. It was released on the Anna label on December 10, 1959, and became the first million selling disc for Berry Gordy's Motown Records empire. *Money* was Barrett Strong's only chart hit as a recording artist, but in partnership with Norman Whitfield, he co-wrote several million selling hits on the Tamla labels in the late Sixties and early Seventies. These include: *I Wish It Would Rain* by The Temptations, a million seller in 1968, which stayed in the US Top 20 for five weeks; *Cloud Nine* which also sold a million for The Temptations, and stayed in the US Top 20 for eight weeks and in the British Top 20 for three weeks; *I Heard It Through The Grapevine* which was a million seller twice over, once for Marvin Gaye, whose version was at No. 1 in the US for seven weeks, and No. 1 for three weeks in Britain, and earlier for Gladys Knight and The Pips, whose version got to No. 2 in America; *War* a million seller for Edwin Starr, which reached No. 1 for

three weeks in the US and No. 3 in Britain, and *Ball Of Confusion* again by The Temptations and also a million seller, which stayed in the Top 20 for eleven weeks in the US and seven weeks in Britain.

After The Beatles released their version of *Money* on the *With The Beatles* LP, Bern Elliott and The Fenmen scored a hit with their version of the song which was in the Top 20 for four weeks during 1964, its highest placing being No. 14.

R 5084—November 29, 1963

This, The Beatles' fifth single, had advance orders of 700,000 by November 6, 1963 and of over 940,000 by November 27, two days before release. As a result, the initial factory pressing of the record was 500,000 before it was released, an unprecedented figure at the time. It entered the charts one week after release on December 4 at No. 1, where it stayed for six weeks, and was in the Top 10 for ten weeks and the Top 30 for fourteen weeks. It had sold 1,250,000 by the end of the year, which was only one month after release, thus making it the second top selling single in Britain for 1963 (*She Loves You* being the top seller with 1,300,000). By January 17, 1964 it had sold 1.5 million in Britain alone, and by 1974 had sold 1,509,000. It is at present the third highest selling single in Britain after *Mull Of Kintyre* and *She Loves You*.

Although not the highest selling single in Britain, it is the highest selling British single world-wide having sold between 12 and 15 million.

34 I WANT TO HOLD YOUR HAND
The Beatles' biggest selling single was written by John and Paul in the basement of Jane Asher's house in Harley Street, London. John and Paul share the lead vocal and George joins them for harmony. Recorded October 19, 1963.

On January 19, 1980, Dollar's recording of *I Want To Hold Your Hand* entered the *NME* Top 30 at No. 28. It rose to No. 11 on February 2, staying in the charts for five weeks. The single was Dollar's fourth chart entry, the first being *Shooting Star* (1978), followed by *Who Were You With In The Moonlight* (1979) and *Love's Got A Hold On Me* (1979), which reached No. 4 in the

BMRB chart. Dollar, a male/female duo, are David Van Day and Thereze Bazar. They were originally members of Guys and Dolls (who had five chart hits between 1975 and 1978), until they broke away towards the end of 1978.

35 THIS BOY

Written by John and sung by John and Paul. Recorded October 19, 1963.

This Boy was used in the first Beatles' film, *A Hard Day's Night*, as incidental music, scored by George Martin, whose orchestral and non-vocal version, which was called *Ringo's Theme*, was played during the towpath scene where Ringo is seen walking by a river, and attempts to take a photograph of himself, something which produces rather amusing results.

Ringo's Theme was released as a single by The George Martin Orchestra on August 7, 1964, backed with *And I Love Her*, but was not a hit in Britain. In the US however, after release on July 31, 1964, the single reached No. 53 in Billboard's Hot 100, and spent eight weeks in that chart.

This Boy also appeared on The George Martin Orchestra's Parlophone LP, *Off The Beatle Track*, which was composed of a dozen Beatle hits, orchestrated by The Beatles producer and performed by a full orchestra made up of session musicians under his leadership. Not only is the LP of interest because of Martin's excellent arrangements but additionally since its sleeve contains photographs of Martin together with various Beatles, plus a picture of John Lennon, who also penned the sleeve notes in his inimitably witty style. The album was released in Britain on August 3, 1964, and in America a few weeks earlier, on July 10, 1964. As well as *This Boy*, it also

contains orchestrated versions of *All My Loving, Don't Bother Me, Can't Buy Me Love, All I've Got To Do, I Saw Her Standing There, She Loves You, From Me To You, There's A Place, Please Please Me, Little Child* and *I Want To Hold Your Hand.*

On February 19, 1965 an EP titled *Music From 'A Hard Day's Night'* was released in Britain by The George Martin Orchestra, and this also included *This Boy*, although with a title of *Ringo's Theme*, as well as *And I Love Her, A Hard Day's Night* and *If I Fell.*

11 ALL MY LOVING

GEP. 8891—February 7, 1964

Continuing their policy of lifting tracks from the group's latest album release, Parlophone released The Beatles' fourth EP containing two tracks from the No. 1 album *With The Beatles*, plus two tracks from *Please Please Me*, both of which were also the "B" sides of their first two singles. As with the previous Beatles' EPs, it was a big hit, entering the Top 30 on February 5 at No. 18 (*With The Beatles* and *Please Please Me* still held the top two positions in the album chart). This EP's highest position was No. 13 and it stayed in the chart for seven weeks.

A SIDE

22a ALL MY LOVING (2.04)
(See *With The Beatles* LP.)

4b ASK ME WHY (2.22)
(See *Please Please Me* single.)

B SIDE

33a MONEY (THAT'S WHAT I WANT)
(2.46)
(See *With The Beatles* LP.)

2b P.S. I LOVE YOU *(2.00)*
(See *Love Me Do* single.)

12 CAN'T BUY ME LOVE *(2.10)*
YOU CAN'T DO THAT *(2.32)*

R 5114—March 20, 1964

The group's sixth single, and their first for 1964, holds the record for the highest advance sales for any single — 2,100,000 in the US and one million in Britain. The million mark for advance orders in Britain was passed on March 17, and inevitably the single entered the charts at No. 1 on March 24, 1964, where it remained for four weeks, by which time it had sold 1,210,000. It was in the Top 10 for seven weeks and the Top 30 for nine weeks.

Total global sales have been estimated at over six million.

36 CAN'T BUY ME LOVE
Written mainly by Paul, but helped by John who also shares lead vocal with Paul. The song was recorded on a four track machine in the Pathé Marconi Studios in Paris on January 29, 1964, although George changed his lead guitar part in London, using his twelve string Rickenbacker, after listening to the final Paris tape at the EMI studios, on February 25, 1964.

Ella Fitzgerald had a minor hit with her version of *Can't Buy Me Love*, in May 1964. It entered the Top 30 at No. 30 for one week on May 6. Ella recorded five other hits during the late Fifties and early Sixties, *Swinging Shepherd Blues*, *But Not For Me*, *Mack The Knife*, *How High The Moon* and *Desafinado*, but was generally regarded as being a high class jazz vocalist — as such, it must have been quite an honour when she recorded a song written by The Beatles.

37 YOU CAN'T DO THAT
Written by John who sings lead with Paul and George supplying harmony while George plays twelve string guitar. The backing track was recorded in Paris at the Pathé Marconi Studios during the *Can't Buy Me Love* session on January 29, 1964, with the vocal added later at EMI on February 25, 1964.

13 LONG TALL SALLY

GEP 8913—June 19, 1964

The Beatles' fifth EP and the first to contain previously unreleased material, which would also be exclusively available on this EP until 1976 when the four tracks were released in stereo on the double album *Rock 'N' Roll Music*. The EP entered the Top 30 on July 1 at No. 13, rising to No. 11 a week later and staying in the Top 30 for six weeks, during which time it was the only EP in the chart. It was No. 1 in the EP charts for seven weeks, and by early 1965 had sold over 250,000 copies in Britain, and with foreign sales has sold over a million globally.

The cover photograph was taken by Robert Freeman, with sleeve notes supplied by Derek Taylor.

The four songs were recorded in late February, 1964.

A SIDE

38 LONG TALL SALLY *(2.00)*
Paul sings solo, and probably supplies the piano, for this number which the group frequently performed during their days in Hamburg.

Written by Enotris Johnson, Richard Penniman (Little Richard) and Robert Blackwell, originally titled *The Thing*, and recorded by Little Richard in New Orleans, it was later re-titled *Bald Headed Sally*, but not released, after which it was re-cut in Los Angeles. Released on March 12, 1956, backed with *Slippin' And Slidin'*, it got to No. 13 in the US Top 20, staying in the charts for seven weeks. It was an even bigger hit in Britain, reaching No. 3 and staying in the Top 20 for fourteen weeks to become Little Richard's second global million seller.

The song also provided a hit for Pat Boone, whose cover version got to No. 18, staying in the Top 20 for two weeks, in both America and Britain.

Little Richard had ten Top 20 hits between 1956 and 1964, including *Lucille*, *Good Golly Miss Molly* — both featured in The Beatles' early repertoire — *Keep A-Knockin'*, *The Girl Can't Help It* and *Rip It Up*. He had seven million selling singles: *Tutti Frutti* 1955; *Long Tall Sally* 1956; *Rip It Up* 1956; *Lucille* 1957; *Jenny Jenny* 1957; *Keep A-Knockin'* 1958 and *Good Golly Miss Molly* 1958.

39   I CALL YOUR NAME *(2.05)*
Written by John, who sings lead vocal which is occasionally double tracked.

This song was given to Billy J. Kramer and The Dakotas as the 'B' side to their *Bad To Me* single, released in Britain on July 26, 1963. *Bad To Me*, written by John for Billy J. Kramer, was No. 1 in Britain for two weeks, staying in the Top 30 for eleven weeks. Originally released in America, backed with *I Call Your Name* on September 23, 1963, *Bad To Me* was re-released, backed with *Little Children*, on March 30, 1964. It was in the American Top 30 for seven weeks, getting to No. 9 for two weeks. The single sold 340,000 in Britain and 540,000 in America, making it a global million seller with the addition of sales in other countries.

B SIDE
40   SLOW DOWN *(2.54)*
John again sings double tracked solo vocal, with Paul probably supplying the piano.

Written and recorded by Larry Williams and released as a single on February 24, 1958, backed with *Dizzy Miss Lizzy*, on the Specialty label in America. Larry Williams did not score a Top 20 hit with this single, although he did have two million selling singles in 1957; *Short Fat Fanny* which got to No. 6 and was in the American Top 20 for twelve weeks and *Bony Moronie*, which reached No. 18 during four weeks in the America Top 20 and No. 11 in Britain during seven weeks in the Top 20.

41   MATCHBOX *(1.55)*
Ringo sings solo.

Written by Carl Perkins, and released by him as a single on February 11, 1957, on the famous Sun label, *Matchbox* was not a Top 20 hit, although during the previous year Perkins had a million selling single with *Blue Suede Shoes*.

In 1964, The Beatles won two Carl Allen Awards for 1963: one for "Most Outstanding Beat Group of The Year" and the other for "Most Outstanding Vocal Record For Dancing" with She Loves You.

14   A HARD DAY'S NIGHT *(2.28)*
THINGS WE SAID TODAY *(2.34)*

R 5160—July 10, 1964

A Hard Day's Night was The Beatles' third single to go straight to No. 1 one week after release. Advance orders for the single totalled 600,000, and by July 23 it had sold 800,000 in less than two weeks. It went to No. 1 on July 15, staying there for four weeks, and remained in the Top 10 for eight weeks and the Top 30 for eleven weeks. It eventually sold a million in Britain, making it the group's fourth British million selling single, while global sales exceed three million.

42   A HARD DAY'S NIGHT
The title song of the first Beatles' film was written by John, who is double tracked on lead vocal, with Paul and George harmonising. It was recorded on April 16, 1964, with piano supplied by George Martin.

Two cover versions of *A Hard Day's Night* have entered the UK Top 30. Peter Sellers' comedy version (backed by *Help*) entered the Top 30 at No. 20 on December 20, 1965, rose to No. 15 for two weeks and was in the Top 30 for five weeks. An instrumental version, by The Ramsey Lewis Trio, reached the chart for one week at No. 30 on April 27, 1966.

43   THINGS WE SAID TODAY
Written by Paul, who takes lead vocal with John backing. The song was recorded between June 1–3, 1964.

The Beatles won five "Ivor Novello Awards" for 1963: John and Paul winning four as composers with "The Year's Most Broadcast Song" — She Loves You; "Highest Selling Record" — She Loves You; "Second Highest Selling Record" — I Want To Hold Your Hand and "Second Most Outstanding Song" — All My Loving. The Beatles, Brian Epstein and George Martin received a special award "For Outstanding Services To British Music".

PCS 3058—August 10, 1964

The soundtrack album of The Beatles' first film, *A Hard Day's Night*, entered the album charts on July 15 at No. 1, where it stayed for twenty one weeks (being replaced by *Beatles For Sale*). It also entered the Top 30 on the same day at No. 29, rising to No. 22 for two weeks, and staying in that chart for four weeks before dropping out. It re-entered the Top 30 two weeks later at No. 30, rose to No. 22 for another week, and dropped out. It stayed in the Top 10 album charts for thirty weeks.

The album had advance orders in Britain of 250,000, and by December 1964 had sold 600,000, eventually selling 750,000 in Britain.

The two American albums *A Hard Day's Night* and *Something New* (both containing songs from the film) sold over three million together and thus global sales of *A Hard Day's Night* can be estimated at around four million.

The seven songs on the first side of the album were all included in the film, and, except for *A Hard Day's Night* and *Can't Buy Me Love*, were recorded between March and April 1964. The six songs on the second side were not used in the film, and were recorded between June 1 and June 3, 1964, with the exception of *I'll Cry Instead*, which was recorded at the same time as the film songs.

A SIDE

42a   A HARD DAY'S NIGHT *(2.28)*
(See single.)

44   I SHOULD HAVE KNOWN BETTER *(2.41)*
Written by John who is double tracked on lead vocals and also plays mouth organ. George plays his brand new twelve string Rickenbacker guitar, a revolutionary instrument at the time, which was also used on some other tracks on the album.

This song gave The Naturals, a five piece band from Harlow, their only chart entry. It was released on the Parlophone label in July, 1964, entered the Top 30 on September 2 at No. 27, and was in the Top 30 for three weeks, rising to No. 26 in its third week.

45   IF I FELL *(2.16)*
Written by John who shares lead vocal with Paul.

46   I'M HAPPY JUST TO DANCE WITH YOU *(1.57)*
Written by John, for George to sing. John and Paul supply backing.

47   AND I LOVE HER *(2.27)*
Paul got the inspiration for this song from Jane Asher, although John helped him write it. Paul takes solo vocal which is double tracked in places.

And I Love Her is the third most popular "cover" song of The Beatles, with 372 different versions recorded up to October 1972, including versions by Mary Wells, Connie Francis, The Count Basie Orchestra, Chet Atkins, Jose Feliciano, Sarah Vaughan, Georgie Fame and Bobby Womack.

48   TELL ME WHY *(2.06)*
Written by John. Paul and John share lead vocals, with George helping out on vocal backing.

36a   CAN'T BUY ME LOVE *(2.10)*
(See single.)

B SIDE

49   ANY TIME AT ALL *(2.09)*
Written by John who sings lead, with Paul and George providing background vocals.

50   I'LL CRY INSTEAD *(1.43)*
Written by John, originally for the *A Hard Day's Night* film. However, the film's director, Dick Lester, thought it unsuitable, so although it was recorded along with the other film songs, it was not included in the film.

John and Paul share lead vocals.

43a   THINGS WE SAID TODAY *(2.34)*
(See *A Hard Day's Night* single.)

51 WHEN I GET HOME *(2.15)*
Written by John who takes lead vocal, with Paul and George providing harmony.

37a YOU CAN'T DO THAT *(2.32)*
(See *Can't Buy Me Love* single.)

52 I'LL BE BACK *(2.20)*
Written by John who sings lead, with Paul and George supplying backing vocals.

16 EXTRACTS FROM THE FILM "A HARD DAY'S NIGHT"

GEP 8920—November 4, 1964

With this and the following EP, Parlophone were trying to get as much mileage as possible from a batch of Beatle songs, but did not manage to procure the record sales attained by their earlier "re-packaging". Neither this nor any of the subsequent Beatles' EPs (until *Magical Mystery Tour*) sold enough to enter the *NME* Top 30.

Three of the tracks on this EP were released as singles in America.

A SIDE
44a I SHOULD HAVE KNOWN BETTER *(2.41)*

45a IF I FELL *(2.16)*

B SIDE
48a TELL ME WHY *(2.06)*

47a AND I LOVE HER *(2.27)*
(See *A Hard Day's Night* LP for all above titles.)

For the week of August 5, 1964, The Beatles achieved the first "double double top" in the record charts; they were No. 1 in the British and American singles and album charts with the same single and album — A Hard Day's Night.

Since The Beatles achieved this feat in 1964, it has rarely been equalled. In 1971, Rod Stewart did it with Maggie May and Every Picture Tells A Story

on October 6 and 13 (for two weeks) and in 1978 The Bee Gees topped the album charts with Saturday Night Fever (a soundtrack album including other artists) and the singles chart with Night Fever.

17 EXTRACTS FROM THE ALBUM "A HARD DAY'S NIGHT"

GEP 8924—November 6, 1964

A SIDE
49a ANY TIME AT ALL *(2.09)*

50a I'LL CRY INSTEAD *(1.43)*

B SIDE
43b THINGS WE SAID TODAY *(2.34)*
(See *A Hard Day's Night* single.)

51a WHEN I GET HOME *(2.14)*
(See *A Hard Day's* Night LP for other three titles.)

18 I FEEL FINE *(2.21)*
SHE'S A WOMAN *(2.59)*

R 5200—November 27, 1964.

With advance orders of 500,000 by November 5 and up to 750,000 just before release, The Beatles' eighth single went straight to No. 1 on December 2, by which date it had sold 800,000, only five days after release. By December 11 it had sold one million, making it The Beatles' fifth consecutive million selling single in Britain, and one of the fastest (if not the fastest) selling single ever in Britain. It stayed at No. 1 for six weeks and was in the Top 10 for eight weeks and the Top 30 for ten weeks.

Global sales can be estimated at over three million.

53 I FEEL FINE *(2.21)*
John wrote this number at a recording session around the opening guitar riff. John takes lead vocal with Paul helping at times and all singing harmony. At the beginning of the song, feedback can be heard — probably the first time this effect has been used on a record. John

and George play the guitar duet. The recording was made in early October 1964.

54   SHE'S A WOMAN

As with *I Feel Fine*, *She's A Woman* was written, by Paul, in the studio on the day it was recorded early in October 1964. Paul sings lead with John and George helping with the chorus, and Paul plays piano.

19   BEATLES FOR SALE

PCS 3062—December 4, 1964

Beatles For Sale entered both the album and Top 30 charts on December 9 at No's 1 and 28 respectively. The album replaced *A Hard Day's Night* at No. 1, staying there for nine weeks, and was in the Top 10 charts for thirty-one weeks. It also remained in the Top 30 for five weeks, rising to No. 22.

A month before its release, advance orders for *Beatles For Sale* stood at 550,000, and rose to 750,000, which at

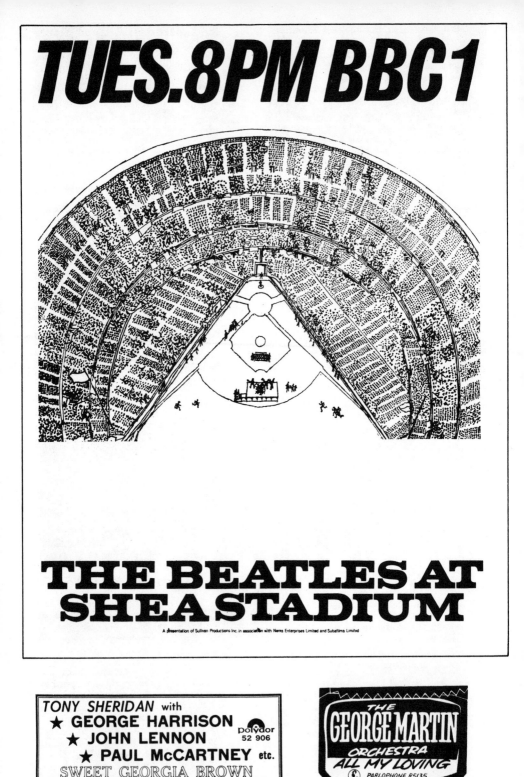

TUES.8PM BBC1

THE BEATLES AT SHEA STADIUM

A presentation of Sullivan Productions Inc. in association with Nems Enterprises Limited and Subafilms Limited

TONY SHERIDAN with
★ GEORGE HARRISON
★ JOHN LENNON
★ PAUL McCARTNEY etc.
polydor 52 906
SWEET GEORGIA BROWN

THE GEORGE MARTIN ORCHESTRA
ALL MY LOVING
PARLOPHONE R5135

the time was the highest advance order for an LP in Britain. The album sold 700,000 copies by December 4, and sales eventually exceeded a million in Britain alone.

The American equivalent of the *Beatles For Sale* album was *Beatles '65*, which sold over three million in six weeks, and with *Beatles For Sale*, combined world sales of the two albums total over four million. In America, six tracks from *Beatles For Sale* were used on the *Beatles VI* LP, which also sold a million bringing the total sales of the *Beatles For Sale* songs to between five and six million.

The album was recorded between late September and mid-October 1964. The usual Beatles' line-up is featured on all tracks, with the addition of other instruments as listed.

of the single included nine other songs in addition to those on the 7" version.

The idea originated in Canada where a DJ edited together several original recordings (including a few Beatles tracks, plus Ringo's *No No No Song* and Wings' *Silly Love Songs*) using a disco back beat, to make a sixteen minute tape. The tape was pressed as an illegal 12" single called *Bits And Pieces III*. Copies of the record eventually found their way to Britain and Europe, where a Dutch producer, Jaap Eggermont, heard the record, and realising its potential, decided to produce a legal "cover" version. The songs were recorded so as to imitate the sound of the originals as faithfully as possible, even down to the vocals (although a

A SIDE

55   NO REPLY *(2.13)*

Written by John, who is double tracked on lead vocals with Paul helping and George joining occasionally for the chorus.

This song was at one time considered as a singles release in Britain.(See *Eight Days A Week*.)

On April 10, 1981, a Dutch group, Starsound, released a medley of songs called *Stars On 45*, containing twelve segued tracks put to a disco beat. Although the idea did not originate from the group, the hit single sparked off a barrage of similar medleys on the British charts. The Starsound single included eight Beatles songs: *No Reply, I'll Be Back, Drive My Car, Do You Want To Know A Secret, We Can Work It Out, I Should Have Known Better, Nowhere Man* and *You're Going To Lose That Girl* along with *Venus* (Shocking Blue) and *Sugar Sugar* (The Archies) as well as two versions of the title song *Stars On 45*. A 12" version

slight Dutch accent can be heard several times, especially on The Beatles' songs).

The record, released on the CBS label, entered the *NME* Top 30 at No. 15 on May 2, 1981, going to No. 1 a week later. It was at No. 1 for one week only, but stayed in the Top 30 for eight weeks.

An album, called *Stars On 45 — The Album* was released on May 8, and on side one contained thirty Beatles' songs segued together. It entered the *NME* Top 30 Album Chart on May 23, 1981, at No. 4, went to No. 1 on June 6, dropping to No. 2 for two weeks, and returning to No. 1 for another week on June 27, during a residency in the album charts of seventeen weeks.

The group followed the "Beatles Medley" with an "Abba Medley" (which reached No. 2 in the *NME* Top 30) and an "Instrumental Medley" (No. 14), which were titled *Stars On 45 Vol 2* and *Stars On 45 Vol 3* respectively. The follow up album *Stars On 45 Vol 2 — The*

Album, stayed in the Top 30 Album charts for two weeks.

56 I'M A LOSER *(2.26)*
Written by John. Paul supports John on the lead vocals.

Again considered for a single in Britain.(See *Eight Days A Week*).

57 BABY'S IN BLACK *(2.03)*
Written by John and Paul who share the vocals.

58 ROCK AND ROLL MUSIC *(2.28)*
John sings solo. George Martin, Paul and John play the same piano.

Written and originally recorded by Chuck Berry, whose version was released on the Chess label on

This song was written by Roy Lee Jackson, recorded by Dr. Feelgood and the Interns, and released on January 15, 1962 on Okeh, but was not a Top 20 hit.

61 KANSAS CITY/HEY HEY HEY HEY *(2.35)*
Paul sings lead vocals with John and George backing him towards the end.

Although credited as *Kansas City* on the record, this track is in fact two songs sung as a medley, starting with *Kansas City* and segueing into *Hey Hey Hey Hey* by Richard Penniman (Little Richard). The Beatles styled their version on the way the songs were performed on stage by Little Richard, who originally sang them as a medley.

September 30, 1957, and became a million seller in America, reaching No. 8, and staying in the Top 20 for nine weeks. Chuck Berry had six million selling singles before 1970, including *Rock And Roll Music; Maybellene*, 1955; *Roll Over Beethoven*, 1956; *School Days*, 1957; *Sweet Little Sixteen*, 1958 and *Johnny B. Goode*, 1958. He had many other hit singles in America including: *Carol, Let It Rock, No Particular Place To Go* and *You Never Can Tell*, but it was not until 1972 that he scored his first No. 1 single in Britain and America, with *My Ding-a-ling*, a live recording.

59 I'LL FOLLOW THE SUN *(1.47)*
Composer Paul sings solo, with double tracking in places.

60 MR. MOONLIGHT *(2.36)*
John sings lead with Paul helping. Paul plays Hammond organ and George plays an African drum.

Hey Hey Hey Hey was also the "B" side to Little Richard's seventh million selling single, *Good Golly Miss Molly*, which reached No. 10 with fifteen weeks in the US charts, while he recorded *Kansas City* on his album *The Fabulous Little Richard*, issued March 9, 1959. *Kansas City* was written by Jerry Leiber and Mike Stoller, and was originally called *K. C. Loving* and recorded by Little Willie Littlefield as a single released on December 29, 1952. After Little Richard had recorded it for his album, Wilbert Harrison released his singles version on March 23, 1959, achieving a million seller, topping the charts for two weeks and staying ten weeks in the US Top 20.

Jerry Leiber and Mike Stoller first met in 1949 in Los Angeles, where they started their songwriting and producing partnership. They originally wrote strictly R&B songs, but later began to provide pop hits for such artists as The Coasters and Elvis Presley, through whom they sold over

30 million records up to 1960. Eleven of their songs sold over a million discs each; these include *Hound Dog* (six million), *Lovin' You* (two million), *Jailhouse Rock* (two million), *Don't* (two million) and *Bossa Nova Baby* by Elvis Presley; *Searchin'* (two million), *Yakety Yak* (two million), *Charlie Brown* and *Poison Ivy* by The Coasters and *Lucky Lips* which was a million seller for Ruth Brown in the US in 1959, and a million seller for Cliff Richard in 1963.

B SIDE

62   EIGHT DAYS A WEEK *(2.42)*
Written jointly by John and Paul, who also share the vocals, with George helping occasionally. This was probably the first song to feature a "fade-in" at the beginning of the record (as opposed to a "fade-out" at the end).

This song (along with *No Reply* and *I'm A Loser*) was originally being considered as a potential single release in Britain, until John came up with *I Feel Fine*. Though not released in Britain as a single, it did find its way onto a 45 in the form of an EP extract from *Beatles For Sale*.

63   WORDS OF LOVE *(2.01)*
John and Paul share the vocals on this Buddy Holly song. Ringo plays packing case!

The song was one of Buddy Holly's early unsuccessful singles, released on the Coral label on June 17, 1957. In September of the same year, he released his first million selling single, *Peggy Sue*, and his second million seller *It Doesn't Matter Anymore* was released in 1958, after two Top 20 hits *Listen To Me* and *Rave On*. With The Crickets he had several big hits: *That'll Be The Day* (1957, million seller); *Oh Boy* (1957); *Maybe Baby* (1958, million seller) and *Think It Over* (1958).

64   HONEY DON'T *(2.55)*
Ringo sings.

Honey Don't was written by Carl Perkins, and released as the "B" side of Perkins' best known song, *Blue Suede Shoes*, on January 2, 1956, on the Sun label. Although little credit for this can accrue to *Honey Don't*, the record reached No. 4 in the US charts, selling two million copies, and remaining in the Top 20 for fourteen weeks, while in Britain it peaked at No. 10 during a Top 20 residency of seven weeks. In Britain, the Perkins record found a commercially more successful rival in Elvis Presley's cover of *Blue Suede Shoes* which achieved a position of No. 9 during an eight week stay in the charts.

65   EVERY LITTLE THING *(2.00)*
Written by John and Paul, who both sing lead. Ringo plays tympani.

66   I DON'T WANT TO SPOIL THE PARTY *(2.33)*
Written by John. John and Paul share the vocals, with George helping on harmony.

67   WHAT YOU'RE DOING *(2.28)*
Written by John and Paul. Paul sings lead with John and George harmonising.

68   EVERYBODY'S TRYING TO BE MY BABY *(2.23)*
George sings solo and is double tracked in places.

The third Carl Perkins number to be recorded by The Beatles (see *Matchbox* and *Honey Don't*), all of which were included on the Perkins LP, *Teen Beat*, released on Sun on August 18, 1958.

20   BEATLES FOR SALE

GEP 8931—April 6, 1965

Three tracks on this EP were originally considered as singles material, until the release of *I Feel Fine*. *Eight Days A Week* was released as a single in America.

A SIDE

55a   NO REPLY *(2.13)*

56a   I'M A LOSER *(2.26)*

B SIDE

58a   ROCK AND ROLL MUSIC *(2.28)*
(Not considered as a single.)

62a   EIGHT DAYS A WEEK *(2.42)*
(See *Beatles For Sale* LP for above titles.)

21   TICKET TO RIDE *(3.03)*
YES IT IS *(2.38)*

R 5265—April 9, 1965

Ticket To Ride went to No. 1 on April 14 making it the fifth Beatles' single to go directly to No. 1 within a week of release. It stayed at No. 1 for five weeks, was in the Top 10 for seven weeks and the Top 30 for nine weeks, selling over 700,000 copies in Britain. Globally, sales amount to between two and three million.

69   TICKET TO RIDE
Written by John, who sings lead, with Paul and George adding vocal support. Paul plays guitar. Recorded February 1965.

Their version of *Ticket To Ride* was The Carpenters' first single, which gave them a minor hit in America in 1969. Their follow up, *Close To You* was a two million selling American No. 1, and the first of a long string of American and British hits, including *Goodbye To Love, Yesterday Once More, Top Of The World, Please Mr. Postman, Only Yesterday* and *Calling Occupants Of Interplanetary Craft*.

70   YES IT IS
Another John composition. John is very prominent vocally, but Paul and George sing in unison with him at times. Recorded February 1965.

22   BEATLES FOR SALE (No. 2.)

GEP 8938—June 4, 1965

The Beatles' ninth EP, which contains selections from their No. 1 album, *Beatles For Sale.*

A SIDE
59a   I'LL FOLLOW THE SUN *(1.47)*

57a   BABY'S IN BLACK *(2.03)*

B SIDE

63a   WORDS OF LOVE *(2.10)*

66a   I DON'T WANT TO SPOIL THE PARTY *(2.33)*
(See *Beatles For Sale* LP for all titles.)

23   HELP! *(2.16)*
I'M DOWN *(2.30)*

R 5305—July 23, 1965

Advance orders for *Help* reached 300,000 by July 21, and the single went straight to No. 1 on July 28, staying there for four weeks. It sold 500,000 in its first week of release, and by August 13, the total had increased to 800,000. Final sales of 900,000 were reported in Britain, following stays in the Top 10 of eight weeks and the Top 30 of ten weeks. World sales are around two million.

71   HELP!
Composer John sings lead, with Paul and George supplying harmony. Recorded April 13, 1965.

72   I'M DOWN
Written by Paul, who sings lead, backed vocally by John and George. John plays Hammond organ. Recorded late May 1965.

24   HELP!

PCS 3071—August 6, 1965

The Beatles' second film soundtrack album entered the charts on August 11, at No's 1 and 26 in the album and Top 30 charts respectively. The album stayed at No. 1 for eleven weeks, was in the album chart for twenty six weeks and in the Top 30 for four weeks, rising to No. 23.

The album had advance sales in Britain of 250,000, and actually sold 270,000 in its first week. This total eventually reached 900,000 in Britain, while world sales are around 2,300,000.

The "A" side of the album contains the songs included in the film. *The Night Before, You've Got To Hide Your Love Away, I Need You, Another Girl* and *You're Gonna Lose That Girl* were recorded between early February and early March 1965. *You Like Me Too Much, Tell Me What You See* and *Dizzy Miss Lizzy* were recorded on

May 10 and May 11, 1965. *Act Naturally, It's Only Love, I've Just Seen A Face* and *Yesterday* were recorded between late May and early June, 1965.

69a   **TICKET TO RIDE** *(3.03)*
(See single.)

A SIDE

B SIDE

71a   **HELP!** *(2.16)*
(See single.)

73   **THE NIGHT BEFORE** *(2.30)*
Written by Paul, who takes lead vocals, supported by George and John in the background. John plays electric piano.

74   **YOU'VE GOT TO HIDE YOUR LOVE AWAY** *(2.06)*
Composer John sings solo with flutes added by session men.

This song was given to The Silkie, a folk group formed by students from Hull University, who were managed by Brian Epstein. Their recording was produced by John and Paul, while George played tambourine and Paul guitar. The single got into the *NME* Top 30 chart for one week at No. 29, on September 29, 1965.

75   **I NEED YOU** *(2.25)*
Written by George, who sings lead, with Paul and John helping out on harmony.

76   **ANOTHER GIRL** *(2.02)*
Composer Paul sings lead with John and George providing backing vocals. Paul plays lead guitar.

77   **YOU'RE GOING TO LOSE THAT GIRL** *(2.14)*
Written by John who sings lead with Paul and George supplying vocal backing.

78   **ACT NATURALLY** *(2.27)*
Ringo sings with Paul helping here and there.

Act Naturally was written by Johnny Russell and Vonie Morrison, and released as a single by Buck Owens on March 11, 1963, when it became a No. 1 Country And Western hit in the US.

79   **IT'S ONLY LOVE** *(1.53)*
Written by John, who sings lead, with Paul helping.

Shortly before his unfortunate death, John Lennon, in one of his "comeback" interviews, expressed his dislike of *It's Only Love*, but ironically, the song became a hit during 1981, when Gary "US" Bonds spent a few weeks near the bottom of the British chart with his version, which was produced with the assistance of several members of Bruce Springsteen's E Street Band. *It's Only Love* was also one of the four tracks on Bryan Ferry's *Extended Play* EP, which was a Top 10 hit in Britain during the summer of 1976.

80   **YOU LIKE ME TOO MUCH** *(2.33)*
Composer George sings lead with Paul supporting. John plays electric piano, while Paul and George Martin play a Steinway acoustic piano.

81   **TELL ME WHAT YOU SEE** *(2.34)*
Written by Paul who shares lead vocals with John. Paul plays electric piano.

LENNON &
McCARTNEY
produce
THE SILKIE
In their new hit
YOU'VE GOT TO
HIDE YOUR
LOVE AWAY
TF 603

fontana

Marianne
Faithfull
YESTERDAY
F 12268
DECCA

The Hit Version
of the
LENNON/McCARTNEY
Composition
MICHELLE
by
the
Overlanders
7N 17034

THE SETTLERS

7N 17065 NOWHERE MAN

Sole Agent : TITO BURNS PRODUCTIONS LTD.,   Personal Manager
3 Vere Street, London, W.1. HYD 8751   GLORIA E. HELLMAN

THE HIT SINGLE VERSION OF THE
LENNON—McCARTNEY SONG by

THE ST. LOUIS UNION
GIRL
Backed with
RESPECT
on DECCA F 12318

... A NATURAL HIT SINGLE ... A NATURAL HIT SINGLE ... A NATURAL HIT SINGLE ... A NATURAL HIT SINGLE ...

THE NATURALS
SING
JOHN LENNON — PAUL McCARTNEY'S
I SHOULD HAVE KNOWN BETTER
(FROM THE FILM : "A HARD DAY'S NIGHT")
PUBLISHED BY
NORTHERN SONGS LTD.
on PARLOPHONE R 5165
ARTISTS' MANAGEMENT
DICK JAMES MUSIC LTD.
(AGENCY DIVISION)
TEM 1687

82 I'VE JUST SEEN A FACE *(2.02)*
Again written by Paul, who this time sings solo.

83 YESTERDAY *(2.02)*
Paul woke up one morning and went to the piano, started playing and a tune came — but he couldn't think of any words at the time, so he called the song "Scrambled Egg". For a couple of days that was the title, but he then thought of *Yesterday*, and began to write appropriate lyrics. Paul sings solo to his own guitar accompaniment, backed by a string quartet. John, George and Ringo do not appear on this track.

Paul allegedly offered the song to Chris Farlowe before anybody else, but Farlowe turned it down — even so, *Yesterday* holds the record for the most popular Beatles composition in terms of cover versions. By December 1967 there were 450 recordings of the song, and by 1975, this number increased to 1,186 — 637 in America, 355 in Britain and 194 in Europe. Along with the 1973 hit by Dawn *Tie A Yellow Ribbon Round The Old Oak Tree*, *Yesterday* is the most covered song of all time.

Yesterday has been covered by many solo vocalists, including Cilla Black, Ray Charles, Vera Lynn, Marianne Faithfull, Tom Jones, Brenda Lee, Kenneth McKellar, Dionne Warwick, Frank Sinatra and Lou Rawls. Among the groups to have recorded *Yesterday* are The Seekers and Jan and Dean, while several Motown artists have done likewise, including Marvin Gaye, Gladys Knight and The Pips, Smokey Robinson and The Miracles, The Supremes, The Temptations and Mary Wells. Probably hundreds of instrumental orchestras and bands have also recorded the song, including Acker Bilk, Liberace, Frank Chacksfield and Frank Pourcel.

However, of all these cover versions only one artist had a Top 30 hit with the song when Matt Monro's version entered the Top 30 on October 13, 1965, at No. 29. Matt Monro had thirteen Top 50 hits between 1960 and 1973, including *Portrait Of My Love*, *My Kind Of Girl*, *Softly As I Leave You*, *From Russia With Love* and *Walk Away*.

Marianne Faithfull had a minor hit with her version in November 1965, and Ray Charles with his in December 1967, both reaching the lower regions of the BMRB Top 50.

The song was not released in Britain as a Beatles' single until 1976, but it was released in single form in many other countries, topping the charts in the USA, Hong Kong, Finland, Norway and Belgium. The single sold 1,800,000 in America alone and has sold well over 2.5 million globally.

84 DIZZY MISS LIZZY *(2.51)*
John sings solo.

Written and originally recorded by Larry Williams, whose version was released as a single on February 24, 1958, backed by *Slow Down* (also recorded by The Beatles for their *Long Tall Sally* EP), although it was not a major hit. (See *Slow Down* for further information on Larry Williams.)

25 DAY TRIPPER *(2.49)*
WE CAN WORK IT OUT *(2.12)*

R 5389—December 3, 1965

The Beatles' first double "A" sided single went straight to No. 1 on December 8, and stayed there for five weeks, selling 750,000 by December 8 and one million by December 20, just eight days after its release. It was the seventh consecutive Beatles' single to enter the charts at No. 1 and their tenth consecutive single to reach No. 1 in Britain, where it figured in the Top 10 for eight weeks and the Top 30 for ten weeks.

With sales of over a million in both Britain and America, the single has sold around three million world-wide.

85 DAY TRIPPER
Written mainly by John, supposedly on the subject of drugs, with Paul's help. John and Paul sing lead, with George assisting on harmony. John played tambourine, and the song was recorded in early November 1965.

86 WE CAN WORK IT OUT
Written mainly by Paul, with John contributing the middle section. Paul sings lead, with John and George helping with backgrounds and harmony. John plays harmonium, and the song was again cut in early November 1965.

Stevie Wonder also scored a hit on both sides of the Atlantic with his version of *We Can Work It Out* during 1971, which peaked at No. 22 in the *NME* Top 30 during a five week chart stay, doing rather better in America where it reached No. 9 during its seven weeks in the Top 30.

PCS 3075—December 3, 1965

The Beatles' sixth British album entered the Top 10 album chart on December 8 at No. 1, making it their fifth album to go directly to No. 1 less than a week after release. The album stayed at No. 1 for twelve weeks and was in the album chart for twenty nine weeks, but did not enter the Top 30 chart, as had their previous four albums.

The album had advance orders of over 500,000, and EMI had shipped that number of copies to dealers by December 6. It eventually sold around 750,000 in Britain, and with American sales of two million, must have sold over three million globally.

All tracks for *Rubber Soul* were recorded between mid-October and early November 1965.

A SIDE

87   DRIVE MY CAR *(2.25)*
Written by John and Paul, who share lead vocal, with George helping out on harmony. Paul plays piano.

88   NORWEGIAN WOOD (THIS BIRD HAS FLOWN) *(2.01)*
John admitted he wrote this song about an affair he had had with another woman in an attempt to describe his feelings without letting his wife know. It was written at his Kenwood home, with Paul helping out with a few words. John sings lead, with Paul helping in places. George plays sitar — the first time this Indian instrument was used on a pop record. (After The Beatles had used the sitar on record, several other groups

featured the instrument on their recordings, e.g. The Rolling Stones' 1966 single, *Paint It Black* and Traffic's 1967 singles, *Paper Sun* and *Hole In My Shoe*.)

89   YOU WON'T SEE ME *(3.18)*
Composer Paul sings lead vocals, with John and George supplying harmony and helping with the chorus. Paul plays piano and Mal Evans plays Hammond organ.

90   NOWHERE MAN *(2.40)*
When John lived in Britain at his Kenwood home, for at least a few hours every day he would sit on the steps of his house just thinking and writing songs. One day he was trying to write a song, but eventually he stopped searching for inspiration, as nothing was occurring to him. Finally, he stopped thinking, but then, imagining himself as doing nothing and going nowhere, he conceived the idea of

himself as a "nowhere man". John wrote the whole song and it was recorded unaltered as he had written it. John, Paul and George sing the lead vocal together, with John singing solo at times.

This was a minor hit for Three Good Reasons in March 1966, when it entered the lower regions of the BMRB Top 50.

91   THINK FOR YOURSELF *(2.14)*
Composer George handles lead vocals, with John and Paul supplying backing vocals. Paul plays fuzz bass and George tambourine.

92   THE WORD *(2.39)*
Both John and Paul wrote this song, and John sings the verse while Paul and George join him for the chorus. Paul

plays piano and George Martin harmonium.

93   MICHELLE *(2.40)*
Written mainly by Paul, but John helped with the bridge. Paul sings lead, with John and George supplying harmony.

By January 8, 1966, a month after the release of the album, there were twenty cover versions of *Michelle* recorded in all parts of the world. The song is the second most covered song written by The Beatles, with over 620 versions recorded by 1975.

The first cover versions of *Michelle* were by The Overlanders and David and Jonathan. The Overlanders' version entered the Top 30 at No. 15 on January 12, 1966, and on February 2 topped the chart for one week. It stayed in the Top 30 for eight weeks and was The Overlanders' only British hit.

David and Jonathan's version entered the Top 30 on January 19 at No. 15 staying in the Top 30 for four weeks and reaching No. 9. They followed this single up with their self-penned *Lovers Of The World Unite*, which was a

THE BEATLES
PAPERBACK WRITER
RAIN

PARLOPHONE R5452

RELEASE DATE 10 JUNE

EMI

bigger hit, reaching No. 7. After the success of this single, the English duo, real names Roger Cook and Roger Greenaway, turned to songwriting and together (and with other songwriters) have written numerous hits for many artists. These hits include for Blue Mink, (with whom Roger Cook was a vocalist), *Good Morning Freedom* (with Albert Hammond and Mike Hazelwood), *Banner Man, Stay With Me, Randy* (with Herbie Flowers) and *Melting*

Pot, and for the Fortunes *You've Got Your Troubles, This Golden Ring,* and *Freedom Come, Freedom Go* (with Hammond and Hazelwood). For Cilla Black, *Conversations* (with Jerry Lordan) and *Something Tells Me,* for The Hollies, *Gasoline Alley Bred* (with Tony MacCauley), for Andy Williams *Home Lovin' Man* (with Tony MacCauley), for Whistling Jack Smith *I Was Kaiser Bill's Batman,* for The Drifters *Like Sister, Like Brother* (with

Geoff Stephens), for White Plains *My Baby Loves Lovin'*, for The Fantastics *Something Old, Something New* (with Tony MacCauley), for Cliff Richard *Sunny Honey Girl* (with Hiller and Goodison) and for The Family Dogg *A Way Of Life*.

B SIDE

94   WHAT GOES ON *(2.43)*
Written by John a few years earlier, but Paul and Ringo wrote a new middle eight when it was being recorded. Ringo sings lead, with John and Paul supplying harmony.

95   GIRL *(2.26)*
Written by John about a "dream" girl. John sings lead and Paul and George support with harmony.

Two cover versions of this song got into the Top 30. The first, by St. Louis Union, a Manchester group, entered the charts on January 26, 1966 at No. 25, rising to No. 19 and staying in the charts for four weeks and was the group's sole chart success. The second version was recorded by Truth, who had a longer run in the charts, of five weeks, entering on February 2 at No. 23 and rising to No. 18.

96   I'M LOOKING THROUGH YOU *(2.21)*
This song was written by Paul when Jane (Asher) left him and went away to Bristol. Paul sings double tracked lead vocal with John helping occasionally. Ringo plays Hammond organ.

97   IN MY LIFE *(2.22)*
Written by John, who sings double tracked lead vocal, with help from Paul. George Martin plays piano.

98   WAIT *(2.10)*
Written by John and Paul. John sings lead in the verses, with Paul and George joining him for choruses.

99   IF I NEEDED SOMEONE *(2.18)*
Written by George, who is double tracked on lead vocals, with assistance from John and Paul.

The Hollies had a UK hit with their version of *If I Needed Someone*, which George Harrison publicly said he didn't like, something that could account for the fact that it didn't do very well in the charts, compared to The Hollies' other hits. It was in the Top 30 for three weeks, entering at No. 28 on December 15, 1965, and reaching No. 24. The Hollies have had more British hits than any other British group,

including the Beatles. Their total up to 1976 was 27, including *Stay, Just One Look, Here I Go Again, We're Through, Yes I Will, I'm Alive* (their first No. 1), *Look Through Any Window, I Can't Let Go, Bus Stop, Stop Stop Stop, On A Carousel, Carrie Anne, Jennifer Eccles, Sorry Suzanne, He Ain't Heavy, He's My Brother, I Can't Tell The Bottom From The Top* and *The Air That I Breathe*, while a medley of their previous hits returned them to the Top 20 in 1981.

100   RUN FOR YOUR LIFE *(2.16)*
Written by John, who sings lead with Paul and George assisting.

This is one song that John always said he disliked, as it was "knocked off" to complete an album.

<table><tr><td>**27**</td><td>**THE BEATLES' MILLION SELLERS**</td></tr></table>

GEP 8946—December 6, 1965

This, the tenth Beatles EP, was obviously intended to appeal to the Christmas market and contained four of their five (up to that time) British million selling singles, *A Hard Day's Night* being the track omitted. Fourteen days after the release of this EP, the Beatles received their sixth British million selling singles award, for *Day Tripper*, which had been released only three days prior to the EP.

The combined British sale of the four singles exceeds 5,350,000: *She Loves You* — 1,600,000; *I Want To Hold Your Hand* — 1,509,000; *Can't Buy Me Love* — 1,250,000 and *I Feel Fine* — 1,000,000. Even more phenomenal is the total world sale for the four singles of over twenty-seven million with *I Want To Hold Your Hand* accounting for over thirteen million, *Can't Buy Me Love* six million, *She Loves You* five million and *I Feel Fine* three million.

A SIDE

18a   SHE LOVES YOU *(2.18)*

34a I WANT TO HOLD YOUR HAND *(2.23)*

B SIDE

36b CAN'T BUY ME LOVE *(2.11)*

53a I FEEL FINE *(2.20)*
(See respective singles for each title.)

28 YESTERDAY

GEP 8948—March 4, 1966

On this EP, each Beatle takes a turn in singing lead vocal; Paul on *Yesterday*; Ringo on *Act Naturally*; George on *You Like Me Too Much* and John on *It's Only Love*.

A SIDE

83a YESTERDAY *(2.03)*

78a ACT NATURALLY *(2.27)*

B SIDE

80a YOU LIKE ME TOO MUCH *(2.34)*

79a IT'S ONLY LOVE *(1.53)*
(See *Help* LP for all above titles.)

29 PAPERBACK WRITER *(2.23)*
RAIN *(2.58)*

R 5452—June 10, 1966

The twelfth Beatles' single entered the charts at No. 2 on June 15, making it the first Beatles' single since *She Loves You* to fail to enter the charts directly at No. 1; all seven singles from *I Want To Hold Your Hand* to *Day Tripper* had simultaneously entered and topped the charts within a week of release. However, *Paperback Writer* did reach No. 1 on June 22, staying in that position for two weeks, which made it the eleventh consecutive Beatles' single to get to No. 1. It remained in the Top 10 for five weeks and the Top 30 for eight weeks.

** *Paperback Writer* sold over 500,000 in Britain and with American sales of over one million, global sales must be over two million. The single was also a No. 1 hit in Holland, Hong Kong, Denmark, Germany, Austria, Ireland, New Zealand, Australia, Malaysia and Singapore.**

** (See also "The Singles Collection 1962—1970" on page 89, for chart re-entry details relating to this single.)**

101 PAPERBACK WRITER
Paul wrote the tune and most of the words, with John contributing the remaining lyric. Paul sings lead, with John and George harmonising. Paul plays Rickenbacker bass and Vox organ. The basic track of guitars, drums and vocals was recorded on Wednesday, April 16, 1966 at EMI Studio No. 3. Some special effects were added a few days later. The entire recording took ten hours.

102 RAIN
Recorded in late April 1966, John sings lead on his own composition, with Paul and George supporting him vocally. At the end of the recording one line of John's vocals ("Rain, when the rain comes they run and hide their heads") is heard backwards, as John had inadvertently played the master tape backwards when at home, liked what he heard, and wished to use it on the finished recording.

The Beatles were nominated in eight sections of the American Grammy Awards for 1966: Eleanor Rigby — "Best Contemporary Solo Vocal Performance", "Best Contemporary Record", "Best Arrangement Accompanying a Vocal" and "Record Of The Year"; Michelle — "Best Song Of The Year" and "Best Instrumental Arrangement"; and Revolver — "Best Album Of The Year" and "Best Album Cover".

* They eventually won in two sections — Michelle became "Song Of The Year" and Eleanor Rigby was judged "Best Contemporary Solo Vocal Performance". Klaus Voorman received an Award for the "Best Graphic-Art Album Cover" for Revolver.*

30 NOWHERE MAN

GEP 8952—July 8, 1966

The twelfth Beatles' EP was a selection from their 1965 album *Rubber Soul*.

A SIDE

90a   NOWHERE MAN *(2.40)*

87a   DRIVE MY CAR *(2.25)*

B SIDE

93a   MICHELLE *(2.33)*

89a   YOU WON'T SEE ME *(3.21)*
(See *Rubber Soul* album for all above titles.)

31   ELEANOR RIGBY *(2.04)*
YELLOW SUBMARINE *(2.36)*

R 5493—August 5, 1966

This, the Beatles' second double "A" sided single to be released in Britain, was the first occasion on which the group had released a single on the same day as the album on which the tracks also appeared, the LP being *Revolver.* **It entered the charts on August 10 at No. 2 and rose a week later to No. 1, where it remained for four weeks, staying in the Top 10 for seven weeks and the Top 30 for ten weeks. The single had advance orders in Britain of 250,000, which EMI had shipped to dealers by August 10. By August 24, it had sold 300,000 in Britain, and by the end of the year had sold 455,000, the highest certified sales for 1966. Global sales must be well over two million since** *Yellow Submarine* **was also No. 1 in Germany, Norway, Sweden, Holland, Canada, Switzerland, Australia and New Zealand.**

103   ELEANOR RIGBY
Written by Paul and John, but Paul had the original idea for the song when he was looking in a shop window in Bristol, and liked the name above the shop — "Daisy Hawkins". Playing with the name in his head, it turned into a rhythm, and then into *Eleanor Rigby.* He had written most of the words by the time the group came to record it, but the last verse was made up in the studio.

Paul recorded the vocal for the number on April 20, and eight days later, four violins, two violas and two cellos played by session men were added.

This song became a very popular choice for "cover" versions by other artists. Ray Charles had a minor hit with his version in August 1968, when it got into the *NME* Top 30 for two weeks, its highest position being No. 25. Aretha Franklin's version in America reached No. 23 and was in the Top 30 there for four weeks.

104   YELLOW SUBMARINE
Written by Paul and John for Ringo, who sings lead with the other Beatles joining him for the chorus. As well as the Beatles, Mal Evans (Beatles' Road Manager), Neil Aspinall (Beatles' Personal Assistant), George Martin (Beatles' Producer), Alf (?), Geoffrey Emerick (Engineer), Patti Harrison (George's wife) and other studio staff and engineers sing the final fade out chorus. The basic track was recorded in June, with special effects — John blowing bubbles through a straw, George swirling water in a bucket, a brass band, submarine noises, etc. — added two weeks later. Paul and John are heard talking in the middle section as the submarine crew, and it's John who repeats some of the words after Ringo sings them.

This song has over the years become very popular as a children's favourite with a contagious chorus.

32   REVOLVER

PCS 7009—August 5, 1966

The Beatles' seventh album was to be titled "Abracadabra", until it was discovered that the title had already been used. *Revolver* **was the group's sixth album to enter the album charts at No. 1, which it did on August 10, when it also entered the Top 30 chart at No. 28, rising to No. 18, and staying in that chart for four weeks, and becoming their fifth album to reach the** *NME* **Top 30. The album stayed at No. 1 for seven weeks during a stay in the album chart lasting twenty weeks.**

Revolver **had advance orders of 300,000 in Britain, and by August 10 had actually sold 200,000. By August 24 it had passed 300,000 and eventually sold around 500,000. World sales probably amount to two million.**

Revolver **must be the most "covered" album ever to appear in Britain, as over half a dozen other**

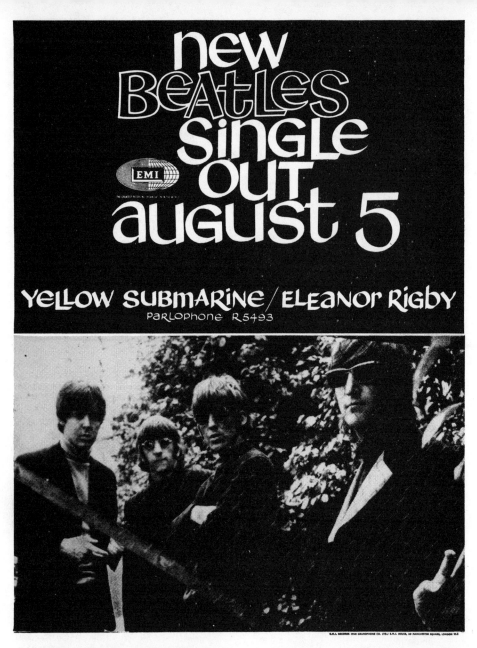

new BEATLES Single OUT august 5

EMI THE GREATEST RECORDING ORGANISATION IN THE WORLD

YELLOW SUBMARINE / ELEANOR RigbY
PARLOPHONE R5493

E.M.I. RECORDS (THE GRAMOPHONE CO. LTD.) E.M.I. HOUSE, 20 MANCHESTER SQUARE, LONDON W.1

artists recorded songs from the album before it was released, followed by several more versions after release. The cover versions included: *Good Day Sunshine/For No One* by Scott Hamilton; *Here There And Everywhere* by The Fourmost; *Good Day Sunshine* by The Tremeloes; *Yellow Submarine* by The She Trinity; *Good Day Sunshine* by Glen Dale; *For No One/Here There And Everywhere* by Brian Withers; *Here There And*

Everywhere by Episode Six; *Taxman* by Loose Ends; *For No One* by Cilla Black and *Got To Get You Into My Life* by Cliff Bennett and The Rebel Rousers, which was the only cover to make the charts (see below).

Recording of *Revolver* began on April 6, 1966, with *Tomorrow Never Knows*. Most of the recordings were done at EMI Studios No. 2, but No. 3 Studio was used on some days.

The album cover for *Revolver* was

designed and drawn by Klaus Voorman, an old friend of the Beatles from their early days in Hamburg. Voorman, one time bass player with Manfred Mann (he replaced Jack Bruce who had left to form Cream), later played bass with The Plastic Ono Band, and on many Beatles' solo albums.

A SIDE

105 TAXMAN (2.35)
Written by George, who is double tracked on lead vocal, with John and Paul supplying harmony.

103a ELEANOR RIGBY (2.04)
(See single.)

106 I'M ONLY SLEEPING (2.58)
John wrote this and sings lead, with Paul and George harmonising.

107 LOVE YOU TO (2.58)
Written by George, who is double tracked on lead vocal and also plays sitar. The tabla, an Indian hand drum, is played by Anil Bhagwat.

108 HERE, THERE AND EVERYWHERE (2.22)
Written by Paul, who sings double tracked lead vocal, assisted by John and George.

Emmylou Harris had a minor hit ten years later with her version of *Here, There And Everywhere*, which entered the Top 30 for one week at No. 28 on March 20, 1976.

104a YELLOW SUBMARINE (2.36)
(See single.)

109 SHE SAID, SHE SAID (2.33)
This was written by John about his second LSD trip in Los Angeles, an occasion when he met Peter Fonda, who said he knew what it was like to be dead. John sings lead, with Paul and George helping.

B SIDE

110 GOOD DAY SUNSHINE (2.07)
Written by Paul, who sings lead, with John and George joining in for the chorus. Paul plays piano.

111 AND YOUR BIRD CAN SING (1.58)
Written by John, who sings lead, helped by Paul and George.

112 FOR NO ONE (1.57)
Written by Paul, who sings solo, and plays piano. The horn was played by Alan Civil.

For No One was also recorded without chart success by Cilla Black.

113 DR. ROBERT (2.13)
Written mainly by John about a man in New York, who the Beatles were told could get them anything "medicinal" they wanted, as he was a "pill" doctor. Paul assisted in writing the middle section. John sings double tracked lead vocal, with Paul helping in places.

114 I WANT TO TELL YOU (2.26)
Written by George, who is double tracked on lead vocal, with John and Paul supplying harmony. Paul plays piano.

115 GOT TO GET YOU INTO MY LIFE (2.26)
Written by Paul, who sings double tracked solo vocal, with brass backing supplied by Ian Hamer, Les Condon and Eddie Thornton on trumpet and Alan Branscombe and Peter Coe on tenor saxophone.

This song was recorded in mid-July by Cliff Bennett and The Rebel Rousers, with Paul McCartney producing, and released as a single on August 5, 1966. It entered the Top 30 on August 17 at No. 30 and rose to No. 8, staying in the Top 30 for eight weeks. The group had scored a previous hit with *One Way Love* (originally recorded by The Drifters, and written by B. Russell and N. Meade), which was in the charts for four weeks. After the disbandment of The Rebel Rousers, Bennett formed an unsuccessful progressive rock band called Toe Fat.

The second cover version of *Got To Get You Into My Life* to enter the charts was by Earth, Wind and Fire, and was from the *Sgt. Pepper's Lonely Hearts*

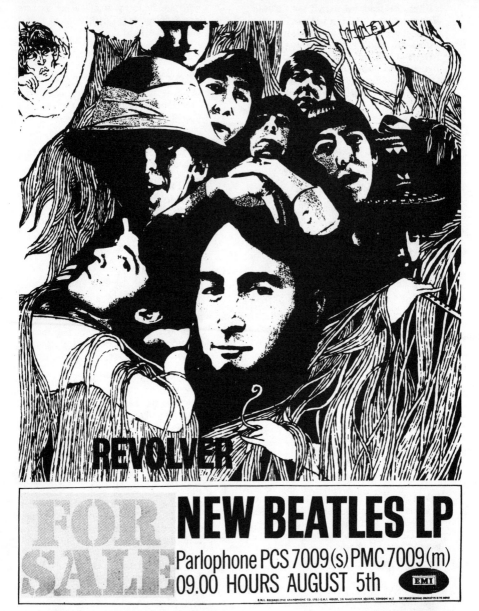

NEW BEATLES LP

Parlophone PCS 7009 (s) PMC 7009 (m)
09.00 HOURS AUGUST 5th

E.M.I. RECORDS (THE GRAMOPHONE CO. LTD.) E.M.I. HOUSE, 20 MANCHESTER SQUARE, LONDON W.I   THE GREATEST RECORDING ORGANISATION IN THE WORLD

Club Band film soundtrack. It entered the US charts at No. 19 on August 15, 1978, remaining in the chart for fourteen weeks and peaking at No. 4 for three weeks. It also made the British charts, but was far less successful, entering for a single week at No. 30 on October 30, 1978. This black American group were formed in Chicago in 1971, and have become one of America's top selling bands, with every album release since their third going gold. Their first US Top 30 hit single came in 1975, when *Shining Star* got to No. 1. They followed

this with *That's The Way Of The World* (13); *Sing A Song* (7), *Getaway* (10), *Saturday Nite* (21) and *Serpentine Fire* (15). Their next hit was *Got To Get You Into My Life*, which was followed by *September* (6), *Boogie Wonderland* and *After The Love Has Gone* (3). In Britain their first Top 30 entry came in 1977 with *Saturday Nite* which reached No. 20, and was followed by *Fantasy* (14). Following *Got To Get You Into My Life, September* gave them their biggest British hit to date, reaching No. 3. (See "Sgt. Pepper" picture disc for further details relating to the "Sgt. Pepper" film.)

116 TOMORROW NEVER KNOWS (2.55)
Written by John, who sings solo. John's voice was put through a Leslie speaker, as he wanted it to sound as though it were coming from a hilltop in Tibet. John made eight tape loops, which were put on eight different tape machines, and each tape was faded in and out when required. It was the first song for the album to be recorded, on April 6, 1966, and was originally titled *The Void*.

33 A COLLECTION OF BEATLES' OLDIES (BUT GOLDIES)

PCS 7016—December 10, 1966

This was the first Beatles' album to fail to reach No. 1 in Britain. It was released for the Christmas market, even though *Revolver* was still selling very well, and entered the album charts at No. 7 on December 14. Its highest position was No. 6, and it stayed in the album charts for ten weeks.

All the tracks on the album, except *Bad Boy*, had been previously released in Britain either as singles or on album. Of the sixteen tracks, thirteen came from eleven singles, which were all million sellers globally. Six achieved gold status in Britain and twelve were million sellers in America (hence the "But Goldies" suffix in the title.) The total global sales of the singles on the album exceeded forty-two million, including over ten million in Britain and nearly twenty million in the United States.

The "Carnaby Street" style cover was designed by David Christian, with the back cover photograph taken by Robert Whitaker.

A SIDE

18b SHE LOVES YOU (2.18)

16b FROM ME TO YOU (1.54)
The stereo version of this song differs from the mono single version, in that the harmonica introduction is missing at the beginning of the song.

86a WE CAN WORK IT OUT (2.12)

71b HELP! (2.16)

93b MICHELLE (2.40)
(See *Rubber Soul* LP.)

83b YESTERDAY (2.03)
(See *Help!* LP.)

53b I FEEL FINE (2.17)
This track differs from the original single release due to the addition of two seconds of whispering at the beginning.

104b YELLOW SUBMARINE (2.36)

B SIDE
36c CAN'T BUY ME LOVE (2.10)

117 BAD BOY (2.17)
(See below.)

85a DAY TRIPPER (2.49)

42b A HARD DAY'S NIGHT (2.28)

69b TICKET TO RIDE (3.03)

101a PAPERBACK WRITER (2.15)

103b ELEANOR RIGBY (2.04)

34b I WANT TO HOLD YOUR HAND (2.22)
(For all above titles see singles, unless otherwise indicated.)

117 BAD BOY (2.17)
John sings solo on this number recorded on May 10-11, 1965, during the *Help!* album sessions. It was the only previously unreleased song on the album, though it had been released in America in 1965 on the *Beatles VI* LP.

Bad Boy was written by Larry Williams, who released the song as a single on January 19, 1959, on the Specialty label, backed with *She Said 'Yeah'*. Although this single was not a Top 20 hit for Larry Williams, he had previously scored with two earlier million selling single hits, *Short Fat Fanny*, which was in the US Top 20 for

THE BEATLES

PARLOPHONE
PCS 7016 (S)
PMC 7016 (M)

EMI RECORDS (The Gramophone Co. Ltd.)
EMI HOUSE · 20 MANCHESTER SQUARE · LONDON W1

twelve weeks, reaching No. 6 and *Bony Moronie*, which was in the US Top 20 for four weeks, reaching No. 18, and in the British Top 20 for seven weeks, reaching No. 11.

34	**PENNY LANE** *(2.57)* **STRAWBERRY FIELDS FOREVER** *(4.03)*

R 5570—February 17, 1967

The Beatles' fourteenth British single,

and the first since *Love Me Do* not to reach No. 1 in Britain. It entered the charts on February 22 at No. 3, and began a two week stay at No. 2 on March 8. It was prevented from reaching the No. 1 position by British million seller, *Release Me* by Engelbert Humperdinck, which topped the chart for six weeks.

The single still sold 100,000 copies on the day of release and 350,000 in three days in Britain, eventually passing the half million mark. It was in the Top 10 for six weeks and the Top 30 for nine weeks. Global sales are well in excess of two million.

118 PENNY LANE

Written mainly by Paul about a street in Liverpool, although John helped with some of the lyrics. Recorded during the first two weeks of January 1967, with Paul singing lead and John helping in places. John and George Martin play piano and John plays conga drum. Other instruments used include: string bass - Frank Clarke; sped-up piccolo B Flat trumpet - David Mason; trumpet solo - Philip Jones, plus flutes, piccolos and a flugelhorn.

119 STRAWBERRY FIELDS FOREVER

Written by John who sings solo. The song was recorded before Christmas 1966, and the final recording consisted of two separate recordings joined together. John was not happy with the first recording, and asked George Martin to write a new score for the strings, which he did, and this was used for the second recording. John was still dissatisfied, but next wanted the first half of the early recording plus the second half of the new recording joined together. George Martin said that this was impossible as the two recordings were in different keys and tempi, but found that if he speeded up the slower recording (the second) by five percent, it brought it into the same key and tempo as the first recording, and thus the two recordings were joined as John had wished.

Paul plays the Mellotron at the beginning using the flute stop. George and Paul played the tympani and bongo drums, while Mal Evans played tambourine. Ringo provided an electric drum track and George played tabla harp. A vast variety of percussion sounds were used, and other instruments added included cellos, flutes, a harpsichord and brass.

This song is also about an actual place in Liverpool.

By February 1967, EMI claim that The Beatles have sold 180,000,000 records world wide.

The Beatles won the following "Ivor Novello Awards" for 1966: "Most Performed Work Of The Year" — 1. Michelle and 2. Yesterday; "'A' Side of a Record which has achieved the Highest Certified Sales of 1966" — Yellow Submarine with 455,000.

In May 1967, EMI claim that The Beatles' world total record sales exceed 200,000,000.

35 SGT. PEPPER'S LONELY HEARTS CLUB BAND

PCS 7027—June 1, 1967

Sgt. Pepper, the Beatles' ninth British album release, sold 250,000 in Britain during its first week on sale. It entered the album charts at No. 1 on May 31, staying at No. 1 for twenty-two weeks, and also entered the Top 30 at No. 26, rising to No. 21 and staying in that chart for five weeks. The LP was in the album charts for forty-five weeks initially, but re-entered at No. 28 for one week on May 14, 1974. As with all Beatles' albums, Sgt. Pepper still sells in large quantities today, and frequently enters the lower regions of the BMRB Top 50 chart. It had sold half a million one month after release, and eventually exceeded one million in Britain by April 1973. It topped the charts all over the world, and in Germany sold 100,000 in its first week, a new sales record for that territory. Up to January 1971, Sgt. Pepper was the biggest selling British album of all time, with sales of over 7.5 million, but this figure was later equalled by the Beatles' own 1969 album, Abbey Road. By 1981, sales of both Sgt. Pepper and Abbey Road exceeded ten million.

The LP was recorded at the EMI Studios at Abbey Road, St. John's Wood, North London, between December 10, 1966 and April 2, 1967.

`PENNY LANE´    `STRAWBERRY FIELDS FOREVER´   THE BEATLES

PARLOPHONE OUT FRIDAY FEBRUARY 17 1967

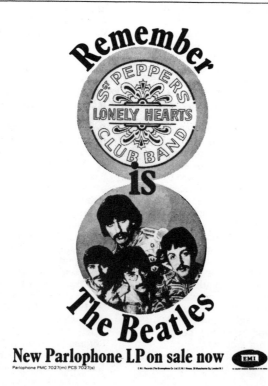

Remember

St PEPPERS
LONELY HEARTS
CLUB BAND

is

The Beatles

New Parlophone LP on sale now

Parlophone PMC 7027(m) PCS 7027(s)

The record is probably the first not to be split into individual tracks — i.e. it is not "banded". There is only a fraction of a second gap between one song and the next, and in some cases, no gap at all, so that tracks merge into one another: *Sgt. Pepper* into *With A Little Help From My Friends*, and *Good Morning, Good Morning* into *Sgt. Pepper* into *A Day In The Life*.

The run-out groove on the second side of the record is used: the first part of the groove contains a sound specially designed for dogs, a high frequency note pitched at eighteen kilocycles per second. This is above the general limit picked up by the human ear, which cannot hear sounds above 17 kilocycles. On the circular groove in the centre of the record is a snatch of jabbering conversation by The Beatles, mixed up and distorted, which sounds like "I never go see any other".

The sleeve of *Sgt. Pepper* has a picture montage of fifty-seven photographs, plus nine waxwork models, The Beatles, a Sgt. Pepper drum, a stone bust, four statuettes, an idol, a doll with "Welcome The Rolling Stones" on its jumper, a portable television set, a gold award and a variety of flower arrangements, one spelling the word "Beatles" and another in the shape of a guitar.

It was Paul's idea to have the

photographs on the sleeve. He said that as the LP was a great work of art, it should have all the people The Beatles liked on its sleeve. However, this wasn't as easy as it sounded, because legal clearance had to be obtained from all the celebrities whom the Beatles planned to portray. Brian Epstein gave the job to Wendy Moger, his Personal Assistant and NEMS employee, who had to get the legal clearance within a week — although EMI were not very keen on the idea, Paul wanted it. Wendy Moger had an enormous job and spent many hours (and pounds) on the telephone to

America to find that some people agreed and others didn't; Fred Astaire, she said, was very sweet, and she got on famously with Marlon Brando, but Shirley Temple said she wanted to hear the record before giving her approval.

Brian Epstein also didn't like Paul's idea for the cover, and early in 1967, while the negotiations were going on,

he was due to fly back to London from New York. Epstein was very superstitious, and was convinced that the plane would crash and that he would be killed, so before boarding the aircraft he wrote a note on a scrap of paper which he gave to Nat Weiss, his New York attorney. The note read "Brown paper Jackets for Sgt. Pepper's Lonely Hearts Club Band (album)".

All the items in the photograph on the cover came from the homes and personal collections of The Beatles, apart from nine waxwork models, loaned from Madame Tussaud's, of Diana Dors, Sonny Liston, Lawrence of Arabia, Dr Livingstone, George Bernard Shaw and the Beatles.

After Wendy Moger had obtained clearance for all the photographs, a montage was prepared by Peter Blake and Jann Haworth, and then assembled with the rest of the paraphernalia in a Chelsea photographic studio owned by Michael Cooper. The costumes worn by the Beatles themselves were specially made by Berman's, the notable theatrical costumiers, after the group had selected materials from satin samples supplied by Berman's, although originally the group had intended to be dressed in Salvation Army uniforms. Michael Cooper finally photographed

the tableau on March 30, 1967.

The front cover photo was not the only part of the album sleeve to cause a problem. Another was the back cover, on which the Beatles wanted the lyrics of the songs printed, something which was previously unheard of, and which caused some publishing difficulties, although these were eventually overcome. Also on the back cover is a

small picture of The Beatles, but one Beatle has his back turned. This is because it isn't a Beatle at all, and is, in fact, Mal Evans — Mal deputised for Paul, who was in America to be with Jane Asher on her twenty-first birthday, a time when Jane was touring with the Bristol Old Vic. As the sleeve had to go into production by the end of April, before Paul was due to return, Mal donned Paul's Sgt. Pepper gear and stood in for him, but turned his back so that people would not suspect that Paul was absent.

Another first for the *Sgt. Pepper* sleeve was the inner paper bag, (the actual record container, which normally remained white), was decorated with a colour wash of reds and pinks, a design created by Seemon and Marijke — it is now very common for albums to have a printed inner sleeve, which often becomes part of the main sleeve design and incorporates lyrics and credits. The decorated inner sleeve for *Sgt. Pepper* only appeared with early pressings of the album, and was discontinued later.

Also contained within the *Sgt. Pepper* sleeve is a set of cardboard cutouts, which include a moustache, picture card of "Sgt. Pepper", sergeant's stripes, a "Sgt. Pepper's Lonely Hearts Club Band" motif

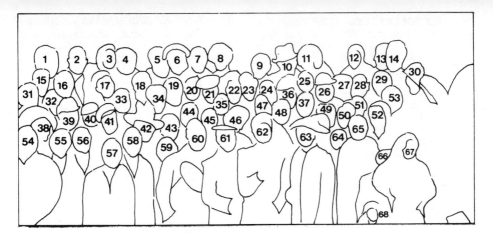

badge, a "Sgt. Pepper" badge and a "stand up" of the Beatles in "Pepper" gear.

Most of the tracks for "Sgt. Pepper" were recorded over several days, or rather nights, as at the time The Beatles preferred to start recording early in the evening, going through until the early hours of the morning. The total recording time spent on *Sgt. Pepper* was over 700 hours, at a cost of around £25,000.

1 **UNKNOWN**

2 **ALEISTER CROWLEY**
Black magician

3 **MAE WEST** — Born 1893.
US actress and film star. First film *Night After Night* 1932. Other films include *She Done Me Wrong* 1933 and *My Little Chickadee* 1940. A legend in showbusiness history.

4 **LENNY BRUCE**
Modern American comedian, who died in disgrace in 1966.

5 **KARLHEINZ STOCKHAUSEN** – Born 1928.
German composer and theorist. One of the foremost successful exponents of electronic music.

6 **W.C. FIELDS** — 1880-1946.
US music-hall and film comedian. Real name William Claude Dukenfield. Films include *Tillie's Punctured Romance* 1928, *My Little Chickadee* 1940 and *Never Give A Sucker An Even Break* 1941.

7 **CARL GUSTAV JUNG** — 1875-1961.
Swiss psychiatrist.

8 **EDGAR ALLAN POE** — 1809-49.
US poet and short story writer. Regarded by many as the creator of the modern detective story. Works include poems *The Raven* 1845 and *Annabel Lee* 1849 and stories *The Fall Of The House Of Usher* 1939 and *The Murders In The Rue Morgue* 1841.

9 **FRED ASTAIRE** — Born 1899.
US dancer and film star. Real name Frederick Austerlitz. Starred with Ginger Rogers in many 1930's musicals. Films include *The Gay Divorcee* 1934, *Top Hat* 1935, *Swing Time* 1936 and *Funny Face* 1957.

10 **MERKIN**
American artist.

11 **BINNIE BARNES** —
Born 1908 in London.
Real name Gertrude Maude Barnes. Film actress who starred in such films as *The Hour Before Dawn, Up In Mabel's Room, Barbary Coast Gent, The Fifth Chair* and *The Spanish Main*.

12 **HUNTZ HALL**
American film star, partner of The Bowery Boys in several notable films.

13 **SIMON RODIA**
Folk artist and creator of *Watts Towers*.

14 **BOB DYLAN** — Born 1941.
US folk/rock singer and composer. Taught himself to play guitar, piano, autoharp and harmonica. One of the originators of folk rock.

15 **AUBREY BEARDSLEY** — 1872-98.
British illustrator in the Art Nouveau style.

16 **SIR ROBERT PEEL** — 1788-1850.
British politician. Was an MP from 1809 to 1850 and twice Prime Minister in 1834-35 and 1841-46. Founder of the British police force.

17 **ALDOUS HUXLEY** — 1894-1963.
British novelist. Most well-known works are *Crome Yellow* 1921, *Antic Hay* 1923, *Point Counter Point* and *Brave New World* 1932, which is a nightmarish look into the future.

18 **TERRY SOUTHERN**
American author of humorous novels including *Candy* and *The Magic Christian*. Ringo starred in the films based on both books.

19 **TONY CURTIS** — Born 1925.
(Bernard Schwarz.) US film actor. Made first film *Criss Cross* 1948. Other films include *Trapeze* 1956, *Some Like It Hot* 1959 and *The Boston Strangler* 1968.

20 **WALLACE BORMAN**
Los Angeles artist.

21 **TOMMY HANDLEY** — 1892-1949.
British radio comedian who appeared in many programmes from 1926, including *ITMA (It's That Man Again)* 1942. Made several films including *Elstree Calling* 1930 and *It's That Man Again* 1942.

22 **MARILYN MONROE** — 1926-62.
US film star. Real name Norma Jean Baker. Talented comedienne, and sex symbol. Committed suicide at the age of thirty-six. Films include *Gentlemen Prefer Blondes* 1953, *The Seven Year Itch* 1955, *Bus Stop* 1956, *Some Like It Hot* 1959 and *The Misfits* 1961.

23 **WILLIAM BURROUGHS** — Born 1914.
US novelist regarded as founder of the "Beat Generation". *Junkie* 1959, one of his most notable works, deals with his addiction to heroin. Other works include *The Ticket That Exploded* 1962 and *The Wild Boys* 1971.

24 **UNKNOWN**

25 **RICHARD LINDNER**
New York artist.

26 **OLIVER HARDY** — 1892-1957.
US comedian teamed with Stan Laurel to star in more than 200 films. Best films include *Leave 'Em Laughing* 1928, *The Music Box* 1932 and *Way Out West* 1937.

27 **KARL HEINRICH MARX** — 1818-83.
German social philosopher and political theorist. Founder (with Friedrich Engels) of world communism.

28 **H.G. (HERBERT GEORGE) WELLS** — 1866-1946.
British author whose most well-known works are his science fiction writings such as *The Time Machine* 1895, *The Invisible Man* 1897, and *War Of The Worlds* 1898. Other works include *Love And Mr. Lewisham* 1900, *Kipps* 1905 and *Tono-Bungay* 1909.

29 **UNKNOWN**

30 **UNKNOWN**

31 **STUART SUTCLIFFE** — 1941-62.
An original member of the Beatles, who died of a brain tumour on April 10, 1962, while in Hamburg.

32 **UNKNOWN**

33 **DYLAN (MARLAIS) THOMAS** — 1914-53.
Welsh poet who wrote radio play *Under Milk Wood* 1954, and inspired Bob (Zimmerman) Dylan's stage name.

34 **DION** — Born 1939.
(Di Mucci) New York pop singer. Formed The Belmonts in 1958, had many American hits, plus worldwide hit with *Teenager In Love*. As solo artist hits included *Runaround Sue* and *The Wanderer*.

35 **DR. DAVID LIVINGSTONE** — 1813-73.
British missionary and explorer.

36 **STAN LAUREL** — 1890-1965.
Real name Arthur Stanley Jefferson. British-born gag inventor and director. Teamed with Oliver Hardy as famous comedy film duo.

37 **GEORGE BERNARD SHAW** — 1856-1950.
Irish dramatist and critic. His plays included *Candida* 1895, *Man And Superman* 1903, *Pygmalion* 1913. He received the 1925 Nobel Prize for Literature.

38 **JULIE ADAMS** —
Born 1926 in Waterloo, Iowa, USA. Film actress who starred in such films as *Where The River Bends, Horizons West, The Lawless Breed, Mississippi Gambler* and *The Man From The Alamo*.

39 MAX MILLER
British comedian and film star, famous for his "double entendre" material.

40 UNKNOWN GIRL.

41 MARLON BRANDO — Born 1924.
US film star. First major film success *A Streetcar Named Desire* 1951. Other films include *The Wild One* 1954, *On The Waterfront* 1954, *Mutiny On The Bounty* 1962, *The Godfather* 1971, *Last Tango In Paris* and *Superman*.

42 TOM MIX
Cowboy film star.

43 OSCAR WILDE — 1854-1900.
Full name Oscar Fingal O'Flahertie Wills Wilde, Irish dramatist and wit. His plays include *Lady Windermere's Fan* 1892, *A Woman Of No Importance* 1893, *An Ideal Husband* 1895 and his masterpiece *The Importance Of Being Earnest*, 1895.

44 TYRONE POWER
US film star and heart-throb.

45 LARRY BELL
Modern painter.

46 JOHNNY WEISSMULLER
US actor who played Tarzan in many films.

47 STEPHEN CRANE — 1871-1900.
US novelist, short story writer, poet and war correspondent. Best known work *The Red Badge Of Courage* 1895.

48 ISSY BONN
Comedian.

49 ALBERT STUBBINS
Liverpool footballer.

50 UNKNOWN.

51 ALBERT EINSTEIN — 1879-1955.
German-American physicist. His "Special Theory Of Relativity" led to the discovery of the atomic bomb.

52 LEWIS CARROLL — 1832-98.
Real name Charles Lutwidge Dodgson. British mathematician, photographer and writer. Well remembered for his children's stories *Alice's Adventures In Wonderland* 1865 and *Alice Through The Looking Glass* 1872.

53 T.E. (THOMAS EDWARD) LAWRENCE — 1888-1935.
British archaeologist, soldier and author, known as "Lawrence Of Arabia".

54 SONNY LISTON
World Heavyweight boxing champion, before he was defeated by Muhammed Ali (then known as Cassius Clay).

55 GEORGE

56 JOHN

57 RINGO

58 PAUL

59 UNKNOWN

60 JOHN

61 RINGO

62 PAUL

63 GEORGE

64 BOBBY BREEN
British dance band vocalist.

65 MARLENE DIETRICH — Born 1904 (Maria Magdalena von Losch) in Germany. Film star and cabaret singer. Films include *The Blue Angel* 1930, *Blonde Venus* 1932, *Destry Rides Again* 1939 and *Roncho Notorius* 1956.

66 UNKNOWN

67 DIANA DORS
British film star and sex symbol of the Fifties.

68 SHIRLEY TEMPLE — Born 1928.
US film actress. As child star appeared in *The Little Colonel* 1935, *Rebecca Of Sunnybrook Farm* 1938 and *The Blue Bird* 1940. Made several films in the Forties but then went into politics as Shirley Temple Black.

A SIDE

120 SGT. PEPPER'S LONELY HEARTS CLUB BAND *(1.59)*
Recording started on February 1, 1967. Paul, who wrote the song, takes lead vocal and is joined by the others for the chorus. The four horns were played by session men, with audience sound effects added. The audience noises were added to this track to give the impression of a "live" recording, as it was Paul's idea that the "Sgt. Pepper" song should be at the start of the album, and be repeated towards the end, so that the album would have a main theme — "The Sgt. Pepper Band Show"

— to resemble a complete "live" recording.

The next song is introduced at the end of this track: "So let me introduce to you, the one and only Billy Shears", "Billy Shears" being Ringo. George Martin plays the organ that links the two songs together.

121 WITH A LITTLE HELP FROM MY FRIENDS (2.41)

Recording began on March 30, the same day as the photo session for the front cover. John and Paul join Ringo, who sings lead, for the vocals. Paul plays piano. This song was originally called *Bad Finger Boogie* and was written by Paul, with John helping out with some of the words.

The Young Idea had a minor hit with their version of *With A Little Help From My Friends*, which charted for a single week at No. 29 on July 26, 1967, although Joe Cocker's version, which topped the British chart in November 1968, has since become his "signature" tune. It is generally regarded as the best cover version of any Beatles song, and some even consider it superior to the original. Cocker is featured in the *Woodstock* film, singing the song live, and it is probably the high spot of the whole film (and triple album). The Cocker version entered the Top 30 on October 9, 1968 at No.29, and was No. 1 on November 6, staying in the chart for nine weeks.

122 LUCY IN THE SKY WITH DIAMONDS (3.25)

Recording started on March 2. John wrote the song, claiming he got the idea from his son, Julian, who had brought home a painting he had done at school. John asked him what it was supposed to be and Julian answered, "It's Lucy in the sky with diamonds". John told this story many times in defence of the song, which was originally banned from being played on many radio stations due to the fact that it was thought that the song was about drugs — as the initials of the song matched those of the hallucinatory drug LSD and the two were therefore connected. John always denied that the song is about drugs or that it was even inspired by drugs.

John sings lead, with Paul and George joining in for the chorus and supplying vocal backing. Paul plays Hammond organ using a special organ stop, which produces a bell-like over- chord, resembling the sound of a celeste.

Elton John recorded *Lucy In The Sky With Diamonds* in late August, 1974, with a certain Dr. Winston O'Boogie playing guitar and singing backing vocals. The song was released as a single on November 15, 1974, and entered the Top 30 on November 19 at No. 30, rising to No. 8 and staying in the Top 30 for nine weeks. The single was advertised as "featuring Dr. Winston O'Boogie and His Reggae Guitars" — Dr. Winston O'Boogie is a pseudonym used by John Lennon (see *Walls And Bridges* album booklet in which he also credits himself as Dr. Winston O'Ghurkin, Hon. John St. John Johnston, Rev. Thumbs Ghurkin, Kaptain Kundalini, Rev. Fred Ghurkin, Dr. Dream, Dr. Winston O'Reggae and Dwarf McDougal). By the end of 1980, Elton John had scored twenty-seven British hits, including *Your Song*, *Rocket Man*, *Crocodile Rock*, *Daniel*, *Saturday Night's Alright For Fighting* and *Pinball Wizard* plus his only No. 1, *Don't Go Breaking My Heart*, a duet sung with Kiki Dee.

123 GETTING BETTER (2.47)

Recording started on March 9. Paul was taking his dog Martha for a walk during a spring afternoon in 1967, when the thought occurred to him that spring had finally arrived. "It's getting better", he said to himself, and the phrase made him smile, as it was one often used by Jimmy Nicol, the drummer who had deputised for Ringo during the latter's absence during a tour in 1964. When Nicol was asked how he was managing in his capacity as stand-in for the most famous drummer in the world, he would invariably reply "It's getting better", and when Paul next saw John, he suggested that they write a song titled *It's Getting Better*. Eventually, Paul wrote the majority of the song, with John assisting with some of the lyrics in the middle eight.

Paul sings lead and John joins him for harmony. George plays an enormous Indian instrument called a tamboura — it stands on the floor, looks like a sitar, and has four strings which produce a droning resonant note, although actual tunes cannot be played on it. George Martin plays an unorthodox piano — he's heard striking the actual strings and not the ivories.

JOE COCKER
"WITH A LITTLE HELP FROM MY FRIENDS"
ON REGAL ZONOPHONE RZ3013/PRODUCED BY DENNY CORDELL

124   FIXING A HOLE *(2.34)*
Recording started on February 21. Paul wrote the song, sings lead and also plays harpsichord. The guitar solo is by George.

125   SHE'S LEAVING HOME *(3.32)*
Recording began on March 17. Paul wrote the basic theme for the song, which was based on a story he saw in the *Daily Mail* about a girl leaving home, and John helped out with some of the words — "We gave her most of our lives", "We gave her everything money could buy", etc.

The lead vocal is shared by Paul and John, who sing as a quartet — their two voices recorded twice to make four. The Beatles are not heard instrumentally on this track. A harp and strings, scored by Mike Leander (who co-wrote several hit songs with Gary Glitter) form the accompaniment. The strings were added to the recording after April 3, when Paul flew to America.

126   BEING FOR THE BENEFIT OF MR. KITE *(2.33)*
Recording started on February 17.

Lead vocal is by John who wrote the song — he got the idea from an old poster he bought in an antique shop in Sevenoaks, Kent, when the group were making a promotional TV film for *Strawberry Fields Forever*. The poster advertised a variety show, which starred Mr. Kite and included most of the words used in the song.

The guitar solo is by Paul and, to help create a fairground effect, a quartet of harmoniums are played by Ringo, George, Neil Aspinall and Mal Evans (who played a large bass harmonium). John originally wanted to use the authentic sound of an old steam organ, but as George Martin pointed out to John, nowhere in the world is there an instrument of this type that can be played by hand — they all work from punched cards. Instead, George Martin played the Wurlitzer organ with John playing Hammond organ — John playing the basic tune with Martin supplying the counter melody. George Martin then built up an electronic tape to give the effect John required, by using tapes of various recordings of old Victorian steam organs, which were cut up into short pieces, and haphazardly spliced together by the studio engineer.

B SIDE

127 WITHIN YOU, WITHOUT YOU *(5.00)*
Recording started on March 15. George wrote this song after dinner at Klaus Voorman's house — Klaus owned a harmonium, an instrument which George had never played before. George began to doodle on it, playing to amuse himself, when he stumbled across the basic idea behind *Within You*, completing the song when he returned to his own home.

George takes the vocal completely by himself, and in fact is the only Beatle heard on the recording. His vocal blends into the instrumental sounds of a dilruba, an Indian bowed instrument rather like a violin and sitar, played by an Indian friend of George's. George plays a tamboura and swordmandel, a zither-like Indian instrument. Indian friends played a tamboura, and a tabla, and Neil Aspinall added a third tamboura. Session men played three cellos and eight violins. At the end of the track there is a sudden burst of laughter. It was thought this was put on by the other three Beatles, to mock George's Indian music, but in fact it was completely George's idea; after five minutes of sad Indian music, he felt some light relief was needed.

128 WHEN I'M SIXTY-FOUR *(2.36)*
Written by Paul in the Cavern days — the age was in honour of his father. Recording started on December 10, 1966, the first session for the album. The lead vocal is by Paul, who also plays piano and sings a wordless chorus along with John and George. John plays lead guitar. Session musicians played the backing sounds of two clarinets and a bass clarinet.

129 LOVELY RITA *(2.40)*
Recording started on February 22. Paul wrote the song when he got the idea from an American visitor to London, who said, "Oh, I see you've got meter maids over here these days".

Paul sings lead and plays piano. George Martin plays the honky tonk piano. John and George join Paul for the backing vocals and a "comb and paper" trio to get special sound effects.

130 GOOD MORNING, GOOD MORNING *(2.42)*
John got the idea for this song from a cornflakes advertisement on television. Recording started on February 16. Lead vocals are by John, and Paul joins him for the chorus. The electric guitar solo is by Paul. Three saxophones, two trombones and a French horn were played by the front line instrumentalists from Sounds Incorporated. An assortment of various animal noises were used at the end of this recording — the track begins with a cock crowing and ends with a chicken clucking, and this blends into the final guitar chord, which in turn becomes the first note of the next song.

131 SGT. PEPPER'S LONELY HEARTS CLUB BAND (Reprise) *(1.16)*
Recording started on the second version of the title track on March 17. The vocals are by Paul, John and George, with Paul slightly to the fore. There are audience sound effects, different chords are used from the first version and there are no horns. The song segues into the final track on the album.

132 A DAY IN THE LIFE *(5.05)*
Recording began on January 19. Lead vocal is shared by John, who wrote the first and last parts of the song, which he sings, and Paul, who sings the middle portion, which he wrote. John's lyrical inspiration came from genuine items of

news published in the *Daily Mail*, which he propped up on the piano in front of him while writing the song. There genuinely was a paragraph noting that 4,000 holes had been found in Blackburn, Lancashire, although the car accident was based less directly on the crash in which Tara Browne, a friend of The Beatles and especially of John's, had been killed, which was also mentioned in the newspaper. One item which did not owe its inclusion to the *Daily Mail*, however, was the film — this is a reference to John's appearance in *How I Won The War*, an ironic black comedy concerning the outcome of the Second World War, which was adapted from a novel.

John had written the three verses which comprise the first and last parts of the song, and these were recorded with Paul on piano and John playing guitar, when it was decided that an additional middle section would enhance the song. Paul mentioned that he had written some lyrics — "Woke up, fell out of bed..." — which he intended to form the basis of another song, but which he suggested might be inserted into *A Day In The Life* if they were appropriate, and after some discussion, his suggestion was adopted, with the proviso that any connecting passage should be heavily rhythmic. George Martin then decreed that the connecting passages should have a definite length of, say, twenty four bars of solely rhythm, and in order to achieve this with precision — it is difficult for untrained musicians to detect the end of a twenty-four bar passage — Mal Evans was enlisted to stand counting out the bars. He also had an alarm clock to time the interval, and both the sound of Mal's counting, and the alarm bell on the clock can be heard on the track during the first big orchestral build-up. Having completed the rhythmic connecting parts, George Martin enquired what the group intended to do about what he termed "those bloody great gaps" between the three sections, whereupon Paul said that he would like a symphony orchestra to "freak out". This was not a suggestion which found favour with Martin, but as Paul was adamant, he agreed to write a score for the orchestra, correctly pointing out that any ninety-eight piece symphony orchestra would probably be uncertain as to what they should do if asked to "freak out", and the likely result would be that the orchestra members would simply feel embarrassed. It was

eventually decided to compromise, and Martin booked a forty-one piece orchestra, for which, in collaboration with John and Paul, he scored the obvious underlying harmonies. During the twenty-four bar sections, John and Paul suggested the inclusion of an enormous shriek, that would start comparatively quietly, but build up to a tremendous noise. In order to achieve this, Martin had to produce a separate score for each individual instrument — at the start of the twenty-four bar passage, he wrote down the lowest note in each instrument's range, and at the end of the passage, the highest note of which the instrument was capable, between the two notes writing the instruction "poco-a-poco gliss", which can be roughly translated as "gentle slide". When it came to actually recording the orchestra, Martin further instructed the musicians to slide very gradually up the scale, also telling the woodwind section to take a fresh breath whenever they found it necessary.

For this part of the recording, The Beatles decided to create a special atmosphere, inviting several friends to attend, who were asked to dress up for the occasion. Mick Jagger, Marianne Faithfull and the entire staff of the Apple boutique were some of the forty or more friends who appeared, while Paul asked that all the members of the orchestra, plus George Martin (who was not the type of person who could be expected to wear fancy dress) should wear evening dress. Paul also provided carnival paraphernalia — funny hats and false noses — which was distributed among the orchestra members.

The orchestral section was recorded on February 10, with John playing lead guitar parts at the start, while at the end, three pianos are played by four people — Ringo, John, Paul and Mal Evans — with George Martin playing harmonium. The final long drawn out chord played by the orchestra lasts forty-two seconds.

36   ALL YOU NEED IS LOVE *(3.57)*
BABY YOU'RE A RICH MAN *(3.02)*

R 5620—July 7, 1967

The Beatles' fifteenth single was their eighth to go directly to No. 1 within a week of release. It went to No. 1 on July 12, staying there for four weeks, in the Top 10 for eight weeks, and the Top 30 for ten weeks. With British sales of

over half a million and American sales of over one million, global sales of the Beatles' thirteenth British No. 1 single are over three million.

All You Need Is Love was the fastest single the Beatles ever made; it was written at the end of May, recorded by June 25, and released a couple of weeks later on July 7, 1967.

133 ALL YOU NEED IS LOVE

The song was specially written for the television programme *Our World*. When the group accepted the invitation to represent Britain in the show, John and Paul agreed to compose a special number. The programme showed the Beatles recording the song at EMI Studios, Abbey Road (the large No. 1 Studio), and was broadcast on June 25, 1967, when it was then screened worldwide "live" to an estimated 400 million viewers by satellite. This international hook-up by twenty-six nations and five continents, involving the TV systems of fourteen countries, was the first occasion on which a truly worldwide satellite broadcast had been attempted.

Recording of *All You Need Is Love* began on June 14 at Olympic Studios, where the first backing track, which lasted ten minutes, was laid down. This consisted of John on harpsichord, Paul on string bass, which he played with a bow, Ringo on drums, and George on violin, which he played for the first time in his life. The song was completed at EMI Studios in St. John's Wood, with Paul playing ordinary bass, Ringo on drums, George on guitar, John singing, and George Martin adding piano. The orchestral accompaniment consists of two trumpets, two trombones, two saxophones, an accordion, four violins and two cellos, all played by session men. The final recording ran for six minutes.

For the show, The Beatles used the backing track made earlier, to which they sang and played live, although this version was not used for the single recording.

John sings lead, with Paul and George backing. Members of the chorus include Mick Jagger, Gary Leeds, Keith Richard, Marianne Faithfull, Jane Asher, Patti Harrison, Keith Moon and Graham Nash.

Snatches of four other tunes can be heard within *All You Need Is Love* — The *Marseillaise* (the French National Anthem), the opening passage of *In The Mood* (originally made famous by Glenn Miller, but more recently the signature tune of Joe Loss), *Greensleeves*, plus a chorus of *She Loves You* sung by Paul during the fade.

134 BABY YOU'RE A RICH MAN

Baby You're A Rich Man, originally called *One Of The Beautiful People*, consists of two songs, one written by John and the other by Paul, and was at one time intended for the soundtrack of the *Yellow Submarine* cartoon film.

Recording began on May 11 at Olympic Studios in Barnes, which was the first time The Beatles had recorded away from EMI Studios, since they had become a hit act. John played a Clavioline, which consists of a keyboard and amplifier, and is heard at the beginning of the song. John and Paul played pianos and a studio engineer played vibes. John sings lead, with Paul and George in support, while Brian Jones plays oboe.

37 HELLO GOODBYE (3.24) I AM THE WALRUS (4.32)

R 5655—November 24, 1967

The Beatles' last single of the "Flower Power Year", 1967, entered the charts on November 29 at No. 3, and on December 6 went to No. 1, where it stayed for six weeks. It sold half a million within three weeks in Britain, and stayed in the Top 10 for nine weeks and the Top 30 for ten weeks.

Global sales are well over two million.

135 HELLO GOODBYE

Written by Paul. Recording started on this song on October 2, 1967, but was spread over a few weeks, as all the group were busy editing and doing other jobs on the "Magical Mystery Tour" film. Paul is lead singer, with George joining him occasionally, and John supplying the answering voices. John and George play the spiky metallic lead guitar chords. Paul plays piano, and two session men play violins. Extra percussion and rhythm instruments were brought in towards the end of the song, while Ringo plays maracas.

136 I AM THE WALRUS

John began this number at the beginning of September 1967, and The Beatles kept working on it all through that month. George Martin scored the strings which follow John's Mellotron opening, these comprising eight violins and four cellos. Three horns were used, and there are "radio" voices which pop up now and then. Members of the Mike Sammes Singers, six boys and six girls, sing the two chorus lines at the end — the boys sing "Oompah Oompah, stick it up your jumper" and the girls sing "Everybody's got one".

Three of the verses for *I Am The Walrus* came to John one day when he was at home in Weybridge. He heard a police car going past in the distance with its siren shrieking. The noise consisted of two notes, up and down, repeated over and over again. In his head he was playing a game of putting words to the rhythm — "mis-ter, ci-ty, p'lice-man, sit-ting, pre-tty".

John wrote two other phrases that day; "Sitting on a cornflake waiting for the man to come" and "Sitting in an English country garden", which John did for at least two hours every day. All these phrases were put together to make *I Am The Walrus*.

38   MAGICAL MYSTERY TOUR

SMMT 1/2—December 8, 1967

The *Magical Mystery Tour* soundtrack was released in Britain as a special double EP package — containing two EP's and a twenty four page booklet — on December 8, 1967. It entered the *NME* singles chart for the week ending December 13 at No. 10 and by its third week in the chart was at No. 2. It was prevented from getting to No. 1 by The Beatles' own single, *Hello Goodbye*, which was No. 1 for six weeks. The EP's were in the charts for nine weeks, becoming the highest placed EP's in the *NME* Top 30 Chart. Previously, The Beatles' *Twist And Shout* was the highest placed EP in the chart at No. 4 in 1963.

In the *Melody Maker* chart, *Magical Mystery Tour* was at No. 1 for one week, toppling *Hello Goodbye* from that position on January 13, 1968, four weeks after the EP was released.

The two-EP set had advance orders in Britain of 400,000, and by mid January 1968 had sold 600,000.

The *Magical Mystery Tour* book was edited by Tony Barrow, with assistance from Neil Aspinall and Mal Evans, with photography by John Kelly and drawings by Bob Gibson.

The six *Magical Mystery Tour* songs were recorded between the end of April and the end of September 1967.

A SIDE RECORD ONE

137   **MAGICAL MYSTERY TOUR** *(2.45)*
The "Tour" title track was recorded at the end of April/beginning of May. Paul, who wrote most of the song, is lead singer with the others behind him. Paul plays piano with special echo effects, and a trio of session musicians play the trumpets at the beginning. The words and most of the music for *Magical Mystery Tour* were not written until recording was started — the song grew organically as it was being recorded. Paul was playing the piano and Mal Evans, (the group's Road Manager during their touring days) was writing down the words as Paul thought them up. They recorded the backing for the song, with only one line of the words made up, first. That line was the opening "Roll up, roll up for the Magical Mystery Tour". After the backing track was finished they began thinking up the other words while Mal wrote them down: "Reservation", "Trip of a lifetime", "Satisfaction guaranteed". But they soon got fed up, so they decided to sing anything that came into their heads, just to see what happened.

After that track was completed Paul added bass guitar to the backing, and then suggested that more instruments should be added. So Paul, John, George, Ringo, Neil (Aspinall) and Mal picked up any instruments that were lying around — maracas, bells and tambourines — and played them.

The backing track was recorded on April 25, the voices were added two nights later and then finally trumpet accompaniment was added on May 3.

138   **YOUR MOTHER SHOULD KNOW** *(2.24)*
Work began on this track on August 22 at Chappell Studios in New Bond Street. Paul, who wrote the song, sings lead and plays piano, while John plays organ. It was re-recorded during

September, after *Flying* but before *Fool On The Hill*, as the group didn't like various things about the first version.

B SIDE RECORD ONE

136a   I AM THE WALRUS *(4.32)*
(See *Hello Goodbye* single.)

A SIDE RECORD TWO

139   THE FOOL ON THE HILL *(2.56)*
Work started on *Fool On The Hill*, which was composed by Paul, on September 25. Paul sings and plays piano, Ringo plays finger cymbals,

George and John use harmonicas and Paul double tracks his playing of the recorder. Solo guitar passage is by George, with Paul also playing flute.

Sergio Mendes and Brazil '66 had a hit with *The Fool On The Hill* in America in 1968, when it was in the Top 30 for nine weeks — its highest position was No. 6.

After her success with *Something*, Shirley Bassey recorded another Beatles song as a follow up, but her version of *The Fool On The Hill* only reached the BMRB Top 50 chart for one week, in January 1971.

140   FLYING *(2.10)*
Flying, the Beatles' first Parlophone instrumental was started on September 8, and was composed by all four Beatles, becoming the first composition to bear all their names.

On this track, John plays the main tune on his Mellotron, while Paul and George play an assortment of guitars. All four Beatles do the chanting later on in the arrangement, and at the end electronic sounds, which John and Ringo built up in the studio using tape loops, take over.

B SIDE RECORD TWO

141   BLUE JAY WAY *(3.50)*
Recording for this song, written by George, began on September 6. George's vocal is double tracked, and he also sings the backing with Paul. George plays a "swirling" Hammond organ — the "swirling" effect was created in the studio using a technical process called "phasing", which was also used on George's vocals. The only other instrument on this track is a single cello, but studio-produced technical effects are used at the very end.

George wrote *Blue Jay Way* in the early summer of 1967 during a visit to California. *Blue Jay Way* is the name of the street in which he and Patti, his wife, rented a house in Los Angeles. After flying in from London, they were waiting for their friend Derek Taylor to visit them, but Derek was delayed so he telephoned George. George told him where the house was and Derek said that he would be able to find it, if necessary by consulting a policeman. George waited and waited — although he was tired after the flight, he didn't want to go to bed until Derek came. Outside, it was foggy, and as it got later and later, partly to keep himself awake, and partly as a joke, George wrote a

song about waiting in Blue Jay Way. George messed around on a little Hammond organ in the corner of the rented house, and later perfected the song at his home in Esher, England. All the words of the song relate to George's wait for Derek Taylor.

39   LADY MADONNA *(2.14)*
THE INNER LIGHT *(2.33)*

R 5675—March 15, 1968

The Beatles' first single of 1968 featured George as a composer for the first time on a single — he wrote *The Inner Light*. The single entered the charts on March 20 at No. 6, and a week later went to No. 1 for two weeks. Selling over 250,000 in Britain, it stayed in the Top 10 for five weeks and in the Top 30 for seven weeks.

Global sales of the disc are over two million. As well as being a No. 1 single in Britain and America, it also topped the charts in Germany, Poland, Denmark, Sweden, France and Australia.

142   LADY MADONNA
Written by Paul. Recording began at the beginning of February 1968, and on the first recording session, George and John played two guitars through the same amplifier, while Ringo played drums. Paul then added bass guitar and his own voice. Four top jazz session musicians — Ronnie Scott, Harry Klein, Bill Povey and Bill Jackson — all played saxophones, a last-minute addition instigated by Paul. Paul plays piano, and the vocal backing is by all four Beatles, singing with their hands cupped around their mouths.

143   THE INNER LIGHT
George's first song to appear on a single. All the music was recorded in India at EMI Studios, Bombay, in January 1968, using Indian musicians under George's control. George added his own voice to the instrumental track in England on February 6, and John and Paul added harmony backing.

40   HEY JUDE *(7.15)*
REVOLUTION *(3.22)*

R 5722—August 26, 1968

The Beatles' first release on their own Apple label, and their eighteenth

NEW PARLOPHONE SINGLE R5620

EMI

ALL YOU NEED IS LOVE

THE · BEATLES

C/W BABY YOU'RE A RICH MAN

E.M.I. Records (The Gramophone Co. Ltd.) E.M.I. House, 20 Manchester Sq. London W.1

single. It entered the Top 30 on September 4 at No. 3, and a week later went to No. 1, where it stayed for three weeks. (It was knocked from the No. 1 position by Mary Hopkin's *Those Were The Days*, the second Apple Records release, which was produced by Paul.) *Hey Jude* stayed in the Top 10 for eight weeks and in the Top 30 for twelve weeks.

By September 4, the single had sold 250,000, and the figure had increased to 558,535 by September 27. The total reached 700,000 by the end of November, and by the end of the year had risen to 800,000. World sales topped the two million mark by September 11, and by October 20 had reached 4,738,000. By the end of November, the total sales were closer to 6,000,000, with American sales of 3.25 million and combined European and Japanese sales of 1.5 million. It also sold over 300,000 in Canada. Total world sales up to October 1972 stood at 7.5 million.

It was also a No. 1 hit in Germany, Holland, Ireland, Belgium, Malaysia, Singapore, New Zealand, Sweden, Norway and Denmark.

144 HEY JUDE

Paul wrote this one day while driving to see John's son Julian. As he was driving, he started to sing "Hey Jules, don't make it bad", which he later changed to "Hey Jude". John and Paul spent most of Friday, July 26, 1968 at Paul's house putting the final touches to the song, which they rehearsed with George and Ringo at EMI Studios the following Monday. On the Tuesday night, they recorded it at EMI Studios while a camera team filmed them for a fifty minute feature about the national music of Britain. On Wednesday, July 31, they moved from EMI to Trident Studios, scrapped the first version and recorded a second. George played electric guitar, Paul piano and Ringo tambourine with John on rhythm. To the first backing track Paul added his solo vocal, after which the others joined him for harmonies. A forty piece orchestra (originally Paul wanted to use a full symphony orchestra of about a hundred musicians, but George Martin said that it was impossible to book one at such short notice) was used on Thursday, August 1. The orchestra held single notes for long periods. Towards the end of the evening the orchestra members were asked if they would clap and sing the "la-la-la" chorus, to which they agreed, although it has been reported that afterwards, several of the musicians asked for extra fees for this additional "work". The following day, the final remix was done on the tapes and by Friday afternoon, the first rough discs, or advance acetates, were made.

Hey Jude is the longest single the Beatles ever released at seven minutes fifteen seconds, and contains one of the longest fade-outs ever recorded — four minutes.

Wilson Pickett's version of *Hey Jude* was in the Top 30 for seven weeks, entering on January 15, 1969 at No. 29. Its highest position was No. 24.

145 REVOLUTION

Written by John while in India. Recording of *Revolution* started in June 1968, when the original ten minute version was cut. During the same month, a second version was completed, and on Tuesday, July 9, the group began version three. No additional instruments were used, besides the usual three guitars and drums, but by the end of July, there were four versions of *Revolution* and the fourth and final version was used as the "B" side of *Hey Jude*. On this final version, John is lead singer, with Paul adding organ and piano.

(See also *The Singles Collection 1962-1970* on page 89, for chart re-entry details of *Hey Jude*.)

41 THE BEATLES

PCS 7067-8—November 22, 1968

With advance sales of over 300,000 in Britain, The Beatles' first double album entered the *NME* album chart on November 27, one week after release, at No. 1, where it stayed for nine weeks. In the same week, it also entered the *NME* Top 30 chart at No. 20, dropping to No. 24 one week later, and falling to No. 29 for its third and last week in the chart. The album is the only double album ever to get into the Top 30 chart, was in the British album chart for twenty-four weeks, and was the first double album to get to No. 1 in that chart.

After one month on the market, at the end of 1968, the album had sold over four million copies around the world, and at the end of 1970, two years after release, estimated global sales amounted to 6.5 million, which made *The Beatles* the biggest selling double album of all time at that point. Although subsequently this figure has been exceeded by the American film soundtrack to *Saturday Night Fever*, a double LP which had sold approximately 25,000,000 copies up to 1980, it would appear that no British made double album has been able to overtake the sales of *The Beatles*, which by now probably total somewhat more than seven million. A measure of its popularity was that it reached the unprecedented position for an album of No. 7 in the Swedish singles chart.

The idea of the sleeve design for the double album was suggested to The Beatles by an artist called Richard Hamilton. He was introduced to The Beatles by Robert Fraser, an art dealer and gallery owner, who had also introduced to them Peter Blake and Jann Haworth (who designed the "Sgt. Pepper" sleeve). Fraser showed them a print by Hamilton based on a collage of newspaper cuttings of The Rolling Stones' drug trial, after which Paul invited Hamilton to do a similar design for the next Beatles' sleeve. Hamilton, however, did not wish to add to the number of garish sleeves in existence,

and suggested that to make the cover look distinctive they should have nothing on it at all. He also recommended that they should make up their own collage of pictures, using an autobiographical theme, and, because he thought that the pure white cover should be defaced in some way, suggested that each sleeve be consecutively numbered to give the impression of a limited edition. The Beatles liked Hamilton's idea, and got Gordon House to "design" it. Included with the album are four colour prints of The Beatles taken by John Kelly, and a large poster, with lyrics on one side and a montage of Beatles photographs (as Hamilton had suggested) on the other. Neil Aspinall and Mal Evans collected a number of old Beatle photographs for the collage, and Jeremy Banks acted as Chief Co-ordinator for the sleeve design. However, controversy surrounded one of the photographs in the montage, when some journalists focussed their attention on a photo of Paul in the nude, and some national "dailies" had a field day, even though the photo was very small, no more than four by two

centimetres, using such headlines as "Paul Goes Nude". The Apple Press Officer at the time, Derek Taylor, summed up the whole daily paper reaction when he said of the reviews, "All this work, all these tracks, all this talent — and all their dirty little minds focus on is one tiny picture".

Over the years, due to the pure white virgin cover, the album has become commonly known to everybody in the music business and to all Beatle people, as simply "The White Album".

(Interesting notes — original copies of the album had a rather unusual sleeve packaging design; the open sides, for insertion of the records, were at the top edge, rather than the 'fore edge', of the sleeve. These sleeves were later replaced with the more conventional type, where the open edges are at the fore edge. The originals also had a black inner paper bag, whereas later copies have the usual white bags. There are also differences between the mono and stereo versions.)

The thirty tracks for the album were recorded between May 30 and October 17, 1968 at EMI Studios, with four tracks at Trident Studios, using the following well-known engineers: Chris Thomas (who has produced albums for Elton John and The Pretenders), Ken Scott (who has worked as engineer and/or producer with David Bowie on *Space Oddity*, *The Man Who Sold The World*, *Hunky Dory*, *Ziggy Stardust*, *Aladdin Sane* and *Pin Ups*, George Harrison on *All Things Must Pass*, Jackie Lomax — an Apple artist — on his George Harrison produced *Is This What You Want* and Mary Hopkin on her Apple album *Postcard* produced by Paul McCartney), Geoff Emerick (Steeleye Span's *All Around My Hat*, Wings'

the beatles
hey jude · revolution
apple records
R5722

EMI

Band On The Run and Badfinger's *Straight Up*) and Barry Sheffield (Bonzo Dog Band and Black Sabbath). Each track took an average of thirty recording hours to put on tape, with some tracks being completed in a single twelve hour all-night session. The last track for the album was started on Sunday, October 13, and on Monday, October 14, Ringo and his family left for a holiday in Sardinia. On Wednesday, George joined Jackie Lomax and Mal Evans in America, leaving John and Paul to assist George

Martin with the final re-mixing of the tapes and to decide on the running order. Work on the final tracks was completed at one of the longest sessions ever, starting early on October 16, and continuing into the next day.

Over the five month recording period, a number of songs were recorded which were not eventually used on the album. These include George's *Not Guilty* (which reputedly features Eric Clapton), John's *What's The New Mary Jane* (which had been recorded before, during the "Sgt. Pepper" sessions) and Paul's *Jubilee* (which later appeared on his solo album *McCartney* under the new title of *Junk*).

A SIDE RECORD ONE

146   BACK IN THE USSR *(2.41)*
Written by Paul, who sings lead and plays electric guitar. John and George provide high "Beach Boy" harmony vocals, while John plays a six string bass with George also playing bass. Recording started at EMI on August 22.

147   DEAR PRUDENCE *(3.59)*
John wrote this in India about Mia Farrow's sister, Prudence, who would spend longer meditating in her room than anybody else. John therefore suggests that she comes out into the sunshine to "greet the brand new day". John plays Epiphone guitar and Paul piano and flugelhorn, John and Mal play tambourines, and John sings lead, with all four Beatles singing the chorus, assisted by Mal, Paul's cousin John, and Jackie Lomax for the clapping. Recording began August 28 at Trident Studios.

148   GLASS ONION *(2.13)*
Written by John, who sings lead, with Paul joining him occasionally. John plays acoustic Gibson and Ringo works with two drum kits. Violins were added at the end of the number. The song includes references to several earlier Beatle songs: *Strawberry Fields Forever*, *I Am The Walrus*, *Lady Madonna*, *Fool On The Hill* and *Fixing A Hole*.

149   OB-LA-DI OB-LA-DA *(3.06)*
Written by Paul, who sings lead, with John and George joining in with the chorus. Paul plays piano. Recording

started on July 2 at EMI.
Both Marmalade and The Bedrocks made cover versions of the song, which got into the *NME* Top 30. Marmalade were No. 1 for two weeks and in the charts for a total of thirteen weeks with their version. This was their biggest British hit, although two of their later singles reached No. 3 in the Top 30; *Reflections Of My Life* (their only American Top 20 hit) and *Rainbow*. They had a total of eight Top 20 hits, including *Cousin Norman* and *Radancer*, and two million selling singles with *Ob-La-Di Ob-La-Da*, which sold over half a million in Britain, and *Reflections Of My Life*.
The Bedrocks' highest position was No. 17 during a chart run of seven weeks. It was their only chart success.

150   WILD HONEY PIE *(0.53)*
Written and produced entirely by Paul, who sings and plays guitar and a bass drum, which is double tracked. Recording began on August 20 at EMI. This is the shortest track on the album.

151   THE CONTINUING STORY OF BUNGALOW BILL *(3.12)*
Written by John. This was recorded immediately after *I'm So Tired* — sometime between midnight and dawn, 9-10 October, at EMI. John sings lead with all joining in for the chorus. Yoko Ono sings the line "Not when he looked so fierce" in the last verse, as well as joining in with The Beatles in the choruses. John plays organ and engineer Chris Thomas the Mellotron.

152   WHILE MY GUITAR GENTLY WEEPS *(4.41)*
Written by George, who sings solo, double tracked in places, John and George play acoustic guitars, John plays organ and Eric Clapton supplies the lead electric guitar. Recording began at EMI on July 25.

153   HAPPINESS IS A WARM GUN *(2.40)*
John got the idea for this song from a gun magazine, which George Martin showed him. On the cover it said "Happiness is a warm gun", which John read, and thinking it was a fantastically insane phrase to use, based the song on that title. John sings lead with Paul and George providing harmony. This was one of the most difficult recordings on the album as the guitars were in 3/4 time and the drumming in 4/4 time. Recording began on September 23 at EMI.

The Beatles

Ballad of John and Yoko

Old brown shoe

Apple Records
R5786 [EMI]

B SIDE RECORD ONE

154   MARTHA MY DEAR *(2.27)*
Written by Paul, about his dog Martha.
Paul sings double tracked solo vocal
and plays piano. Brass and violins were
used in the backing. Recording began
on October 4 at Trident.

155   I'M SO TIRED *(2.02)*
Written by John, who sings solo.
Recorded in a single early evening
session at EMI on October 9.

156   BLACKBIRD *(2.18)*
Composer Paul sings solo vocal, which
is double tracked at times, to his own

acoustic guitar accompaniment, plus a
blackbird singing in the background.
Paul is heard tapping out the beat
possibly with a drum-stick on a table.
Recording began on June 11 at EMI
Studios.

157   PIGGIES *(2.03)*
Written by George, who sings with his
voice filtered through special studio
equipment to create a nasal effect
halfway through the number, while
John and Paul help out at the end. Chris
Thomas, who was George Martin's
assistant at that time, played
harpsichord, Ringo tambourine, and
John supplied the tape loops.

Recording started on September 19 at EMI.

158 ROCKY RACCOON *(3.32)*
This was written by Paul, with the assistance of John and Donovan, while in India. The three were sitting on the roof of a building at the Maharishi's camp, playing their guitars, when the idea came to Paul — it was originally called "Rocky Sassoon" but was later changed to "Raccoon". Paul sings solo and swaps with George on lead guitar, George playing bass. John plays harmonium and George Martin supplies honky tonk piano. This was recorded in one all night session at EMI on August 15.

159 DON'T PASS ME BY *(3.48)*
Ringo's first recorded solo songwriting effort, on which he takes complete solo vocal, as well as playing piano. Ringo had tried writing songs many times before, but whenever he played his new songs to the other Beatles, they always told him that they sounded like other songs, with which he agreed after hearing the similarity.

The country fiddle was played by a session musician. Recording began on July 12 at EMI.

160 WHY DON'T WE DO IT IN THE ROAD *(1.39)*
Written and completely played by Paul. Paul sings, plays guitar, piano, bass and drums. The vocals are double tracked in places. Recorded on October 10 at EMI.

161 I WILL *(1.43)*
Paul singing solo, double tracked in places, with an acoustic guitar and bongo backing. Written by Paul. John plays skulls. Recording began September 16 at EMI.

162 JULIA *(2.52)*
Written by John with help from Yoko. John sings solo and is double tracked in places, and plays guitar which is also double tracked. The last number to be started, it was recorded on Sunday evening, October 13, at EMI.

A SIDE RECORD TWO

163 BIRTHDAY *(2.41)*
Written by Paul and John, with the others contributing ideas, at EMI studio, where it was recorded on September 18. Paul and John sing lead, with George, who wore a glove to avoid getting any more blisters, playing tambourine, and Ringo and Mal clapping. Yoko Ono, Patti Harrison and other famous people sing the "birthday" chorus, while Paul plays a carefully prepared upright piano, which sounds like an electric harpsichord.

164 YER BLUES *(3.59)*
John, who composed this number, sings solo. Recording began at EMI on August 13. The wailing guitar behind John is, of course, played by George. Ringo is heard at the beginning of the song doing the "2-3" count in.

165 MOTHER NATURE'S SON *(2.46)*
Written by Paul in India. Paul sings solo. This was recorded at EMI on August 9 at 3 o'clock in the morning, and was done after the other three Beatles had gone home. Paul sang and played acoustic guitar. The singing is double tracked in places.

166 EVERYBODY'S GOT SOMETHING TO HIDE EXCEPT ME AND MY MONKEY *(2.25)*
Written by John who sings lead with Paul and George helping. Originally called "Come On, Come On" from the first line of the words. Recording began at EMI on July 31.

167 SEXY SADIE *(3.13)*
Written by John in India about the Maharishi, who was said to have made unseemly advances to Mia Farrow and several other ladies while The Beatles were in his camp. John sings lead with Paul and George supplying harmony. John plays Gibson acoustic guitar, George Gibson electric and Paul piano. Recording began July 19 at EMI.

168 HELTER SKELTER *(4.28)*
Paul wrote this after he had read a review of a record in a paper, which said that a group had really gone wild with echo and screaming. Paul was initially disappointed that another group had adopted this technique, as he would have liked to do something similar, but when he actually heard the record it was nothing like the review, so he decided to record a song as wild and noisy as the one suggested by the review.

Paul sings lead with vocal harmony by all four. John plays bass, as well as saxophone, and Mal Evans plays trumpet. The track was recorded on a new eight track machine just installed at EMI, making The Beatles the first to use the machine. Ringo is heard at the end of the number shouting "I got blisters on my fingers" — this does not appear on mono versions of the record.

The original recording, started on July 18 at EMI, was twenty-four minutes long, but the final released version, recorded during the second week of September, is of the usual length.

It was this song, and several others on the album, that prompted Charles Manson, a Jesus-like cult leader, to instruct some of his followers to commit the grisly and apparently motiveless Tate and La Bianca murders of August, 1969 in Los Angeles. Manson thought The Beatles were telling him, through *Helter Skelter*, that the end of the world was imminent, and that when *Helter Skelter* came, the Black Panthers, led by *Rocky Raccoon*, would rise and eliminate the *Piggies*.

169 LONG, LONG, LONG (3.04)
Composer George sings double tracked solo vocal and plays acoustic guitar. Paul plays Hammond organ as well as his usual bass. Extra fast drumming at the end comes courtesy of Ringo. Recording began on October 8 at EMI.

B SIDE RECORD TWO

170 REVOLUTION 1 (4.13)
This is a slower version of *Revolution* than the recording on the "B" side of *Hey Jude*, although the lyrics are identical, except that after the eighth line of the song which reads "Don't you know that you can count me out", John adds "in".

John wrote the song, sings lead, and helps George and Paul provide harmony and "shoo be doos". Paul plays piano and there is added brass backing.

171 HONEY PIE (2.38)
Written by Paul, who sings solo and plays piano, with John on electric guitar and George on bass. Fifteen session musicians supply the brass backing, mainly of saxophones, scored by George Martin. Recording began at Trident Studios on October 1.

172 SAVOY TRUFFLE (2.52)
Written by George, who sings double tracked lead, with John and Paul helping occasionally. Brass backing instruments are two baritone and four tenor saxophones. The song's lyrics include references to various kinds of sweets and candies that can be found in "Good News" chocolate boxes; the words "good news" are also used in the song. Recording began at Trident on October 3

173 CRY BABY CRY (3.00)
This nursery rhyme type song was written by John, who sings the verses, with Paul and George joining him for the chorus. John plays piano and organ, and George Martin harmonium. Recording began July 15 at EMI.

174 REVOLUTION 9 (8.15)
This number is completely different to *Revolution* and *Revolution 1*, and contains no singing, only jumbled up noises and voices. It was made mainly by John using thirty tape loops. It is the longest individual track released by The Beatles.

Recording of *Revolution 9* began on May 30 at EMI.

175 GOODNIGHT (3.09)
Written by John for Ringo, who sings solo to the accompaniment of a thirty piece orchestra (including a harp) and a choir of four boys and four girls. No other Beatles are heard on this recording. The orchestration was written by George Martin. Recording began on June 11 at EMI.

42 YELLOW SUBMARINE

PCS 7070—January 17, 1969

The cartoon film of *Yellow Submarine* is thought to be the first film based on a song. The film was produced by Al Brodax, head of the TV and Motion Pictures Division of King Features Syndicate, and written by Lee Minoff and Al Brodax, from an original story by Lee Minoff. Based on the song and *Sgt. Pepper's Lonely Hearts Club Band*, it tells the story of The Beatles' journey in a yellow submarine and their defence of "Pepperland" against the "Blue Meanies" and other anti-music monsters. Apart from the soundtrack music, and a brief appearance at the end (in the flesh), The Beatles had nothing to do with the film; their voices were supplied by actors.

The soundtrack album was originally scheduled for release in December 1968, although it failed to

appear until January 17, 1969. It entered the *NME* album charts five days later at No. 9, peaking for two weeks at No. 3. The Beatles' double album, *The Beatles*, was still at No. 1 in the charts, which possibly provides a good reason for *Yellow Submarine's* not topping the charts, thus becoming the second Beatles' album not to get to No. 1 in Britain. The LP was in the charts for eight weeks, and had sold 800,000 globally within three months, reaching one million later in 1969.

For the first time in Britain, a Beatles' album contained non-Beatles' material, in the shape of the original musical score for the film by George Martin, which appeared on the "B" side. (In America, this had been normal practice with their film soundtrack albums — *A Hard Day's Night* and *Help!*)

The new songs for the film were recorded in mid-June, 1967 (*All Together Now* and *It's All Too Much*) during the "Sgt. Pepper" sessions, and in mid-February 1968 (*Only A Northern Song* and *Hey Bulldog*). Other recordings heard in the film are: *Yellow Submarine*, *Eleanor Rigby*, *Within You, Without You* (part), *A Day In The Life* (orchestral build-up only), *When I'm Sixty-Four*, *Nowhere Man*, *Lucy In The Sky With Diamonds*, *Sgt. Pepper's Lonely Hearts Club Band*, *With A Little Help From My Friends* (part), *All You Need Is Love* and *Baby You're A Rich Man* (part), although not all appear on the soundtrack.

The original film score, composed and orchestrated by George Martin, was as follows: *Pepperland*, *Sea Of Time*, *Sea Of Holes*, *Sea Of Monsters*, *March Of The Meanies*, *Pepperland Laid Waste* and *Yellow Submarine In Pepperland* (which is an orchestrated version of Lennon and McCartney's *Yellow Submarine*).

A SIDE

104c YELLOW SUBMARINE (2.36)
(See single.)

176 ONLY A NORTHERN SONG (3.20)
Written by George, and the last song written for the film. At two o'clock one morning at EMI Studios, with the London Symphony Orchestra waiting

patiently to go home, producer Al Brodax insisted that the *Yellow Submarine* film was one song short. George told Brodax to sit tight while he knocked out another tune, and after an hour or two, returned to the studio with the final song. "Here, Al" said George, "It's only a northern song".

George sings solo vocal with brass backing and organ. His vocal is double tracked in places. There are various percussion instruments, bells, etc., in the background.

177 ALL TOGETHER NOW (2.07)
Paul wrote this number, and he sings the verse, with John singing the "Bom bom — look at me" part and all four Beatles providing the chorus. John probably added the mouth-organ, and Paul the acoustic guitar opening.

178 HEY BULLDOG (3.07)
Written by John. This is probably the quickest post-touring song ever cut by The Beatles, as it was completed in February 1968 in less than one day from start to finish. A three minute promotional film to go with *Lady Madonna* was required for television screening, and because they would need to be in the studio one Saturday, Paul suggested that the group should also record a new song to save wasting time. He asked John if he would write something, and as John had a few words lying around at his home, he brought them in.

They finished off the words in the studio, and after John had indicated roughly how he heard the song in his head, the group created the backing between them simply by playing together, while they were being filmed.

The lyrics of the song changed as they recorded it. As Paul misread John's handwriting, he sang "measured out in you", which should have been "measured out in news", although they agreed "you" sounded better. There is no mention of a bulldog in the song, but there was a bullfrog, because of which, Paul, as a joke, started barking to make John laugh. Thus, the barking was retained and the title altered.

John sings lead with Paul assisting. Piano is probably by Paul.

179 IT'S ALL TOO MUCH (6.16)
Composer George sings double tracked lead, with John and Paul joining in for the long fade out chorus. Clapping and brass backing can also be heard.

(The film soundtrack version of this song is longer than the version which appears on the album.)

133a ALL YOU NEED IS LOVE (3.44)
(See single.)

---

43 GET BACK (3.09)
DON'T LET ME DOWN (3.30)

R 5777—April 11, 1969

Get Back **entered the Top 30 on April 23 at No. 3, and went to No. 1 on April 30. It stayed at No. 1 for five weeks, and was in the Top 10 for ten weeks and the Top 30 for eleven weeks. It sold over 530,000 in Britain and was a No. 1 hit in many other countries including Canada, Germany, France, Spain, Norway, Denmark, Holland, Belgium, Malaysia, Singapore, Australia and New Zealand. With sales of over two million in America, world sales are estimated at over 4,500,000.**

(See also *The Singles Collection 1962 - 1970* **on page** 89, **for re-entry details.)**

180 GET BACK
This was written in the recording studio by Paul and was recorded immediately after he had finished the song. It was cut at Apple Studios in January 1969 during the filming of the *Let It Be* motion picture, which was premiered in 1970, and was the first occasion on which Apple Studios had been used to record a Beatles' single. Before release, on Monday, April 7, the original tape of *Get Back* was remixed. Paul sang lead and

played bass, with John on lead guitar and George on rhythm, while Ringo played drums and Billy Preston added electric piano. Preston was the first guest artist actually to be credited as playing on a Beatles single — the label credits read "The Beatles with Billy Preston" — and he also received a Gold Disc for his contribution to this track.

Rod Stewart has always been noted for his excellent versions of songs made famous by other artists, e.g. *Oh No Not My Baby, Sailing, This Old Heart Of Mine, Pretty Flamingo, The First Cut Is The Deepest, You Keep Me Hanging On, It's All Over Now*, etc., but his version of *Get Back* seemed not to come up to his usual standard, although it still managed to reach No. 10 in the Top 30, staying in the chart for six weeks. Since 1971, Rod Stewart has had numerous big hits including *Maggie May, You Wear It Well* (both No. 1's), *Angel* (written by Jimi Hendrix), *Oh No Not My Baby* (written by Goffin and King, and previously a hit in Britain for Manfred Mann in 1965), *Sailing* (written by Gavin Sutherland of The Sutherland Brothers, who originally recorded the song), *This Old Heart Of Mine* (written by Holland Dozier and Holland and originally a hit for The Isley Brothers in 1966 in America), *Tonight's The Night* and *The Killing Of Georgie* (both self penned).

Stewart's version of *Get Back* was taken from the soundtrack album of *All This And World War II*, which was made up of Lennon and McCartney songs sung by well-known artists such as The Bee Gees, Elton John, Roy Wood, Leo Sayer, Status Quo, Peter Gabriel and others, backed by The London Symphony Orchestra and The Royal Philharmonic Orchestra. The film consisted of newsreel footage from the Second World War, with appropriate songs to accompany it. The whole project was conceived by Lou Reizner, who took several years in producing the album and getting approval from various record companies for their artists to appear. The album entered the album charts on November 27 at No. 27, where it remained for four weeks, peaking at No. 21.

181 DON'T LET ME DOWN
Written by John who sings a double tracked lead vocal, with Paul helping, backed by the usual Beatles' line-up plus Billy Preston's electric piano.

44 THE BALLAD OF JOHN AND YOKO (2.58)
OLD BROWN SHOE (3.17)

R 5786—May 30, 1969

The Beatles' twentieth single, and their first to appear in stereo, was No. 1. It entered the charts on June 4 at No. 11, by which time *Get Back* had dropped to No. 2, rose to No. 2 the following week, and reached No. 1 after three weeks, while *Get Back* was still in the charts at No. 6. It was at No. 1 for two weeks, in the Top 10 for six weeks and in the Top 30 for ten weeks, selling in the region of 300,000 in Britain and 2.5 million globally.

The single was also a No. 1 hit in Germany, Austria, Holland, Norway, Spain, Belgium, Denmark and Malaysia.

182 THE BALLAD OF JOHN AND YOKO
Written by John about his marriage to Yoko, their trips to Paris and Amsterdam, and their life. John sings lead with Paul helping towards the end. George and Ringo do not play on this number — John plays guitar and Paul plays drums and piano. Recorded April 22, 1969.

183 OLD BROWN SHOE
Written by George, who sings solo, backed up by the usual Beatles' line-up with the addition of piano.

45 ABBEY ROAD

PCS 7088—September 26, 1969

The Beatles' twelfth British album, *Abbey Road* went directly to No. 1 one week after release, their ninth album to do so, and became their tenth No. 1 LP in all. The record had advance sales in Britain of 190,000, stayed at No. 1 for eighteen weeks, and was in the British charts for thirty six weeks.

By the end of November 1969 (six weeks after release) the estimated world sales were four million, reaching well over five million by the end of 1969. In America the album sold a million and won a Grammy Award for the Best Engineered Non-Classical Recording.

By 1980, world sales totalled around ten million, making it one of the biggest selling British albums of all time.

The album was recorded beween April and August, 1969, at EMI Studios in Abbey Road, St. John's Wood, with some tracks being recorded in January, 1969 at Apple Studios, but re-recorded later in the year at the Abbey Road sessions, in No. 2 Studio. The recordings were engineered by Geoff Emerick and Philip McDonald (who also engineered such recordings as: Deep Purple — *Deep Purple In Rock*; The Rolling Stones — *Black And Blue*; George Harrison — *All Things Must Pass, Living In The Material World* and *Dark Horse*; John Lennon — *John Lennon/Plastic Ono Band* and *Imagine*; Yoko Ono — *Yoko Ono/Plastic Ono Band* and Ringo Starr — *Sentimental Journey*).

The album was, of course, named after Abbey Road, where EMI Studios are situated. The studio complex at Abbey Road contains four studios, known as No's 1, 2, 3 and 4, the largest being No. 1, which is mainly used for orchestral and opera recordings. The Beatles used the next largest studio, No. 2, which is known as the "pop studio", although they have, from time to time, used No's 3 and 4. It was in No. 2 that most of their singles and albums were recorded.

The cover photograph was taken in Abbey Road on August 8, 1969 at about 10 o'clock in the morning, by Iain Macmillan. Compared to *Sgt. Pepper* and *The Beatles*, the cover design was kept very simple, using only two photographs, and with no title on the front cover and no lyric sheet.

As with most Beatles' albums, there were many cover versions recorded of the *Abbey Road* songs, but with this album, one group made a complete cover version of the whole album, right down to the sleeve photograph. Booker T and the M.G.s recorded all the *Abbey Road* songs using their own arrangements, as a tribute to The Beatles. They named the album *McLemore Avenue*, after the Memphis street in which their recording studios were situated, and their sleeve photograph also shows the group walking across the avenue which gave their LP its title.

As with *Sgt. Pepper* and *The Beatles*, there is little or no gap between tracks on *Abbey Road*. The second side of the album is almost continuous, with only minimal breaks between *Here Comes The Sun* and *Because*, and between *Because* and *You Never Give Me Your Money*. From *You Never Give Me Your Money*, the numbers all blend into one another, except for a short break between *She Came In Through The Bathroom Window* and *Golden Slumbers*. It was Paul's idea to segue these numbers together, as the LP contained several short tracks which might have sounded incomplete if they had been separated.

A SIDE

184   COME TOGETHER *(4.16)*
Written by John, who sings lead, with Paul supporting him to emphasise certain words. John wrote this just after his car accident in 1969.

It was the last song to be recorded for the album, and was started on July 21.

(See the single *Something/Come Together* for chart information.)

In 1978, Aerosmith's version of *Come Together*, taken from the "Sgt. Pepper's Lonely Hearts Club" film sountrack, entered the US chart at No. 27 on September 16 and stayed in the Top 30 for four weeks, reaching No. 20 for one week. An American five-piece band, Aerosmith, was formed in the state of Massachusetts, in 1970. By 1975 they had a million selling album *Get Your Wings*, and in 1976 a smash hit single, *Dream On*, which reached No. 6 in the US Top 30. They followed this with *Last Child*, which made No. 21, and *Walk This Way* (12). *Come Together* was their next single. (See "Sgt. Pepper" picture disc for further details of the "Sgt. Pepper" film.)

185   SOMETHING *(2.58)*
George wrote this just after the double album, *The Beatles*, was completed. He sings lead and is double tracked in places, while Paul and Ringo supply background vocals. The song was initially recorded during January and February 1969, at Apple Studios, but was re-recorded on May 2 at EMI No. 1

Studio, using an orchestra. It wasn't until July 12 that George added his vocal, and Paul and Ringo added their singing and handclapping several days later.

(See the single *Something/Come Together* for chart information.)

Shirley Bassey had one of her biggest hits with her cover version, which entered the Top 30 on June 24, 1970 at No. 26. It was at No. 4 for two weeks and in the Top 30 for thirteen weeks, thus outperforming The Beatles' own version. Shirley Bassey scored twenty seven hit singles between 1957 and 1973, including *Banana Boat Song*, *Kiss Me Honey Honey Kiss Me*, *As I Love You*, *As Long As He Needs Me*, *Reach For The Stars*, *What Now My Love*, *I (Who Have Nothing)*, *Goldfinger*, *For All We Know* and *Never Never Never*.

186   MAXWELL'S SILVER HAMMER *(3.24)*
Written by Paul in 1968, it was the first song to be worked on in 1969, during a January 13 session at Apple Studios, although a subsequent re-recording of the song started on July 9 at Abbey Road. Paul sings lead and plays guitar and piano, and is joined by George on four string guitar and Ringo on anvil (the January 13 recording featured Mal Evans on anvil). On July 11, backing vocals were added by Paul, George and Ringo and George played acoustic guitar and George Martin organ. George used his Moog Synthesiser for the first time on this track.

The Beatles can be seen recording an early version of *Maxwell's Silver Hammer* in the *Let It Be* film, and this is probably the January 13 session.

On release of the album, several cover versions of the most popular songs on the album were made, including four of *Maxwell's Silver Hammer* — by George Howe, Brownhill's Stamp Duty, Format and The Good Ship Lollypop — none of which made the charts.

187   OH DARLING *(3.25)*
Written by Paul, *Oh Darling* was first recorded at Apple Studios in January, re-recorded in July at EMI and finished on Friday, July 18. During the cutting of this track, Paul went into the studio earlier than the others, in order to run through the song by himself, because at first his voice was too clean, and he wanted to sound as though he had been performing the song on stage for a week. As well as singing lead, Paul also

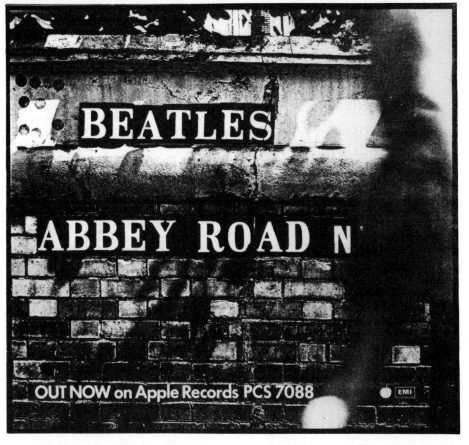

BEATLES

ABBEY ROAD N

OUT NOW on Apple Records PCS 7088

EMI

plays piano, with John and George supplying harmony.

Robin Gibb's version of *Oh Darling*, from the "Sgt. Pepper's Lonely Hearts Club Band" film soundtrack, entered the US Top 30 on September 16, 1978, at No. 28, and stayed in the chart for three weeks, peaking at No. 24. Robin Gibb is one third of The Bee Gees, who started singing as a group when they were children in Australia, where they had their own TV show. They moved back to Britain, their home country, in 1967 and enjoyed their first British hit with *New York Mining Disaster 1941*. This was followed by a string of Top 30 hits, including *Massachusetts* (which reached No. 1), *World, Words, I've Got To Get A Message To You, First Of May* and *Lonely Days*, before they split up in 1970.

They re-formed in 1971, with little success, and it wasn't until 1975 that they achieved superstar status after moving to America, when they emulated their early successes with a string of British and American disco-oriented hits including *Jive Talkin', You Should Be Dancing, Love So Right, How Deep Is Your Love, Stayin' Alive, Night Fever, Too Much Heaven* and *Tragedy*. Four of their hits, *You Should Be Dancing, Stayin' Alive, Night Fever* and *How Deep Is Your Love* were from the *Saturday Night Fever* soundtrack, which is the biggest selling album ever, with over 25 million sold worldwide.

(See "Sgt. Pepper" picture disc for further details of the "Sgt. Pepper" film.)

188   OCTOPUS'S GARDEN *(2.48)*
Written by Ringo. Recording started on April 26, and the group returned to it on July 17. Ringo sings and plays drums, with Paul on bass and piano, and John and George playing guitars. Paul and George supply backing vocals and, halfway through the song, their high pitched vocals were put through special amplifiers to give a gurgling underwater effect. Ringo blew bubbles in a glass of water to add to the atmosphere.

In the *Let It Be* film, Ringo can be seen singing this song for the first time, to George Martin, who is seen working out an arrangement for it with Ringo and George.

189 I WANT YOU (SHE'S SO HEAVY) *(7.44)*
This was written by John about Yoko. It features John playing lead guitar and singing to blend with his guitar riffs. Paul and George support John vocally halfway through the song. Organ appears throughout and various tape loops were used towards the end.

B SIDE

190 HERE COMES THE SUN *(3.04)*
Written by George on a very sunny day in Eric Clapton's garden. Work started on this early in July with George singing lead vocals and playing acoustic guitar, Paul on bass and Ringo on drums — John was absent and did not play on the original recording. Later John, with the others, added some intricate vocal harmony and clapping. George used his Moog on this number.

For the first time in his career, Steve Harley recorded a song that he hadn't composed himself, when his version of *Here Comes The Sun* was released on July 24, 1976. It entered the Top 30 on August 7 at No. 27, staying in the chart for five weeks. Steve Harley and Cockney Rebel had four Top 30 hits before *Here Comes The Sun*, with *Judy Teen, Mr Soft, Make Me Smile (Come Up And See Me)* (No. 1) and *Mr Raffles (Man It Was Mean).*

191 BECAUSE *(2.44)*
Because was written by John about Yoko and himself — Yoko was playing some Beethoven chords, John told her to play them backwards and the result became *Because*. John, Paul and George join together to sing the very intricate lead vocals in harmony. The three rehearsed this number very thoroughly before they attempted to record it. Moog was once again used on this number.

192 YOU NEVER GIVE ME YOUR MONEY *(3.57)*
Written by Paul, when Apple was experiencing financial difficulties. The song was started on Tuesday, July 15, and is divided into three vocal parts. Paul sings lead in all the parts, with John assisting in the first part, and supplying harmony between the second and third parts. At the end, the harmony is by Paul, John and George. Paul plays

piano. The number fades away, blending into the beginning of the next track.

193 SUN KING *(2.32)*
Sun King starts with cow bells and forest noises, crickets, bubbling water and bird whistles, and features several acoustic guitars. The song was written by John and was started on Thursday, July 24. John, Paul and George again sing very intricate lead vocals in harmony. Additional instruments include John on maracas, Paul on harmonium, Ringo on bongos and George Martin on organ. (John originally called the song *Los Paranoias* — probably because of the very Spanish feel and the inclusion of some "Spanish" sounding lyrics.)
The track blends straight into the next:

194 MEAN MR. MUSTARD *(1.06)*
Written by John in India in 1968. John sings lead with Paul and George joining in for the last verse. Paul plays piano with added tambourine. Recording started on July 24.
This song segues to the next:

195 POLYTHENE PAM *(1.18)*
Written by John in India about a mythical Liverpool "scrubber", it was almost included on the previously released "white" double album. Recording began on July 28, with John playing maracas and singing lead and Paul and George providing backing vocals. Paul played cow-bells and piano and George tambourine.
This song is immediately followed by the next track :

196 SHE CAME IN THROUGH THE BATHROOM WINDOW *(1.52)*
Written by Paul, who sings lead, with John and George helping with backing vocals. Originally recorded on January 13, it was re-started on Friday, July 25. Paul plays piano.
There is a very short gap between this and the next song.

197 GOLDEN SLUMBERS *(1.31)*
Paul borrowed one verse for this number from the traditional song, which was shown to him by his stepsister, Ruth, when he was doodling on the piano at his father's house in Cheshire. Ruth asked whether he could play the song, but as Paul is unable to read music, he was forced to admit that he couldn't. However, in reading the song's lyrics, he noticed

THE BEATLES 'Something'|'Come Together' **OUT NOW** Apple Records ●

that they would fit something he was writing but had not completed as a whole song. So he put his own music to the original *Golden Slumbers* lyrics and added the other verses to form The Beatles version of *Golden Slumbers.*

Recording started on the last day of July. Paul sings solo, and plays piano with orchestral backing.

The song changes abruptly into the next:

198   CARRY THAT WEIGHT *(1.37)*

This was written by Paul, but all four Beatles sing the "Carry that weight" chorus, with Paul, John and George singing the "I never give you my pillow" verse in the middle. Orchestral backing completes the track.

Trash (formerly White Trash) recorded this as their second single for

British Section   77

Apple — their version in fact included both *Golden Slumbers* and *Carry That Weight* as arranged on the album — and reached the *NME* Top 30 for two weeks, its highest position being No. 27. Orange Bicycle also recorded *Golden Slumbers/Carry That Weight* as a single, but it did not make the charts.

Carry That Weight segues into the penultimate track on the album.

199 THE END *(2.04)*

Written by Paul, who sings lead with all singing harmony. The number opens with the first recorded drum solo by Ringo on a Beatles record, which is followed by three guitar solos, one each played by John, Paul and George, with orchestral backing.

A gap of twenty seconds silence follows *The End* before the final number, which is not listed on the album sleeve:

200 HER MAJESTY *(0.23)*

Written by Paul, as a tribute to the Queen. Paul sings solo and plays guitar. Complimentary copies of the album were sent to Buckingham Palace. This remains the shortest recorded Beatle song.

46 SOMETHING *(2.58)*
COME TOGETHER *(4.16)*

R 5814—October 31, 1969

This, The Beatles' twenty-first single, was their first British single to be taken from an already released album — *Abbey Road*. It was also George's first "A" side contribution to a single, although both tracks are regarded as "A" sides. It entered the *NME* Top 30 at No. 17 (the lowest entry position for any Beatles' single since *Love Me Do*) on November 5, while its highest position in the chart was No. 5 for two weeks, making it the third Beatles' single not to get to No. 1 (*Penny Lane* in 1967 only got to No. 2 and the first single, *Love Me Do*, got to No 27). It was in the Top 10 for four weeks and the Top 30 for nine weeks.

Global sales can be estimated at 2.5 million.

It was due to Allen Klein's insistence that this single was released in America, and then in Britain, Klein being the group's manager at this time.

185a SOMETHING

184a COME TOGETHER
(See *Abbey Road* for both titles.)

NO ONE'S GONNA CHANGE OUR WORLD

SRS 5013—December 12, 1969

At a meeting of the World Wildlife Fund on December 21, 1976, at Buckingham Palace, Spike Milligan suggested, on behalf of several people from the entertainment world who were present, that an album should be released, and everyone involved — artists, composers, publishers and record companies — should donate all fees towards the Wildlife Fund. Two years later, this album was the result, with all royalties going towards funds dealing with rare animals in danger of extinction. The album was only ever released in Britain, with George Martin co-ordinating the project. Prince Philip and Spike Milligan supplied sleeve notes, and the front cover artwork was drawn by Michael Grimshaw.

The version of *Across The Universe* on this charity album did not appear on a Beatles' album until the release of *The Beatles Collection* in 1978, when it was included on the free *Rarities* album included with this boxed set. As the charity album was deleted only a few years after its release, this Beatles track did indeed become a rarity for many years, until its appearance in *The Beatles Collection* set. It was the first time that an "official" Beatles track had appeared on an album featuring other artists, and this was not to happen again until 1978 when the *All You Need Is Love* **album included the title track by The Beatles.**

Tracks and artists on the album are as follows:

A SIDE

ACROSS THE UNIVERSE (The Beatles) (See below)

WHAT THE WORLD NEEDS NOW IS LOVE (Cilla Black)

CUDDLY OLD KOALA (Rolf Harris)

WINGS (The Hollies)

NING NANG NONG/THE PYTHON (Spike Milligan)

B SIDE

MARLEY PURT DRIVE (The Bee Gees)

I'M A TIGER (Lulu)

BEND IT (Dave Dee, Dozy, Beaky, Mick & Tich)

IN THE COUNTRY (Cliff Richard & The Shadows)

WHEN I SEE AN ELEPHANT FLY (Bruce Forsyth)

LAND OF MY FATHERS (Harry Secombe)

201   ACROSS THE UNIVERSE (Version 1) *(3.44)*
This is not the version featured on the *Let It Be* album, but is the original recording made in February 1968. The song was written by John when he woke up one morning at about 7 o'clock with the words "pools of sorrow, waves of joy" going through his head. So he got up and wrote them down, ending up with about ten lines in all. The group started recording the song on Sunday, February 4 (*Lady Madonna* had been recorded the day before) with George playing sitar, John singing lead and Ringo playing drums and Coca Cola tin. Later during the recording, John and Paul decided at the last minute that they needed girls to sing a high falsetto passage. Paul went out and started talking to the crowd of Beatle fans gathered outside the recording studio gates, and eventually

invited two girls into the studio for a try out, the privileged pair being Lizzie Bravo of 16 Compayne Gardens, London, N.W.6, and Gayleen Pease of 17 Amhurst Road, London N.16. The Beatles found the two girls were ideal, and they sing the line "nothing's going to change my world" over and over again.

David Bowie recorded this song, with John Lennon playing guitar, in January, 1975, for his album, *Young Americans*.

47   LET IT BE *(3.49)*
YOU KNOW MY NAME (LOOK UP THE NUMBER) *(4.17)*

R 5833—March 6, 1970

The last Beatles' single to be released before they split up entered the Top 30 on March 11 at No. 9. It went to No. 3 the following week, but made no further progress, thus becoming the fourth Beatles' single not to reach No. 1 in Britain. It was in the Top 10 for five weeks and the Top 30 for seven weeks.

The single sold over 1½ million in the USA and world sales are well over three million.

202   LET IT BE
Written by Paul, who sings lead, with John and George supplying harmony. Paul plays piano, John bass guitar and George lead. Billy Preston is on organ. Recorded late January 1969.

203   YOU KNOW MY NAME (LOOK UP THE NUMBER)
A song recorded at about the same time as the tracks used on the "Sgt. Pepper" LP in early 1967. Written by John who sings solo, with Mal Evans supplying background vocals. There are supposed to be several well-known musicians on this recording, including the late Brian Jones on saxophone.

The song was originally to be released as a Plastic Ono Band single (backed with another still unreleased Beatles' gem, *What's The New Mary Jane*, also recorded in 1967) as a follow up to the *Cold Turkey* hit, but was scrapped in favour of *Instant Karma*. It is interesting to note that some kind of pressing of *You Know My Name/What's The New Mary Jane* probably does exist, as its allocated catalogue number, "APPLES 1002", appears scratched out on the "B" side of the *Let It Be* single. Therefore, it seems safe to assume that, as a master was made for the "A" side of the withdrawn P.O.B. single, a similar master was produced for the "B" side, that is, *What's The New Mary Jane*.

Up to September, 1970, The Beatles total world sales have been estimated at 133 million (74 million singles, three million EPs and 56 million albums) the equivalent of 416 million singles.

PXS 1—May 8, 1970
PCS 7096—November 6, 1970

Let It Be, the thirteenth and last Beatles' album to be released before the group eventually split up, was the "soundtrack" to their fourth film, which showed the group rehearsing and recording the album. It was released in Britain as a boxed set (PXS 1), which included the album and an 11 by 8½ inch (280 by 215mm) paperback book called *The Beatles Get Back*, containing stills and (unused) dialogue from the film. The album was released separately as PCS 7096 on November 6, 1970. The paperback book was not sold separately, and the boxed set is no longer available.

The album entered the *NME* Top 20 album chart at No. 3 on May 13, within a week of release, and by June 3 it was at No. 1, staying there for three weeks, then dropping down to No. 2 for two weeks, and returning to No. 1 for one week. It dropped down again to No. 3 and went back to No. 1 for two weeks, thus being at No. 1 for a total of six weeks. The album continued to move up and down the chart for a total of

twenty four weeks until October 21, when it dropped out of the Top 20. When the *NME* introduced their new Top 30 album chart later in the year, the album returned to the chart at No. 26 on December 9 for one week and returned again on December 29 at No. 26, this time staying in the chart for six weeks and rising to No. 11 in its sixth week, after which it was absent from the chart before spending three more weeks near the foot of the lists.

It was in the charts for a total of thirty four weeks between May 13, 1970 and March 10, 1971.

Let It Be achieved the highest initial sale of any album in the history of the American recording industry. Advance orders for the album in the USA totalled 3,700,000 — representing a gross retail value of 25,900,000 dollars (the album cost $7 in America and £2 19s 11d. in Britain).

World sales of the album must be well over four million and have probably reached five million.

The story behind the conception and recording of *Let It Be* is long and complex, starting in November 1968 and ending in May 1970, when the album was finally released.

In November, 1968, The Beatles had decided to perform before a live audience, the show to be filmed, and subsequently screened worldwide on television. The original idea was to do three shows, which would be recorded on colour video tape, with the television show being made up of the best parts from each of the three shows, which the group decided would mainly comprise songs from the just released double album, *The Beatles*, plus a few oldies. During December, 1968, camera and technical crews were booked for the week January 17 to 24, 1969, but Paul's return from Portugal held up any decision on the venue, which at one time was to be The Roundhouse in North London.

Rehearsals for the shows started on January 2, at Twickenham Film Studios, with January 18, or thereabouts, as a tentative show date. At this point, The Beatles' idea for the show ran along similar lines to that used for the *Hey Jude* film clip, where they would perform live in front of an audience, letting the fans join in to get a party mood going, and thus making an hour-long TV film of Beatles numbers, although later, the length of the show was increased to ninety minutes.

At the same time, it was agreed that all rehearsal work should be filmed to make a documentary production separate from the TV show. During their time at Twickenham, The Beatles had written and rehearsed eight new songs for the show (thus changing their original plan of performing material from the double album). While the rehearsal work was in progress, possible venues for the shows were being sought without success. Many suggestions were put forward — Michael Lindsay-Hogg, the show's director, favoured Africa, as at one point the idea had been to perform outside, which necessitated a warm climate. Lindsay-Hogg and producer Denis O'Dell knew of an old Roman amphitheatre on the coast of Tripoli, which sounded the ideal site, and Mal Evans was due to fly to Africa to inspect it on Monday, January 13, but on Sunday, January 12, The Beatles finally abandoned the idea of a TV show.

The reason for the sudden change in plans was that although Paul, John and Ringo were in favour of the idea, George was not, and on January 10 at Twickenham, George announced his disagreement and told the others he was going home, as he could not continue to rehearse for something he did not believe in. With George's departure, the original project could not progress, so it was mutually agreed by all four that they should continue with rehearsals and finish writing the new material, but use it for an album instead. They agreed that the filming at Twickenham should continue, and that a film crew should also capture the recording of the new numbers at Apple Studios.

On Thursday, January 16, rehearsals ended at Twickenham, and operations moved to Apple Studios, in Savile Row, on Monday, January 20. The installation of recording equipment at Apple had not been completed, so EMI brought in an eight track tape machine and console as temporary equipment. The initial recording and filming at Apple continued from January 20 to May 28, 1969, and on January 30, the group recorded five numbers on the roof of the Apple building, giving a free lunchtime show to passers-by and other office workers who positioned themselves on surrounding buildings.

At the end of June, 1969, Apple Records reported that a new Beatles album should be out in late August. Neil Aspinall, Apple's managing director, confirmed that the album had been given a tentative title of *The Beatles Get Back*, but added that it could be changed before the official release date. The Beatles had the idea of using similar wording to that used on their first album *Please Please Me* something like *The Beatles Get Back, Don't Let Me Down And Nine Others.*

The *Beatles Get Back* album consisted of the following tracks: *One After 909* (the only roof top recording used), *Save The Last Dance For Me, Don't Let Me Down* (a different version to that on the "B" side of the *Get Back* single), *Dig A Pony, I've Got A Feeling* and *Get Back* constituting side one, plus *For You Blue, Teddy Boy* (later recorded by Paul as a solo number on his *McCartney* album), *Two Of Us On Our Way Home, Maggie Mae, Dig It* (the full length version), *Let It Be* and *The Long And Winding Road* on side two.

The original idea for the *Get Back* album was to record The Beatles in as live a situation as possible, without the technical studio effects and techniques used on their previous three albums, and to try to re-create their original sound as it had appeared on the first two albums, *Please Please Me* and *With The Beatles*, using the three guitars and drums line-up. The album would include studio floor conversation, with The Beatles chatting to each other, preparing for the next number and shouting comments up to the control room. The album sleeve was also to be similar to that of *Please Please Me* — the photograph that was to be used on the *Get Back* album cover was taken in exactly the same place and by the same photographer, Angus McBean, as the photograph on the *Please Please Me* album, and the group positioned themselves over the staircase at the offices of EMI Records in Manchester Square, London, as they had done six years earlier for the *Please Please Me* cover photo session. (As can be seen later, with the change of album title, the original idea for the cover was also changed, and eventually stills from the film were used as cover photographs. The photograph taken for the *Get Back* album was not

Apple Records

THE BEATLES

Let it be
You know my name (Look up the number)

out now

The Beatles
"Let it be"
apple PCS 7096

LET IT BE

39/11
Recommended
retail price

Now available excluding the book at standard price

E.M.I Records (The Gramophone Co. Ltd.) E.M.I House, 20 Manchester Square, London W1A 1ES

wasted, as it was later used on the two double albums, *The Beatles 1962 - 1966* and *The Beatles 1967 - 1970*, released in 1973. It appears on the back cover of the "62 - 66" album, and on the front cover of the "67 - 70" album, with a similar shot, taken at the original *Please Please Me* session, but not identical to the *Please Please Me* cover picture, on the remaining surfaces.)

The *Get Back* album was scheduled for release by Apple Records at the end of August, 1969, but a last minute decision by The Beatles led to its postponement, because they felt the album should not be released until the documentary film of them recording it was ready for general viewing on television (at this point the film was still intended for television, and it wasn't until later that it was decided to make it a film for cinema release). As they wanted to get an album ready for rush release, the group returned to the studios for a concentrated series of recording sessions in July, to complete some tracks that they had already started, and to record some new ones. The results appeared on *Abbey Road*, which was released in September, 1969.

In the September, 1969 issue of *Beatles Monthly*, the News page reported that the *Get Back* album was scheduled for December release, and that a book had been prepared by John Kosh, with photographs by Ethan Russell and Mal Evans. The album did not appear in December, but music papers reported that the new Beatles' single, *Let It Be*, from the film *Get Back* (which was the working title), would be released on February 20, 1970, with the *Get Back* album following immediately.

While the *Get Back* film was being completed, things were happening, both at Apple (courtesy of Allen Klein) and with the Beatles themselves, which caused plans for the *Get Back* album to be totally altered. By this time, the *Get Back* recordings, produced by George Martin, and engineered by Glyn Johns, had been lying around for a year, and when The Beatles listened to the tapes they decided that the whole project was worthless and should be abandoned immediately, but as Apple had a large amount of capital tied up in the venture, the group reportedly gave the tapes to Glyn Johns for re-mixing.

In January, 1970, the *NME* reported that The Beatles, minus John Lennon, who was in Denmark, had recorded *I Me Mine*, a George Harrison number, as the last track for their new *Get Back* album. It also reported that the title of the album might be changed to *Let It Be*, also the name of their new single, and that they had decided to change their original plans for the album, and to change the order of the tracks.

During the problems at Apple, John and George had become friendly with Phil Spector, the well-known record producer and songwriter. In Paul's absence (he was busy recording his first solo album *McCartney*), John and George decided to give the *Get Back* tapes to Phil Spector to re-produce and re-mix. In doing so, the original idea of the *Get Back* album, to record the Beatles as near to playing live as was possible, was ruined, as Spector altered the whole concept by adding an orchestra and female choir to several tracks: *Across The Universe, I Me Mine, Let It Be* and *The Long And Winding Road*. The playing order of the tracks was altered, and three numbers from the original recording were scrapped altogether: *Save The Last Dance For Me, Don't Let Me Down* and *Teddy Boy*. The *Dig It* track was cut by at least 4 minutes to run for only 48 seconds. When Paul heard the remixed tapes, he was not pleased with the Spectorisation, especially the treatment given to his *The Long And Winding Road*, which he thought had been overly orchestrated.

So, sixteen months after the initial recording sessions for the album, the *Let It Be* LP finally appeared in May, 1970. After Phil Spector's treatment, the music on the album does not live up to the sleeve note on the back of the cover:

"This is a new phase BEATLES album...essential to the content of the film, LET IT BE was that they performed live for many of the tracks; in comes the warmth and the freshness of a live performance; as reproduced for disc by Phil Spector." (sic)

This could have been said of the original *Get Back* recordings, albeit in superior grammatical form.

The *Let It Be* package was designed by John Kosh, and many record reviewers saw his black sombre design as a fitting choice for the last Beatles' album.

With the Spectorisation of the *Let It*

Be album, it no longer became the soundtrack of the film, as the songs on the actual film soundtrack escaped the Spector treatment. The album contained only twelve of the twenty three songs featured in the film. The film songs were as follows: *Don't Let Me Down, Maxwell's Silver Hammer, Two Of Us, I Got A Feeling, Oh Darling, One After 909, Jazz Piano Song, Two Of Us* (No. 2), *Across The Universe, Dig A Pony, Suzy Parker, I Me Mine, For You Blue, Besame Mucho, Octopus's Garden, You Really Got A Hold On Me, The Long And Winding Road* (reggae version), *The Long And Winding Road* (short version), *Shake Rattle And Roll, Kansas City, Lawdy Miss Clawdy, Dig It* (full version) *Two Of Us* (No. 3), *Let It Be, The Long And Winding Road* (full version), *Get Back, Don't Let Me Down* (No. 2), *I Got A Feeling* (No. 2), *One After 909* (No. 2), *Dig A Pony* (No. 2), *Get Back* (No. 2) and *The "Laughing" Get Back*, which is played over the credits.

A total of ninety-six hours of filming was accumulated during the *Get Back* recording sessions, and around thirty hours of music was recorded. Before The Beatles started to rehearse or record their own numbers, they would very often warm up by singing and playing some old standards, and the following oldies played during rehearsals, were probably recorded and thus lie "in the can" somewhere in the Apple/EMI vaults: *Stand By Me, Baby I Don't Care, Thirty Days, Hippy Hippy Shake, Short Fat Fanny, Fools Like Me, You Win Again, Turn Around, Blue Suede Shoes, True Love, The Right String But The Wrong Yo Yo, Sure To Fall, Memphis Tennessee, Maybellene, Johnny B. Goode, Sweet Little Sixteen, Little Queenie, Roll Over Beethoven, Rock And Roll Music, Singing The Blues, Midnight Special, Michael Row The Boat Ashore, She Said, She Said, Devil In Her Heart, You Can't Do That, Hitch Hike, Money, Three Cool Cats, Good Rockin' Tonight, All Shook Up, Don't Be Cruel, Lucille, Send Me Some Lovin', Dizzy Miss Lizzy, Be-Bop A-Lula, Lotta Lovin', House Of The Rising Sun, Tea For Two, Blowin' In The Wind, I Shall Be Released, All Along The Watchtower, High Heel Sneakers, It's Only Make Believe, C'mon Everybody, Some-*

thing Else, Bad Boy, Rock Island Line, Third Man Theme, Piece Of My Heart, Good Golly Miss Molly and *Love Me Do.*

It is very likely that all the above tracks were recorded, because in the July, 1969 issue of *Beatles Monthly*, in an early review of the *Get Back* album, Mal Evans reported that, "Although this LP has only eleven main numbers on it, far more tracks have been recorded. The Beatles didn't want to repeat the 'double disc' idea and make everybody buy a pair of LP records together. Instead all the other tracks are held 'in the can' so that they can be used later.

"Amongst the stuff that 'stays on file' so to speak is enough material for a special rock'n'roll LP — including famous American rock hits like *Shake Rattle And Roll* and *Blue Suede Shoes*".

In the September, 1969 issue of the same monthly, in an article titled "In The Studio", about the *Abbey Road* recordings, Frederick James reported, "We thought there'd be a special rock'n'roll LP — but there's no scheduled issue date for the wealth of rock material like *Shake Rattle And Roll, Blue Suede Shoes* and the revamped *Love Me Do* which the lads started putting on tape as long ago as January 26, 1969."

From these two reports it is safe to assume that there must be a great many unreleased recordings from the *Get Back* sessions.

A SIDE

204   TWO OF US (3.33)

This number was written by Paul for Mortimer, the teenage group from New York. It was recorded by them for their first Apple single, but for some unknown reason the record never came out.

Paul sings lead, and shares the vocals with John in places for the harmony work. The number starts with John saying, "*I Dig A Pigmy* by Charles Hawtrey on the deaf aids. Phase one in which Doris gets her oats", which is followed by some laughter. No bass guitar was used on this track, but George reached low down on his electric guitar to get the bass notes. Acoustic guitar is prominent and the number fades out with a whistled tune.

205 DIG A PONY *(3.52)*
Written by John, who sings lead with Paul helping in places. Billy Preston plays electric piano. This was the first number to be recorded, and was started at the Apple Studios on January 20, 1969. The number begins with a false start and ends with John saying, "Thank you, brothers".

206 ACROSS THE UNIVERSE (Version 2) (3.43)

John was not pleased with the original recording of *Across The Universe* (see *No One's Gonna Change Our World* album) so he decided to re-record it for the *Let It Be* album. He sings solo, backed by a choir and orchestra, plus acoustic guitars but without drumming.

207 I ME MINE (2.24)

George's number, which he sings, with Paul helping for the chorus. John was not present when this number was recorded on January 3, 1970. This track and *Across The Universe* were the only songs not recorded during the original *Get Back* recordings in January, 1969.

In the *Let It Be* film, George introduces *I Me Mine* as a waltz, and John and Yoko are seen dancing to it.

208 DIG IT (0.48)

This is an edited version of the original five minute number written by all four Beatles. John sings lead and plays bass, with Paul on piano and George on acoustic guitar.

At the end of this track, John introduces the next number with, "That was 'Can You Dig It' by Georgie Wood. Now we'd like to do "Ark The Angels Come'".

209 LET IT BE (Version 2) (4.02)

Written by Paul, who sings lead, with John and George supplying harmony. Paul plays piano, John bass guitar and George his Lesley guitar, which resembles an organ at times. Orchestral backing is again added. This is a different version from the single release, and features a different guitar passage from George.

210 MAGGIE MAE (0.39)

John and Paul sing this traditional song, and it is the first non-Beatles composition to be released by The Beatles since *Bad Boy* on the *Collection Of Oldies* album in 1966.

B SIDE

211 I'VE GOT A FEELING (3.34)

This was written by Paul and John — Paul wrote the first part "I've got a feeling..." and sings that part, while John wrote and sings the second part "Everybody had a...". At the end they both sing their own parts at the same time.

212 ONE AFTER 909 (2.50)

This number was written by John and Paul in 1959. It was recorded on the Apple roof with The Beatles playing their usual instruments plus Billy Preston on electric piano, and is the only Apple roof-top recording to be used. Altogether five numbers were recorded on the roof, the others being *I've Got A Feeling, Don't Let Me Down, Get Back* and *Dig A Pony*, but none of these recordings was used for the album, all being re-recorded in the Apple Studios.

At the end of the track, John sings a line from *Danny Boy*.

213 THE LONG AND WINDING ROAD (3.34)

Written by Paul, who sings solo and plays piano, with John taking over the bass guitar. The backing includes a complete orchestra, with violins, brass and harp plus a female choir but no drumming.

Between this track and the next, John is heard very quietly saying, "The Queen says 'No' to pot smoking FBI members".

214 FOR YOU BLUE (2.24)

Written by George who sings solo and plays acoustic guitar. John plays slide steel guitar, Paul is on piano and Ringo on drums. Half-way through the number George says, "Dig those rhythm and blues" and "Elmore James got nothing on this, baby".

215 GET BACK (Version 2) (3.07)

At the beginning of this number, when the group are warming up, John sings, "Sweet Loretta fart, she thought she was a cleaner, but she was a frying pan". Paul sings solo, with John playing lead guitar, George on rhythm, Paul bass and Ringo drums. Billy Preston supplied the electric piano. At the end of the number Paul says, "Thanks Mo" to Maureen (Starkey — Ringo's wife) who was clapping the loudest and John says, "I'd like to say thank you on behalf of the group and ourselves and I hope we pass the audition". This piece of conversation appears in the *Let It Be* film, just after the group has completed its roof-top concert.

This is a different version from the one released as a single.

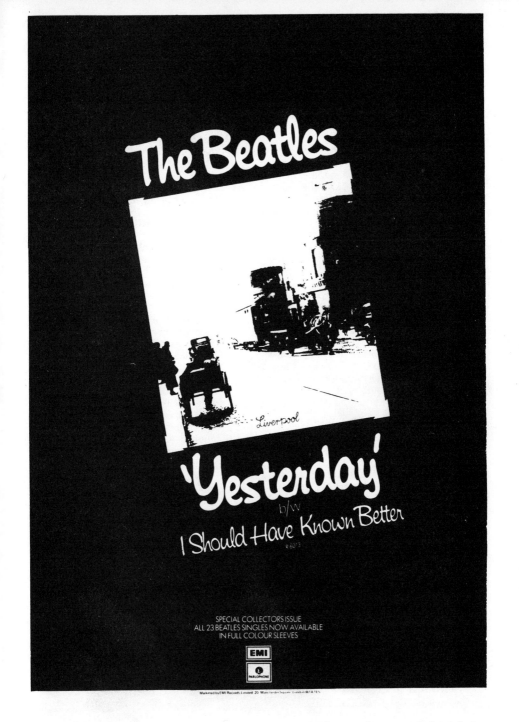

205 **DIG A PONY** *(3.52)*
Written by John, who sings lead with
Paul helping in places. Billy Preston
plays electric piano. This was the first
number to be recorded, and was
started at the Apple Studios on January
20, 1969. The number begins with a
false start and ends with John saying,
"Thank you, brothers".

206 ACROSS THE UNIVERSE (Version 2) *(3.43)*
John was not pleased with the original recording of *Across The Universe* (see *No One's Gonna Change Our World* album) so he decided to re-record it for the *Let It Be* album. He sings solo, backed by a choir and orchestra, plus acoustic guitars but without drumming.

207 I ME MINE *(2.24)*
George's number, which he sings, with Paul helping for the chorus. John was not present when this number was recorded on January 3, 1970. This track and *Across The Universe* were the only songs not recorded during the original *Get Back* recordings in January, 1969.

In the *Let It Be* film, George introduces *I Me Mine* as a waltz, and John and Yoko are seen dancing to it.

208 DIG IT *(0.48)*
This is an edited version of the original five minute number written by all four Beatles. John sings lead and plays bass, with Paul on piano and George on acoustic guitar.

At the end of this track, John introduces the next number with, "That was 'Can You Dig It' by Georgie Wood. Now we'd like to do "Ark The Angels Come'".

209 LET IT BE (Version 2) *(4.02)*
Written by Paul, who sings lead, with John and George supplying harmony. Paul plays piano, John bass guitar and George his Lesley guitar, which resembles an organ at times. Orchestral backing is again added. This is a different version from the single release, and features a different guitar passage from George.

210 MAGGIE MAE *(0.39)*
John and Paul sing this traditional song, and it is the first non-Beatles composition to be released by The Beatles since *Bad Boy* on the *Collection Of Oldies* album in 1966.

B SIDE

211 I'VE GOT A FEELING *(3.34)*
This was written by Paul and John — Paul wrote the first part "I've got a feeling..." and sings that part, while John wrote and sings the second part "Everybody had a...". At the end they both sing their own parts at the same time.

212 ONE AFTER 909 *(2.50)*
This number was written by John and Paul in 1959. It was recorded on the Apple roof with The Beatles playing their usual instruments plus Billy Preston on electric piano, and is the only Apple roof-top recording to be used. Altogether five numbers were recorded on the roof, the others being *I've Got A Feeling, Don't Let Me Down, Get Back* and *Dig A Pony*, but none of these recordings was used for the album, all being re-recorded in the Apple Studios.

At the end of the track, John sings a line from *Danny Boy*.

213 THE LONG AND WINDING ROAD *(3.34)*
Written by Paul, who sings solo and plays piano, with John taking over the bass guitar. The backing includes a complete orchestra, with violins, brass and harp plus a female choir but no drumming.

Between this track and the next, John is heard very quietly saying, "The Queen says 'No' to pot smoking FBI members".

214 FOR YOU BLUE *(2.24)*
Written by George who sings solo and plays acoustic guitar. John plays slide steel guitar, Paul is on piano and Ringo on drums. Half-way through the number George says, "Dig those rhythm and blues" and "Elmore James got nothing on this, baby".

215 GET BACK (Version 2) *(3.07)*
At the beginning of this number, when the group are warming up, John sings, "Sweet Loretta fart, she thought she was a cleaner, but she was a frying pan". Paul sings solo, with John playing lead guitar, George on rhythm, Paul bass and Ringo drums. Billy Preston supplied the electric piano. At the end of the number Paul says, "Thanks Mo" to Maureen (Starkey — Ringo's wife) who was clapping the loudest and John says, "I'd like to say thank you on behalf of the group and ourselves and I hope we pass the audition". This piece of conversation appears in the *Let It Be* film, just after the group has completed its roof-top concert.

This is a different version from the one released as a single.

PCSP 717—April 19, 1973

In early 1973, an unauthorised Beatles anthology entitled *The Beatles Alpha Omega* (a four record set distributed by Audio Tape Inc., catalogue No ATRBH 3583) was released in America, with heavy advertising on radio and television. It was this album which prompted EMI to release two double albums, *The Beatles 1962 - 1966* and *The Beatles 1967 - 1970*, in America and Britain.

The two double albums appeared in Britain on April 19, 1973, just over two weeks after the American release date. As with most Beatles albums, they entered the *NME* chart one week later, the "62 - 66" album at No. 17 and the "67 - 70" album at No. 27. (For further chart details of the "67 - 70" album see appropriate album entry.) In its third week, the "62 -66" album jumped from No. 15 to No. 3, where it stayed for four weeks, after which it went to No. 1 for a single week. After its thirtieth week in the chart, the album dropped out for one week, but returned at No. 25 for another chart week. It re-entered for one week at No. 27 on December 4, and again for two weeks on January 1, 1974, in the mid-twenties. On January 29, it began another seven week chart stay at No. 29, rising to No. 22 in the final week, and re-entered once more in 1974 at No. 29 on May 14. Exactly two years later, on May 15, 1976, it was back for one more week at No. 24. The album was in the Top 10 for fourteen weeks, the Top 20 for nineteen weeks and the Top 30 for forty-three weeks over a period of three years.

The estimated global sale for the album is around 1½ million.

The front cover photograph on this album was taken at the same session that supplied the *Please Please Me* cover shot. The back cover photograph was originally to be used on the never released *The Beatles Get Back* album, which eventually became the *Let It Be* album (see *Let It Be* album for complete details).

All the tracks on the album had been previously released as singles or on albums. For details of singles, see appropriate singles entry and for details of album tracks see appropriate album (title given in brackets).

A SIDE RECORD ONE

10 c   **LOVE ME DO** *(2.18)*

3c   **PLEASE PLEASE ME** *(1.58)*

16c   **FROM ME TO YOU** *(1.54)*
The stereo version of *From Me To You* — with the harmonica introduction missing.

18c   **SHE LOVES YOU** *(2.18)*

34c   **I WANT TO HOLD YOUR HAND** *(2.22)*

22b   **ALL MY LOVING** *(2.04)*
(With The Beatles LP)

36d   **CAN'T BUY ME LOVE** *(2.10)*

B SIDE RECORD ONE

42c   **A HARD DAY'S NIGHT** *(2.28)*

47b   **AND I LOVE HER** *(2.27)*
(A Hard Day's Night LP)

62b   **EIGHT DAYS A WEEK** *(2.42)*
(Beatles For Sale LP)

53c   **I FEEL FINE** *(2.17)*

69c   **TICKET TO RIDE** *(3.03)*

83c   **YESTERDAY** *(2.03)*
(Help LP)

A SIDE RECORD TWO

71c   **HELP!** *(2.16)*

74a **YOU'VE GOT TO HIDE YOUR LOVE AWAY** *(2.06)*
(*Help* LP)

86b **WE CAN WORK IT OUT** *(2.12)*

85b **DAY TRIPPER** *(2.49)*

87b **DRIVE MY CAR** *(2.25)*
(*Rubber Soul* LP)

88a **NORWEGIAN WOOD (THIS BIRD HAS FLOWN)** *(2.02)*
(*Rubber Soul* LP)

B SIDE RECORD TWO

90b **NOWHERE MAN** *(2.40)*
(*Rubber Soul* LP)

93c **MICHELLE** *(2.40)*
(*Rubber Soul* LP)

97a **IN MY LIFE** *(2.23)*
(*Rubber Soul* LP)

95a **GIRL** *(2.26)*
(*Rubber Soul* LP)

101b **PAPERBACK WRITER** *(2.15)*

103c **ELEANOR RIGBY** *(2.04)*

104d **YELLOW SUBMARINE** *(2.36)*

50   **THE BEATLES 1967 — 1970**

PCSP 718—April 19, 1973

This double album was released along with *The Beatles 1962 - 1966* (see entry for this album for further details), and entered the *NME* Album chart one week after release at No. 27. The next three weeks saw the album rise

progressively to No. 16, No. 2 and No. 1 before it dropped back, although it accumulated stays of nineteen weeks in the Top 10, and thirty-seven consecutive weeks in the Top 30. After a single week's absence from the chart, it returned on January 29, 1974, for two weeks, dropped out for another week, and came back for a five week stay on February 19. By April 23, it was back again, this time for four weeks, and also spent single weeks (on May 28 and September 10) at the lower end of the Top 30, altogether spending fifty weeks in the chart over a sixteen month period.

The estimated global sale for the album is almost two million. The cover photos are the same as on "62 - 66" except that they are on opposite covers, i.e. the front cover photo of "62 - 66" becomes the back cover of "67 -70" and vice versa.

All the tracks on the album had been previously released as singles or included on albums or EP's. For details of singles, see appropriate singles entry and for details of album or EP tracks, see appropriate album or EP (title given in brackets)

A SIDE RECORD ONE

119a STRAWBERRY FIELDS FOREVER
(4.03)

118a PENNY LANE *(2.57)*

120a SGT. PEPPER'S LONELY HEARTS CLUB BAND *(1.59)*
(Sgt Pepper LP)

121a WITH A LITTLE HELP FROM MY FRIENDS *(2.41)*
(Sgt Pepper LP)

122a LUCY IN THE SKY WITH DIAMONDS *(3.25)*
(Sgt Pepper LP)

132a A DAY IN THE LIFE *(5.05)*
(Sgt Pepper LP)

133b ALL YOU NEED IS LOVE *(3.44)*

B SIDE RECORD ONE

136b I AM THE WALRUS *(4.32)*
(Hello Goodbye single)

135a HELLO GOODBYE *(3.24)*

139a THE FOOL ON THE HILL *(2.56)*
(Magical Mystery Tour EP)

137a MAGICAL MYSTERY TOUR *(2.45)*
(Magical Mystery Tour EP)

142a LADY MADONNA *(2.14)*

144a HEY JUDE *(7.07)*

145a REVOLUTION *(3.22)*
(Hey Jude single)

A SIDE RECORD TWO

146a BACK IN THE USSR *(2.41)*
(The Beatles LP)

152a WHILE MY GUITAR GENTLY WEEPS *(4.41)*
(The Beatles LP)

149a OB-LA-DI OB-LA-DA *(3.06)*
(The Beatles LP)

180a GET BACK *(3.09)*

181a DON'T LET ME DOWN *(3.30)*
(Get Back single)

182a THE BALLAD OF JOHN AND YOKO *(2.58)*

183a OLD BROWN SHOE *(3.17)*
(The Ballad Of John And Yoko single)

B SIDE RECORD TWO

190a HERE COMES THE SUN *(3.04)*
(Abbey Road LP)

184b COME TOGETHER *(4.16)*
(Abbey Road LP)

185b SOMETHING *(2.58)*
(Abbey Road LP)

188a OCTOPUS'S GARDEN *(2.48)*
(Abbey Road LP)

202a LET IT BE *(3.49)*

206a ACROSS THE UNIVERSE *(3.43)*
(Let It Be LP)

213a THE LONG AND WINDING ROAD *(3.34)*
(Let It Be LP)

THE SINGLES COLLECTION 1962 — 1970

March 6, 1976

During March, 1976, EMI released all twenty-three Beatles' singles simultaneously in special picture sleeves. Although they were advertised as being re-released, they were not re-issues, as all The Beatles' singles were still available at that time. (For a few years, several early singles were deleted, these being *Love Me Do, Please Please Me, From Me To You, She Loves You, Can't Buy Me Love, A Hard Day's Night, I Feel Fine* and *Ticket To Ride,* but they were later reinstated before the "picture sleeve" releases.)

Common front cover.

All twenty-three reached the Top 100 singles chart, and four entered the *NME* Top 30 chart. At one point all twenty-three singles were in the Top 100 singles chart (British Market Research Bureau) simultaneously.

Yesterday was at No. 10, *Hey Jude* 45, *Paperback Writer* 46, *Strawberry Fields Forever* 53, *Get Back* 55, *She Loves You* 59, *Help* 61, *Love Me Do* 62, *Yellow Submarine* 63, *Let It Be* 64, *A Hard Day's Night* 66, *Can't Buy Me Love* 68, *I Want To Hold Your Hand* 69, *All You Need Is Love* 71, *From Me To You* 72, *Hello Goodbye* 74, *Please Please Me* 75, *Lady Madonna* 76, *We Can Work It Out* 79, *I Feel Fine* 81, *Ticket To Ride* 83, *Something* 84 and *The Ballad Of John And Yoko* 88. Of the four singles which reached the *NME* Top 30, three were re-entries, having previously been hits, and these were *Paperback Writer* (highest position No. 18 and three weeks in chart), *Hey Jude* (No. 13, four weeks) and *Get Back* (No. 27, two weeks). The fourth was *Yesterday* (see below).

Back Cover Pictures:

One: *Love Me Do* to *A Hard Day's Night*

Two: *I Feel Fine* to *Yellow Submarine*

Three: *Penny Lane* to *Lady Madonna*

Four: *Hey Jude* to *Let It Be*

51 YESTERDAY *(2.03)*
I SHOULD HAVE KNOWN BETTER *(2.41)*

R 6013—March 8, 1976

The first 'new' Beatles' single since the group's break up, *Yesterday* had already been released in America as a single in 1965, when it sold a million, but had never previously appeared in Britain in single form, although it had been included on an EP in 1966. The single entered the Top 30 on March 20 at No. 21, reached No. 5 for one week, and was in the Top 10 for four weeks and the Top 30 for six weeks.

This single was released along with the 're-issue' of all The Beatles' previous twenty-two singles. All twenty-three singles were packaged in special picture sleeves, with this single being produced in stereo.

83d YESTERDAY
(See *Help* LP.)

44b I SHOULD HAVE KNOWN BETTER
(See *A Hard Day's Night* LP.)

52 ROCK'N'ROLL MUSIC

PCSP 719—June 10, 1976

On February 6, 1976, The Beatles' nine year recording contract, which they had signed in 1967, expired, thus leaving EMI with the rights to re-

release anything from their back catalogue of previously released material. This album was the first release over which EMI had been able to exert complete control.

The album entered the *NME* Top 30 chart on June 19, 1976, at No. 19. Its highest position was No. 10, and it was in the Top 30 for eleven weeks. The album has sold over a million globally, is a certified million seller in the USA.

As with the two previous double albums, EMI provided a somewhat unimaginative sleeve design; art direction was by Roy Kohara (who also designed covers for John Lennon's *Walls And Bridges*, *Rock'N' Roll* and *Shaved Fish* albums and Ringo Starr's *Goodnight Vienna* and *Blast From Your Past* albums) and illustrations by Ignacio Gomez. John had written to EMI offering to design a cover for the album, but EMI declined. John was less than pleased, both with EMI's reply and with the design of the cover.

All the tracks on the album had been previously released on either singles,

EP's or albums. The four *Long Tall Sally* tracks and *I'm Down* appeared both in stereo and on album for the first time in Britain.

For details of each song see main entry under title given in brackets.

A SIDE RECORD ONE

15b **TWIST AND SHOUT** (*2.31*)
(*Please Please Me* LP)

5b **I SAW HER STANDING THERE**(*2.50*)
(*Please Please Me* LP)

37b **YOU CAN'T DO THAT** (*2.32*)
(*Can't Buy Me Love* single)

30a **I WANNA BE YOUR MAN** (*1.56*)
(*With The Beatles* LP)

39a **I CALL YOUR NAME** (*2.05*)
(*Long Tall Sally* EP)

9a **BOYS** (*2.22*)
(*Please Please Me* LP)

38a **LONG TALL SALLY** (*2.00*)
(*Long Tall Sally* EP)

B SIDE RECORD ONE

58b **ROCK AND ROLL MUSIC** (*2.28*)
(*Beatles For Sale* LP)

40a **SLOW DOWN** (*2.54*)
(*Long Tall Sally* EP)

61a **KANSAS CITY/HEY HEY HEY HEY** (*2.35*)
(*Beatles For Sale* LP)

33b **MONEY (THAT'S WHAT I WANT)** (*2.46*)
(*With The Beatles* LP)

117a BAD BOY *(2.17)*
(*A Collection Of Beatles Oldies* LP)

41a MATCHBOX *(1.55)*
(*Long Tall Sally* EP)

27a ROLL OVER BEETHOVEN *(2.42)*
(*With The Beatles* LP)

A SIDE RECORD TWO

84a DIZZY MISS LIZZY *(2.51)*
(*Help* LP)

49b ANY TIME AT ALL *(2.09)*
(*A Hard Day's Night* LP)

87c DRIVE MY CAR *(2.25)*
(*Rubber Soul* LP)

68a EVERYBODY'S TRYING TO BE MY BABY *(2.23)*
(*Beatles For Sale* LP)

73a THE NIGHT BEFORE *(2.30)*
(*Help* LP)

72a I'M DOWN *(2.30)*
(*Help* single)

145b REVOLUTION *(3.22)*
(*Hey Jude* single)

B SIDE RECORD TWO

46b BACK IN THE USSR *(2.41)*
(*The Beatles* LP)

168a HELTER SKELTER *(4.28)*
(*The Beatles* LP)

105a TAXMAN *(2.35)*
(*Revolver* LP)

115a GOT TO GET YOU INTO MY LIFE *(2.26)*
(*Revolver* LP)

178a HEY BULLDOG *(3.07)*
(*Yellow Submarine* LP)

163a BIRTHDAY *(2.41)*
(*The Beatles* LP)

215a GET BACK *(3.05)*
(*Let It Be* LP)

53	**BACK IN THE USSR** *(2.41)*
	TWIST AND SHOUT *(2.31)*

R 6016—June 25, 1976

Released as a promotional single for the *Rock'N'Roll Music* double album, this was the first track to be taken from *The Beatles* (double white album) as a single. It entered the Top 30 on July 17 at No. 24, rose to No. 18 for one week, and was in the Top 30 for three weeks.

The single was released in a picture sleeve to match *The Singles Collection*, and both tracks appear in stereo.

146c BACK IN THE USSR
(See *The Beatles* double LP.)

15c TWIST AND SHOUT
(See *Please Please Me* LP and *Twist And Shout* EP.)

54	**MAGICAL MYSTERY TOUR**

PCTC 255—November 19, 1976

The decision on EMI's part to release this album has never been satisfactorily explained, and in many ways was somewhat unnecessary, in view of the fact that the identical US album (albeit in electronically re-processed stereo) had been available as an import in Britain since 1968, and was in fact EMI's biggest selling import in Britain, with sales of over 50,000. The British release is exactly the same as the album released in the United States in 1967, at which time the *Magical Mystery Tour* tracks had

THE BEATLES
ROCK 'N' ROLL Music

ROCK·OLA

TWIST AND SHOUT · THE NIGHT BEFORE · I CALL YOUR NAME · YOU CAN'T DO THAT
ANYTIME AT ALL · SLOW DOWN · GOT TO GET YOU INTO MY LIFE · LONG, TALL SALLY
DRIVE MY CAR · I SAW HER STANDING THERE · ROLL OVER BEETHOVEN · HELTER SKELTER
REVOLUTION · BACK IN THE U.S.S.R. · I WANNA BE YOUR MAN · BAD BOY · HEY BULLDOG
KANSAS CITY · ROCK 'N' ROLL MUSIC · EVERYBODY'S TRYING TO BE MY BABY · TAXMAN · BOYS
BIRTHDAY · GET BACK · I'M DOWN · DIZZY MISS LIZZY · MATCHBOX · MONEY
28 ROCK 'N' ROLL CLASSICS ON ONE DOUBLE ALBUM
ALBUM PCSP 719 ALSO AVAILABLE ON TAPE
Marketed by EMI Records Limited, 20, Manchester Square, London W1A 1ES.

been released in the form of two EP's.
This LP did not feature in the album
charts, which was possibly the result
of another unexplained decision on
EMI's part — this release was not
advertised in any way.

A SIDE

137b **MAGICAL MYSTERY TOUR** *(2.45)*

139b **THE FOOL ON THE HILL** *(2.56)*

140a **FLYING** *(2.10)*

THE BEATLES
BACK IN THE U.S.S.R.
B/W TWIST AND SHOUT
FROM THE ALBUM ROCK 'N' ROLL MUSIC

R6016

Marketed by EMI Records Limited, 20, Manchester Square, London W1A 1ES

141a BLUE JAY WAY *(3.50)*

138a YOUR MOTHER SHOULD KNOW *(2.24)*

(See *Magical Mystery Tour* EP for details of above titles.)

136c I AM THE WALRUS *(4.32)*
(See *Hello Goodbye* single.)

B SIDE

135b HELLO GOODBYE *(3.27)*

119b STRAWBERRY FIELDS FOREVER *(4.08)*

118b PENNY LANE *(2.57)*

134a BABY YOU'RE A RICH MAN *(3.04)*

(See appropriate single for above titles.)

133c ALL YOU NEED IS LOVE *(4.00)*
This stereo version is slightly longer than the mono singles version, whereas previous stereo versions had been shorter.

---

55   THE BEST OF GEORGE HARRISON

PAS 10011—November 20, 1976

This compilation of George's "best" numbers from both his Beatles' days and his solo work was put together by EMI. George was not happy with it, as he would have preferred to restrict the selections used to those from his solo albums, and not include any Beatles material (as happened with John and Ringo's "Best Of" albums, *Shaved Fish* and *Blast From Your Past*). The album did not appear in the British chart.

A SIDE

185c SOMETHING *(2.58)*
(See *Abbey Road* LP)

99a IF I NEEDED SOMEONE *(2.19)*
(See *Rubber Soul* LP)

190b HERE COMES THE SUN *(3.04)*
(See *Abbey Road* LP)

105b TAXMAN (2.35)
(See *Revolver* LP)

91a THINK FOR YOURSELF *(2.14)*
(See *Rubber Soul* LP)

214a FOR YOU BLUE *(2.24)*
(See *Let It Be* LP)

152b WHILE MY GUITAR GENTLY WEEPS *(4.41)*
(See *The Beatles* LP)

B SIDE

MY SWEET LORD

GIVE ME LOVE (GIVE ME PEACE ON EARTH)

YOU

BANGLA DESH

DARK HORSE

WHAT IS LIFE

---

56   THE BEATLES AT THE HOLLYWOOD BOWL

EMTV 4—May 6, 1977

Before the Beatles recorded their first album, their producer, George Martin, had considered recording the group at the Cavern Club for a live album which would become their first LP, but in fact fourteen years elapsed before the Beatles' first live album appeared, consisting of recordings made over twelve years earlier in 1964 and 1965. The group's Hollywood Bowl concerts in 1964 and 1965 were taped by Capitol Records using a three track recorder, under the supervision of George Martin, but due to the poor recording conditions (The Beatles could not hear what they were singing, as they had no "fold back" speakers on stage) and the continuous screaming from 17,000 fans, the results were therefore technically

disappointing to George Martin, and neither he nor The Beatles, at the time, considered the tapes good enough to release. As a result, the recordings were forgotten for over a decade, until Capitol's President, Bhaskar Menon, unearthed them, and asked George Martin to listen to them, as Capitol wished to release an album. After reluctantly listening to the tapes, Martin was impressed by the electric atmosphere and raw energy emanating from the performances, and with his recording engineer, Geoff Emerick, attempted to enhance the tapes sufficiently for commercial release by transferring the three track recording to multi-track tape, remixing, filtering and generally cleaning up the sound. The performances heard on the album come from both concerts, and include the best numbers from each, carefully edited to give the best overall result. No over-dubbing of additional vocals or instruments was undertaken — the record contains only the original performances. All the work on the tapes was carried out in January, 1977, at George Martin's own AIR Studios in London.

The original recordings at the Hollywood Bowl were produced by Voyle Gilmore, and the recording engineers were Hugh Davies (1964) and Pete Abbott (1965).

The release of the album in Britain was backed by a £200,000 TV advertising campaign (thus the EMTV catalogue number) and was released on the Parlophone label. The album entered the Top 30 album charts on May 14 at No. 16, and on June 25, reached No. 1 for one week. It stayed in the Top 10 for nine weeks, and in the Top 30 for twelve weeks.

The album was the fourth in a series of TV advertised albums from EMI. Up to April 1978, ten albums were released by EMI in this series, the first being *The Beach Boys 20 Golden Greats* followed by similar albums by Glen Campbell, Diana Ross and The Supremes, The Shadows, Buddy Holly, Nat 'King' Cole and Frank Sinatra, plus *30 Golden Greats* from The Black and White Minstrels and *40 Golden Greats* (a double album) from Cliff Richard. Of the first ten albums, six reached No. 1 in the LP charts: The Beach Boys, Glen Campbell, The Shadows, The Beatles, Diana Ross and The Supremes, and Nat 'King' Cole. Both Cliff Richard and Buddy Holly got to No. 2, and The Minstrels to No. 14, while Frank Sinatra peaked at No. 6.

The album has sold over a million globally, as it has been certified a million seller in the States by the R.I.A.A.

For details of each song, see main entry under title given in brackets.

A SIDE

216 TWIST AND SHOUT *(1.20)*
(*Please Please Me* LP)

217 SHE'S A WOMAN *(2.47)*
(*I Feel Fine* single)

218 DIZZY MISS LIZZY *(3.03)*
(*Help* LP)

219 TICKET TO RIDE *(2.20)*
(Single)

220 CAN'T BUY ME LOVE *(2.12)*
(Single)

221 THINGS WE SAID TODAY *(2.10)**
(*A Hard Day's Night* single)

222 ROLL OVER BEETHOVEN *(2.12)**
(*With The Beatles* LP)

B SIDE

223 BOYS *(1.57)**
(*Please Please Me* LP)

224 A HARD DAY'S NIGHT *(2.29)*
(Single)

225 HELP! *(2.15)*
(Single)

226 ALL MY LOVING *(1.55)**
(*With The Beatles* LP)

227 SHE LOVES YOU *(2.10)**
(Single)

228 LONG TALL SALLY *(1.54)**
(*Long Tall Sally* EP)

Tracks marked * were recorded on August 23, 1964, and all other tracks were recorded August 30, 1965.

The programme of songs for the two concerts at The Hollywood Bowl were as follows:

August 23, 1964 —

Twist And Shout
You Can't Do That
* All My Loving
* She Loves You
* Things We Said Today
* Roll Over Beethoven
Can't Buy Me Love
If I Fell
I Want To Hold Your Hand
* Boys
A Hard Day's Night
* Long Tall Sally

August 30, 1965 —

* Twist And Shout
* She's A Woman
I Feel Fine
* Dizzy Miss Lizzy
* Ticket To Ride
Everybody's Trying To Be My Baby
* Can't Buy Me Love
I Wanna Be Your Man
* A Hard Day's Night
* Help
I'm Down
*Indicates performances used on *The Beatles At The Hollywood Bowl* album.

---

57 THE BEATLES COLLECTION

Autumn, 1977

During the Autumn of 1977, EMI's mail order subsidiary, World Records, released a boxed set entitled *The Beatles Collection*, of the twenty-four singles from *Love Me Do* to *Back In The USSR*, available by mail order only, and not through the usual retail outlets. The twenty-four singles were presented in the same sleeves as the March, 1976, re-releases, and packaged in a special gold embossed case. The collection was heavily advertised in the national press with full page advertisements, and also with postal circulars, which included a promotional flexi-disc, to World Records regular customers. The *Sgt. Pepper* single was added to the collection after its release in June, 1978. Unlike the later album and EP collections, the singles collection does not have a special catalogue number. It was deleted from World Records catalogue in April, 1981.

---

58 LOVE SONGS

PCSP 721—November 19, 1977

The second compilation album of old Beatles tracks to appear after their recording contract ended in 1976, this

two record set was released at the end of 1977, with very little publicity, and failed to reach the album charts until nine weeks after it first appeared. It entered the Top 30 LP chart on January 21, 1978, at No. 26, and rose to No. 12 for three weeks, staying in the Top 30 for nine weeks.

The album, like *Rock 'N' Roll Music*, had an uninspired sleeve design containing a minimum of information although, again like *Rock 'N' Roll Music*, it includes tracks never previously available in Britain on an album, and therefore never previously available in Britain in stereo, these being *Yes It Is* and *This Boy*, which were "B" sides to *Ticket To Ride* and *I Want To Hold Your Hand* respectively.

For details of each song, see main entry under title given in brackets.

A SIDE RECORD ONE

83e   **YESTERDAY** *(2.03)*
(*Help* LP)

59b   **I'LL FOLLOW THE SUN** *(1.47)*
(*Beatles For Sale* LP)

75a   **I NEED YOU** *(2.25)*
(*Help* LP)

95b   **GIRL** *(2.26)*
(*Rubber Soul* LP)

97b   **IN MY LIFE** *(2.23)*
(*Rubber Soul* LP)

63b   **WORDS OF LOVE** *(2.01)*
(*Beatles For Sale* LP)

108a   **HERE THERE AND EVERYWHERE** *(2.22)*
(*Revolver* LP)

B SIDE RECORD ONE

185d   **SOMETHING** *(2.58)*
(*Abbey Road* LP)

47c   **AND I LOVE HER** *(2.27)*
(*A Hard Day's Night* LP)

45b   **IF I FELL** *(2.16)*
(*A Hard Day's Night* LP)

52a   **I'LL BE BACK** *(2.20)*
(*A Hard Day's Night* LP)

81a   **TELL ME WHAT YOU SEE** *(2.34)*
(*Help* LP)

70a   **YES IT IS** *(2.38)*
(*Ticket To Ride* single)

A SIDE RECORD TWO

93d   **MICHELLE** *(2.40)*
(*Rubber Soul* LP)

79b   **IT'S ONLY LOVE** *(1.53)*
(*Help* LP)

77a   **YOU'RE GOING TO LOSE THAT GIRL** *(2.14)*
(*Help* LP)

65a EVERY LITTLE THING *(2.00)*
(*Beatles For Sale* LP)

112a FOR NO ONE *(1.57)*
(*Revolver* LP)

125a SHE'S LEAVING HOME *(3.36)*
(*Sgt Pepper* LP)

B SIDE RECORD TWO

213b THE LONG AND WINDING ROAD
(3.34)
(*Let It Be* LP)

35a THIS BOY *(2.11)*
(*I Want To Hold Your Hand* single)

**88b NORWEGIAN WOOD (THIS BIRD
HAS FLOWN)** *(2.02)*
(*Rubber Soul* LP)

**74b YOU'VE GOT TO HIDE YOUR LOVE
AWAY** *(2.06)*
(*Help* LP)

161a I WILL *(1.43)*
(*The Beatles* LP)

2c P.S. I LOVE YOU *(1.59)*
(*Love Me Do* single)

**ALL YOU NEED IS LOVE - A STORY
OF POPULAR MUSIC**

9199 995—February, 1978

This was the "tie in" album for Tony
Palmer's documentary series on the
history of rock music, called *All You
Need Is Love*. The series included The
Beatles' history, and the album was
the first compilation to include a
Beatles track, apart from the specially
conceived *No One's Gonna Change
Our World*. The album was released
by Theatre Projects Records.

Tracks and artists on the album are
as follows:

A SIDE

133d ALL YOU NEED IS LOVE *(3.53)*
This is the original mono single version
electronically enhanced for stereo.
(See single.)

WHOLE LOTTA SHAKIN' GOIN' ON
(Jerry Lee Lewis)

ONLY YOU (The Platters)

THE MIGHTY QUINN (Manfred Mann)

BLUEBERRY HILL (Fats Domino)

SWEET LITTLE SIXTEEN
(Chuck Berry)

APACHE (The Shadows)

I'M WAITING FOR THE MAN
(Velvet Underground)

BREAKING UP IS HARD TO DO
(Neil Sedaka)

NEW YORK MINING DISASTER
(The Bee Gees)
(N.B. The correct title of this track is
New York Mining Disaster 1941, but the
date was omitted by mistake.)

**YOU'VE LOST THAT LOVING
FEELING** (The Righteous Brothers)

B SIDE

MAMA, WEER ALL CRAZEE NOW
(Slade)

PICTURES OF LILY (The Who)

ROOM TO MOVE (John Mayall)

LAYLA (Eric Clapton)

SUNSHINE OF YOUR LOVE (Cream)

CRAZY HORSES (The Osmonds)

MAGGIE MAY (Rod Stewart)

I'M NOT IN LOVE (10 CC)

ROLL OVER LAY DOWN (Status Quo)

**59 SGT. PEPPER'S LONELY HEARTS
CLUB BAND** *(1.59)*
**WITH A LITTLE HELP FROM MY
FRIENDS** *(2.41)*
A DAY IN THE LIFE *(5.05)*

R 6022—September 30, 1978

The Beatles twenty-fifth British single, and the first to feature tracks from the *Sgt. Pepper* album. The single was released due to the interest generated in the *Sgt. Pepper* album by the film *Sgt. Pepper's Lonely Hearts Club Band*, which was based on both the *Sgt. Pepper* and *Abbey Road* albums, and featured Peter Frampton and The Bee Gees. EMI were perhaps a little premature in releasing the record, as the film had not been premiered in America, and would not reach Britain until early 1979. Consequently, the single did not register in the Top 30, thus becoming the first Beatles' single not to enter the charts.

A SIDE

120b   SGT. PEPPER'S LONELY HEARTS CLUB BAND

121b   WITH A LITTLE HELP FROM MY FRIENDS

B SIDE

132b   A DAY IN THE LIFE
(See *Sgt. Pepper* album for all titles.)

60   THE BEATLES 1962 — 1966 (red vinyl)

PCSPR 717

61   THE BEATLES 1967—1970 (blue vinyl)

PCSPB 718—September 30, 1978

EMI were several months behind other countries in cashing in on the coloured vinyl boom — as a result, these albums had been available on import for many months before EMI decided to officially release them in Britain. In accordance with what had become EMI's normal practice, they were released unadvertised until over a month later, when, a week before Christmas, a full page advert appeared showing The Beatles'

twelve original albums, and two coloured doubles and the boxed collection. Until the end of 1978, there were six Beatles' albums available on import on coloured vinyl: *Sgt. Pepper* (marble and at least four other colours); *The Beatles* double album (white); *Abbey Road* (green); *Let It Be* (white) and the two red and blue doubles. *Sgt. Pepper* was also available as a picture disc from the States at about £10, but this was of very poor quality. EMI were hoping to release a *Sgt. Pepper* picture disc of superior quality for the Christmas period of 1978, but this was unfortunately delayed for various reasons.

62   THE BEATLES COLLECTION

BC 13—December 2, 1978

After the "Singles Collection" of 1976, the "Album Collection" had to follow. EMI collected all twelve original studio albums together, plus one 'free' album of "Rarities" and a poster, and presented them in a gold blocked box for £51.39. The box was of a very simple design, and the *Rarities* album, the sleeve of which matched the box, contained seventeen tracks, most of which were either previously unavailable on LP, or had never been released at all in Britain.

The collection contained the following albums: *Please Please Me; With The Beatles; A Hard Day's Night; Beatles For Sale; Help!; Rubber Soul; Revolver; Sgt. Pepper's Lonely Hearts Club Band; The Beatles* (White double album); *Yellow Submarine; Abbey Road* and *Let It Be* plus *Rarities*. For obvious reasons the *A Collection Of Beatles Oldies* was omitted, but why the *Magical Mystery Tour* album was not included, only EMI can say. As well as the free "sampler" album, a free poster was included in the box, but as this showed enlargements of the four pictures included in the "White Album", Beatle fans were acquiring nothing really new. There are a total of 199 different songs in the collection, with only one song repeated twice, *Yellow Submarine*, which appears on *Revolver* and *Yellow Submarine*, thus making exactly 200 tracks in all.

It is interesting to note that on the *Rarities* album, nine of the seventeen tracks are indicated as being stereo, but of these nine, only four are actually in stereo. (See below — tracks marked M are listed as being mono on the label; tracks marked S are listed as being stereo, and those marked * are listed as being stereo but are not.)

RARITIES

PSLP 261

A SIDE

201a ACROSS THE UNIVERSE *(3.44)* S
This first appeared on the World Wildlife Fund charity album, *No-One's Gonna Change Our World*, and a later version of the song is included on the *Let It Be* album. (See *No-One's Gonna Change Our World* LP.)

70b YES IT IS *(2.38)* M
This was originally the "B" side of *Ticket To Ride* and later appeared on the *Love Songs* double album in stereo. (See *Ticket To Ride* single.)

35b THIS BOY *(2.11)* M
The "B" side of the biggest selling British single, *I Want To Hold Your Hand*. It appeared on the *Love Songs* double album in stereo. (See *I Want To Hold Your Hand* single.)

143a THE INNER LIGHT *(2.33)* M
Appearing for the first time on an album, this was originally the flipside of the *Lady Madonna* single, but unfortunately appears here in mono. (See *Lady Madonna* single.)

19a I'LL GET YOU *(2.02)* *
The "B" side of *She Loves You*. The song appears on the American *The Beatles Second Album* in stereo. (See *She Loves You* single.)

17b THANK YOU GIRL *(1.59)* M
Originally the "B" side of *From Me To You*, and also appearing on the EP *The Beatles' Hits*. Here it appears on album for the first time, but in mono, although it appeared in stereo on the American *The Beatles Second Album* . (See *From Me To You* single.)

229 KOMM, GIB MIR DEINE HAND *(2.24)* S
I Want To Hold Your Hand sung in German, and appearing on a British record for the first time. (See American *Sie Liebt Dich* single on Page 133.)

203a YOU KNOW MY NAME (LOOK UP THE NUMBER) *(4.17)* *
The "B" side of the *Let It Be* single, appearing here on an album for the first time, but although indicated as being in stereo, the track has no clear instrumental or vocal separation whatsoever. (See *Let It Be* single.)

230 SIE LIEBT DICH *(2.16)* S
She Loves You sung in German, and also appearing on a British record for the first time. (See American *Sie Liebt Dich* single on Page 133.)

B SIDE

102a RAIN *(2.58)* M
The "B" side of the 1966 single *Paperback Writer*. Appearing here on an album for the first time in Britain, although not in stereo; on the American *Hey Jude* album it is in stereo. (See *Paperback Writer* single.)

54a SHE'S A WOMAN *(2.59)* *
Originally the coupling for *I Feel Fine* , but again this is not in stereo, although on the American *Beatles '65* album it is in perfect stereo. (See *I Feel Fine* single.)

41b MATCHBOX *(1.55)* M
Along with *Long Tall Sally, I Call Your Name* and *Slow Down*, this track is taken from the *Long Tall Sally* EP, and later appeared with the other tracks in stereo on the *Rock 'N' Roll Music* album. Here they appear in mono. (See *Long Tall Sally* EP.)

39b I CALL YOUR NAME *(2.05)* M
See *Matchbox* above.

117b BAD BOY *(2.17)* S
Originally on *A Collection Of Beatles Oldies*, and later appearing on the *Rock 'N' Roll Music* album. (See *A Collection Of Beatles Oldies* album.)

40b SLOW DOWN (2.54) M
See *Matchbox* above.

72b I'M DOWN (2.30)*
Originally the "B" side of the *Help!* single, this later appeared in true stereo on the *Rock 'N' Roll Music* album, although this version is not in stereo. (See *Help!* single.)

38b LONG TALL SALLY (2.00)*
See *Matchbox* above.
N.B. Of the thirteen original non-album "B" sides, EMI omitted four of these from the above album. Although all four songs, *Baby You're A Rich Man, Don't Let Me Down, Old Brown Shoe* and *Revolution*, have appeared on various compilation albums, they perhaps should have been included on the *Rarities* album, thus collecting all these "rare" tracks into one package.

63 SGT. PEPPER'S LONELY HEARTS CLUB BAND (Picture Disc)

PHO 7027—January 1979

EMI eventually managed to release the *Sgt. Pepper* picture disc, albeit at least one month after its scheduled appearance. Although of far superior sound quality to the American release, EMI could not match the superb American packaging. Having the original sleeve, with a hole in the middle, detracts from the impact of the picture disc, whereas with the American version, the sleeve bears no resemblance to the picture disc, and therefore highlights it. The British version contains the same picture on both sides of the record, whereas the American version shows a blow up of the *Sgt. Pepper* drum on the B side.
The disc was manufactured by

Metronome Records of West Germany (who also produced one of the very first picture discs, by Curved Air, called *Air Conditioning* in 1970 — this record is now a valuable collector's item). Again EMI failed to advertise the release of the record in the British music press, and coupled with its £6.99 price tag, this probably accounted for its failure to register in the charts.
The release of the *Sgt. Pepper* picture disc and *Sgt. Pepper* single in Britain and America was directly due to the film *Sgt. Pepper's Lonely Hearts Club Band* which was made in America, and starred Peter Frampton and The Bee Gees. The story of the film was written by Henry Edwards and was based on the *Sgt. Pepper* and *Abbey Road* albums, with Peter Frampton playing Billy Shears and The Bee Gees the *Sgt. Pepper* band. The film contained most of the songs from the two albums, some of which were performed and visualised in true Hollywood style. Frampton and The Bee Gees performed most of the songs, with guest performers and groups handling the rest. Other artists appearing in the film included George Burns, Alice Cooper, Earth Wind and Fire, Aerosmith, Paul Nicholas and Frankie Howerd. All but two of the songs were produced by George Martin, the original Beatles producer, although of the three hit singles which resulted (see below), Martin produced only *Oh Darling*.
The soundtrack album from the film did not chart in Britain, but in America it reached No. 4 for three weeks, staying in the Top 30 album chart for fourteen weeks. Several singles were released from the album, although only three made the Top 30 in America. Aerosmith's *Come Together* reached No. 20, staying four weeks in the Top 30, Robin Gibb got to No. 24 with *Oh Darling*, which stayed in the Top 30 for two weeks, while Earth, Wind and Fire's *Got To Get You Into My Life* was the most successful, reaching No. 11 for two weeks, and staying eight weeks in the Top 30. In Britain, only *Got To Get You Into My Life* entered the Top 30, reaching No. 30 for a single week.

64 THE BEATLES (white vinyl)

PCS 7067-8—?, 1979

65 ABBEY ROAD (green vinyl)

66   LET IT BE (white vinyl)

PCS 7096—?, 1979

67   MAGICAL MYSTERY TOUR
(yellow vinyl)

PCTC 255—May ?, 1979

The above four coloured vinyl records were released in limited editions in Britain, without any advertising or mention in the music press. The exact dates of release are unknown.

A MONUMENT TO BRITISH ROCK VOLUME 1

20 Rock/Pop Classics From EMI - Vol. I.
EMTV 17—May ?, 1979

The second compilation album to feature a Beatles track, *A Monument To British Rock* was EMI's seventeenth album in their TV advertised series, which had in the past included albums by The Shadows, The Supremes, The Hollies, Glen Campbell and The Beatles (the *Hollywood Bowl* album). This album, released on EMI's Harvest label, entered the *NME* Top 30 album charts at No. 18 on June 2, 1979, where it remained for four weeks, reaching No. 17 for two weeks. It dropped out for one week, but re-entered at No. 22 on July 7 for a further single week.

Tracks and artists on the album are as follows:

A SIDE

ROLL OVER BEETHOVEN (Electric Light Orchestra)

MY SWEET LORD (George Harrison)

HERE COMES THE NIGHT (Them)

GOT TO GET YOU INTO MY LIFE
(Cliff Bennett & The Rebel Rousers)

SHAKIN' ALL OVER (Johnny Kidd & The Pirates)

WHEN I'M DEAD AND GONE
(McGuinness Flint)

NATURAL BORN BUGIE
(Humble Pie)

WILD THING (The Troggs)

DOWN DOWN (Status Quo)

OUT OF TIME (Chris Farlowe)

B SIDE

180b   GET BACK *(3.07)*
This is the original singles track electronically re-processed for stereo. (See single.)

ITCHYCOO PARK (Small Faces)

THE RESURRECTION SHUFFLE
(Ashton, Gardner & Dyke)

BLACK NIGHT (Deep Purple)

IMAGINE (John Lennon)

APACHE (The Shadows)

MAKE ME SMILE (COME UP AND SEE ME) (Steve Harley & Cockney Rebel)

A WHITER SHADE OF PALE
(Procol Harum)

THE HIPPY HIPPY SHAKE
(The Swinging Blue Jeans)

SEE MY BABY JIVE (Wizzard)

68   HEY JUDE

PCS 7184—June ?, 1979

This is identical to the LP released in America in 1970, which reached No. 2 in the US charts, selling nearly four million. Both the American *Hey Jude* album and its French equivalent, *The Beatles Again*, had been available as imports in Britain since 1970, and were among EMI's biggest selling import albums — as a result, EMI once again seemed to be displaying a lack of imagination, and as they also failed to advertise the album in any of the music papers, it seems doubtful that the album's sales can have exceeded a few thousand copies in Britain.

This album is identical to the American release in every significant respect, and each track had previously appeared on album in Britain, including the three "B" sides, *Rain, Old Brown Shoe* and *Don't Let Me Down.* It is interesting to note that on the *Rarities* album included in the *Beatles Collection, Rain* appears in mono, but on *Hey Jude,* it is in stereo. It is therefore difficult to understand why the *Rarities* album contains a mono version of the track.

For details of each song see main entry under title given in brackets.

A SIDE

36e   CAN'T BUY ME LOVE *(2.09)*
(See single.)

44c   I SHOULD HAVE KNOWN BETTER *(2.41)*
(See *A Hard Day's Night* LP)

101c   PAPERBACK WRITER *(2.15)*
(See single.)

102b   RAIN *(2.58)*
(See *Paperback Writer* single.)

142b   LADY MADONNA *(2.14)*
(See single.)

145c   REVOLUTION *(3.22)*
(See *Hey Jude* single.)

B SIDE

144b   HEY JUDE *(7.06)*
(See single.)

183b   OLD BROWN SHOE *(3.17)*
(See *The Ballad Of John and Yoko* single.)

181b   DON'T LET ME DOWN *(3.30)*
(See *Get Back* single.)

182b   THE BALLAD OF JOHN AND YOKO *(2.58)*
(See single.)

69   RARITIES

PCM 1001—October ?, 1979

When the boxed set of original Beatles albums was released in 1978, EMI stated that the bonus *Rarities* album would not be made available separately, and would only appear in the £51.39 boxed collection. After some record shops separated the *Rarities* album from the box set, and sold it for as much as £8, EMI decided to release the album officially as a separate LP. Unfortunately, they decided to retain the rather grotesque sleeve design and used the original masters as used for the *Beatles Collection* version, and therefore most of the songs still appear in mono although EMI did correct their earlier credit errors on the label by stating that twelve out of the seventeen tracks are in mono. (See *Rarities* album under *The Beatles Collection*.)

The sleeve design was altered slightly to include a review of the album and the songs by Hugh Fielder of *Sounds*, who makes one mistake concerning *This Boy*. He states, quite correctly, that *This Boy*, being the "B" side of *I Want To Hold Your Hand*, is therefore the biggest selling rarity in the world, but is incorrect when he goes on to say that *I Want To Hold Your Hand* sold five million copies worldwide. In fact, *I Want To Hold Your Hand* sold between thirteen to fifteen million copies worldwide (five million in the States, where the "B" side was not *This Boy* but *I Saw Her Standing There*).

At the end of the review, he states "Only true Beatles followers could claim to have more than half the tracks on this album. And only die-hard fanatics could boast over eighty percent." "True Beatles followers" would presumably own all the original singles and EPs, and "die-hard fanatics" would have purchased the *Beatles Collection*! He concludes "So on any level this album represents a collector's item...and some fine rock'n'roll to boot." In the *Beatles Collection*, perhaps a collector's item, but as a separate album retailing at £3.45?...

(Tracks and numbering same as *Beatles Collection*.)

| 70 | THE BEATLES BALLADS — 20 ORIGINAL TRACKS |

PCS 7214—October 20, 1980

The first twenty track Beatles' album, and the first Beatles' album of the Eighties, was released unheralded with no pre-publicity or any media advertising whatsoever. Initially, it did not sell well enough to enter the charts, but after the tragic murder of John Lennon on December 8th, 1980, sales of this, and virtually all items in The Beatles catalogue, escalated, and it entered the *NME* Top 30 album chart at No. 21 on January 3rd, 1981, for one week only.

The track selection is not dissimilar to the *Love Songs* album, with ten out of twenty tracks on *Ballads* also being on *Love Songs*.

The front cover painting, by John Patrick Byrne, first appeared in Alan Aldridge's book *The Beatles Illustrated Lyrics*, which featured many famous artists' and painters' interpretations of The Beatles' lyrics in paintings, photographs and sculptures. The painting acted as a "frontispiece" for the book and Byrne also illustrated *Here, There And Everywhere* in the same publication. Byrne, who normally signs his work "Patrick", has also painted artwork for other album covers, including Donovan's *HMS Donovan* (1971) and Gerry Rafferty's *Can I Have My Money Back* (1971).

For details of each song see main entry under title given in brackets.

A SIDE

83f   **YESTERDAY** *(2.03)*
(*Help!* LP)

88c   **NORWEGIAN WOOD (THIS BIRD HAS FLOWN)** *(2.02)*
(*Rubber Soul* LP)
This track features a re-mixed version of the song.

12b   **DO YOU WANT TO KNOW A SECRET**
(1.54)

(*Please Please Me* LP)

112b   FOR NO ONE *(1.57)*
(*Revolver* LP)

93e   MICHELLE *(2.40)*
(*Rubber Soul* LP)

90c   NOWHERE MAN *(2.40)*
(*Rubber Soul* LP)

**74c   YOU'VE GOT TO HIDE YOUR LOVE
AWAY** *(2.06)*
(*Help!* LP)

201b   ACROSS THE UNIVERSE *(3.44)*
(*No-One's Gonna Change Our World*
LP)

22c   ALL MY LOVING *(2.04)*
(*With The Beatles* LP)

144c   HEY JUDE *(7.07)*
(Single.)

B SIDE

185e   SOMETHING *(2.58)*
(*Abbey Road* LP)

139c   THE FOOL ON THE HILL *(2.56)*
(*Magical Mystery Tour* EP)

25a   TILL THERE WAS YOU *(2.10)*
(*With The Beatles* LP)

213c   THE LONG AND WINDING ROAD
(3.34)
(*Let It Be* LP)

190c   HERE COMES THE SUN *(3.04)*
(*Abbey Road* LP)

156a   BLACKBIRD *(2.18)*
(*The Beatles* LP)

47d   AND I LOVE HER *(2.27)*
(*A Hard Day's Night* LP)

125b   SHE'S LEAVING HOME *(3.36)*
(*Sgt. Pepper* LP)

108b   HERE, THERE AND EVERYWHERE
(2.22)
(*Revolver* LP)

202b   LET IT BE *(3.49)*
(Single.)

*On October 15 and 16, 1980, EMI held
an auction at their Abbey Road Studios
to help pay for a new penthouse studio
being built there. Among the many*

*items of studio equipment to come
under the hammer was the Studer J37
four track recording machine on which
Sgt. Pepper was recorded, which was
sold for £500. Also from the Sgt. Pepper
sessions was the Mellotron, which still
contains several original Beatles
tapes, used for recording the album,
and this was sold to a certain Mr Mike
Oldfield for £1,000. Mr Oldfield also
purchased two Belcamen Valve
Limiters, which he had used to record
his own Tubular Bells album. Other
articles of interest included a brass
ashtray (as used by Ringo), which
fetched £130; a copy of Brian Epstein's
A Cellarful Of Noise, autographed by
all four Beatles and George Martin
(£210); limiter compressors as used by
Joe Meek during the recording of
Telstar (by The Tornadoes) and a 1967
Neve Console (as used by The Dave
Clark Five).*

*Up to October, 1980 The Beatles
Collection had sold 25,000 copies in
Australia, thus qualifying for a "Gold
Box", and had also entered the Top 40
there. (At the British price of £51.39,
this amounts to a gross sale of
£1,284,750.)*

71   ROCK'N'ROLL MUSIC VOLUME 1

MFP 50506—October 27, 1980

The first ever Beatles album to be
repackaged on a budget label, this and
Rock 'N' Roll Music Volume 2, were
part of a package of five Beatle albums
re-released on EMI's budget label,
Music For Pleasure. The three other
"Beatles" albums included in the
release were Ringo Starr's *Ringo*, John
Lennon's *Mind Games* and George
Harrison's *Dark Horse*. (Note no Paul
McCartney repackage, due to the fact
that he was still signed to EMI,
whereas the other three Beatles'
contracts with EMI had long since
expired.) All five albums sold for the
very reasonable price of £1.99 each,
but it wasn't until John Lennon was
murdered in New York on December
8th that they started to sell.

The two *Rock 'N' Roll Music* albums
are re-packages of the original double
album *Rock 'N' Roll Music* PCSP 719,
with new identical sleeves. The front
cover photograph shows The Beatles
just prior to their departure for
America on February 7, 1964, and was
probably taken by Leslie Bryce, one of

the photographers from *Beatles Monthly*. Although the track listings for the two albums are identical to the original double album, the records differ from the originals in that they were re-mastered using the American tapes which George Martin remixed for the American release of the original double album in 1976. (See the *Rock 'N' Roll Music* double album in the American section.)

For details of each song see main entry under title given in brackets.

A SIDE

15d	**TWIST AND SHOUT** *(2.31)*
	(Please Please Me LP)

5c **I SAW HER STANDING THERE** *(2.50)*
(*Please Please Me* LP)

37c **YOU CAN'T DO THAT** *(2.32)*
(*Can't Buy Me Love* single.)

30b **I WANNA BE YOUR MAN** *(1.56)*
(*With The Beatles* LP)

39c **I CALL YOUR NAME** *(2.05)*
(*Long Tall Sally* EP)

9b **BOYS** *(2.22)*
(*Please Please Me* LP)

38c **LONG TALL SALLY** *(2.00)*
(*Long Tall Sally* EP)

B SIDE

58c **ROCK 'N' ROLL MUSIC** *(2.28)*
(*Beatles For Sale* LP)

40c **SLOW DOWN** *(2.54)*
(*Long Tall Sally* EP)

61b **KANSAS CITY/HEY HEY HEY HEY**
(2.35)
(*Beatles For Sale* LP)

33c **MONEY (THAT'S WHAT I WANT)**
(2.46)
(*With The Beatles* LP)

117c **BAD BOY** *(2.16)*
(*A Collection Of Beatles Oldies But Goldies* LP)

41c **MATCHBOX** *(1.55)*
(*Long Tall Sally* EP)

27b **ROLL OVER BEETHOVEN** *(2.42)*
(*With The Beatles* LP)

72   ROCK'N'ROLL MUSIC VOLUME 2

MFP 50507—October 27, 1980

This album was released with its companion Volume 1. (See *Rock 'N' Roll Music Volume 1*.)

A SIDE

84b **DIZZY MISS LIZZY** *(2.51)*
(*Help!* LP)

49c **ANY TIME AT ALL** *(2.09)*
(*A Hard Day's Night* LP)

87d **DRIVE MY CAR** *(2.25)*
(*Rubber Soul* LP)

68b **EVERYBODY'S TRYING TO BE MY BABY** *(2.23)*
(*Beatles For Sale* LP)

73b **THE NIGHT BEFORE** *(2.30)*
(*Help!* LP)

72c **I'M DOWN** *(2.30)*
(*Help!* single)

145d **REVOLUTION** *(3.22)*
(*Hey Jude* single)

B SIDE

146d **BACK IN THE USSR** *(2.41)*
(*The Beatles* LP)

168b **HELTER SKELTER** *(4.28)*
(*The Beatles* LP)

105c **TAXMAN** *(2.35)*
(*Revolver* LP)

115b GOT TO GET YOU INTO MY LIFE
(2.25)
(*Revolver* LP)

178b HEY BULLDOG *(3.07)*
(*Yellow Submarine* LP)

163b BIRTHDAY *(2.41)*
(*The Beatles* LP)

215b GET BACK *(3.06)*
(*Let It Be* LP)

73   THE BEATLES BOX

SM 701-SM 708—December 1980

World Records, the mail-order subsidiary of EMI, have released over fifty boxed sets of albums covering the careers of EMI's top artists, such as Cliff Richard, The Supremes, The Shadows, Frank Sinatra, Nat 'King' Cole, Hank Williams, Mantovani, The Beach Boys, etc, and obviously their ultimate release would be a Beatles collection. Ten years after The Beatles' split, and following many years of negotiation, World Records were given the right to release this Beatles' boxed collection. Unlike the EMI *Beatles Collection* of 1978, it is a collection of completely new albums, in new sleeves and a highly original box. The collection was advertised for the first time in the national press on November 5, 1980, with repeat ads monthly into 1981. As the album was only sold by mail order, its sales would not register in the charts, but at a very reasonable price of £29.75 for eight albums, it was a very good purchase, and its sales must have been increased by the tragic death of John Lennon.

Each sleeve contains very well written notes (by Hugh Marshall), being a short biography of The Beatles from 1960 to 1970, with notes on the songs on each album. All eight sleeves contain a different picture to depict the period from which the songs on each album were taken, sleeve designs being undertaken by Frank Watkin of *Out Of Town Creative*.

The track selections were compiled in chronological order, by Simon Sinclair.

As can be seen from the track listing below, each LP in the box is a selection of songs from each of The Beatles original albums, plus the singles and two EP's. The breakdown is as follows:

Album 1
Side One — Please Please Me (8 songs)
Side Two — With The Beatles (5 songs)
    + 3 singles tracks

Album 2
Side One — A Hard Day's Night (6 songs)
    + 2 singles tracks
Side Two — A Hard Day's Night (2 songs)
    Long Tall Sally EP (4 songs)
    + 2 singles tracks

Album 3
Side One — Beatles For Sale (8 songs)
Side Two — Help! (7 songs)
    + 1 single track

Album 4
Side One — Help! (6 songs)
    + 2 singles tracks
Side Two — Rubber Soul (8 songs)

Album 5
Side One — Revolver (5 songs)
    + 2 singles tracks
Side Two — Revolver (5 songs)
    + 2 singles tracks

Album 6
Side One — Sgt. Pepper (7 songs)
Side Two — Sgt. Pepper (2 songs)
    + 2 singles tracks +
    Magical Mystery Tour EP
    (4 songs)

Album 7
Side One — The Beatles (3 songs)
    + 4 singles tracks
Side Two — The Beatles (7 songs)
    Yellow Submarine (1 song)

Album 8
Side One — Let It Be (7 songs)
    + 1 singles track
Side Two — Abbey Road (10 songs)

The versions of certain songs included on these albums differ from the original releases; variations are indicated after each track. For details of each song, see under title given in brackets.

A SIDE

1a   **LOVE ME DO** *(2.23)*
This is the first album appearance of the original version of *Love Me Do*, featuring Ringo on drums, which appeared on the original "red label" pressings of the single. (See *Love Me Do* single for full details.)

2d   **P.S. I LOVE YOU** *(1.59)*
(See *Love Me Do* single.)

5d   **I SAW HER STANDING THERE** *(2.50)*
(See *Please Please Me* LP.)

3d   **PLEASE PLEASE ME** *(1.58)*
(See single.)

6b   **MISERY** *(1.46)*

12c   **DO YOU WANT TO KNOW A SECRET** *(1.54)*

13b   **A TASTE OF HONEY** *(1.59)*

15e   **TWIST AND SHOUT** *(2.31)*

(All above, see *Please Please Me* LP unless otherwise indicated.)

B SIDE

16d   **FROM ME TO YOU** *(1.54)*
This is the stereo version which does not include the harmonica introduction. (See single.)

17c   **THANK YOU GIRL** *(1.59)*
(See *From Me To You* single.)

18d   **SHE LOVES YOU** *(2.18)*
(See single.)

20a   **IT WON'T BE LONG** *(2.09)*

26a   **PLEASE MR. POSTMAN** *(2.30)*

22d   **ALL MY LOVING** *(2.06)*
This track is two seconds longer than the original on the *With The Beatles* album, due to the "hi-hat" introduction.

27c   **ROLL OVER BEETHOVEN** *(2.42)*

33d   **MONEY (THAT'S WHAT I WANT)** *(2.46)*

(All above, see *With The Beatles* LP, unless otherwise indicated.)

A SIDE

34d   **I WANT TO HOLD YOUR HAND** *(2.22)*
(See single.)

35c   **THIS BOY** *(2.11)*
This track is in mono. (See *I Want To Hold Your Hand* single.)

36f   **CAN'T BUY ME LOVE** *(2.10)*
(See single.)

37c   **YOU CAN'T DO THAT** *(2.32)*
(See *Can't Buy Me Love* single.)

42d   **A HARD DAY'S NIGHT** *(2.28)*
(See single.)

44d   **I SHOULD HAVE KNOWN BETTER** *(2.41)*

45c   **IF I FELL** *(2.16)*

47e   **AND I LOVE HER** *(2.35)*
This track is eight seconds longer than that on the *A Hard Day's Night* album. The original track has only four "guitar phrases" at the end of the song, while

this version has six. (For above tracks see *A Hard Day's Night* LP, unless otherwise indicated.)

B SIDE

43c THINGS WE SAID TODAY *(2.34)*
(See *A Hard Day's Night* single.)

52b I'LL BE BACK *(2.20)*
(See *A Hard Day's Night* LP.)

38d LONG TALL SALLY *(2.05)*

39d I CALL YOUR NAME *(2.05)*

41d MATCHBOX *(1.55)*

40d SLOW DOWN *(2.52)*
This and the above two tracks, are indicated on the record label as being in mono; they are in fact, in stereo. (For this and previous three tracks, see *Long Tall Sally* EP.)

54b SHE'S A WOMAN *(2.59)*
This track appears for the first time in stereo on a British release. On the *Rarities* album it is listed on the label as being in stereo, but the track is in fact in mono. (See *I Feel Fine* single.)

53d I FEEL FINE *(2.17)*
This is a different version from that released on 45, as it features two seconds of whispering at the beginning. (See single.)

A SIDE

62c EIGHT DAYS A WEEK *(2.42)*

55b NO REPLY *(2.13)*

56b I'M A LOSER *(2.26)*

59c I'LL FOLLOW THE SUN *(1.47)*

60a MR. MOONLIGHT *(2.36)*

65b EVERY LITTLE THING *(2.00)*

66b I DON'T WANT TO SPOIL THE PARTY *(2.29)*

61c KANSAS CITY/HEY HEY HEY HEY *(2.35)*

(For above tracks, see *Beatles For Sale* LP.)

B SIDE

69d TICKET TO RIDE *(3.03)*
(See single.)

72d I'M DOWN *(2.30)*
(See *Help!* single.)

71d HELP! *(2.16)*
(See single.)

73c THE NIGHT BEFORE *(2.30)*

74d YOU'VE GOT TO HIDE YOUR LOVE AWAY *(2.06)*

75b I NEED YOU *(2.25)*

76a ANOTHER GIRL *(2.02)*

77b YOU'RE GOING TO LOSE THAT GIRL *(2.14)*

(For above tracks see *Help!* LP, except where otherwise indicated.)

A SIDE

83g YESTERDAY *(2.03)*

78b ACT NATURALLY *(2.27)*

81b TELL ME WHAT YOU SEE *(2.34)*

79c **IT'S ONLY LOVE** *(1.53)*

80b **YOU LIKE ME TOO MUCH** *(2.33)*

82a **I'VE JUST SEEN A FACE** *(2.02)*

(For above tracks, see *Help!* LP.)

85c **DAY TRIPPER** *(2.49)*
This is a different stereo mix to those previously available in Britain, and originally appeared on the American *Yesterday...And Today* album. (See single.)

86c **WE CAN WORK IT OUT** *(2.12)*
(See single.)

B SIDE

93f **MICHELLE** *(2.36)*

87e **DRIVE MY CAR** *(2.25)*

88e **NORWEGIAN WOOD (THIS BIRD HAS FLOWN)** *(2.02)*

89b **YOU WON'T SEE ME** *(3.18)*

90d **NOWHERE MAN** *(2.40)*

95c **GIRL** *(2.26)*

96a **I'M LOOKING THROUGH YOU** *(2.21)*

97c **IN MY LIFE** *(2.23)*
(See *Rubber Soul* LP.)

A SIDE

101d **PAPERBACK WRITER** *(2.15)*
This version of *Paperback Writer* is a re-mixed version of the recording previously available.

102c **RAIN** *(2.58)*
(See *Paperback Writer* single.)

108c **HERE, THERE AND EVERYWHERE** *(2.22)*

105d **TAXMAN** *(2.35)*

106a **I'M ONLY SLEEPING** *(2.58)*

110a **GOOD DAY SUNSHINE** *(2.07)*

(See *Revolver* LP for above titles.)

104e **YELLOW SUBMARINE** *(2.36)*
(See single.)

B SIDE

103d **ELEANOR RIGBY** *(2.04)*
(See single.)

111a **AND YOUR BIRD CAN SING** *(1.58)*

112c **FOR NO ONE** *(1.57)*

113a **DR. ROBERT** *(2.13)*

115c **GOT TO GET YOU INTO MY LIFE** *(2.26)*

(For above titles see *Revolver* LP.)

118c **PENNY LANE** *(2.56)*
This version of *Penny Lane* differs from the original in that about eight seconds before the song finishes, there is an additional trumpet coda. This version was originally released as a promotional record to radio stations in the States only, and the additional trumpet riff was removed for the commercial release. This is the first time it has appeared on a British release.

119c **STRAWBERRY FIELDS FOREVER** *(4.03)*
(See single for this and previous title.)

A SIDE

120c **SGT. PEPPER'S LONELY HEARTS CLUB BAND** *(1.59)*

121c WITH A LITTLE HELP FROM MY FRIENDS *(2.41)*

122b LUCY IN THE SKY WITH DIAMONDS *(3.25)*

124a FIXING A HOLE *(2.34)*

125c SHE'S LEAVING HOME *(3.32)*

126a BEING FOR THE BENEFIT OF MR. KITE *(2.33)*

132c A DAY IN THE LIFE *(5.05)*

(For above titles see *Sgt. Pepper* LP.)

B SIDE

128a WHEN I'M SIXTY FOUR *(2.36)*

129a LOVELY RITA *(2.40)*

(For above titles see *Sgt. Pepper* LP.)

133e ALL YOU NEED IS LOVE *(3.57)*
This is the original mono version of the song which appeared as a single. All subsequent stereo versions to appear on albums are thirteen seconds shorter than the mono singles version. (See single.)

134b BABY YOU'RE A RICH MAN *(2.58)*
(See *All You Need Is Love* single.)

137c MAGICAL MYSTERY TOUR *(2.45)*

138b YOUR MOTHER SHOULD KNOW *(2.24)*

139d THE FOOL ON THE HILL *(2.56)*

(For last three titles, see *Magical Mystery Tour* EP.)

136d I AM THE WALRUS *(4.32)*
The original British single version of *I Am The Walrus* featured the organ introduction repeated four times, while it was repeated six times on the stereo version of the *Magical Mystery Tour* EP. The American single version is identical to the British single having the organ intro repeated four times, but it also has a few extra beats before the fourth verse, which starts "Yellow Matter Custard". The *Beatles Box* version of the song features the six times organ intro and the extra beats. (See *Hello Goodbye* single.)

A SIDE

135c HELLO GOODBYE *(2.24)*
(See single.)

142c LADY MADONNA *(2.14)*
(See single.)

144d HEY JUDE *(7.07)*
(See single.)

145e REVOLUTION *(3.22)*
(See Hey Jude single.)

146e BACK IN THE USSR *(2.41)*

149b OB-LA-DI OB-LA-DA *(3.06)*

152c WHILE MY GUITAR GENTLY WEEPS *(4.40)*

(For above titles see *The Beatles* double album, unless otherwise indicated.)

B SIDE

151a THE CONTINUING STORY OF BUNGALOW BILL *(3.05)*

153a HAPPINESS IS A WARM GUN *(2.40)*

154a MARTHA MY DEAR *(2.27)*

155a I'M SO TIRED *(2.02)*

157a PIGGIES *(2.03)*

159a DON'T PASS ME BY *(3.48)*

162a JULIA *(2.52)*

(For above titles, see *The Beatles* double album.)

177a ALL TOGETHER NOW *(2.07)*
(See *Yellow Submarine* LP.)

A SIDE

215c GET BACK (Version 2) *(3.05)*
(See *Let It Be* album for song details and *Get Back* single.)

181c DON'T LET ME DOWN *(3.30)*
(See *Get Back* single.)

182c THE BALLAD OF JOHN AND YOKO
(2.58)
(See single.)

206b ACROSS THE UNIVERSE (Version 2)
(3.43)

214b FOR YOU BLUE *(2.24)*

204a TWO OF US *(3.33)*

213d THE LONG AND WINDING ROAD
(3.35)

209a LET IT BE *(4.00)*

(For above titles see *Let It Be* LP, unless
otherwise indicated.)

B SIDE

184c COME TOGETHER *(4.16)*

185f SOMETHING *(2.58)*

186a MAXWELL'S SILVER HAMMER
(3.24)

188b OCTOPUS'S GARDEN *(2.48)*

190d HERE COMES THE SUN *(3.04)*

191a BECAUSE *(2.44)*

197a GOLDEN SLUMBERS *(1.31)*

198a CARRY THAT WEIGHT *(1.37)*

199a THE END *(2.04)*

200a HER MAJESTY *(0.23)*
(For above songs see *Abbey Road* LP.)

74	THE BEST OF GEORGE HARRISON

MFP 50523—November, 1981

A year after the first selection of
"Beatles" albums appeared on the
Music For Pleasure label, EMI
released a second ration comprising
this album, plus Ringo's *Blast From
Your Past* and John's *Rock 'N' Roll*
(about which EMI consulted Yoko Ono
prior to release). This album was
originally released with the same title
on Parlophone PAS 10011, but the re-
release boasted a new sleeve
featuring the photograph of George
included in *The Beatles* double album
of 1968. It might have been wiser for
EMI to have used the original
American sleeve, which was far
superior to the original 1976 British
album cover.

A SIDE

185g SOMETHING *(2.58)*
(See *Abbey Road* LP.)

99b IF I NEEDED SOMEONE *(2.19)*
(See *Rubber Soul* LP.)

190e HERE COMES THE SUN *(3.04)*
(See *Abbey Road* LP.)

105e TAXMAN *(2.35)*
(See *Revolver* LP.)

91b THINK FOR YOURSELF *(2.14)*
(See *Rubber Soul* LP.)

214c FOR YOU BLUE *(2.24)*
(See *Let It Be* LP.)

**152d WHILE MY GUITAR GENTLY
WEEPS** *(4.41)*
(See *The Beatles* LP.)

B SIDE

MY SWEET LORD

GIVE ME LOVE (GIVE ME PEACE ON EARTH)

YOU

BANGLA DESH

DARK HORSE

WHAT IS LIFE

SAVILE'S TIME TRAVELS — 20 GOLDEN HITS OF 1963

MFP 50541—November, 1981

This album was the first in a series of twenty-five LPs to be released by Music For Pleasure under the title of *Savile's Time Travels* (*20 Golden Hits Of 1960* was released at the same time). Each album contains twenty hits by both British and American artists from a particular year. Part of the royalties from the sale of each album went towards disc jockey Jimmy Savile's Stoke Mandeville Charity Fund, to help rebuild the hospital's Spinal Unit. Each album contains a well written sleeve note, as well as giving highest chart positions for each song.

1963 was a very big year for the Beatles in Britain, as they had four chart topping singles, as well as two No. 1 albums and three top selling EP's, and also wrote seven chart hits for other acts. This album features *She Loves You*, which was the top selling single in Great Britain for 1963, plus two Lennon and McCartney compositions, *Do You Want To Know A Secret* and *Hello Little Girl* recorded by Billy J. Kramer and The Dakotas and The Fourmost respectively, both being Top Ten hits.

A SIDE

18e   SHE LOVES YOU *(2.18)*

HOW DO YOU DO IT
(Gerry & The Pacemakers)

DO YOU WANT TO KNOW A SECRET
(Billy J Kramer & The Dakotas)

IF YOU GOTTA MAKE A FOOL OF SOMEBODY
(Freddy And The Dreamers)

STAY (The Hollies)

THE HIPPY HIPPY SHAKE
(The Swinging Blue Jeans)

I'LL NEVER GET OVER YOU
(Johnny Kidd & The Pirates)

HELLO LITTLE GIRL (The Fourmost)

FOOT TAPPER (The Shadows)

SUMMER HOLIDAY (Cliff Richard)

B SIDE

THE NIGHT HAS A THOUSAND EYES
(Bobby Vee)

BROWN EYED HANDSOME MAN
(Buddy Holly)

MY WAY (Eddie Cochran)

PIPELINE (The Chantays)

MY LITTLE GIRL (The Crickets)

ALL ALONE AM I (Brenda Lee)

THE FOLK SINGER (Tommy Roe)

MR. BASS MAN (Johnny Cymbal)

WIPE OUT (The Surfaris)

SURFIN' USA (The Beach Boys)

75   THE BEATLES EPs COLLECTION

BEP 14—December 7, 1981

Following the singles and albums collections of 1976 and 1978, 1981 saw the release of the EP collection, housed in a matching box to the album collection. The collection contained all of the original twelve EPs in mono, the *Magical Mystery Tour* **double EP in stereo, plus a bonus EP containing previously unavailable stereo versions of four songs.**

The EPs contained in the box are as follows: *The Beatles' Hits, Twist And Shout, The Beatles No. 1, All My Loving, Long Tall Sally, Extracts From The Film 'A Hard Day's Night', Extracts From The Album 'A Hard Day's Night', Beatles For Sale, Beatles For Sale No. 2, The Beatles' Million Sellers* **(this pressing is correctly titled on the label — the original pressings were titled** *Beatles' Golden Discs***),** *Yesterday, Nowhere Man, Magical Mystery Tour* **(original releases included white inner sleeves for each record; here black inner sleeves are used) plus the bonus EP called simply** *The Beatles* **(the front cover picture of which is identical to that used on the 1967** *Penny Lane* **single picture sleeve).**

THE BEATLES

SGE 1

A SIDE

143b THE INNER LIGHT *(2.33)*
Originally appeared on the flipside of *Lady Madonna* in 1968 and later on the *Rarities* album of 1978 in mono. This is the first time it has appeared in stereo in Britain. (See *Lady Madonna* single.)

134c BABY YOU'RE A RICH MAN *(2.58)*
First appeared in 1967 on the "B" side of

All You Need Is Love, and later in "mock" stereo on the British *Magical Mystery Tour* album. This true stereo (and slightly shorter) version originally appeared on the British cassette of *Magical Mystery Tour*, and later in the boxed set *The Beatles Box*, issued by World Records.

54c SHE'S A WOMAN *(3.02)*
She's A Woman first appeared in mono on the flip of the 1964 single *I Feel Fine*, and later on the *Rarities* album of 1978. In 1980 a stereo version was included in the boxed set *The Beatles Box* issued by World Records. This slightly longer stereo version differs from the "Box" version in that it starts with a "One, Two, Three, Four" introduction by Paul (which is also absent on the original mono version).

35d THIS BOY *(2.11)*
The sleeve of the EP states that this song has never been issued in stereo in the UK before, but this is incorrect, as it appeared in the same stereo version on the *Love Songs* album of 1977. It originally appeared on the flip side of *I Want To Hold Your Hand* in 1963, and again appeared in mono on the *Rarities* album of 1978.

With the release of these four stereo versions, only one Beatles track remains unreleased in true stereo, *You Know My Name (Look Up The Number)*, which appeared on the back of the *Let It Be* single in mono, and on the *Rarities* album in "mock" stereo.

EMI estimate that during 1981 nearly 75 million Beatles records and tapes were sold worldwide.

76 REEL MUSIC

PCS 7218—March 29, 1982

Yet another compilation album, again originating from Capitol Records in America, where the album was co-ordinated by Randall Davis. This selection features songs from the Beatles' five films; four from *A Hard Day's Night*, **three from** *Help!*, **two from** *Magical Mystery Tour*, **two from** *Yellow Submarine* **and three from** *Let It Be*. **It was the first new Beatles' compilation album (i.e. excluding budget price reissues) not to enter the album charts.**

The album was compiled by Randall Davis (who also supplied the sleeve notes), with Steve Meyer selecting the track listing. The sleeve artwork was drawn by David McMacken, with design by Michael Diehl, who assisted Roy Kohara with art direction. The album included a twelve page four colour booklet featuring an article and a photographic selection from each film. The back cover of the booklet depicts sixteen film posters supplied by the Ron Furmanek archives, and also contains the Capitol Records logo, indicating that EMI Records imported the booklet from America for the British release. The printed inner sleeve of the album also features a selection of stills from the five films. For details of each song see main entry under title given in brackets.

A SIDE

42e   A HARD DAY'S NIGHT *(2.32)*
(See *A Hard Day's Night* LP)

44e   I SHOULD HAVE KNOWN BETTER
(2.41)
(See *A Hard Day's Night* LP)

36g   CAN'T BUY ME LOVE *(2.09)*
(See single)

47f   AND I LOVE HER *(2.27)*
(See *A Hard Day's Night* LP)

71e   HELP! *(2.16)*
(See single)

**74e   YOU'VE GOT TO HIDE YOUR LOVE
AWAY** *(2.06)*
(See *Help!* LP)

69e   TICKET TO RIDE *(3.07)*
(See single)

137d   MAGICAL MYSTERY TOUR *(2.45)*
(See *Magical Mystery Tour* EP)

B SIDE

136e   I AM THE WALRUS *(4.32)*
This is the EP version of the song with the organ intro riff repeated six times.
(See *Magical Mystery Tour* EP)

104f   YELLOW SUBMARINE *(2.36)*
(See single)

133f   ALL YOU NEED IS LOVE *(3.44)*
(See single)

209b   LET IT BE *(4.00)*
(See *Let It Be* LP)

215d   GET BACK *(3.07)*
(See *Let It Be* LP)

213e   THE LONG AND WINDING ROAD
(3.34)
(See *Let It Be* LP)

**77   THE BEATLES' MOVIE
MEDLEY** *(4.01)*
**I'M HAPPY JUST TO DANCE
WITH YOU** *(1.54)*

R6055—May 24, 1982

The Beatles' twenty-sixth Parlophone single release in Britain, and their twenty-fifth to enter the *NME* Top 30 — it appeared on June 12, 1982, at No. 29. It peaked at No. 10 on July 10, its fifth week in the chart, and eventually stayed in the Top 30 for eight weeks.

The seven tracks making up the medley were edited together by John Palladino in America, where the idea for the single originated. It was Capitol's idea to put the single together after the world-wide success of the Star Sound "Stars On 45" medleys of Beatles' songs. Initially, EMI Records did not consider the single good enough for release in Britain, even though a catalogue number was assigned to it; however, due to demand for imported copies from the US, they eventually relented, and the record was released using the same sleeve design and "B" side coupling as the American release.

A SIDE

137   MAGICAL MYSTERY TOUR *(0.31)*

133	**ALL YOU NEED IS LOVE** *(1.05)*
74	**YOU'VE GOT TO HIDE YOUR LOVE AWAY** *(0.36)*
44	**I SHOULD HAVE KNOWN BETTER** *(0.46)*
42	**A HARD DAY'S NIGHT** *(0.23)*
69	**TICKET TO RIDE** *(0.31)*
215	**GET BACK** *(0.38)*

B SIDE

46a **I'M HAPPY JUST TO DANCE WITH YOU** *(1.54)*

Originally appearing on the *A Hard Day's Night* album, this is the first reappearance of the song.

78	**LOVE ME DO** *(2.18)* **P.S. I LOVE YOU** *(1.59)*

R 4949—October 4, 1982

In his editorial (subtitled "A Note To E.M.I.") in *Record Collector* magazine (April 1982), Johnny Dean made a special plea to EMI to celebrate the twentieth anniversary of the release of the Beatles' first Parlophone single by re-releasing that single in a picture sleeve, on October 5, 1982. And thereafter reissuing all subsequent releases on their twentieth anniversary date. Dean also offered to assist in compiling the releases. Up to this point (April 1982) EMI had no plans whatsoever to celebrate the anniversary; however, on October 4, 1982, the repackage of *Love Me Do* appeared. (As EMI's releases were now scheduled for a Monday, as opposed to a Friday, the single came out one day before the official anniversary.)

The single entered the *NME* Top 30 on October 23 at No. 5, rising to No. 3 (its highest position) the following week, and staying in the chart for five weeks.

The single was pressed using a red Parlophone label; it differs from the original release as it has several label credit changes: the 1962 release credits "Ardmore & Beechwood Ltd" as the song publishers, while the new release credits "MPL Communications Ltd" (Paul McCartney's own company, who purchased

the early Lennon & McCartney compositions from Ardmore & Beechwood Ltd). The 1982 release credits George Martin as producer, states that the recordings are mono and marks the "A" and "B" sides accordingly, while none of this information appeared on the original release.

10d **LOVE ME DO**

Although EMI were trying to duplicate the original release with the red label, they did not use the original version of *Love Me Do* which appeared on the first release. This version is the second recording of *Love Me Do* — featuring Andy White on drums, with Ringo playing tambourine — that appeared on the *Please Please Me* album and the black label pressing of the single. (See first *Love Me Do* single.)

2e **P.S. I LOVE YOU**

(See first *Love Me Do* single.)

79	**LOVE ME DO** *(2.18)* (picture disc) **P.S. I LOVE YOU** *(1.59)*

RP 4949—October 4, 1982

To further celebrate the twentieth anniversary of the release of the Beatles' first Parlophone single, EMI released a limited edition picture disc of the *Love Me Do* single — this being the first official release of its kind to feature the Beatles. The disc used the same pictures as those on the sleeve of the normal black vinyl re-release.

10e **LOVE ME DO**

(See 1962 *Love Me Do* single.)

2f **P.S. I LOVE YOU**

(See 1962 *Love Me Do* single.)

PCTC 260—October 18, 1982

The Beatles' second twenty track compilation album, and the first to feature singles tracks only, entered the *NME* album chart on October 30 at No. 24. It rose to No. 9 the next week staying in the chart for a total of six weeks. The album went gold (100,000 copies) in Britain by October 26.

The album, containing all of the Beatles' No. 1 singles based on the BMRB chart (thus *Please Please Me* is missing as it only reached No. 2 in this chart, whereas in the *NME* and *Melody Maker* charts it did reach No. 1) includes both sides of the two double "A"-sided hits. Also included is *Love Me Do* (a timely choice due to the twentieth anniversary celebration, and also of current interest in view of its contemporary chart presence).

It is the first Beatles' hits album to feature singles tracks only; the 1966 *A Collection Of Oldies* featured two album tracks, *Michelle* and *Yesterday*, as well as *Bad Boy*, and the two compilation double albums *1962 — 1966* and *1967 — 1970* also included selected album tracks (although all twenty-two original singles were included).

The eighteen singles featured on the album have sold well over fourteen million in Britain, with six being million sellers; all have sold over a million globally, with total sales world-wide of around sixty-seven million.

EMI had originally scheduled a double album titled *The Beatles Greatest Hits*, featuring all twenty-two original singles, making a total of twenty-six tracks (including the four double "A"-sided singles, giving a total running time of over seventy-five minutes). The album (catalogue number EMTV 34), was due for release on October 11, 1982. The album was to be TV advertised, and as it would have been the first Beatles' album to contain all their original singles — without any album fillers — it would almost certainly have been a massive seller. It wasn't until a few single-sided white label copies of the double album had been pressed that EMI decided to withdraw the release, in favour of the twenty track single album.

EMI's reason for shelving the double album (making it the first withdrawn British Beatles' album) was that other countries were releasing twenty track albums; therefore EMI had to follow suit, and they were afraid of criticism that the double album idea was duplicating the *1962 — 1966* and *1967 — 1970* compilations.

The *20 Greatest Hits* album, despite not having a TV catalogue number, did receive TV advertising. Roy Kohara and Peter Shea organised the sleeve design, while the inner sleeve collage of various photographs of the Beatles was by Chuck Ames.

A SIDE

| 10f | **LOVE ME DO** *(2.18)* |

| 16e | **FROM ME TO YOU** *(1.55)* |

This is the stereo version which appeared on *A Collection Of Oldies*, with no harmonica introduction.

| 18f | **SHE LOVES YOU** *(2.18)* |

| 34e | **I WANT TO HOLD YOUR HAND** *(2.24)* |

| 36h | **CAN'T BUY ME LOVE** *(2.09)* |

| 42f | **A HARD DAY'S NIGHT** *(2.30)* |

| 53e | **I FEEL FINE** *(2.18)* |

This is the stereo version with the whispered introduction.

| 69f | **TICKET TO RIDE** *(3.07)* |

| 71f | **HELP!** *(2.16)* |

| 85d | **DAY TRIPPER** *(2.48)* |

| 86d | **WE CAN WORK IT OUT** *(2.12)* |

B SIDE

101e PAPERBACK WRITER *(2.15)*

104g YELLOW SUBMARINE *(2.36)*

103e ELEANOR RIGBY *(2.04)*

133g ALL YOU NEED IS LOVE *(3.44)*

135d HELLO GOODBYE *(3.24)*

142d LADY MADONNA *(2.14)*

144e HEY JUDE *(7.07)*

180c GET BACK *(3.09)*

182d THE BALLAD OF JOHN AND YOKO
(2.57)

(For all above titles see respective singles.)

---

81 LOVE ME DO *(2.18)*
P.S. I LOVE YOU *(1.59)*/**LOVE ME DO** *(2.21)* (twelve-inch single)

12R 4949—November 1, 1982

With *Love Me Do* high in the Top Ten singles charts, EMI released the first official Beatles' twelve-inch single record in Britain to try and boost sales by pushing the single to the No. 1 position. They met with no success.

When the *Love Me Do* single was re-released on October 5, it was realised that the original version of the song had not been used. EMI explained that the original master for the recording had been lost. It was reported, in the *NME* of October 30, that EMI had discovered the masters of the two versions of *Love Me Do* had accidentally been switched at the factory. This explained why only the Andy White version had been available for the past twenty years;

the missing master had been discovered. With the rediscovery of the original masters, and with the interest in the whole *Love Me Do* saga, EMI decided to release both versions on a twelve-inch single in a picture sleeve (using the same photographs used on the seven-inch version.)

A SIDE

10g LOVE ME DO
The second version of the song, recorded on September 11, 1962, with Andy White on drums and Ringo on tambourine. Andy White is a member of the BBC Radio Orchestra in Glasgow.

2g P.S. I LOVE YOU

B SIDE

1b LOVE ME DO
The first version of the song as recorded on September 4, 1962, with Ringo on drums. This version of the song also appeared on *The Beatles Box* collection of 1980.

---

82 THE BEATLES/THE COLLECTION
(Original Master Recordings™)

(No special package number) — Mobile Fidelity Sound Lab— November, 1982

This release was not manufactured in Britain, but was the American album imported by TEK Marketing, retailing at the princely sum of £299. (For full details see the American release on page 166.)

---

83 THE BEATLES SINGLES COLLECTION

BSC 1 — December 6, 1982

To further celebrate the twentieth anniversary of the Beatles' first singles release, EMI put together the third collection in their trilogy of box sets. This set contained all twenty-six British Beatles' singles. It is the third "reissue" of their singles: *The Singles Collection* appeared in 1976, with all twenty-two original releases available in picture sleeves, with four different common back cover illustrations, plus the new single *Yesterday*.

This collection was not available to the public in a box set, although promotional boxed sets were supplied by EMI to disc jockeys and other notable music business personnel. In 1977, *The Singles Collection* was available from EMI's mail order subsidiary, World Records, as a box set called *The Beatles Collection*; this included the subsequent release *Back In The USSR* and, later, *Sgt. Pepper's Lonely Hearts Club Band.*

Of the twenty-six singles in the collection, twenty-two appear in new individual picture sleeves; the remaining four, *Penny Lane, Let It Be, Sgt. Pepper* and *The Beatles Movie Medley* all retain their original picture sleeves. (*Penny Lane* and *Let It Be* were the only original singles to be packaged in picture sleeves when first released.) The blue box matches the LP and EP boxed sets, with the heading and Beatles' signatures in gold lettering; it is completed with an insert listing the singles in chronological order, giving original release date, recording dates and highest chart position, with weeks at No. 1 (all chart statistics based on the BMRB chart).

The set was originally scheduled to include an extra bonus single, probably the picture disc of *Love Me Do*, but wisely this idea must have been dropped (any Beatle fan paying around £38 for a boxed set would almost certainly have purchased the picture disc anyway). A more realistic and interesting choice would have been the never released Plastic Ono Band single *You Know My Name (Look Up The Number)/ What's The New Mary Jane* (which, as everybody knows, is a Beatles' recording). As a matrix does exist of the single, it would presumably have been relatively easy for EMI to have produced such a single. (Think about it EMI?)

Except for *Love Me Do* and *Please Please Me*, the singles are the same as the original *Singles Collection* 1976 releases or later issues. *Love Me Do* and *Please Please Me* appear on the red Parlophone labels — like their original releases — although there are differences between the 1962/3 red labels and the new 1982

versions. Most of the pressings use the same matrices as those for *The Singles Collection*; some, however, have had new ones cut, notably the "B" side of *Let It Be*, which no longer contains the scratched out legend "APPLES 1002" (see *Let It Be* in British section), although a new engraving — "NICK W" — appears (probably the signature of the cutting engineer).

84 PLEASE PLEASE ME *(1.58)*
ASK ME WHY *(2.21)*

R 4983—January 10, 1983

The second anniversary re-release did not enter the *NME* charts, although it did manage a four week stay in the BMRB Top 100. It entered the chart on January 22, at No. 32, rising to No. 29 the following week. The single was the same pressing as used in *The Beatles Singles Collection* of 1982, with the same picture sleeve and red Parlophone label.

3e PLEASE PLEASE ME
(See original single.)

4c ASK ME WHY
(See original *Please Please Me* single.)

85 PLEASE PLEASE ME *(1.58)*
(picture disc)
ASK ME WHY *(2.21)*

RP 4983—January 10, 1983

As with the *Love Me Do* anniversary release, EMI produced a limited edition picture disc of *Please Please Me*, utilising the same illustrations as used on the sleeve of the black vinyl reissue.

3f PLEASE PLEASE ME
(See original single.)

4d ASK ME WHY
(See original *Please Please Me* single.)

CHRONOLOGICAL RECORD RELEASES IN GREAT BRITAIN

The following is a chronological list of The Beatles' record releases on the Parlophone and Apple labels, giving the "record number", the catalogue number and release date. Albums are listed as underlined UPPER CASE headings, EP's in UPPER CASE only, while all other entries relate to singles.

Rec. No.	Record Title	Cat. No.	Rel. Date
1962			
1a	Love Me Do/P.S. I Love You (red label)	R 4949	5/10
1963			
2	Please Please Me/Ask Me Why	R 4983	11/1
3	PLEASE PLEASE ME	PCS 3042	22/3
1b	Love Me Do/P.S. I Love You (black label)	R 4949	?/4
4	From Me To You/Thank You Girl	R 5015	12/4
5	TWIST AND SHOUT	GEP 8882	12/7
6	She Loves You/I'll Get You	R 5055	23/8
7	THE BEATLES' HITS	GEP 8880	6/9
8	THE BEATLES (No.1)	GEP 8883	1/11
9	WITH THE BEATLES	PCS 3045	22/11
10	I Want To Hold Your Hand/This Boy	R 5084	29/11
1964			
11	ALL MY LOVING	GEP 8891	7/2
12	Can't Buy Me Love/You Can't Do That	R 5114	20/3
13	LONG TALL SALLY	GEP 8913	19/6
14	A Hard Day's Night/Things We Said Today	R 5160	10/7
15	A HARD DAY'S NIGHT	PCS 3058	10/8
16	EXTRACTS FROM THE FILM "A HARD DAY'S NIGHT"	GEP 8920	4/11
17	EXTRACTS FROM THE ALBUM "A HARD DAY'S NIGHT"	GEP 8924	6/11
18	I Feel Fine/She's A Woman	R 5200	27/11
19	BEATLES FOR SALE	PCS 3062	4/12
1965			
20	BEATLES FOR SALE	GEP 8931	6/4
21	Ticket To Ride/Yes It Is	R 5265	9/4
22	BEATLES FOR SALE (No. 2)	GEP 8938	4/6
23	Help!/I'm Down	R 5305	23/7
24	HELP!	PCS 3071	6/8
25	Day Tripper/We Can Work It Out	R 5389	3/12
26	RUBBER SOUL	PCS 3075	3/12
27	THE BEATLES' MILLION SELLERS	GEP 8946	6/12
1966			
28	YESTERDAY	GEP 8948	4/3
29	Paperback Writer/Rain	R 5452	10/6
30	NOWHERE MAN	GEP 8952	8/7
31	Eleanor Rigby/Yellow Submarine	R 5493	5/8
32	REVOLVER	PCS 7009	5/8
33	A COLLECTION OF BEATLES' OLDIES (BUT GOLDIES)	PCS 7016	10/12
1967			
34	Penny Lane/Strawberry Fields Forever	R 5570	17/2
35	SGT. PEPPER'S LONELY HEARTS CLUB BAND	PCS 7027	1/6
36	All You Need Is Love/Baby You're A Rich Man	R 5620	7/7
37	Hello Goodbye/I Am The Walrus	R 5655	24/11
38	MAGICAL MYSTERY TOUR	SMMT 1/2	8/12

Rec. No.	Record Title	Cat. No.	Rel. Date
1968			
39	**Lady Madonna/The Inner Light**	R 5675	15/3
40	**Hey Jude/Revolution**	R 5722	26/8
41	**THE BEATLES**	PCS 7067-8	22/11
1969			
42	**YELLOW SUBMARINE**	PCS 7070	17/1
43	**Get Back/Don't Let Me Down**	R 5777	11/4
44	**The Ballad Of John And Yoko/Old Brown Shoe**	R 5786	30/5
45	**ABBEY ROAD**	PCS 7088	26/9
46	**Something/Come Together**	R 5814	30/10
	NO ONE'S GONNA CHANGE OUR WORLD	SRS 5013	15/12
1970			
47	**Let It Be/You Know My Name (Look Up The Number)**	R 5833	6/3
48	**LET IT BE**	PXS 1	8/5
		PCS 7096	6/11
1971—1972	**No Releases**		
1973			
49	**THE BEATLES 1962—1966**	PCSP 717	19/4
50	**THE BEATLES 1967—1970**	PCSP 718	19/4
1974—1975			
No Releases			
1976			
	The Singles Collection 1962—1970		6/3
51	**Yesterday/I Should Have Known Better**	R 6013	8/3
52	**ROCK 'N' ROLL MUSIC**	PCSP 719	10/6
53	**Back In The USSR/Twist And Shout**	R 6016	25/6
54	**MAGICAL MYSTERY TOUR**	PCTC 255	18/11
55	**THE BEST OF GEORGE HARRISON**	PAS 10011	20/11
1977			
56	**THE BEATLES AT THE HOLLYWOOD BOWL**	EMTV 4	6/5
57	**The Beatles Collection (singles box set)**	(No no.)	autumn
58	**LOVE SONGS**	PCSP 721	19/11
1978			
	ALL YOU NEED IS LOVE (Theatre Projects Records)	9199 995	?/2
59	**Sgt. Pepper's Lonely Hearts Club Band/With A Little Help From My Friends/A Day In The Life**	R 6022	30/9
60	**THE BEATLES 1962—1966** (red vinyl)	PCSPR 717	?/11
61	**THE BEATLES 1967—1970** (blue vinyl)	PCSPB 718	?/11
62	**THE BEATLES COLLECTION** (box set)	BC 13	2/12
1979			
63	**SGT. PEPPER'S LONELY HEARTS CLUB BAND** (picture disc)	PHO 7027	?/1
64	**THE BEATLES** (white vinyl)	PCS 7067-8	?/?
65	**ABBEY ROAD** (green vinyl)	PCS 7088	?/?
66	**LET IT BE** (white vinyl)	PCS 7096	?/?
67	**MAGICAL MYSTERY TOUR** (yellow vinyl)	PCTC 255	?/5
	A MONUMENT TO BRITISH ROCK VOL. 1 (Harvest)	EMTV 17	?/5
68	**HEY JUDE**	PCS 7184	?/6
69	**"RARITIES"**	PCM 1001	?/10

Rec. No.	Record Title	Cat. No.	Rel. Date
1980			
70	THE BEATLES BALLADS	PCS 7214	20/10
71	ROCK 'N' ROLL MUSIC VOL. 1	MFP 50506	27/10
72	ROCK 'N' ROLL MUSIC VOL. 2	MFP 50507	27/10
73	THE BEATLES BOX (box set)	SM 701-8	?/12
1981			
74	THE BEST OF GEORGE HARRISON	MFP 50523	?/11
	SAVILE'S TIME TRAVELS — 20 GOLDEN HITS OF 1963	MFP 50541	?/11
75	THE BEATLES EPs COLLECTION	BEP 14	7/12
1982			
76	REEL MUSIC	PCS 7218	29/3
77	The Beatles Movie Medley/I'm Happy Just to Dance With You	R 6055	24/5
78	Love Me Do/P.S. I Love You	R 4949	4/10
79	Love Me Do/P.S. I Love You (picture disc)	RP 4949	4/10
80	20 GREATEST HITS	PCTC 260	18/10
81	Love Me Do/P.S. I Love You/Love Me Do (twelve-inch single)	12R 4949	1/11
82	THE BEATLES COLLECTION (half-speed masters — Tek Marketing)		?/11
83	The Beatles singles collection (box set)	BSC 1	6/12

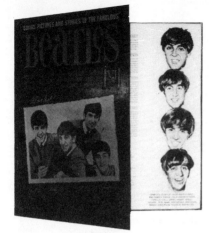

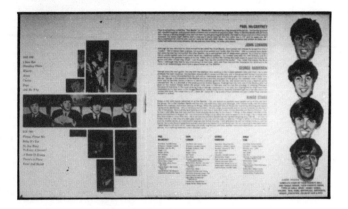

*See 'Songs, Pictures And Stories Of
The Fabulous Beatles', page 135.*

AMERICAN SECTION

As with the British section, all records are listed chronologically, and given a record number. These obviously do not relate to the British numbers. The layout of all entries is similar to the British section, except that "song entries" have not been repeated, although song titles are listed for each record. The song numbers used are the same as for the British section, except that the repeat "suffix" letters refer to the American releases, and therefore song numbers do not necessarily fall in chronological order according to the American record releases, although repeat "suffix" letters do.

This section covers all record releases on Vee Jay, Tollie, Swan, Capitol and Apple, but not those of MGM and ATCO, which appear in Appendix 4.

1 (3) PLEASE PLEASE ME (4) ASK ME WHY

VJ 498 Vee Jay—February 25, 1963

On January 25, 1963, Vee Jay Records, an American independent label, signed The Beatles for US release, although the group had yet to score a major British hit. This was the first release in America of Beatle material which originated from Parlophone/EMI, but was not a hit.

2 (16) FROM ME TO YOU (17) THANK YOU GIRL

VJ 522 Vee Jay—May 27, 1963

The second single, released in America by Vee Jay, which again failed to reach the charts.

3 INTRODUCING THE BEATLES

VJLP 1062 Vee Jay—July 22, 1963

The first album released by The Beatles in America on the Vee Jay label was the equivalent of the British *Please Please Me* album, with the exclusion of two tracks, *Please Please Me* and *Ask Me Why*, which had been released as a single by Vee Jay. The album did not make the charts in this form. (See *Introducing The Beatles* re-release — record No. 7.)

A SIDE

5   I SAW HER STANDING THERE

6   MISERY

7   ANNA (GO TO HIM)

8   CHAINS

9   BOYS

10   LOVE ME DO

B SIDE

2   P.S. I LOVE YOU

11   BABY IT'S YOU

12   DO YOU WANT TO KNOW A SECRET

13   A TASTE OF HONEY

14   THERE'S A PLACE

15   TWIST AND SHOUT

4 (18) SHE LOVES YOU (19) I'LL GET YOU

4152 Swan—September 16, 1963

The third American single was released on the Swan label, but not an immediate hit record, failing to enter the charts until January 25, 1964, when *I Want To Hold Your Hand*, released on Capitol, was in the Top Ten. *She Loves You* entered the Hot 100 at No. 69, rising to No. 2 in its fourth week. It stayed at No. 2 for five weeks (with *I Want To Hold Your Hand* at No. 1), and then rose to No. 1 for two weeks (with *I Want To Hold Your Hand* dropping to No. 2 for two weeks). It was in the American Top 30 for thirteen weeks and sold three million in America.

The week *She Loves You* rose to No. 1, The Beatles also had the following records in the Hot 100: *I Want To Hold Your Hand* — No. 2; *Please Please Me* — No. 3; *Twist And Shout* — No. 7; *I Saw Her Standing There* — No. 14; *From Me To You* — No. 58 and *Roll Over Beethoven* — No. 79, as well as

the earlier *My Bonnie* (by Tony Sheridan and The Beatles) at No. 42.

---

5   **(34) I WANT TO HOLD YOUR HAND (5a) I SAW HER STANDING THERE**

5112—January 13, 1964

In December 1963, Brian Epstein signed The Beatles to Capitol Records, the US subsidiary of EMI, for all future American releases. At first, Capitol Records were not keen to sign The Beatles, which is why the group's previous singles had been released on small American labels, but after their British successes in 1963, Capitol changed their minds. On January 18, *I Want To Hold Your Hand* entered the Hot 100 at 45, rising to No. 3 on January 25, and finally hitting the top spot on February 1, at which time *She Loves You* was at No. 21, *Please Please Me* at No. 69, and *I Saw Her Standing There* at No. 117. *I Want To Hold Your Hand* was at No. 1 for seven weeks, before being replaced by *She Loves You*, and was in the Top 30 for fourteen weeks. The record sold over a million in its first three weeks on release, making it Capitol's fastest selling disc up to that time, and their biggest seller, with total American sales of 4.9 million.

The "B" side of the single, *I Saw Her Standing There*, also entered the Billboard charts. It was in the Top 100 for eleven weeks, and in the Top 30 (highest position No. 14) for five weeks.

---

6   **MEET THE BEATLES**

ST 2047—January 20, 1964

The first Capitol Beatles album was the equivalent of the British *With The Beatles*, with the exclusion of five tracks: *Please Mr. Postman, Roll Over Beethoven, You've Really Got A Hold On Me, Devil In Her Heart* and *Money* and the addition of *I Want To Hold Your Hand, I Saw Her Standing There* and *This Boy.*

The album entered the Top 100 at No. 92 on February 1, jumping to No. 3 the following week, and then hitting the No. 1 spot on February 15, after three weeks in the chart. It stayed at No. 1 for eleven weeks, and was in the Top 30 for twenty-five weeks, the Top 100 for sixty-two weeks and the Top 200 for seventy-one weeks. The album sold 750,000 in its first week on release, and by mid-February had sold 1,600,000. By early March, the total was 2,800,000 and by mid-March, 3,650,000. An estimated 4.5 million were sold by December 1965, and five million by December 1966.

A SIDE

34a   **I WANT TO HOLD YOUR HAND**

5b   **I SAW HER STANDING THERE**

35   **THIS BOY**

20   **IT WON'T BE LONG**

21   **ALL I'VE GOT TO DO**

22   **ALL MY LOVING**

B SIDE

23   **DON'T BOTHER ME**

24   **LITTLE CHILD**

25   **TILL THERE WAS YOU**

7 INTRODUCING THE BEATLES (Re-release)

VJLP 1062 Vee Jay—January 27, 1964

With the success of the Capitol releases *I Want To Hold Your Hand* and *Meet The Beatles*, Vee Jay reissued *Introducing The Beatles*, changing two tracks from the original release by replacing *Love Me Do* and *P.S. I Love You* with *Please Please Me* and *Ask Me Why*, and this time the album became a hit. It entered the Top 100 on February 8 at No. 59, and by February 29 was at No. 2, where it stayed for nine weeks, *Meet The Beatles* being at No. 1, and was in the Top 30 for twenty-three weeks. It stayed in the Top 100 for forty-one weeks and in the Top 200 for forty-nine weeks. The album sold well over a million in America.

A SIDE

5c I SAW HER STANDING THERE

6a MISERY

7a ANNA (GO TO HIM)

8a CHAINS

9a BOYS

4a ASK ME WHY

B SIDE

3a PLEASE PLEASE ME

11a BABY IT'S YOU

12a DO YOU WANT TO KNOW A SECRET

13a A TASTE OF HONEY

14a THERE'S A PLACE

15a TWIST AND SHOUT

8 (3b) PLEASE PLEASE ME (16a) FROM ME TO YOU

VJ 581 Vee Jay—January 30, 1964

Having experienced no success with their first two Beatle releases, Vee Jay coupled both previous "A" sides to form the third Vee Jay Beatles' single release, and this time scored two hits. *Please Please Me* began a ten week chart residency on February 6 at No. 55, rising to No. 3 for two weeks, although *From Me To You* only reached No. 41, staying in the Top 100 for six weeks. The record sold over a million in America.

9 JOLLY WHAT! THE BEATLES AND FRANK IFIELD ON STAGE

VJLP 1085—February 26, 1964

This was not, as the title suggests, a live Beatles album; "On Stage" refers to Frank Ifield only. As only a limited number of Beatle songs were available to Vee Jay, the company inevitably attempted to issue the tracks in as many different formats as possible. The album entered the Billboard Album Chart on April 4 at No. 135, but only reached No. 104, bubbling under the Hot 100 for six weeks. The album was later re-packaged in June as *The Beatles and Frank Ifield (On Stage)*, with the same tracks and catalogue number.

A SIDE

3c PLEASE PLEASE ME (Track one)

16b FROM ME TO YOU (Track six)

B SIDE

4b ASK ME WHY (Track two)

17a THANK YOU GIRL (Track three)

THE BEATLES & FRANK IFIELD
ON STAGE

PLEASE, PLEASE ME
THANK YOU GIRL
FROM ME TO YOU
ASK ME WHY

Want To Hold Your Hand No. 2, Twist And Shout No. 3, Please Please Me No. 4, I Saw You Standing There No. 27, and four other Beatles discs were at Nos. 50, 71, 75 and 78. The "B" side, You Can't Do That, entered at No. 115 the same week. One week later, on April 4, Can't Buy Me Love went to No. 1, and headed the greatest monopoly of the sales charts by any group or artist in the history of the recording industry — The Beatles, as well as being at No. 1, were also at No. 2 (Twist And Shout), No. 3 (She Loves You), No. 4 (I Want To Hold Your Hand), No. 5 (Please Please Me), with I Saw Her Standing There No. 31, From Me To You No. 41, Do You Want To Know A Secret No. 46, All My Loving No. 58, You Can't Do That No. 65, Roll Over Beethoven No. 68 and Thank You Girl No. 79. They were also in the top two places in the album charts with Meet The Beatles and Introducing The Beatles.

(On March 27, 1964, the first six records in the Australian Top Ten were as follows: No. 1 I Saw Her Standing There, No. 2 Love Me Do, No. 3 Roll Over Beethoven, No. 4 All My Loving, No. 5 She Loves You and No. 6 Want To Hold Your Hand.)

After its first week on release in the U S, Can't Buy Me Love had sold 1,500,000, an all time high. It was at No. 1 for five weeks and stayed in the Top 30 for nine weeks. You Can't Do That was in the Top 100 for four weeks, rising to No. 48. The record sold three million copies in the USA.

| 10 | (15b) TWIST AND SHOUT |
| | (14b) THERE'S A PLACE |

9001 Tollie—March 2, 1964

This was the first release on the Tollie label, a subsidiary of Vee Jay Records. It entered the Billboard Top 100 on March 14 at No. 55, jumped to No. 7 the following week, was at No. 2 for four weeks, and stayed in the Top 30 for nine weeks. There's A Place entered the Top 100 for one week at No. 74.

The record sold over a million within three weeks of its release in America.

| 11 | (36) CAN'T BUY ME LOVE |
| | (37) YOU CAN'T DO THAT |

5150—March 16, 1964

This, the second Beatles' single release on the Capitol label, holds the record for the biggest advance sales for any single disc — 2,000,000 in the US (1,000,000 in Britain). It entered the Billboard charts on March 28 at No. 27, a time when She Loves You was No. 1, I

| 12 | SOUVENIR OF THEIR VISIT TO |
| | AMERICA (THE BEATLES) |

VJEP 1-903 Vee Jay—March 23, 1964

Vee Jay initially produced this record as an EP at the usual price of $1.29, but after stopping manufacture of the original cardboard jacket, the company issued it in a paper sleeve. Printed on the paper sleeve was information stating that the EP was being sold as a single, with Ask Me

Why being promoted as the main song. The EP is reputed to have sold a million. All the tracks on the record are from the American Vee Jay album, *Introducing The Beatles*.

A SIDE

6b   **MISERY**

13b   **A TASTE OF HONEY**

B SIDE

4c   **ASK ME WHY**

7b   **ANNA (GO TO HIM)**

13   **(12b) DO YOU WANT TO KNOW A SECRET**
(17b) THANK YOU GIRL

VJ 587 Vee Jay—March 23, 1964

The third single to be taken from the *Introducing The Beatles* album sold a million in America. It was in the Top 30 for eight weeks after entering the chart on March 28 at No. 78, rising to No. 2 for one week, while *Thank You Girl* was in the Top 100 for seven weeks, peaking at No. 35, after entering the chart on April 4, one week after *Do You Want To Know A Secret*.

14   **THE BEATLES' SECOND ALBUM**

ST 2080—April 10, 1964

The second Capitol album was made up of five tracks remaining from *With*

The Beatles, plus four tracks from American singles and two other previously unreleased tracks from the (yet to be released) British EP, *Long Tall Sally*. The album sold 250,000 on its first day of release, and entered the Top 100 at No. 16 on April 25. The following week it was at No. 1, staying there for five weeks, in the Top 30 for twenty-three weeks, in the Top 100 for fifty-three weeks and in the Top 200 for fifty-five weeks. The album sold a million, and was Capitol's fastest selling LP up to that point.

On May 2, The Beatles were at No. 1 (*The Beatles' Second Album*), No. 2 (*Meet The Beatles*) and No. 4 (*Introducing The Beatles*) in the album chart.

A SIDE

38   **LONG TALL SALLY**
(From British *Long Tall Sally* EP.)

39   **I CALL YOUR NAME**
(From British *Long Tall Sally* EP.)

26   **PLEASE MR. POSTMAN**

19a   **I'LL GET YOU**
(Previously Swan single 4152 c/w *She Loves You*.)

18a   **SHE LOVES YOU**
(Previously Swan single 4152 c/w *I'll Get You*.)

(All other tracks from *With The Beatles* British LP.)

B SIDE

27   **ROLL OVER BEETHOVEN**

17c THANK YOU GIRL
(Previously Vee Jay single VJ 522 c/w
From Me To You.)

29 YOU REALLY GOT A HOLD ON ME

31 DEVIL IN HER HEART

33 MONEY (THAT'S WHAT I WANT)

37a YOU CAN'T DO THAT
(Previously Capitol single 5150 c/w
Can't Buy Me Love.)

**15   (10a) LOVE ME DO
      (2a) P.S. I LOVE YOU**

9008 Tollie—April 27, 1964

The second Beatle single to be
released on the Tollie label entered the
Top 100 on April 11 at No. 81, topping
the chart for one week on May 30. It
was in the Top 30 for ten weeks, and
sold a million in the USA. The "B" side,
P.S. I Love You, was in the Top 30 for
five weeks, rising to No. 10.

16   FOUR BY THE BEATLES

EAP 2121—May 11, 1964

The first Capitol Beatles' EP
comprised two tracks from each of
their Capitol albums, *Meet The
Beatles* and *The Beatles Second
Album*. The EP was in the Top 100 for
three weeks, rising to No. 92.

A SIDE

27a ROLL OVER BEETHOVEN

22a ALL MY LOVING

B SIDE

35a THIS BOY

26a PLEASE MR. POSTMAN

CHARTBUSTERS VOLUME 4

ST 2094—May 11, 1964

The first of many "Various Artists"
compilation albums to feature The
Beatles. Other artists included on the
album are The Beach Boys, Al Martino, Nat "King" Cole, The Kingston
Trio, The Drew-Vels, Donna Lynn
and Jody Miller.

A SIDE (Track 1)
34b I WANT TO HOLD YOUR HAND

B SIDE (Track 5)
5d I SAW HER STANDING THERE

**17   (230) SIE LIEBT DICH (SHE LOVES
      YOU)
      (19b) I'LL GET YOU**

4182 Swan—May 21, 1964

Along with *Komm, Gib Mir Deine
Hand, Sie Liebt Dich* was originally
released in Germany on the Odeon
label, (Cat. No 22671) on March 5,
1964. Coupled with *I'll Get You* (the
original "B" side of the English
version), its only contemporary
release outside Germany was on the
Swan label in America. It entered the
Hot 100, after bubbling under for four
weeks, for one week at No. 97 on June
27, 1964.

230 SIE LIEBT DICH
This was recorded, with *Komm, Gib
Mir Deine Hand,* at the Pathé Marconi
Studios in Paris on January 29, 1964, with
George Martin producing and Norman
Smith engineering. On the same day.
the group also recorded *Can't Buy Me
Love.*

UAS 6366 United Artists—June 26, 1964

In America, the *A Hard Day's Night* soundtrack album was released by United Artists, who had exclusive rights to the film soundtrack as they were the film distributors, and included only the songs from the film plus four orchestral items from the film soundtrack performed by George Martin and his Orchestra. The album had advance sales of one million in the USA, and sold two million by October, 1964, making it one of the fastest selling albums in the history of the record industry — it entered the Top 100 charts on July 18 at No. 12, and the following week was No. 1, where it stayed for fourteen weeks. It was in the Top 30 for thirty-eight weeks, the Top 100 for forty-nine weeks and the Top 200 for fifty-one weeks,

A SIDE

42   A HARD DAY'S NIGHT

48   TELL ME WHY

132   The Long And Winding Road

50   I'LL CRY INSTEAD

This United Artists album version of the song includes an extra verse that is not present on the original British release.

(I SHOULD HAVE KNOWN BETTER)

46   I'M HAPPY JUST TO DANCE WITH YOU

(AND I LOVE HER)

B SIDE

44   I SHOULD HAVE KNOWN BETTER

45   IF I FELL

47   AND I LOVE HER

(RINGO'S THEME)

36a   CAN'T BUY ME LOVE

(A HARD DAY'S NIGHT)

(Titles within brackets are those performed by George Martin and his Orchestra.)

19   (42a) A HARD DAY'S NIGHT (44a) I SHOULD HAVE KNOWN BETTER

5222—July 13, 1964

On July 18, less than a week after its release, *A Hard Day's Night* entered the US charts at No. 21, the highest ever for a new disc up to 1964. By its third chart week, it was No. 1, where it stayed for two weeks, and was in the Top 30 for twelve weeks. The record sold a million in America and won a Grammy Award for the "Best Vocal Group Performance" of 1964.

The "B" side, *I Should Have Known Better*, was in the Top 100 for four weeks, reaching No. 53.

20   (50a) I'LL CRY INSTEAD (46a) I'M HAPPY JUST TO DANCE WITH YOU

5234—July 20, 1964

The second singles release from the soundtrack album, *A Hard Day's Night, I'll Cry Instead* reached No. 25, and was in the Top 30 for two weeks, and in the Top 100 for seven weeks. *I'm Happy Just To Dance With You* got to No. 95, and was in the Top 100 for one week only, despite "bubbling under" for six weeks. Both tracks entered the chart on August 1.

21 (47a) AND I LOVE HER
(45a) IF I FELL

5235—July 20, 1964

The third single to be taken from *A Hard Day's Night*, which left only one track on the album, *Tell Me Why* not released as a single, achieved more success than *I'll Cry Instead*, peaking at No. 12 for two weeks, and staying in the Top 30 for six weeks and the Top 100 for nine weeks. Its "B" side, *If I Fell*, got to No. 53 and was in the Top 100 for nine weeks, entering the chart one week after *And I Love Her* on August 1.

22 SOMETHING NEW

ST 2108—July 20, 1964

The third Capitol album included five songs from the United Artist's *A Hard Day's Night* album, three from the British *A Hard Day's Night* album, two from the British *Long Tall Sally* EP and the German version of *I Want To Hold Your Hand*. The album had advance orders of half a million, and subsequently sold a million. It entered the Top 200 on August 8 at No. 125, jumping to No. 6 the following week, and in its third week was at No. 2, where it stayed for nine weeks, *A Hard Day's Night* being at No. 1. It was in the Top 30 for twenty-eight weeks, the Top 100 for thirty-eight weeks and the Top 200 for forty-one weeks.

A SIDE

50b I'LL CRY INSTEAD

43   THINGS WE SAID TODAY
(From British *A Hard Day's Night* LP.)

49   ANY TIME AT ALL
(From British *A Hard Day's Night* LP.)

51   WHEN I GET HOME
(From British *A Hard Day's Night* LP.)

40   SLOW DOWN
(From *Long Tall Sally* EP.)

41   MATCHBOX
(From *Long Tall Sally* EP.)

B SIDE

48a TELL ME WHY

47b AND I LOVE HER

46b I'M HAPPY JUST TO DANCE WITH YOU

45b IF I FELL

229 KOMM, GIB MIR DEINE HAND
(See *Sie Liebt Dich* Swan single for details.)

23 **(12c) DO YOU WANT TO KNOW A SECRET**
(17d) THANK YOU GIRL

OL 149 Oldies 45—August 10, 1964

24 **(63d) PLEASE PLEASE ME)**
(16c) FROM ME TO YOU

OL 150 Oldies 45—August 10, 1964

25 **(10b) LOVE ME DO**
(2b) P.S. I LOVE YOU

OL 151 Oldies 45—August 10, 1964

26 **(15c) TWIST AND SHOUT**
(14c) THERE'S A PLACE

OL 152 Oldies 45—August 10, 1964

Before Vee Jay finally went out of business, the above four singles were incorporated in the "Oldies 45" re-issue series. None of them made any impression on the charts.

27 **(40a) SLOW DOWN**
(41a) MATCHBOX

5255—August 24, 1964

In the wake of the "Oldies 45" re-issues from Vee Jay, Capitol released these two tracks from the *Something New* album. *Matchbox* made No. 17 in the Top 30, staying in the chart for four weeks, while *Slow Down* scraped in for two weeks, reaching No. 25, both tracks entering the chart on September 5.

THE BIG HITS FROM ENGLAND AND THE USA

DT 2125—September 7, 1964

The second compilation album to feature The Beatles. The American artists featured on the album are The Beach Boys, Nat "King" Cole and Al Martino, while the other English artists are Peter and Gordon (who sing two Lennon and McCartney numbers, *A World Without Love* and *Nobody I Know*) and Cilla Black.

B SIDE (Track 1)

36b **CAN'T BUY ME LOVE**

(Track 2)

37b **YOU CAN'T DO THAT**

28 **THE BEATLES VS. THE FOUR SEASONS**

VJDX 30 Vee Jay—October 1, 1964

This double album contained one album of Beatles numbers (*Introducing The Beatles*) and one of the Four Seasons, which includes several of their hits. The album entered the Top 200 for three weeks, its highest position being No. 142, after entering the chart on October 10.

A SIDE

5e **I SAW HER STANDING THERE**

6c **MISERY**

7c **ANNA (GO TO HIM)**

8b **CHAINS**

9b **BOYS**

4d **ASK ME WHY**

B SIDE		B SIDE	
3e	PLEASE PLEASE ME	3f	PLEASE PLEASE ME
11b	BABY IT'S YOU	11c	BABY IT'S YOU
12d	DO YOU WANT TO KNOW A SECRET	12e	DO YOU WANT TO KNOW A SECRET
13c	A TASTE OF HONEY	13d	A TASTE OF HONEY
14d	THERE'S A PLACE	14e	THERE'S A PLACE
15d	TWIST AND SHOUT	15e	TWIST AND SHOUT

29 SONGS, PICTURES AND STORIES OF THE FABULOUS BEATLES

VJLP 1092 Vee Jay—October 12, 1964

Less than two weeks after the double album release *The Beatles Vs. The Four Seasons*, Vee Jay re-packaged and re-titled *Introducing The Beatles* and released it for the fourth time as *Songs, Pictures and Stories of The Fabulous Beatles*. The album entered the Top 200 on October 31 at No. 121 and rose to No. 63, being in the Top 100 for six weeks and in the Top 200 for eleven weeks.

A SIDE

5f	I SAW HER STANDING THERE
6d	MISERY
7d	ANNA (GO TO HIM)
8c	CHAINS
9c	BOYS
4e	ASK ME WHY

30 THE BEATLES STORY

STBO 2222—November 23, 1964

Capitol released this double album to commemorate the first anniversary of The Beatles first Capitol single *I Want To Hold Your Hand* and the record industry revolution that it started. The album is a narrative and musical biography of Beatlemania, including interviews with each Beatle, Brian Epstein and George Martin, plus a Beatles medley and a very short excerpt from a Beatles concert. The album hit the million dollar sales mark in its first week, and subsequently sold a million copies. It entered the Top 100 at No. 97 on December 12, rising to No. 7 for four weeks, and was in the Top 30 for nine weeks, the Top 100 for fifteen weeks and the Top 200 for seventeen weeks.

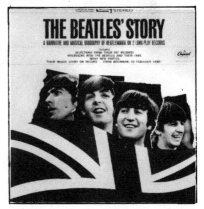

Tracks:

SIDE ONE
On Stage With The Beatles
How Beatlemania Began
Beatlemania In Action
Man Behind The Beatles —
Brian Epstein

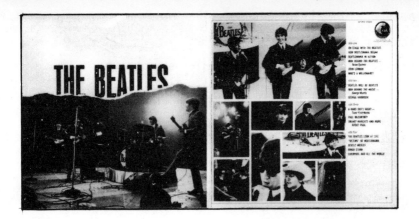

John Lennon
Who's A Millionaire?

SIDE TWO
Beatles Will Be Beatles
Man Behind Their Music — George
Martin
George Harrison

SIDE THREE
A Hard Day's Night — Their First Movie
Paul McCartney
Sneaky Haircuts and More About Paul

SIDE FOUR
TWIST AND SHOUT
This live cut was recorded on August 23, 1964 at the Hollywood Bowl.
The Beatles Look At Life
Beatle Medley
Things We Said Today
I'm Happy Just To Dance With You
Little Child
Long Tall Sally
She Loves You
Ringo Starr
Liverpool And All The World

The album was written and narrated by John Babcock, Al Wiman and Roger Christian.

31	(53) I FEEL FINE
	(54) SHE'S A WOMAN

5327—November 23, 1964

I Feel Fine sold a million in its first week of release in America, and one week after release entered the US charts at No. 22. On December 26 it reached No. 1, where it stayed for three weeks. It was in the Top 30 for ten weeks.

She's A Woman rose to No. 4 for two weeks, and was in the Top 30 for seven weeks.

32	BEATLES '65

ST 2228—December 15, 1964

Beatles '65 is the American equivalent of the British *Beatles For Sale* LP, and contains eight tracks from that album, plus one track left over from *A Hard Day's Night* and two tracks from a single.

The album had advance orders of 750,000 and sold over a million in its first week, 2,124,000 in four weeks, and over three million in six weeks, making it the fastest selling album up to 1964. It entered the charts at No. 98 on January 2, 1965, and went to No. 1 the following week, where it remained for nine weeks. It was in the Top 30 for twenty-nine weeks, the Top 100 for fifty weeks and the Top 200 for seventy-one weeks.

On January 9, 1965, The Beatles had all their eight American albums in the Top 200 album chart:- No. 1 (*Beatles '65*); No. 6 (*A Hard Day's Night*); No. 7 (*The Beatles Story*); No. 13 (*Something*

New); No. 69 (*Meet The Beatles*); No. 70 (*The Beatles Second Album*); No. 138 (*Songs, Pictures And Stories Of The Fabulous Beatles*); and No. 146 (*Introducing The Beatles*).

A SIDE

55   NO REPLY

56   I'M A LOSER

57   BABY'S IN BLACK

58   ROCK AND ROLL MUSIC

59   I'LL FOLLOW THE SUN

60   MR. MOONLIGHT

B SIDE

64   HONEY DON'T

52   I'LL BE BACK
(From British *A Hard Day's Night* album.)

54a SHE'S A WOMAN
("B" side of *I Feel Fine* single.)

53a I FEEL FINE
(Single)

68   EVERYBODY'S TRYING TO BE MY BABY
(All other tracks from British *Beatles For Sale* LP.)

33   4 BY THE BEATLES

R 5365—February 1, 1965

The second Capitol EP, a selection from the *Beatles '65* album, was in the Top 100 for five weeks, rising to No. 68, after entering the chart on February 27 at No. 81.

A SIDE

64a HONEY DON'T

56a I'M A LOSER

B SIDE

60a MR. MOONLIGHT

68a EVERYBODY'S TRYING TO BE MY BABY

**34   (62) EIGHT DAYS A WEEK
(66) I DON'T WANT TO SPOIL THE PARTY**

5371—February 15, 1965

For various reasons, Capitol Records always contrived to stretch a British LP release into several different forms for American release, and this single was the result of such a process with regard to *Beatles For Sale*. Eight tracks from the album were included on *Beatles '65*, leaving six additional cuts which could be used elsewhere. The two tracks on this single were among the six extras — *Eight Days A Week* had been considered as a potential British single, but was eventually discarded in favour of *I Feel Fine*. In the United States, this single sold over one million copies and topped the chart for two weeks during a chart stay of ten weeks, having entered on February 20 at No. 53.

I Don't Want To Spoil The Party charted for six weeks, achieving a highest position of No. 39 after entering on the same day as *Eight Days A Week* at No. 81.

24, and rose to No. 43. It stayed in the Top 100 for fourteen weeks and in the Top 200 for thirty-four weeks.

The album sold a million by the end of 1973, being awarded a Gold Disc by R.I.A.A. on January 8, 1974.

A SIDE

10c	LOVE ME DO
15f	TWIST AND SHOUT
7e	ANNA (GO TO HIM)
8d	CHAINS
9d	BOYS
4f	ASK ME WHY

B SIDE

3g	PLEASE PLEASE ME
2c	P.S. I LOVE YOU
11d	BABY IT'S YOU
13e	A TASTE OF HONEY
12f	DO YOU WANT TO KNOW A SECRET

35 THE EARLY BEATLES

ST 2309—March 22, 1965

After Vee Jay Records finally went out of business, Capitol released this album of the tracks which made up the *Introducing The Beatles* Vee Jay album, which had been re-packaged and released four times by Vee Jay in the space of fifteen months. This album included both the singles *Love Me Do/P.S. I Love You* and *Please Please Me/Ask Me Why*, but excluded *I Saw Her Standing There* and *There's A Place*. *Please Please Me*, *Twist And Shout* and *Do You Want To Know A Secret* appeared on record here for the seventh time in America. The record entered the Top 200 at No. 132 on April

36 (69) TICKET TO RIDE (70) YES IT IS

5407—April 14, 1965

Ticket To Ride had an advance sale of 750,000 in the US and entered the Top 100 on April 24 at No. 59. It reached No. 1 for one week on May 22, and was in the Top 30 for nine weeks.

An interesting fact concerning Capitol's release of *Ticket To Ride* is that the label credits for the song state 'From the United Artists Release *"Eight Arms To Hold You"*'. Capitol jumped the gun somewhat here, as "Eight Arms..." was only a tentative

title for the film which was later re-titled *Help!*.

    Yes It Is was in the Top 100 for four weeks, rising to No. 46.

37   BEATLES VI

ST 2358—June 14, 1965

The sixth Capitol album was composed of the remaining six tracks from the *Beatles For Sale* not used on *Beatles '65*, three tracks from the yet to be released British *Help!* album, and two additional items.

    The album sold 500,000 in five days, and a million by July 1, 1965. Entering the Top 200 at No. 149 on June 26, it reached No. 1 in its third week in the chart, remaining there for six weeks, and was in the Top 30 for twenty weeks. The disc stayed in the Top 100 for thirty-nine weeks and in the Top 200 for forty-one weeks.

A SIDE

61   KANSAS CITY/HEY, HEY, HEY, HEY
(*Beatles For Sale*)

62a   EIGHT DAYS A WEEK
(*Beatles For Sale*)

80   YOU LIKE ME TOO MUCH
(*Help!*)

117   BAD BOY
(This track was not released in Britain until 1966, when it•appeared on *The Collection Of Beatles Oldies* LP.)

66a   I DON'T WANT TO SPOIL THE PARTY
(*Beatles For Sale*)

63   WORDS OF LOVE
(*Beatles For Sale*)

B SIDE

67   WHAT YOU'RE DOING
(*Beatles For Sale*)

70a   YES IT IS
("B" side of *Ticket To Ride* single.)

84   DIZZY MISS LIZZY
(*Help!*)

81   TELL ME WHAT YOU SEE
(*Help!*)

65   EVERY LITTLE THING
(*Beatles For Sale*)

38   (71) HELP!
(72) I'M DOWN

5476—July 19, 1965

Help! sold a million in the US in one week, and entered the Top 100 on August 7 at No. 41. On September 4, it rose to No. 1, topping the chart for three weeks. It stayed in the Top 30 for eleven weeks and spent thirteen weeks in the Top 100. *I'm Down* did not enter the Top 100, but "bubbled under" for seven weeks.

39   HELP!

SMAS 2386—August 13, 1965

The American *Help!* album contained the seven film songs plus six orchestral tracks from the soundtrack by Ken Thorne. *Help!* qualified for an immediate Gold Disc, as it had a definite order of a million before release, something which had never previously occurred in the history of the record industry. The album entered the Top 200 on August 28 at No. 148, jumped to No. 61 on September 4, and went to No. 1 on September 11 in its third week in the chart. It stayed at No. 1 for nine weeks, was in the Top 30 for thirty-one weeks, the Top 100 for forty-two weeks and the Top 200 for forty-four weeks.

77 YOU'RE GOING TO LOSE THAT GIRL

(The Chase)

76 ANOTHER GIRL

A SIDE

(James Bond Theme)

71a HELP!

73 THE NIGHT BEFORE

(From Me To You Fantasy)

74 YOU'VE GOT TO HIDE YOUR LOVE AWAY

75 I NEED YOU

(In The Tyrol)

B SIDE

(The Bitter End/You Can't Do That)

(Another Hard Day's Night)

69a TICKET TO RIDE

(Titles within brackets are those performed by Ken Thorne and his Orchestra.)

**40   (83) YESTERDAY
       (78) ACT NATURALLY**

5498—September 13, 1965

These two songs from the British *Help!* album were not included on the American album, but instead were released as a single, which sold over one million in ten days. *Yesterday* entered the chart twelve days after release, eventually making No.1 for four weeks in October. Although it entered the chart on the same day, at No. 87, *Act Naturally* peaked at No. 47, for two weeks, and was in the Top 100 for seven weeks. The single eventually sold 1,800,000 in America.

41	(15g) TWIST AND SHOUT (14f) THERE'S A PLACE

6061 Capitol Starline—October 11, 1965

42	(10d) LOVE ME DO (2d) P.S. I LOVE YOU

6062 Capitol Starline—October 11, 1965

43	(3h) PLEASE PLEASE ME (16d) FROM ME TO YOU

6063 Capitol Starline—October 11, 1965

44	(12g) DO YOU WANT TO KNOW A SECRET (17e) THANK YOU GIRL

6064 Capitol Starline—October 11, 1965

45	(27b) ROLL OVER BEETHOVEN (6e) MISERY

6065 Capitol Starline—October 11, 1965

46	(9e) BOYS (61a) KANSAS CITY/HEY HEY HEY HEY

6066 Capitol Starline—October 11, 1965

After Vee Jay Records went out of business, Capitol acquired the rights to the earlier Beatles material that had originally been leased to the Vee Jay and Tollie labels. The first four singles in the series had been re-issued by Vee Jay on their Oldies label, but the last two had never been released as singles. None of the singles made any impression on the charts, except *Boys*, which bubbled under for one week, on October 30, at No. 102.

47	(86) WE CAN WORK IT OUT (85) DAY TRIPPER

5555—December 6, 1965

This single sold over a million in America. In Britain, *Day Tripper* was considered the stronger side of the double "A" sided release, but in America *We Can Work It Out* was preferred, entering the chart on December 18 at No. 36, and reaching No. 1 on January 8 for two weeks. It dropped to No. 2 for one week, returned to No. 1 for another week on January 29, 1966, and was in the Top 30 for ten weeks. *Day Tripper* peaked at No. 5 for one week, and was in the Top 30 for seven weeks, entering on December 18 at No. 56.

48	RUBBER SOUL

ST 2442—December 6, 1965

The American *Rubber Soul* album contained ten tracks included on the British version of the LP plus two tracks from the British *Help!* album. With this release, The Beatles broke all their previous sales records, as it sold 1,200,000 in its first nine days, and qualified for an instant Gold Disc, the group's tenth American gold album. With sales continuing at a tremendous rate into 1966, the album soon passed the two million mark. It entered the Top 200 at No. 106 on December 25, and jumped to No. 60 the following week, making No. 1 in its third week of the chart, remaining at the top of the chart for six weeks, in the Top 30 for twenty-nine weeks, the Top 100 for forty-four weeks and the Top 200 for fifty-one weeks. The sleeve for this album is identical to that of the British release. See page 36 of British section.

**49   (90) NOWHERE MAN
        (94) WHAT GOES ON**

5587—February 21, 1966

Two songs included on the British *Rubber Soul* LP, but omitted from the American release of the album, were instead released as a single, which sold a million within three weeks of release. *Nowhere Man* entered the Top 30 at No. 25 on March 5, and rose to No. 3 on March 26. It was in the Top 30 for nine weeks. *What Goes On* featured in the Top 100 for two weeks only, entering at No. 89 on March 12.

**50   (101) PAPERBACK WRITER
        (102) RAIN**

5651—May 30, 1966

Paperback Writer entered the charts on June 11 at No. 28, and two weeks later was at No. 1 for one week, dropping to No. 2 for one week, but returning to No. 1 for a second week. It was in the Top 30 for nine weeks. *Rain*, which also first charted on June 11, but at No. 72, peaked at No. 23 for two weeks, and was in the Top 30 for four weeks. The single sold one million in America,

51   YESTERDAY AND TODAY

ST 2553—June 20, 1966

The original cover for *Yesterday And Today* showed The Beatles wearing butcher's smocks and surrounded by lumps of meat and mutilated dolls, but various parties disapproved of the photo, and it was withdrawn at the last minute. Only a few copies of the "Butcher sleeve" survive today. The

album contains tracks from the British *Help!*, *Rubber Soul* and *Revolver* LPs that were omitted from the American albums with those titles. The album was awarded a Gold Disc on July 8, 1966, and subsequently sales exceeded one million. It entered the Top 200 on July 9 at No. 120, and after three weeks reached No. 1, where it stayed for five weeks. It was in the Top 30 for thirteen weeks, the Top 100 for twenty-three weeks and the Top 200 for thirty-one weeks.

A SIDE

87 **DRIVE MY CAR**
(*Rubber Soul*)

106 **I'M ONLY SLEEPING**
(*Revolver*)

90a **NOWHERE MAN**
(*Rubber Soul*)

113 **DOCTOR ROBERT**
(*Revolver*)

83a **YESTERDAY**
(*Help!*)

78a **ACT NATURALLY**
(*Help!*)

B SIDE

111 **AND YOUR BIRD CAN SING**
(*Revolver*)

99 **IF I NEEDED SOMEONE**
(*Rubber Soul*)

86a **WE CAN WORK IT OUT**
(Single)

94a **WHAT GOES ON**
(*Rubber Soul*)

85a **DAY TRIPPER**
(Single)

52   (104) YELLOW SUBMARINE (103) ELEANOR RIGBY

5715—August 8, 1966

This single sold 1,200,000 in its first four weeks in America, and The Beatles received their 21st Gold Disc Award from the R.I.A.A., the most ever earned by any act in R.I.A.A. history. *Yellow Submarine* was in the Top 30 for seven weeks, rising to No. 2 for one week. *Eleanor Rigby* peaked at No. 11 for two weeks, staying in the Top 30 for five weeks. Both tracks entered the chart within three weeks of release.

53   REVOLVER

ST 2576—August 8, 1966

Revolver was awarded a Gold Disc after three weeks on the market, and entered the Top 200 charts on September 3 at No. 45. The following week it was No. 1, where it stayed for six weeks, being in the Top 30 for twenty-four weeks. It was in the Top 100 for thirty-seven weeks and the Top 200 for seventy-seven weeks. This sleeve is identical to the British release. See page 41 of British section.

A SIDE

105 **TAXMAN**

103a **ELEANOR RIGBY**

107 **LOVE YOU TO**

108 **HERE, THERE AND EVERYWHERE**

104a **YELLOW SUBMARINE**

109 **SHE SAID, SHE SAID**

110   **GOOD DAY SUNSHINE**

112   **FOR NO ONE**

114   **I WANT TO TELL YOU**

115   **GOT TO GET YOU INTO MY LIFE**

116   **TOMORROW NEVER KNOWS**

54   **(118) PENNY LANE**
        (119) STRAWBERRY FIELDS FOREVER

5810—February 13, 1967

With this single, The Beatles made history for Capitol Records, as over 1,000,000 were ordered, the highest quantity of any one single ever pressed and shipped in a three day period by the label. US sales passed the million mark in March, and eventually exceeded 1,500,000. *Penny Lane* reached No. 1 for one week, and was in the Top 30 for eight weeks. *Strawberry Fields Forever* rose to No. 8 and made the Top 30 for seven weeks, after both tracks had entered the chart on February 25, *Penny Lane* at No. 83 and *Strawberry Fields Forever* two places lower. This sleeve is identical to the British release. See page 46 of British section.

55   **SGT. PEPPER'S LONELY HEARTS CLUB BAND**

SMAS 2653—June 2, 1967

Sgt. Pepper had advance sales in America of one million, and sold over 2.5 million in three months. The album entered the Top 30 at No. 8 on June 24, and went to No. 1 the following week. It was at No. 1 for fifteen weeks and stayed in the Top 30 for forty-five weeks, the Top 100 for eighty-five weeks and the Top 200 for eighty-eight weeks, dropping out after February 22, 1969. It remained outside the Top 200 for thirty-seven weeks, and on November 15, 1969, re-entered at No. 124, rising to No. 101 on January 3, 1970. It continued in the chart until April 4, 1970, dropping out the following week, but returned again on July 25, 1970, at No. 159, for a further four weeks, and was in the Top 200 for a total of 113 weeks.

The album won four Grammy Awards for Best Contemporary Album, Best Performance, Best Album Cover and Best Engineered Recording of 1967.

For the first time, Capitol's release of a Beatles' album was identical to the British release — therefore, tracks and numbering are the same as the British release, as is the cover. See page 47 of the British section.

56   **(133) ALL YOU NEED IS LOVE**
        (134) BABY YOU'RE A RICH MAN

5964—July 17, 1967

Another million seller in the States for The Beatles, *All You Need Is Love* entered the charts five days after release, and was in the Top 30 for nine weeks and at No. 1 for one week. *Baby You're A Rich Man* was in the Top 100 for five weeks, rising to No. 34 for one week, having entered at No. 64 on July 29.

57   **(135) HELLO GOODBYE**
        (136) I AM THE WALRUS

2056—November 27, 1967

Hello Goodbye sold a million in America by December 15, within three weeks of release. It entered the Top 100 at No. 45 on December 2, jumping to No. 8 the following week, and was No. 1 on December 30, for the first of three weeks. It was in the Top 30 for nine weeks. *I Am The Walrus*

reached No. 56 and was in the Top 100 for four weeks, after entering the chart on December 9 at No. 64.

58 MAGICAL MYSTERY TOUR

SMAL 2835—November 27, 1967

In Britain the *Magical Mystery Tour* songs appeared on two EP's, but Capitol's release was padded out into an album by including the singles released in 1967. The album had the biggest initial sale of any album in Capitol's history up to that time, with sales passing eight million dollars within three weeks. By mid-January 1968, it had sold 1.75 million, and subsequent sales have increased that total to over three million. The album entered the Top 200 at No. 157 on December 23, 1967, and by January 6, 1968 it reached No. 1, where it stayed for eight weeks. Initially, it was in the Top 30 for twenty-five weeks, the Top 100 for fifty-three weeks and the Top 200 for fifty-nine weeks, but dropped out of the Top 200 after February 1, 1969. It re-entered forty weeks later on November 27, 1969, at No. 146, rising to No. 109 on January 3, 1970, and stayed in the Top 200 for a further seventeen weeks up to March 7, when it dropped out, only to re-enter again on July 25, at No. 194, for two weeks. It was in the Top 200 for a total of seventy-eight weeks.

The re-entry of *Sgt. Pepper* and *Magical Mystery Tour* into the charts at the end of 1969 was the direct result of the "Paul is dead" rumours that were sweeping the USA at the time. The rumour was perpetrated by Russ Gibb , a Programme Co-ordinator for WKNR Radio, Detroit, Michigan. (See Appendix 2.) This album contains electronically created stereo tracks.
The sleeve is identical to the British release. See page 59 of British section.
A SIDE

137 **MAGICAL MYSTERY TOUR**

139 **THE FOOL ON THE HILL**

140 **FLYING**

141 **BLUE JAY WAY**

138 **YOUR MOTHER SHOULD KNOW**

136a **I AM THE WALRUS**

B SIDE

135a **HELLO GOODBYE**

119a **STRAWBERRY FIELDS FOREVER**

118a **PENNY LANE**

134a **BABY YOU'RE A RICH MAN**

133a **ALL YOU NEED IS LOVE**

**59 (142) LADY MADONNA
(143) THE INNER LIGHT**

2138—March 18, 1968

Although it failed to reach No. 1 in America, *Lady Madonna* sold a million in its first week, and entered the Top 100 at No. 23, a week after release. Its highest position in the charts was No. 4 for three weeks, and it stayed in the Top 30 for nine weeks. *The Inner Light* entered the Top 100 for one week at No. 96 on March 30.

**60 (144) HEY JUDE
(145) REVOLUTION**

2276 Apple—August 26, 1968

Hey Jude entered the American charts on September 14 at No. 10, the highest for any disc (beating Herman's Hermits' 1965 single *Mrs Brown You've Got A Lovely Daughter*, which entered at No. 12) and went to No. 3 the following week, and then to No. 1. It stayed at No. 1 for nine consecutive weeks, the longest stay at the top for any single since 1960, when Percy Faith's *Theme From A Summer Place* also topped the chart for nine weeks. Since the Billboard charts started in 1950, there have been only seven singles that have topped the chart for longer than nine weeks:
Song From 'Moulin Rouge' by Percy Faith, 1953 — 10 weeks; *Cherry Pink*

And Apple Blossom White by Perez Prado, 1955 — 10 weeks; *Third Man Theme* by Anton Karas, 1950 — 11 weeks; *Cry* by Johnny Ray, 1951-2 — 11 weeks; *Vaya Con Dios* by Les Paul & Mary Ford, 1953 — 11 weeks; *Hound Dog* by Elvis Presley, 1956 — 11 weeks; and *Goodnight Irene* by Gordon Jenkins & The Weavers, 1950 — 13 weeks.

There have been seven other singles to stay at No. 1 for nine weeks since 1950:

Tennessee Waltz by Patti Page, 1950-1; *Wheel Of Fortune* by Kay Starr, 1952; *Auf Wiederseh'n Sweetheart* by Vera Lynn, 1952; *Little Things Mean A Lot* by Kitty Kallen, 1954; *Singing The Blues* by Guy Mitchell, 1957; *Mack The Knife* by Bobby Darin, 1959 and *Theme From 'A Summer Place'* by Percy Faith, 1960.

Hey Jude sold over a million in eight days, and eventually around four million in America, and was in the Top 30 for eighteen weeks. *Revolution* peaked at No. 12 for three weeks, and stayed in the Top 30 for ten weeks, entering at No. 38 on September 14.

61   THE BEATLES

SWBO 101—November 25, 1968

Advance orders in America for *The Beatles* double LP amounted to 1,900,000. Thus, the album was awarded an immediate Gold Disc by the R.I.A.A. and was the fastest selling disc ever for Capitol Records, with US sales over three million. The album entered the Top 30 charts at No. 11 on December 14, went to No. 2 the following week and made No. 1 in its third week in the chart. It stayed at No. 1 for nine weeks, and was in the Top 30 for twenty-three weeks, the Top 100 for fifty-four weeks and the Top 200 for sixty-five weeks.

Tracks and numbering are the same as British release as is the sleeve. See page 63 of British section.

62   YELLOW SUBMARINE

SW 153—January 13, 1969

Yellow Submarine entered the Top 100 on February 8 at No. 86, and went to No. 2 for one week. It was in the Top 30 for eleven weeks, the Top 100 for twenty-one weeks and the Top 200 for twenty-four weeks. It was awarded a

Gold Disc in February 1969. The record sleeve is identical to that of the British release. See page 70 of British section.

A SIDE

104b	YELLOW SUBMARINE
176	ONLY A NORTHERN SONG
177	ALL TOGETHER NOW
178	HEY BULLDOG
179	IT'S ALL TOO MUCH
133b	ALL YOU NEED IS LOVE

B SIDE

(PEPPERLAND)

(SEA OF TIME)

(SEA OF HOLES)

(SEA OF MONSTERS)

(MARCH OF THE MEANIES)

(PEPPERLAND LAID WASTE)

(YELLOW SUBMARINE IN PEPPERLAND)

(All "B" side numbers performed by George Martin and his Orchestra.)

FIRST VIBRATION

5000—May, 1969

A mail order album from the "Do It Now" Foundation.

As well as the one Beatle cut, the album includes tracks by The Animals, Hoyt Axton, Buffalo Springfield, The Byrds, Canned Heat, Chad and Jeremy, Donovan, Genesis, Jefferson Airplane, Jimi Hendrix, The Peanut Butter Conspiracy, Ravi Shankar and Things To Come.

B SIDE (Track 2)

90b	NOWHERE MAN

63   (180) GET BACK
(181) DON'T LET ME DOWN

2490 Apple—May 5, 1969

Get Back equalled *Hey Jude*'s feat in entering the American charts at No.

10, the highest entry position for any single, within a week of release on May 10. It sold a million within two weeks of release, and eventually sold two million in America. It reached No. 1 on May 24, staying there for five weeks, and in the Top 30 for twelve weeks. Billy Preston received a gold disc from the R.I.A.A. in May, 1970, for his organ accompaniment on the disc. *Don't Let Me Down*'s highest position was No. 35, and it was in the Top 100 for four weeks, entering on May 10 at No. 40.

64 (182) THE BALLAD OF JOHN AND YOKO
(183) OLD BROWN SHOE

2531 Apple—June 4, 1969

The Ballad Of John And Yoko entered the American Top 100 at No. 71 on June 14, with *Get Back* still at No. 1. Its highest position was No. 8, for two weeks, while *Get Back* was still in the charts at No. 12. The record sold a million by July 16, and eventually sold 1,250,000. It was in the Top 30 for eight weeks. *The Ballad Of John And Yoko* was banned in America because of the chorus "Christ you know it ain't easy, You know how hard it can be. The way things are going, they're going to crucify me", which probably accounts for its comparatively low position in the chart. The American charts are partially based on the number of radio requests received from the public, and not solely on record sales as in Britain. *Old Brown Shoe* did not make the charts.

65 ABBEY ROAD

SO 383—October 1, 1969

Abbey Road entered the US Top 200 on October 18 at No. 178, in one week jumped 174 places to No. 4, and went to No. 1 the following week. It stayed at No. 1 for eleven weeks, and was in the Top 30 for thirty-one weeks, the Top 100 for forty-seven weeks and the Top

200 for eighty-three weeks. The album sold five million in America, and was awarded a Gold Disc on October 27, 1969.

Between November 15, 1969 and March 7, 1970, The Beatles had four albums in the charts at the same time: *Abbey Road* 1 - 3; *The Beatles* 79 - 178; *Sgt. Pepper* 101 - 160 and *Magical Mystery Tour* 109 - 190.

Tracks and numbering are the same as British release, as is the sleeve. See page 73 of British section.

66 (185a) SOMETHING
(184a) COME TOGETHER

2654 Apple — October 6, 1969

Something entered the Top 30 on October 18 at No. 20, with *Come Together* entering at No. 23. Separately, *Something* rose to No. 3 and *Come Together* to No. 2, but on November 29 they were combined at No. 1 for one week. (Billboard's policy of charting both sides of a disc separately was discontinued from November, 1969.) The disc was in the Top 30 for sixteen weeks, and sold a million by October 27. Total US sales were around 1,750,000.

It was Allen Klein's decision to release this single in America, and it was only released in Britain following its American success.

67 HEY JUDE

SW 385/SO 385—February 26, 1970

Hey Jude was released with *Abbey Road* still high in the charts, and with the help of a massive advertising campaign, attracted over two million advance orders. It entered the Top 200 at No. 3 on March 21, and peaked at No. 2 for four weeks, staying in the Top 30 for thirteen weeks, the Top 100 for twenty-five weeks and the Top 200 for thirty-three weeks. By March, 1970, it had sold a million, by May, 3.3 million, and eventually 3,750,000. The album sleeve is identical to that of the British sleeve. See page 61 of British section.

A SIDE

36c   CAN'T BUY ME LOVE

44b   I SHOULD HAVE KNOWN BETTER

101a PAPERBACK WRITER

102a **RAIN**

142a **LADY MADONNA**

145a **REVOLUTION**

B SIDE

144a **HEY JUDE**

183a **OLD BROWN SHOE**

181a **DON'T LET ME DOWN**

182a **THE BALLAD OF JOHN AND YOKO**

2764 Apple—March 11, 1970

With this single, The Beatles broke their own record set up by *Hey Jude* and *Get Back* for the highest entry position into the charts. *Hey Jude* and *Get Back* had both debuted at No. 10, while *Let It Be* entered at No. 6, on March 21, ten days after release. It was No. 1 for two weeks, after four weeks in the charts, and stayed in the Top 30 for thirteen weeks. It sold a million within a month, and eventually sales exceeded 1½ million.

2832 Apple—May 11, 1970

This was not released as a single in Britain, but in America entered the Top 100 at No. 35 on May 23, when *Let It Be* was at No. 6. It reached No. 1 on June 13, the first of two weeks at the top, and was in the Top 30 for nine weeks. The single sold 1,200,000 within two days of release.

AR 34001—May 18, 1970

Let It Be achieved the highest initial sale of any album in the history of the American recording industry. Advance orders for the album in the States totalled 3,700,000 representing a gross retail value of nearly 26 million dollars, and it entered the Top 200 on May 30 at No. 104, reaching No. 2 the following week. In its third week it went to No. 1, where it resided for four weeks. It was in the Top 30 for sixteen weeks, the Top 100 for thirty-seven weeks and the Top 200 for fifty-five weeks. The album was awarded a Gold Disc on May 26, 1970, and subsequently sold over three million in the States.

On May 23, The Beatles were at No. 1 (*Let It Be*), No. 32 (*Hey Jude*) and No. 50 (*Abbey Road*) in the US Album charts. On July 25, 1970 they had five albums in the Top 200: No. 2 — *Let It Be*; No. 52 — *Abbey Road*; No. 57 — *Hey Jude*; No. 159 — *Sgt. Pepper* and No. 194 — *Magical Mystery Tour*.

The American release featured a gatefold sleeve, using stills from the film, although the front cover is identical to the British release. See page 80 of British section.

A SIDE

204   **TWO OF US**

205   **DIG A PONY**

206   **ACROSS THE UNIVERSE** (Version 2)

207   **I ME MINE**

208   **DIG IT**

209   **LET IT BE** (Version 2)

210   **MAGGIE MAE**

B SIDE

211   **I'VE GOT A FEELING**

212   **ONE AFTER 909**

213a   **THE LONG AND WINDING ROAD**

214a   **FOR YOU BLUE**

215   **GET BACK** (Version 2)

DO IT NOW: 20 GIANT HITS

LP 1001—February, 1971

The US mail order Do It Now Foundation album distributed by K-Tel. The other well-known artists on this charity album include Neil Diamond, Janis Joplin, Jimi Hendrix, Melanie, Richie Havens, Donovan, Jefferson Airplane, Eric Burdon, The Association, The Byrds, Buffalo Springfield and The Turtles.

A SIDE (Track 1)

90c   **NOWHERE MAN**

71   THE BEATLES 1962 — 1966

SKBO 3403—April 2, 1973

In early 1973, an unauthorised Beatles anthology album titled *The Beatles Alpha Omega* (a four record set distributed by Audio Tape Inc. catalogue No. ATRBH 3583) was released in America, with heavy advertising on radio and television. It was this album which prompted Apple to release the two double albums *The Beatles 1962 - 1966* and *The Beatles 1967 - 1970* in America and Britain.

The two albums appeared in America two weeks prior to the British release. Both albums entered the charts on April 14, the "62 - 66" at No. 94 and the "67 - 70" album at No. 97. The "62 - 66" album rose to No. 3 for two weeks and stayed in the Top 30 for seventeen weeks, the Top 100 for thirty-one weeks and the Top 200 for seventy-seven weeks. It was awarded a Gold Disc on April 13, 1973. The album sleeve is identical to that of the British release. See page 87 of British section.

A SIDE RECORD ONE

10e   **LOVE ME DO**

3i   **PLEASE PLEASE ME**

16e   **FROM ME TO YOU**

18b   **SHE LOVES YOU**

34c   **I WANT TO HOLD YOUR HAND**

22b   **ALL MY LOVING**

36d   **CAN'T BUY ME LOVE**

B SIDE RECORD ONE

42b   **A HARD DAY'S NIGHT**

47c   **AND I LOVE HER**

62b   **EIGHT DAYS A WEEK**

53b   **I FEEL FINE**

69b   **TICKET TO RIDE**

83b   **YESTERDAY**

A SIDE RECORD TWO

(JAMES BOND THEME)

71b   **HELP**

74a   **YOU'VE GOT TO HIDE YOUR LOVE AWAY**

86b   **WE CAN WORK IT OUT**

85b   **DAY TRIPPER**

87a   **DRIVE MY CAR**

88a   **NORWEGIAN WOOD**

B SIDE RECORD TWO

90d   **NOWHERE MAN**

93a   **MICHELLE**

97a   **IN MY LIFE**

95a   **GIRL**

101b   **PAPERBACK WRITER**

103b   **ELEANOR RIGBY**

104c   **YELLOW SUBMARINE**

72   THE BEATLES 1967 — 1970

SKBO 3404—April 2, 1973

This double album was released along with *The Beatles 1962 - 1966* album (see this entry for details of release) and entered the Top 200 on April 14 at No. 97. In its seventh week in the chart it reached No. 1 for one week, and was in the Top 30 for eighteen weeks. It stayed in the Top 100 for forty-four weeks and in the Top 200 for seventy-seven weeks, and was awarded a Gold Disc on April 13, 1973. The album sleeve is identical to that of the British release. See page 88 of British section.

A SIDE RECORD ONE

119b   STRAWBERRY FIELDS FOREVER

118b   PENNY LANE

120a   SGT. PEPPER'S LONELY HEARTS CLUB BAND

121a   WITH A LITTLE HELP FROM MY FRIENDS

122a   LUCY IN THE SKY WITH DIAMONDS

132a   A DAY IN THE LIFE

133c   ALL YOU NEED IS LOVE

B SIDE RECORD ONE

136b   I AM THE WALRUS

135b   HELLO GOODBYE

139a   THE FOOL ON THE HILL

137a   MAGICAL MYSTERY TOUR

142b   LADY MADONNA

144b   HEY JUDE

145b   REVOLUTION

A SIDE RECORD TWO

146a   BACK IN THE USSR

152a   WHILE MY GUITAR GENTLY WEEPS

149a   OB-LA-DI OB-LA-DA

180a   GET BACK

181b   DON'T LET ME DOWN

182b   THE BALLAD OF JOHN AND YOKO

183b   OLD BROWN SHOE

B SIDE RECORD TWO

190a   HERE COMES THE SUN

184b   COME TOGETHER

185b   SOMETHING

188a   OCTOPUS'S GARDEN

202a   LET IT BE

206a   ACROSS THE UNIVERSE

213b   THE LONG AND WINDING ROAD

73   (115a) GOT TO GET YOU INTO MY LIFE
(168a) HELTER SKELTER

4274—May 31, 1976

Interest in The Beatles' *White Album* had been rekindled by the television dramatisation of the Charles Manson murder trials of 1969. The two part film *Helter Skelter*, based on the best selling book by the prosecuting attorneys, Vincent Bugliosi and Curt Gentry, featured several tunes from the *White Album* including *Helter Skelter*. Because of the film's popularity, Capitol rushed radio stations a special limited edition DJ single (P 4274) of *Helter Skelter* on April 30, 1976, but for commercial release relegated *Helter Skelter* to the B side, preferring *Got To Get You Into My Life* as the A side, as they rightly felt that exploiting the Manson case would not be the best way to get a hit single.

And a hit it was. The Beatles' forty-fifth American single entered the Top 30 at No. 27 on June 26. It rose to its highest position, No. 3, on August 7, and stayed in the chart for twelve weeks.

SKBO 11537—June 7, 1976

Rock 'N' Roll Music, The Beatles' twenty-first Capitol album, entered the Billboard Album charts on June 26, 1976, rising to No. 2, and staying there for thirty weeks.

The album was certified Gold (i.e. one million dollars worth of sales) on its day of release, and Platinum (one million copies sold) on June 14, a week after release, by the R.I.A.A.

The American release of the *Rock 'N' Roll Music* double album differs from the British version in that George Martin re-mixed the early material for the re-issue in America. In his book, *All You Need Is Ears*, George Martin explains that when EMI/Capitol decided to release *Rock 'N' Roll Music*, which included some early material, it was discovered that The Beatles had issued an order that the tapes were not to be touched in any way, and that if they were to be re-issued, they must remain exactly as they were recorded. Bhaskar Menon, President of Capitol Records, had phoned George Martin telling him that he was proposing to issue the album using early Beatles material, and asked Martin to approve the tapes, as he was unable to contact any of The Beatles. When Martin heard the tapes he was "appalled", as EMI had taken The Beatles' order literally, and were going to re-master the original two track tapes intended for mono reproduction, into stereo, with potentially disastrous results. George Martin explains that when the original two track tapes were made, one track was used for the rhythm and one for the vocal, with the rhythm track deliberately recorded at low volume to prevent distortion, thus pushing the vocals artificially forward. As the vocals were on a separate track, when the singing stopped a certain amount of "dirt" could be heard as the mikes were left "open" during recording. This hadn't mattered in mono, but when transferred directly into stereo, the result was terrible. George Martin stated his disapproval, but Capitol Records felt unable to alter the tapes in view of the group's instructions. Martin, however, was unwilling to allow the tracks to be released in such a poor condition, so he spent two days re-dubbing the tapes — filtering here, adding echo there, and eventually producing improved versions more to his satisfaction. Even though Martin didn't get paid for re-mixing the tapes, EMI in England were not pleased by his efforts, and it was later quite obvious that the British version of *Rock 'N' Roll Music* was mastered from the untouched original tapes. The album sleeve is identical to that of the British version. See page 90 of British section.

A SIDE RECORD ONE

15h	**TWIST AND SHOUT**
5g	**I SAW HER STANDING THERE**
37c	**YOU CAN'T DO THAT**
30a	**I WANNA BE YOUR MAN**
39a	**I CALL YOUR NAME**
9f	**BOYS**
38a	**LONG TALL SALLY**

B SIDE RECORD ONE

58a	**ROCK AND ROLL MUSIC**
40b	**SLOW DOWN**
61b	**KANSAS CITY/HEY HEY HEY HEY**
33a	**MONEY (THAT'S WHAT I WANT)**
117a	**BAD BOY**
41b	**MATCHBOX**
27c	**ROLL OVER BEETHOVEN**

A SIDE RECORD TWO

84a	**DIZZY MISS LIZZY**
49a	**ANY TIME AT ALL**
87b	**DRIVE MY CAR**
68b	**EVERYBODY'S TRYING TO BE MY BABY**
73a	**THE NIGHT BEFORE**
72a	**I'M DOWN**

145c REVOLUTION

B SIDE RECORD TWO

146b BACK IN THE USSR

168b HELTER SKELTER

105a TAXMAN

115b GOT TO GET YOU INTO MY LIFE

178a HEY BULLDOG

163a BIRTHDAY

215a GET BACK

**75 (149b) OB-LA-DI OB-LA-DA
(162a) JULIA**

4347—November 8, 1976

To continue their million dollar Beatles 1976 revival programme, (which included The Beatles albums advertised on T.V. and Beatles filmstrips shown in record stores), Capitol lifted two tracks from the *White Album* as a single. The "A" side song, *Ob-La-Di Ob-La-Da*, had already proved itself as singles material, charting for two British groups, The Marmalade and The Bedrocks, in 1968, although neither act scored in America with the song. Even so, the single rose to only No. 49 in the Billboard charts, where it stayed for six weeks, thus becoming the first Beatles' Capitol single not to enter the American Top 30.

76 THE BEST OF GEORGE HARRISON

ST 11578—November 8, 1976

The American version of this album had a different sleeve from that of the British release, and, also unlike the British album, entered the charts, making the Billboard album charts for fifteen weeks from November 27, 1976, and rising to No. 31. The album was awarded a Gold Disc on February 15, 1977, by the R.I.A.A.

A SIDE

185c SOMETHING

99a IF I NEEDED SOMEONE

190b HERE COMES THE SUN

152 The Long And Winding Road

105b TAXMAN

91a THINK FOR YOURSELF

214b FOR YOU BLUE

152b WHILE MY GUITAR GENTLY WEEPS

B SIDE

MY SWEET LORD

GIVE ME LOVE (GIVE ME PEACE ON EARTH)

YOU

BANGLA DESH

DARK HORSE

WHAT IS LIFE

77 THE BEATLES AT THE HOLLYWOOD BOWL

SMAS 11638—May 4, 1977

This album entered the Billboard charts on May 21, 1977, for seventeen weeks, rising to No. 2. It was certified Gold on May 5, 1977, one day after release, and Platinum by August 12, 1977.

(Tracks and numbering same as British release, as is the sleeve. See page 95 British section.)

78 LOVE SONGS

SKBL 11711—October 21, 1977

The Beatles' sixth American double album stayed in the Billboard charts for twenty-four weeks, after entering on November 12, 1977, and rising to its highest position of No. 24.

During November 1977, Capitol decided to release a single from *Love Songs* to help boost the poor sales of the re-package. Promotional copies of the selected tracks, *Girl* backed with *You're Going To Lose That Girl* (Capitol 4506) in a picture sleeve, were sent out to radio stations, but at the last minute Capitol withdrew the single. Suggested reasons for the withdrawal are varied, but these include that the choice of songs wasn't strong enough, and that the Wings' single *Girl's School* had just been released on November 14, and Capitol did not want a single, with a similar title, to compete with this release (which was also selling less well than expected.)

Although the album sleeve for the American edition was the same as in Britain, the American version contained a lyric insert. See page 97 British section.

A SIDE RECORD ONE

83c **YESTERDAY**

59a **I'LL FOLLOW THE SUN**

75a **I NEED YOU**

95b **GIRL**

97b **IN MY LIFE**

63a **WORDS OF LOVE**

108a **HERE THERE AND EVERYWHERE**

B SIDE RECORD ONE

185d **SOMETHING**

47d **AND I LOVE HER**

45c **IF I FELL**

52a **I'LL BE BACK**

81a **TELL ME WHAT YOU SEE**

70b **YES IT IS**

A SIDE RECORD TWO

93b **MICHELLE**

79a **IT'S ONLY LOVE**

77a **YOU'RE GOING TO LOSE THAT GIRL**

65a **EVERY LITTLE THING**

112a **FOR NO ONE**

125a **SHE'S LEAVING HOME**

B SIDE RECORD TWO

213c **THE LONG AND WINDING ROAD**

35b **THIS BOY**

88b **NORWEGIAN WOOD**

74b **YOU'VE GOT TO HIDE YOUR LOVE AWAY**

161a **I WILL**

2e **P.S. I LOVE YOU**

79   SGT. PEPPER'S LONELY HEARTS CLUB BAND (picture disc)

SEAX 11840—August, 1978

Capitol Records of America always seemed to be one step ahead of EMI Records in Britain when it came to a viable Beatles re-package (they had taken the lead with both the red and blue double albums of 1973 and the *Rock 'N' Roll Music* double of 1976). With the release of the *Sgt. Pepper's Lonely Hearts Club Band* film, featuring Peter Frampton and the Bee Gees, Capitol immediately attempted to stimulate sales of the Beatles' original album, helped by the extra interest that the film would inevitably provoke. However, rather than leaving the punters to purchase the original album, which had by this time sold well over three million copies in the States, Capitol used the very popular ploy of a picture disc release. As the cover design for *Sgt. Pepper* was such an innovation when it had originally appeared, and had since become regarded as not only the classic album sleeve, but also as a contemporary work of art, it was the ideal album to use in this particular disc medium. The "A" side of the disc illustrates the front cover of the original album, with a blow-up of the *Sgt. Pepper* drum pictured on the "B" side. The album sleeve is designed in a completely different way from the original album, highlighting the picture disc which appears in the large circular hole in the front of the sleeve. Unfortunately the very impressive packaging did not attract enough buyers to qualify for a place in the American Top 30.

Up to 1980, the *Sgt. Pepper* film was the eighth highest grossing rock film in America and Canada, with a total of nearly 13,000,000 dollars theatre rentals. Despite its popularity with the public, it did not fare as well with the critics and is generally regarded as one of the worst "rock" films ever made.

(Tracks and numbering same as original release.)

| 80 | THE BEATLES (white vinyl) |

SEBX 11841—August, 1978

| 81 | THE BEATLES 1962 — 1966 (red vinyl) |

SEBX 11842—August, 1978

| 82 | THE BEATLES 1967—1970 (blue vinyl) |

SEBX 11843—August, 1978

These three double albums are straight re-releases of the original albums, but in appropriate coloured vinyls. The original *The Beatles* double album had over the years become known simply as the "White Album", so it was an obvious marketing ploy to produce it in white vinyl. Likewise, the two 1973 double albums, the sleeves of which were predominantly red and blue, were pressed in the appropriate coloured vinyl to match the sleeves.

All Capitol's coloured vinyl and picture disc releases were limited to pressings of 150,000 copies.

(Tracks and numbering same as original releases.)

| 83 | (120b) SGT. PEPPER'S LONELY HEARTS CLUB BAND (121b) WITH A LITTLE HELP FROM MY FRIENDS (132b) A DAY IN THE LIFE |

4612—August 14, 1978

Along with EMI Records in Britain, Capitol released this, the first single from the *Sgt. Pepper* album, which managed only seven weeks in the Billboard chart, rising to No. 71.

| 84 | ABBEY ROAD (picture disc) |

SEAX 11900—December, 1978

The second American Beatles picture disc featured the *Abbey Road* album, and again Capitol's designers excelled themselves, featuring the front and back of the original album sleeve on the "A" and "B" sides of the disc respectively, with a sleeve design which further enhanced the package. As with the *Sgt. Pepper* picture disc, it did not enter the American Top 30 album chart.

(Tracks and numbering same as original release.)

| 85 | THE BEATLES COLLECTION |

December, 1978

With EMI in Britain releasing *The Beatles Collection* of all twelve UK albums, Capitol released this very limited Limited Edition de luxe boxed set also containing the Beatles original British releases. Instead of the British bonus album of rarities, Capitol added their own version of the release (Capitol SPRO — 8969) which was identical to the British album (PSLP 261), although instead of the German versions of *She Loves You* and *I Want To Hold Your Hand*, Capitol substituted the English versions of these songs. As with the

British release, the *Rarities* album in the American set was to be exclusively available in the limited edition boxed set, and was issued in a paper sleeve: other countries issuing *The Beatles Collection* supplied the album in a conventional cardboard sleeve.

The boxed set was limited to 3,000 numbered copies (selling at $132.98), but an extra fifty sets were distributed to Capitol executives and record industry VIPs as Christmas gifts. The thirteen albums were presented in a box identical to that containing the British set, and included the following albums (see appropriate album releases in British section for sleeves):

RECORD ONE — PLEASE PLEASE ME PCS 3042

A SIDE

5h   I SAW HER STANDING THERE

6f   MISERY

7f   ANNA (GO TO HIM)

8e   CHAINS

9g   BOYS

4g   ASK ME WHY

3j   PLEASE PLEASE ME

B SIDE

10f   LOVE ME DO

2f   P.S. I LOVE YOU

11e   BABY IT'S YOU

12h   DO YOU WANT TO KNOW A SECRET

13f   A TASTE OF HONEY

14g   THERE'S A PLACE

15i   TWIST AND SHOUT

RECORD TWO — WITH THE BEATLES PCS 3045

A SIDE

20a   IT WON'T BE LONG

21a   ALL I'VE GOT TO DO

22c   ALL MY LOVING

23a   DON'T BOTHER ME

24a   LITTLE CHILD

25a   TILL THERE WAS YOU

26b   PLEASE MR. POSTMAN

B SIDE

27d   ROLL OVER BEETHOVEN

28a   HOLD ME TIGHT

29a   YOU REALLY GOT A HOLD ON ME

30b   I WANNA BE YOUR MAN

31a   DEVIL IN HER HEART

32a   NOT A SECOND TIME

33b   MONEY (THAT'S WHAT I WANT)

RECORD THREE — A HARD DAY'S NIGHT PCS 3058

A SIDE

42c   A HARD DAY'S NIGHT

44c   I SHOULD HAVE KNOWN BETTER

45d   IF I FELL

46c   I'M HAPPY JUST TO DANCE WITH YOU

47e   AND I LOVE HER

48b   TELL ME WHY

36e   CAN'T BUY ME LOVE

B SIDE

49b   ANY TIME AT ALL

50c   I'LL CRY INSTEAD

43a   THINGS WE SAID TODAY

51a   WHEN I GET HOME

37a   YOU CAN'T DO THAT

52b   I'LL BE BACK

RECORD FOUR — BEATLES FOR SALE PCS 3062

111a AND YOUR BIRD CAN SING

112b FOR NO ONE

113a DR. ROBERT

114a I WANT TO TELL YOU

115c GOT TO GET YOU INTO MY LIFE

116a TOMORROW NEVER KNOWS

RECORD EIGHT — SGT. PEPPER'S LONELY HEARTS CLUB BAND PCS 7027
(Tracks and numbering same as original release.)

RECORD NINE — THE BEATLES PCS 7067-7068
(Tracks and numbering same as original release.)

RECORD TEN — YELLOW SUBMARINE PCS 7070
(Tracks and numbering same as original release.)

RECORD ELEVEN — ABBEY ROAD PCS 7088
(Tracks and numbering same as original release.)

RECORD TWELVE — LET IT BE PCS 7096
(Tracks and numbering same as original release.)

RECORD THIRTEEN — THE BEATLES "RARITIES" Capitol SPRO 8969

A SIDE

201 ACROSS THE UNIVERSE
The first appearance of the original version of *Across The Universe* on an American album. The song was originally donated to the World Wildlife Fund for inclusion on their UK only release, *No One's Gonna Change Our World*. (See British section.)

70 YES IT IS
Originally the "B" side to *Ticket To Ride* in both Britain and America, it also appeared on the American album *Beatles VI* in 1965, as well as the *Love Songs* double LP compilation of 1977.

35c THIS BOY
In Britain, the "B" side to *I Want To Hold Your Hand*; in America the song originally appeared on their first Capitol album, *Meet The Beatles* — the American coupling for *I Want To Hold Your Hand* being *I Saw Her Standing There*. *This Boy* also appeared on the 1977 double album, *Love Songs*.

143a THE INNER LIGHT
The first appearance on album of George's *The Inner Light* in America, where — as in Britain — it originally appeared as the "B" side to *Lady Madonna*.

19c I'LL GET YOU
In America, as in Britain, *I'll Get You* was the "B" side to *She Loves You*; it also appeared on the American LP, *The Beatles Second Album*, in 1964.

17f THANK YOU GIRL
Originally the coupling for the *From Me To You* single on the Vee Jay label in 1963, it also appeared on their 1964 album, *Jolly What! The Beatles and Frank Ifield On Stage*. Its second appearance on single as the "B" side to *Do You Want To Know A Secret* on the Vee Jay label in 1964 was followed by two reissues of the same single on the Oldies label, and later by Capitol on its Starline label. This is the first appearance of the song on a Capitol album.

34d I WANT TO HOLD YOUR HAND
This is the third appearance on album in America of the first Capitol single, the one which opened up the US charts to the Beatles and the English invasion that followed.

203a YOU KNOW MY NAME (LOOK UP THE NUMBER)
Appearing on an American album for the first time, this song was originally released as the "B" side of *Let It Be* in both Britain and America.

18c SHE LOVES YOU
The song appeared originally on the Swan label as a single in 1963, and was first released by Capitol on *The Beatles Second Album* in 1964. Its second album appearance was in 1973 on the *1962 — 1966* double album, and it appears on this album for the third time in LP form.

B SIDE

102b RAIN
The "B" side to *Paperback Writer*, this song was released on album in America in 1970 on the *Hey Jude*

compilation (this appearance being its second on album).

54b   SHE'S A WOMAN
As with the British release, *She's A Woman* backed *I Feel Fine* as a single in America in 1964; it later appeared on the Capitol album, *Beatles '65*, in 1964. This LP marks its second appearance on album.

41c   MATCHBOX
This track originally appeared on the Capitol album, *Something New*, and was later coupled as a single with *Slow Down* (in 1964). Its second album appearance was in 1976 on the *Rock'n'Roll Music* double album.

39b   I CALL YOUR NAME
Originally included on the 1964 album *The Beatles Second Album*, and later on the *Rock'n'Roll Music* double album of 1976, this appearance becomes its third on an American album.

117b   BAD BOY
In Britain this song was hidden away on the 1966 album *A Collection of Beatles Oldies*; in America it had appeared over a year earlier on the 1965 album, *Beatles VI*. Its second appearance was in 1976 on the *Rock'n'Roll Music* double album; this is its third inclusion on an American LP.

40c   SLOW DOWN
Originally appearing on the 1964 Capitol album, *Something New*, this song was coupled with *Matchbox* as a single later the same year. Included on the 1976 double album, *Rock'n'Roll Music*, this is its third album appearance.

72b   I'M DOWN
The "B" side to the 1965 single, *Help!*, it was not included on an album until 1976 (when it appeared on the double album *Rock'n'Roll Music*). This is its second appearance on album in America.

38b   LONG TALL SALLY
The third appearance on album in America of *Long Tall Sally*; it first appeared on the 1964 release, *The Beatles Second Album*, and later on the 1976 double album *Rock'n'Roll Music*.

As can be seen from the number of previous appearances of each song on other American albums, this package did not present a true collection of American Beatles rarities (as did the equivalent British album for the British market). The British album presented six single "B" sides which had not previously appeared on album in Britain; this American version presented only two "B" sides not previously available on album in America. The British album also featured two previously unreleased recordings with *Komm, Gib Mir Deine Hand* and *Sie Liebt Dich*, while the US album included only one song previously unreleased in America, *Across The Universe*.

86   LET IT BE

Capitol SW 11922—March, 1979

Both *Let It Be* and *A Hard Day's Night* soundtrack albums had been distributed in the US by United Artists; *Let It Be* had been out of print for several years, until Capitol reissued it on their own label (though the re-release was not packaged in a gatefold sleeve as the original had been). (Tracks and numbering same as original release.)

87   ABBEY ROAD

Mobile Fidelity/Capitol MFSL 1-023— December 28, 1979

This release of the *Abbey Road* album by Mobile Fidelity Sound Laboratory, in conjunction with Capitol, was in the MFSL "Original Half-Speed Master Recording" series, which guaranteed exceptionally high fidelity sound by using Capitol's own sub-master of the album. (Ideally the original master tape should have been used, but this was obviously unobtainable, as it is kept by EMI in London.) Using their exclusive half-speed mastering technique, MFSL produced a top quality master which was sent to Japan, where discs were custom pressed using the highest quality vinyl in a limited edition of 200,000. Such careful preparation requires equally sophisticated protection, which comes in the shape of three forms of packaging: a static-free inner sleeve, a heavy duty cardboard sleeve and an extra thick album jacket. (Tracks and numbering same as original American release.)

SHAL 12060–March 24, 1980

When Capitol released their limited edition, *The Beatles Collection*, in December 1978, it was clearly stated that the extra album, *Rarities* (SPRO 8969), would not be available separately. However, during 1979 Capitol announced that the *Rarities* album would be released on their budget line series in November 1979. The company started pressing the album (SN 12009) in October, but an interesting situation arose with the appearance (supposedly in the summer of 1979) of another apparently official Capitol album of rarities with the title *Collectors Items*.

The story behind this album (catalogue number SPRO 9462) was that Capitol had originally scheduled the package of "rare" Beatles tracks for 1979, with a track listing on side one of: *Love Me Do* (the original recording with Ringo on drums), *From Me To You, Thank You Girl, All My Loving* (with hi hat introduction), *This Boy* (which had never been released in true stereo in the US), *Sie Liebt Dich, I Feel Fine, She's A Woman* (never before released in true stereo in the US), *Help!* and *I'm Down* (supposedly never before available in stereo in the US). And, on side two, *Penny Lane* (the promo version), *Baby, You're A Rich Man* (again never previously available in stereo in US), *I Am The Walrus, The Inner Light, Across The Universe* and *You Know My Name (Look Up The Number)*.

However, after Capitol realized that *I'm Down* had already been released in stereo on the *Rock'n'Roll Music* double album, this track was replaced by a different stereo mix of *Paperback Writer* (and the catalogue number for the album changed to SPRO 9463). Copies of both albums were supposedly manufactured by Capitol, but then came another change of plan from Capitol management — and the *Collectors Items* LP was scrapped altogether. Although Capitol ordered that all copies of the *Collectors Items* LP be destroyed, the albums found their way into the hands of the public; "bootleg" versions of both albums are available (SPRO 9462: *I'm Down*, and SPRO 9463: *Paperback Writer*).

The front covers of both albums show a selection of Beatles memorabilia, while the back covers show Beatles records available on Capitol Records (out of order on the first album, but in chronological release order on the second version). Whether these two albums were originally Capitol ventures or just compilations put together by bootleggers is difficult to say. The budget line *Rarities* album, however, was eventually scrapped, and the revised *Rarities* album (SHAL 12060) prepared, including several tracks that appeared on the *Collectors Items* albums.

The story of Capitol's *Rarities* albums is further complicated by the appearance of another bootleg Capitol album called *Casualties*; this album, like the bootlegged *Collectors Items* albums, has an authentic and well-produced sleeve, with a Capitol logo and credits as well as the legend "for promotional use only — not for sale". The track listing for this album on the first side is: *Please Please Me, I Want To Hold Your Hand, Money, A Hard Day's Night, I'll Cry Instead, Ticket To Ride, Yes It Is, Day Tripper* and *I'm Only Sleeping*; with *Strawberry Fields Forever, I Am The Walrus* (which is the backing track only, featuring the Beatles singing and playing only, i.e. with no special sound effects and orchestral accompaniment), *Only A Northern Song, Revolution, Her Majesty* and *Let It Be* on the second side. Most of the recordings are different stereo or mono mixes from the originally released versions. The sleeve note on the album states:

"Capitol Records proudly presents another collection of 'oddities', unfamiliar versions of well-known Beatles' tunes. None of these tracks have previously appeared on a Capitol album. Most have been issued by EMI in foreign countries. Some have appeared on U.S. singles. Also included are three previously unreleased recordings. So sit back, relax and enjoy the timeless music of the Beatles, the most phenomenal group in entertainment history."

This album, catalogue number SPRO — 9469 (Capitol's promotional series), was produced in 1980, probably after the *Rarities* release; only the record company can say whether it is another aborted Capitol release.

Capitol's decision not to release the British "boxed" version of the *Rarities* album was a wise one: in

America few of the early Beatles' records were identical to corresponding British releases, and many of the so-called "rarities" in Britain were already available on American albums. Therefore the revised *Rarities* album was compiled using rare recordings which would appeal to the American market; the package also boasted an excellent sleeve design (containing a reproduction of the notorious "Butcher sleeve"), as well as many other previously unpublished pictures of the Beatles. The album was compiled by Randall Davis, who also supplied the very interesting sleeve notes, with research by Ron Furmanek and Walter Podrazik.

For the ardent American Beatles fan, the tracks on the album presented many previously unavailable recordings, although some items merely boasted different stereo mixes, and were therefore not actually different recordings. Many American releases of Beatles songs differ from British versions in the mixing and stereo separation, which came about due to the original method by which the Americans assembled a Beatles record: the original multi-tracked master tapes recorded in England were sent to Capitol, who would then transfer them to the two track stereo master required for the production of a record, almost inevitably achieving a different balance and stereo separation from the British release. This can be illustrated by an incident which occurred in late 1968, when George Harrison was in Los Angeles producing tracks for the Jackie Lomax album, *Is This What You Want*. George happened to hear Capitol's master record for the yet to be released album *The Beatles* (The White Album) and immediately realised that it had been mixed incorrectly, thus altering half of the effects originally recorded by the Beatles in England. If George had not worked on the tapes himself to correct Capitol's error, the American "White Album" would have sounded greatly different to the British release. *Rarities* entered the Billboard album charts on April 12, 1980, rising to No. 21. It became the Beatles twenty-fifth Top 30 American album, and stayed in the Top 200 for fifteen weeks.

A SIDE

1   **LOVE ME DO**
This was the first time this version of *Love Me Do* had appeared on record in America, as it is the original recording, with Ringo on drums, which appeared on the first British single. In America the second version of the song, with Andy White on drums and Ringo relegated to maracas, was used for all releases prior to *Rarities*. This *Rarities* track was remastered from a record, as the original master tape for the song had disappeared.

6g   **MISERY**
Misery originally appeared in America on the Vee Jay album, *Introducing The Beatles* and later on a Vee Jay E.P. (*Souvenir Of Their Visit To America*) and two Vee Jay albums (*The Beatles Versus The Four Seasons* and *Songs, Pictures And Stories Of The Fabulous Beatles*). When Capitol Records took over the floundering Vee Jay label in 1965, *Misery* was released on a Starline label single with *Roll Over Beethoven*, but they failed to include it on the album *The Early Beatles*, which was a re-vamp of the original Vee Jay album *Introducing The Beatles*. Capitol had never released the song on an album, and therefore no Capitol stereo version existed before the release of *Rarities*.

The song did appear in stereo on the *Please Please Me* UK Parlophone album included in the Capitol boxed set *The Beatles Collection* of 1978.

14h   THERE'S A PLACE
This song has a similar history to that of *Misery*, first appearing on the *Introducing The Beatles* Vee Jay album, and later as the coupling for *Twist And Shout* as a single, plus two more album appearances on *The Beatles Versus The Four Seasons* and *Songs, Pictures And Stories Of The Fabulous Beatles*. Capitol included it in the Starline singles series, again as the "B" side to *Twist And Shout*, but it had never previously appeared in stereo on an album.

a Capitol album, although appearing in stereo on the *Please Please Me* UK Parlophone album — included in the Capitol boxed set *The Beatles Collection* of 1978.

230a   SIE LIEBT DICH
This German version of *She Loves You* originally appeared in America on a Swan label single, but had never before been available on an album in stereo.

47c   AND I LOVE HER
The original American version of this song on the United Artists album *A Hard Day's Night* and the Capitol *Something New* album was mixed differently from the British and European versions. The vocal on the original British version on the *A Hard Day's Night* album features Paul, mainly double tracked and singing solo only in places, whereas the American version is the opposite, with Paul's vocal mainly solo, and double tracked only in places. The song on the German version of the *Something New* album is similar to the British version, except that the guitar riff at the end of the song is repeated six times, instead of four, and it is this German version that appears on the *Rarities* album.

71c   HELP!
Apparently the American album version of *Help!* differs from the American singles version, due to a different lead vocal, which is rarer, and is therefore included on the *Rarities* album, using a cleaner British version.

106a   I'M ONLY SLEEPING
The record sleeve states that there are two different stereo mixes of this song, the British and American versions, the British version differing from the

American due to the verses being re-arranged and "strange" guitar sounds inserted. This is an example of the Americans mixing the original master tapes differently to the correct British versions. The British version is included on the *Rarities* album.

136c   I AM THE WALRUS
With this song, Capitol have deliberately produced another version of the song by editing two previous versions together — the Capitol singles version, containing a few extra beats in the middle of the song, is combined with the English version, which has the intro riff repeated six times instead of four.

B SIDE

118c   PENNY LANE
When *Penny Lane* was originally scheduled for release in the States, promotional copies were pressed for distribution to radio stations, but this version of the song was different from the later commercial release, having an added horn riff towards the end of the song. The promotional single was in mono, and as no true stereo version had ever been released in the States, Capitol dubbed the extra horn riff onto a stereo version for inclusion on the *Rarities* album.

168c   HELTER SKELTER
In America the "White Album" was available in stereo only, but it was released in both mono and stereo in Britain, and it seems that the Beatles and George Martin made a different mix for the two versions, as there are considerable differences between the two on many tracks on the album. The mono version of *Helter Skelter* differs from the stereo, in that the vocals are more pronounced, with laughter at the beginning and "beeping" sounds heard throughout. The drumming at the end of the song is different, and there is no fade out and in when the song ends, and therefore the statement "I got blisters on my fingers" cannot be heard. It is this mono version that is included on the *Rarities* album.

159a   DON'T PASS ME BY
This mono version of *Don't Pass Me By* from the "White Album", differs from the stereo version in the changes in the violin and vocal sounds, with Ringo's voice seemingly at a higher pitch than on the stereo version.

143b THE INNER LIGHT

The second album appearance of George's *The Inner Light* in America, where — as in Britain — it originally appeared on the "B" side of *Lady Madonna*, as well as on the *Rarities* album included with *The Beatles Collection*. It appears here in mono; a stereo version does exist, even though the album sleeve notes state otherwise — it appeared on a bonus EP included in the British release of 1981, *The Beatles EPs Collection*.

201a ACROSS THE UNIVERSE

To the majority of the American market, this was probably the most interesting track on the album; it had previously only been available on the very limited edition *The Beatles Collection* of 1978, appearing here for the second time on album. This is the original recording of the song donated to the World Wildlife Fund for inclusion in their UK only release, *No One's Gonna Change Our World* (see British section). According to the *Rarities* sleeve notes, Phil Spector doctored this first recording of the song to produce the *Let It Be* version, but this is incorrect: John re-recorded the song in January 1969 for the original *Get Back* album, and it was this version that Spector used for inclusion on the *Let It Be* album. This version and the *Let It Be* version are two completely different recordings. The first was recorded in February 1968, the latter in January 1969 during the *Let It Be* film rehearsals.

203b YOU KNOW MY NAME (LOOK UP THE NUMBER)

The second album appearance for the "B" side to *Let It Be*, but only in mono, like all previous releases.

SGT. PEPPER INNER GROOVE

These two seconds of Beatles gibberish are from the inner groove of the British *Sgt. Pepper* album, and never appeared on the American version of that release. (See British *Sgt. Pepper* album.)

89   A HARD DAY'S NIGHT

SW 11921—August, 1980

As with *Let It Be*, this album had originally been distributed by United Artists; Capitol were scheduled to re-

release it in March 1979 at the same time as the *Let It Be* album, but legal difficulties caused a delay and it finally appeared in August 1980. (Sleeve design, tracks and numbering same as original release.)

90   ROCK'N'ROLL MUSIC VOLUME I

SN 16020—October, 1980

Like EMI in Britain, Capitol Records deleted the original double album, *Rock'n'Roll Music* of 1976, and replaced it with two single albums on their budget label. The albums differ from the British release, having a slightly altered sleeve design.

A SIDE

15j   **TWIST AND SHOUT**

5i   **I SAW HER STANDING THERE**

37e   **YOU CAN'T DO THAT**

30c   **I WANNA BE YOUR MAN**

39c   **I CALL YOUR NAME**

9h   **BOYS**

38c   **LONG TALL SALLY**

B SIDE

58c   **ROCK'N'ROLL MUSIC**

40d   **SLOW DOWN**

61d   **KANSAS CITY/HEY HEY HEY HEY**

33c   **MONEY (THAT'S WHAT I WANT)**

117c   **BAD BOY**

41d MATCHBOX

27e ROLL OVER BEETHOVEN

91 ROCK'N'ROLL MUSIC VOLUME 2

SN 16021—October, 1980

(See *Rock'n'Roll Music Volume 1*.)

A SIDE

84c DIZZY MISS LIZZY

49c ANY TIME AT ALL

87d DRIVE MY CAR

68d EVERYBODY'S TRYING TO BE MY BABY

73c THE NIGHT BEFORE

72c I'M DOWN

145d REVOLUTION

B SIDE

146c BACK IN THE USSR

168d HELTER SKELTER

105d TAXMAN

115d GOT TO GET YOU INTO MY LIFE

178b HEY BULLDOG

163h BIRTHDAY

215b GET BACK

92 MAGICAL MYSTERY TOUR

Mobile Fidelity/Capitol MFSL 1-047— January 30, 1981

This was the second Beatles album to be released in the "Half-Speed Master Series" by Mobile Fidelity Sound Laboratory. Again, the original master tape could not be used, so Capitol supplied the manufacturers with their sub-master tape, which contained three tracks (*Penny Lane, All You Need Is Love* and *Baby You're A Rich Man*) in re-processed stereo. (Tracks and numbering same as original American release.)

93 (34e) I WANT TO HOLD YOUR HAND
(5j) I SAW HER STANDING THERE

A-6278 Capitol Starline—November 30, 1981

94 (36f) CAN'T BUY ME LOVE
(37f) YOU CAN'T DO THAT

A-6279 Capitol Starline—November 30, 1981

95 (42d) A HARD DAY'S NIGHT
(44d) I SHOULD HAVE KNOWN BETTER

A-6281 Capitol Starline — November 30, 1981

96 (50d) I'LL CRY INSTEAD
(46d) I'M HAPPY JUST TO DANCE WITH YOU

A-6282 Capitol Starline — November 30, 1981

97 (47g) AND I LOVE HER
(45e) IF I FELL

A-6283 Capitol Starline—November 30, 1981

98 (41e) MATCHBOX
(40e) SLOW DOWN

A-6284 Capitol Starline—November 30, 1981

99 (53c) I FEEL FINE
(54c) SHE'S A WOMAN

A-6286 Capitol Starline—November 30, 1981

100 (62d) EIGHT DAYS A WEEK
(66c) I DON'T WANT TO SPOIL THE PARTY

A-6287 Capitol Starline—November 30, 1981

101 (69d) TICKET TO RIDE
(70d) YES IT IS

A-6288 Capitol Starline—November 30, 1981

102 (71e) HELP!
(72d) I'M DOWN

A-6290 Capitol Starline—November 30, 1981

103 **(83e) YESTERDAY**
(78c) ACT NATURALLY

A-6291 Capitol Starline—November 30, 1981

104 **(86c) WE CAN WORK IT OUT**
(85c) DAY TRIPPER

A-6293 Capitol Starline—November 30, 1981

105 **(90f) NOWHERE MAN**
(94c) WHAT GOES ON

A-6294 Capitol Starline—November 30, 1981

106 **(101c) PAPERBACK WRITER**
(102c) RAIN

A-6296 Capitol Starline—November 30, 1981

107 **(104e) YELLOW SUBMARINE**
(103d) ELEANOR RIGBY

A-6297 Capitol Starline — November 30, 1981

108 **(118d) PENNY LANE**
(119c) STRAWBERRY FIELDS FOREVER

A-6299 Capitol Starline—November 30, 1981

109 **(133d) ALL YOU NEED IS LOVE**
(134b) BABY YOU'RE A RICH MAN

A-6300 Capitol Starline—November 30, 1981

In 1965 Capitol re-released six singles on the Starline label; 1981 saw the reissue of Capitol's first seventeen Beatles' singles on this label (thus deleting the original Capitol releases). The singles were originally scheduled to appear on August 31, but were held up on account of problems at the pressing plant; they did not appear until November 1981. None of the reissues appeared in the picture sleeves sported by the original releases, but came enclosed in special "Starline" bags.

110 **THE BEATLES**

Mobile Fidelity/Capitol MFSL 2-072— January 7, 1982

Mobile Fidelity's third Beatles "Half-Speed Master" recording.

(Tracks and numbering same as original American release.)

111 **(231) THE BEATLES MOVIE MEDLEY**
(46e) I'M HAPPY JUST TO DANCE WITH YOU

B-5107—March 22, 1982

Due to the popularity of the imitation Beatles' medley singles by Star Sound in 1981, Capitol put together this single using tracks from the *Reel Music* album, (released simultaneously with the single). The seven tracks were edited together by John Palladino. The single was originally scheduled for release on March 15, 1982, with a "B" side featuring an interview recorded during the filming of *A Hard Day's Night* called "Fab Four On Film".

Promotional copies of the single (B-5100) in this format, with an appropriate picture sleeve, were sent out to radio stations; however, due to legal difficulties, the "B" side interview had to be substituted with *I'm Happy Just To Dance With You* for the commercial release — held up until a week later due to this problem.

The single entered the Billboard Hot Hundred on April 3, 1982, at No. 50, rising to its highest position on May 8, at No. 12, where it remained for three weeks. It featured in the Top 60 for nine weeks.

(See British release for tracks included in medley and sleeve.)

112 **REEL MUSIC**

SV-12199—March 22, 1982

Another compilation that originated from Capitol Records. (See British release.) With an extensive promotional campaign from Capitol, the album entered the Billboard album charts on April 10, 1982, at No. 40, rising to No. 19 — its highest position — on May 8. It stayed at No. 19 for three weeks, and remained in the Top 60 album chart for eight weeks.

A SIDE

42e	A HARD DAY'S NIGHT
44e	I SHOULD HAVE KNOWN BETTER
36g	CAN'T BUY ME LOVE
47h	AND I LOVE HER
71f	HELP!
74d	YOU'VE GOT TO HIDE YOUR LOVE AWAY
69e	TICKET TO RIDE
137b	MAGICAL MYSTERY TOUR

B SIDE

136d	I AM THE WALRUS
104f	YELLOW SUBMARINE
133e	ALL YOU NEED IS LOVE
209a	LET IT BE
215d	GET BACK
213d	THE LONG AND WINDING ROAD

113   20 GREATEST HITS

– SV-12245—October, 1982

In America Capitol compiled their own *20 Greatest Hits* album, as the Beatles' American No. 1's differed slightly from their British chart toppers. The Beatles had twenty No. 1 hits in the US, while in Britain only seventeen hit the top spot. The American charts of the sixties charted both sides of a record independently, and many Beatles' singles appeared in the Billboard charts in this manner. This resulted in the individual sides of a double "A"-sided single reaching different positions in the chart (*We Can Work It Out*, for instance, got to No. 1, while *Day Tripper* only reached No. 5). In Britain, both sides of a double "A" sider were counted as chart toppers when the single reached No. 1.

With the Capitol *20 Greatest Hits*, all twenty singles reached the No. 1 position; all were American million sellers, with *She Loves You*, *Can't Buy Me Love* and *Get Back* selling three million, *Hey Jude* over four million, and *I Want To Hold Your Hand* a staggering five million, making a grand total of over thirty-six million in the US. Collectively, the singles were at No. 1 for a total of fifty-nine weeks, with *Can't Buy Me Love* and *Get Back* topping the chart for five weeks each, *I Want To Hold Your Hand* for seven weeks and *Hey Jude* for a marathon nine weeks.

As from *A Hard Day's Night*, Capitol placed the singles in American release order; the previous four tracks, however, do not conform to any discernible order — neither release order, chronological order of date to No. 1 or recording order. Although the singles were released as follows: *She Loves You* (September 26, 1963), *I Want To Hold Your Hand* (January 13, 1964), *Can't Buy Me Love* (March 16, 1964), and *Love Me Do* (April 27, 1964), they did not reach the No. 1 position in the same order. *I Want To Hold Your Hand* went to No. 1 first on February 1, 1964, followed by *She Loves You* on March 21, 1964, *Can't Buy Me Love* on April 4, 1964, and *Love Me Do* on May 30, 1964. Thus, Capitol's order for these first four songs seems rather baffling.

The album had a similar sleeve design to the British release, with the same printed inner sleeve.

A SIDE

18d	SHE LOVES YOU
10g	LOVE ME DO
34f	I WANT TO HOLD YOUR HAND
36h	CAN'T BUY ME LOVE
42f	A HARD DAY'S NIGHT
53d	I FEEL FINE
62e	EIGHT DAYS A WEEK
69f	TICKET TO RIDE

71g   HELP!

83f   YESTERDAY

86d   WE CAN WORK IT OUT

101d PAPERBACK WRITER

     B SIDE

118e PENNY LANE

133f ALL YOU NEED IS LOVE

135c HELLO GOODBYE

144c HEY JUDE

This is the first appearance in America of *Hey Jude* in edited form (the song was shortened by two minutes to run for just over five minutes). The track has not yet been released in this abbreviated form in Britain.

180b GET BACK

184c COME TOGETHER

202b LET IT BE

213e THE LONG AND WINDING ROAD

114   THE BEATLES/THE COLLECTION

(Original Master Recordings™)*

(No special package number)— Mobile Fidelity Sound Lab—1982

During January 1982, Mobile Fidelity Sound Lab released their third half-speed master Beatles' album — *The Beatles* (White Album), preceded by *Abbey Road* in 1979 and *Magical Mystery Tour* in 1981. With this fourteen album half-speed master collection, retailing at $325, Mobile Fidelity produced what must be one of the most extravagant and expensive pop music packages ever. The set comprised all twelve original British albums, plus the *Magical Mystery Tour* release, together with a forty page full colour booklet and an instrument for the precision alignment of the cartridge on a transcription deck — all beautifully housed in a large black case.

After releasing the three Beatles' individual *Original Master Recordings,* reactions from the public convinced Mobile Fidelity to produce this limited edition collection of the Beatles' British albums. To produce each album, Mobile Fidelity borrowed the "original master tapes" from Abbey Road Studios to cut the master lacquer discs. Normal master discs are cut at 33⅓ rpm, using a second or third generation tape; for the *Original Master Recordings* the disc is cut at half speed, thus allowing twice as much time for the master disc cutting system to capture every detail from the original tapes. The master lacquer disc is flown to The Victor Company Of Japan (JVC), where the various procedures for record pressing are undertaken using the strictest quality control conditions to produce a limited number of records.

The records are not pressed on ordinary vinyl, but use an exclusive "Super Vinyl", which is heavier, harder and purer than ordinary vinyl, and lasts much longer. Ordinary inner paper sleeves are also not used (the super quality vinyl deserves better protection). Each record is inserted into a special rice paper sleeve with anti-static and anti-abrasive qualities. The record and inner sleeve are then enclosed in a re-enforced stiff insert folder, which in turn is then housed in the outer sleeve.

The fourteen albums, stored in the specially partitioned case, feature completely new sleeve designs, supposedly depicting the original master tapes for each album. Each picture shows the tape as well as the tin container box; a label on the box shows various details concerning each tape. From these labels it can be ascertained that not all of the tapes used were the "original master tapes" for each album; some are marked as being re-mix tapes from the original four track recordings. The albums cut from the original master tapes are: *Please Please Me, With The Beatles, A Hard Day's Night, Revolver* and *The Beatles.* Those cut using a re-mix from the original four track recordings are: *Beatles For Sale, Rubber Soul, Sgt. Pepper* and *Yellow Submarine. Help!* and *Abbey Road* are marked as merely "re-mix tapes"; *Magical Mystery Tour* is a "copy tape" and *Let It Be* a "corrected copy tape".

Also marked on each label are the dates when each tape was removed and returned to its box, and the reason for its removal (many different countries are listed, such as Brazil, Portugal, Yugoslavia, Egypt, Sweden and Guatemala!, along with other operations: "Stereo master remake", "Mast/Lac"(meaning "master lacquer"), "Copy for Apple", "Quad Remix", "Safety Copy" and "Re-cutting", etc.). Close inspection and comparisons of each cover also reveals that the same tape was photographed for each sleeve picture — identical marks can be seen on the spools, moreover each tape has eight tracks, a white leader tape separating each apparent recording. So the tapes depicted on each sleeve are not the original tapes for that particular album. Further scrutiny reveals that although the lid for each tape container is different, the bottom parts of each tin are not, indicating that only three bottoms were used: one for *Please Please Me, With The Beatles, A Hard Day's Night, Beatles For Sale, Sgt. Pepper* and *The Beatles*, a second for *Help!, Rubber Soul, Revolver, Yellow Submarine* and *Let It Be*, and a third for *Abbey Road* and *Magical Mystery Tour*. Why Mobile Fidelity resorted to this seemingly rather expensive and cunning deception is not known.

The colour booklet includes reproductions of the original British album sleeve, and an explanation of the "Original Master Recordings™"* technique. On the inside front cover of the booklet a "Certificate Of Authenticity" appears, proclaiming that the set is one of a limited number, and contains a handwritten "Limited Edition Number" (mine is 9756). The "Geo-Disc™"* instrument is a twelve-inch plastic platter, used to adjust and re-set the stylus and cartridge of a transcription deck (to a claimed accuracy of 3/1000th of an inch) so as to simulate as closely as possible the position of the stylus used in the cutting of the original lacquer.

Mobile Fidelity utilised their three original individual Beatles' half-speed master albums, *Abbey Road, Magical Mystery Tour* and *The Beatles*, each using the same catalogue number. The remaining original albums are all numbered in release order, except *Sgt. Pepper*, which, for unknown reasons, contains the lowest number. Another irregularity concerns the *Magical Mystery Tour* album; this is out of chronological sequence with the other albums (numbered from one to fourteen). According to the British release order it should be the last album, as it was not issued in Britain until 1976 (after *Let It Be*); but the obvious order would have been after *Sgt. Pepper*, when the recordings appeared in EP form. Mobile Fidelity have, for unknown reasons, placed *Magical Mystery Tour* between *Abbey Road* and *Let It Be*.

The fourteen albums contain 185 of the Beatles' 215 original songs, plus the six orchestral tracks from *Yellow Submarine*, making a total of 192 tracks (*Yellow Submarine* appears twice). Tracks and numbering are as the original British albums included in the American edition of *The Beatles Collection* of December 1978.

RECORD ONE — PLEASE PLEASE ME MFSL 1-101

RECORD TWO — WITH THE BEATLES MFSL 1-102

RECORD THREE — A HARD DAY'S NIGHT MFSL 1-103

RECORD FOUR — BEATLES FOR SALE MFSL 1-104

RECORD FIVE — HELP! MFSL 1-105

RECORD SIX — RUBBER SOUL MFSL 1-106

RECORD SEVEN — REVOLVER MFSL 1-107

RECORD EIGHT — SGT. PEPPER'S LONELY HEARTS CLUB BAND MFSL 1-100

RECORD NINE — THE BEATLES MFSL 2-072 A/B

RECORD TEN — THE BEATLES MFSL 2-072 C/D

RECORD ELEVEN — YELLOW SUBMARINE MFSL 1-108

RECORD TWELVE — ABBEY ROAD MFSL 1-023

RECORD THIRTEEN — MAGICAL MYSTERY TOUR MFSL 1-047

RECORD FOURTEEN — LET IT BE MFSL 1-109

(*"Original Sound Recordings" and "Geo-Disc" are trademarks of Mobile Fidelity Sound Lab.)

The following is a chronological list of The Beatles' American record releases, excluding the "Hamburg" recordings. Listing is as the British list, except that record labels are noted in brackets after each title, apart from releases on the Capitol label.

Rec. No.	Record Title (Record label)	Cat. No.	Rel. Date
1963			
1	Please Please Me/Ask Me Why (Vee Jay)	VJ 498	25/2
2	From Me To You/Thank You Girl (Vee Jay)	VJ 522	27/5
3	INTRODUCING THE BEATLES (Vee Jay)	VJLP 1062	22/7
4	She Loves You/I'll Get You (Swan)	4152	16/9
1964			
5	I Want To Hold Your Hand/I Saw Her Standing There	5112	13/1
6	MEET THE BEATLES	ST 2047	20/1
7	INTRODUCING THE BEATLES (Vee Jay)	VJLP 1062	27/1
8	Please Please Me/From Me To You (Vee Jay)	VJ 581	30/1
9	JOLLY WHAT! THE BEATLES & FRANK IFIELD ON STAGE (Vee Jay)	VJLP 1085	26/2
10	Twist And Shout/There's A Place (Tollie)	9001	2/3
11	Can't Buy Me Love/You Can't Do That	5150	16/3
12	SOUVENIR OF THEIR VISIT TO AMERICA (THE BEATLES) (Vee Jay)	VJEP 1-903	26/2
13	Do You Want To Know A Secret/Thank You Girl (Vee Jay)	VJ 587	23/3
14	THE BEATLES' SECOND ALBUM	ST 2080	10/4
15	Love Me Do/P.S. I Love You (Tollie)	9008	27/4
16	FOUR BY THE BEATLES	EAP 2121	11/5
	CHARTBUSTERS VOL. 4	ST 2094	11/5
17	Sie Liebt Dich/I'll Get You (Swan)	4182	21/5
18	A HARD DAY'S NIGHT (United Artists)	UAS 6366	26/6
19	A Hard Day's Night/I Should Have Known Better	5222	13/7
20	I'll Cry Instead/I'm Happy Just To Dance With You	5234	20/7
21	And I Love Her/If I Fell	5235	20/7
22	SOMETHING NEW	ST 2108	20/7
23	Do You Want To Know A Secret/Thank You Girl (Oldies)	OL 149	10/8
24	Please Please Me/From Me To You (Oldies)	OL 150	10/8
25	Love Me Do/P.S. I Love You (Oldies)	OL 151	10/8
26	Twist And Shout/There's A Place (Oldies)	OL 152	10/8
27	Slow Down/Matchbox	5255	24/8
	THE BIG HITS FROM ENGLAND AND THE USA	DT 2125	7/9
28	THE BEATLES VS. THE FOUR SEASONS (Vee Jay)	VJDX 30	1/10
29	SONGS, PICTURES AND STORIES OF THE FABULOUS BEATLES (Vee Jay)	VJLP 1092	12/10
30	THE BEATLES STORY	STBO 2222	23/11
31	I Feel Fine/She's A Woman	5327	23/11
32	BEATLES '65	ST 2228	15/12
1965			
33	4 BY THE BEATLES	R 5365	1/2
34	Eight Days A Week/I Don't Want To Spoil The Party	5371	15/2
35	THE EARLY BEATLES	ST 2309	22/3
36	Ticket To Ride/Yes It Is	5407	14/4
37	BEATLES VI	ST 2358	14/6
38	Help!/I'm Down	5476	19/7
39	HELP!	SMAS 2386	13/8
40	Yesterday/Act Naturally	5498	13/9
41	Twist And Shout/There's A Place (Capitol Starline)	6061	11/10
42	Love Me Do/P.S. I Love You (Capitol Starline)	6062	11/10
43	Please Please Me/From Me To You (Capitol Starline)	6063	11/10

Rec. No.	Record Title	Cat. No.	Rel. Date
44	Do You Want To Know A Secret/Thank You Girl (Capitol Starline)	6064	11/10
45	Roll Over Beethoven/Misery (Capitol Starline)	6065	11/10
46	Boys/Kansas City (Capitol Starline)	6066	11/10
47	We Can Work It Out/Day Tripper	5555	6/12
48	RUBBER SOUL	ST 2442	6/12
1966			
49	Nowhere Man/What Goes On	5587	21/2
50	Paperback Writer/Rain	5651	30/5
51	YESTERDAY AND TODAY	ST 2553	20/6
52	Yellow Submarine/Eleanor Rigby	5715	8/8
53	REVOLVER	ST 2576	8/8
1967			
54	Penny Lane/Strawberry Fields Forever	5810	13/2
55	SGT. PEPPER'S LONELY HEARTS CLUB BAND	SMAS 2653	2/6
56	All You Need Is Love/Baby You're A Rich Man	5964	17/7
57	Hello Goodbye/I Am The Walrus	2056	27/11
58	MAGICAL MYSTERY TOUR	SMAL 2835	27/11
1968			
59	Lady Madonna/The Inner Light	2138	18/3
60	Hey Jude/Revolution (Apple)	2276	26/8
61	THE BEATLES (Apple)	SWBO 101	25/11
1969			
62	YELLOW SUBMARINE (Apple)	SW 153	13/1
	FIRST VIBRATION (Do It Now Foundation)	5000	?/5
63	Get Back/Don't Let Me Down (Apple)	2490	5/5
64	The Ballad Of John And Yoko/Old Brown Shoe (Apple)	2531	4/6
65	ABBEY ROAD (Apple)	SO 383	1/10
66	Something/Come Together (Apple)	2654	6/10
1970			
67	HEY JUDE (Apple)	SW 385	26/2
68	Let It Be/You Know My Name (Look Up The Number) (Apple)	2764	11/3
69	The Long And Winding Road/For You Blue (Apple)	2832	11/5
70	LET IT BE (Apple)	AR 34001	18/5
1971			
	DO IT NOW: 20 GIANT HITS (Do It Now Foundation)	LP 1001	?/2
1972 **No Releases**			
1973			
71	THE BEATLES 1962—1966 (Apple)	SKBO 3403	2/4
72	THE BEATLES 1967—1970 (Apple)	SKBO 3404	2/4
1974—1975 **No Releases**			
1976			
73	Got To Get You Into My Life/Helter Skelter	4274	31/5
74	ROCK 'N' ROLL MUSIC	SKBO 11537	7/6
75	Ob-La-Di Ob-La-Da/Julia	4347	8/11
76	THE BEST OF GEORGE HARRISON	ST 11578	8/11

1977

77	**THE BEATLES AT THE HOLLYWOOD BOWL**	SMAS 11638	4/5
78	**LOVE SONGS**	SKBL 11711	21/10

1978

79	**SGT. PEPPER'S LONELY HEARTS CLUB BAND** (picture disc)	SEAX 11840	?/8
80	**THE BEATLES** (white vinyl)	SEBX 11841	?/8
81	**THE BEATLES 1962—1966** (red vinyl)	SEBX 11842	?/8
82	**THE BEATLES 1967—1970** (blue vinyl)	SEBX 11843	?/8
83	Sgt. Pepper's Lonely Hearts Club Band/With A Little Help From My Friends/A Day In The Life	4612	14/8
84	**ABBEY ROAD** (picture disc)	SEAX 11900	?/12
85	**THE BEATLES COLLECTION** (limited edition box set)		?/12

1979

86	**LET IT BE**	SW 11922	?/3
87	**ABBEY ROAD** (Mobile Fidelity/Capitol)	MFSL 1-023	28/12

1980

88	**THE BEATLES RARITIES**	SHAL 12060	24/3
89	**A HARD DAY'S NIGHT**	SW 11921	?/8
90	**ROCK'N'ROLL MUSIC VOLUME 1**	SN 16020	?/10
91	**ROCK'N'ROLL MUSIC VOLUME 2**	SN 16021	?/10

1981

92	**MAGICAL MYSTERY TOUR** (Mobile Fidelity/Capitol)	MFSL 1-047	30/1
93	**I Want To Hold Your Hand/I Saw Her Standing There** (Starline)	A-6278	30/11
94	**Can't Buy Me Love/You Can't Do That** (Starline)	A-6279	30/11
95	**A Hard Day's Night/I Should Have Known Better** (Starline)	A-6281	30/11
96	**I'll Cry Instead/I'm Happy Just To Dance With You** (Starline)	A-6282	30/11
97	**And I Love Her/If I Fell** (Starline)	A-6283	30/11
98	**Matchbox/Slow Down** (Starline)	A-6284	30/11
99	**I Feel Fine/She's A Woman** (Starline)	A-6286	30/11
100	**Eight Days A Week/I Don't Want To Spoil The Party** (Starline)	A-6287	30/11
101	**Ticket To Ride/Yes It Is** (Starline)	A-6288	30/11
102	**Help!/I'm Down** (Starline)	A-6290	30/11
103	**Yesterday/Act Naturally** (Starline)	A-6291	30/11
104	**We Can Work It Out/Day Tripper** (Starline)	A-6293	30/11
105	**Nowhere Man/What Goes On** (Starline)	A-6294	30/11
106	**Paperback Writer/Rain** (Starline)	A-6296	30/11
107	**Yellow Submarine/Eleanor Rigby** (Starline)	A-6297	30/11
108	**Penny Lane/Strawberry Fields Forever** (Starline)	A-6299	30/11
109	**All You Need Is Love/Baby You're A Rich Man** (Starline)	A-6300	30/11

1982

110	**THE BEATLES** (Mobile Fidelity/Capitol)	MFSL 2-072	7/1
111	The Beatles Movie Medley/I'm Happy Just To Dance With You	B-5107	22/3
112	**REEL MUSIC**	SV 12199	22/3
113	**20 GREATEST HITS**	SV 12245	?/10

See 'The Beatles/The Collection', page 166.

APPENDICES

WITH A LITTLE HELP TO THEIR FRIENDS

Between 1963 and 1969, twenty-one songs written by "Lennon And McCartney" were recorded by other artists, but were neither officially recorded nor released by The Beatles. Some of the songs were recorded by The Beatles, but have only appeared on bootleg albums. George Harrison wrote two numbers that were recorded by other artists; these have been included in the following breakdown of the *Lennon & McCartney* songs, which only lists singles (the songs also appear on albums, but these are too numerous to mention).

1   DO YOU WANT TO KNOW A SECRET I'LL BE ON MY WAY

Billy J. Kramer And The Dakotas
R 5023 Parlophone (UK)—April 26, 1963
55586 Liberty (US)—June 10, 1963

For chart information on this single see *Do You Want To Know A Secret* under *Please Please Me* album in British section. The "B" side, *I'll Be On My Way,* was written by Paul for Billy.

2   BAD TO ME I CALL YOUR NAME

Billy J. Kramer And The Dakotas
R 5049 Parlophone (UK)—July 26, 1963
55626 Liberty (US)—September 23, 1963

This was Billy J. Kramer's second single, and the song was written for him by John in Spain. It entered the Top 30 on July 31, at No. 19, and rose to No. 1 for

two weeks on August 21. The record was in the Top 30 for eleven weeks. In America it entered the charts at No. 120 on May 23, rose to No. 9 for two weeks, and was in the Top 30 for seven weeks.

The single sold 340,000 in Britain and 540,000 in America, and with other world sales, exceeded one million copies sold.

3   TIP OF MY TONGUE (HEAVEN ONLY KNOWS)

Tommy Quickly
7N 35137 Piccadilly (UK)—July 30, 1963

Tip Of My Tongue was written by Paul. The single did not chart, although Tommy Quickly had a minor hit in October, 1964, with *Wild Side Of Life*, which was in the BMRB Top 50 for eight weeks, rising to No. 33.

4   HELLO LITTLE GIRL (JUST IN CASE)

The Fourmost
R 5056 Parlophone (UK)—August 30, 1963
6280 Atco (US)—November 15, 1963

Written by John, *Hello Little Girl* entered the UK Top 30 on September 18, 1963, at No. 30, and stayed in the chart for nine weeks, its highest position being No. 10. It did not make the US charts.

5   LOVE OF THE LOVED (SHY OF LOVE)

Cilla Black
R 5065 Parlophone (UK)—September 27, 1963

Written by Paul for Cilla, *Love Of The Loved* scraped into the British Top 30 for one week at No. 30 on October 14.

6   I'LL KEEP YOU SATISFIED (I KNOW)

Billy J. Kramer And The Dakotas
*R 5073 Parlophone (UK)—November 1,
1963
55643 Liberty (US)—November 11, 1963*

Billy's third Lennon & McCartney single was written by Paul, and entered the Top 30 on November 6 at No. 22, reaching No. 4 in its third week, and featuring in the chart for ten weeks. In America the single made the Top 30 for one week at No. 30, and was in the Top 100 for seven weeks, entering on July 25, after being re-released on July 10, 1964.

**7   I'M IN LOVE
    (RESPECTABLE)**

The Fourmost
*R 5078 Parlophone (UK)—November
15, 1963
6285 Atco (US)—February 10, 1964*

I'm In Love was written by John for The Fourmost. The single entered the British Top 30 on January 8, 1964, at No. 25 and rose to No. 12 in its third week. It was in the Top 30 for seven weeks, but did not make the US charts.

**8   A WORLD WITHOUT LOVE
    (IF I WERE YOU)**

Peter and Gordon
*DB 7225 Columbia (UK)—February 28,
1964
5175 Capitol (US)—April 27, 1964*

A World Without Love was written by Paul. The single entered the British Top 30 on March 18 at No. 21, and topped the chart for two weeks from April 22. It stayed in the Top 30 for ten weeks, selling 550,000 in Britain. In the US, it entered the charts on April 21 at No. 30, and reached No. 1 on April 18, staying there for two weeks, and in the charts for seventeen weeks, selling 400,000. With combined British, American and other world sales, the record has sold a global million.

**9   ONE AND ONE IS TWO
    (TIME AND THE RIVER)**

The Strangers with Mike Shannon
BF 1355 Philips (UK)—May 8, 1964

Another Paul composition, but this one did not make the charts, and neither did The Strangers.

**10   NOBODY I KNOW
     (YOU DON'T HAVE TO TELL ME)**

Peter and Gordon
*DB 7292 Columbia (UK)—May 29, 1964
5211 Capitol (US)—June 15, 1964*

Paul's second composition for Peter and Gordon, which again provided them with a global million seller. It entered the British Top 30 on June 3, 1964 at No. 25 and rose to No. 9 for two weeks. It stayed in the Top 30 for nine weeks, but did not enter the US charts.

**11   LIKE DREAMERS DO
     (EVERYBODY FALL DOWN)**

The Applejacks
*F 11916 Decca (UK)—June 5, 1964
9681 London (US)—July 6, 1964*

Written by Paul for The Applejacks, giving them their second Top 30 hit. Their first was *Tell Me When* , which was in the charts for thirteen weeks, rising to No. 7 while *Like Dreamers Do* was in the Top 30 for four weeks, rising to No. 23. The Applejacks, from Solihull in Warwickshire, had another hit after *Like Dreamers Do* with *Three Little Words*.

**12   FROM A WINDOW
     (SECOND TO NONE)**

Billy J. Kramer And The Dakotas
*R 5156 Parlophone (UK)—July 17, 1964
66061 Imperial (US)—August 12, 1964*

Billy's fourth and last single credited to Lennon and McCartney, although the song was written by Paul. The single entered the British charts on July 29 at No. 17 and stayed in the Top 30 for six weeks, peaking at No. 13. In America, the single was in the Top 30 for four weeks, and the Top 100 for ten weeks, its highest position being No. 23.
    Billy had two other Top 30 hits — *Trains And Boats And Plains,* and *Little Children*, which was a million seller in 1964.

**13   IT'S FOR YOU
     (HE WON'T ASK ME)**

Cilla Black
*R 5162 Parlophone (UK)—July 31, 1964
5258 Capitol (US)—August 17, 1964*

Paul wrote *It's For You* for Cilla, and it was her fourth hit. It entered the UK Top

30 on August 5 at No. 15, staying in the Top 30 for seven weeks, reaching No. 8 for one week. In America, the single entered the lower regions of the Top 100 for three weeks.

14 I DON'T WANT TO SEE YOU AGAIN (I WOULD BUY YOU PRESENTS)

Peter and Gordon
DB 7356 Columbia (UK)—September 11, 1964
5272 Capitol (US)—September 21, 1964

Another song written by Paul. This did not give Peter and Gordon a hit in Britain, but provided them with their third US chart entry. It entered the Top 100 on October 3 at No. 84, and was in the chart for nine weeks, rising to No. 16.

15 THAT MEANS A LOT (UK) (MY PRAYER) THAT MEANS A LOT (US) (LET THE WATER RUN DOWN)

P.J. Proby
10215 Liberty (UK)—September 17, 1965
55806 Liberty (US)—July 5, 1965

This Paul song gave P.J. his sixth British Top 30 hit. It entered the Top 30 at No. 27 on September 29, and stayed in the chart for four weeks, rising to No. 24. It was not a hit in America, and neither were his other big British hits, which included *Hold Me, Together, Somewhere, I Apologise, Let The Water Run Down* and *Maria*, which was his follow up to *That Means A Lot*.

16 WOMAN (WRONG FROM THE START)

Peter and Gordon
DB 7834 Columbia (UK)—February 11, 1966
5579 Capitol (US)—January 10, 1966

Although the record credits "Webb" as the composer, *Woman* was actually written by Paul, who used a pseudonym to see whether a "Lennon And McCartney" song would be a hit if the public were unaware of its composers' identity. The song was a minor hit, entering the Top 30 for two weeks only at Nos. 23 and 22. In the US, it entered the Top 100 at No. 83 on February 12, 1966, rose to No. 14, and

stayed in the Top 30 for eight weeks.

Peter and Gordon had seven Top 30 hits between 1964 and 1966 in Britain, including, as well as their Lennon And McCartney hits, *True Love Ways, To Know You Is To Love You, Baby I'm Yours* and *Lady Godiva*.

17 CATCALL (MERCY MERCY MERCY)

The Chris Barber Band
598-005 Marmalade—October 20, 1967

Written by Paul, *Catcall* was not a hit. The Chris Barber Jazz Band had a big hit with *Petite Fleur*, which was in the charts for twenty-two weeks in 1959, and reached No. 3.

18 STEP INSIDE LOVE (I COULDN'T TAKE MY EYES OFF YOU)

Cilla Black
R 5674 Parlophone (UK)—May 8, 1968
726 Bell (US)—May 6, 1968

Paul wrote this as the theme for Cilla's television series. The single entered the Top 30 on March 13 at No. 23, reached No. 7 for two weeks, and was in the Top 30 for eight weeks. It was not a hit in the US. Between 1963 and 1974, Cilla had nineteen hits, including *Anyone Who Had A Heart* (No. 1 and a million seller), *You're My World* (No. 1 and a million seller), *You've Lost That Lovin' Feelin', Love's Just A Broken Heart, Alfie, Conversations* and *Something Tells Me (Something Is Gonna Happen Tonight)*.

19 THINGUMYBOB YELLOW SUBMARINE

John Foster and Sons Ltd. Black Dyke Mills Band
Apple 4 Apple (UK)—August 26, 1968
1800 Apple (US)—August 30, 1968

Paul wrote this theme for the television programme, *Thingumybob*, and produced the record. It was not a hit.

20 GOODBYE (SPARROW)

Mary Hopkin
Apple 10 Apple (UK)—March 28, 1969
1806 Apple (US)—April 7, 1969

Paul wrote and produced Mary's follow

up to her debut hit, *Those Were The Days*, which was No. 1 for five weeks and sold five million. *Goodbye* entered the Top 30 at No. 26 on April 2, was at No. 2 for three weeks and stayed in the Top 30 for eleven weeks. It also made the US Top 30 for seven weeks, getting to No. 13.

Mary Hopkin had seven hits, including *Temma Harbour* and *Knock Knock Who's There*, before retiring to become a full-time mother during the 1970s.

21 GIVE PEACE A CHANCE (REMEMBER LOVE)

Plastic Ono Band
Apple 13 Apple (UK)—July 4, 1969
1809 Apple (US)—July 7, 1969

This "Lennon & McCartney" number was written by John for his own group, The Plastic Ono Band. The single was in the UK Top 30 for ten weeks, reaching No. 2, and selling two million copies worldwide. It entered the US Top 100 at No. 62 on July 26 and eventually reached No. 14, staying in the chart for nine weeks.

22 SOUR MILK SEA (THE EAGLE LAUGHS AT YOU)

Jackie Lomax
Apple 3 Apple (UK)—September 6, 1968
1802 Apple (US)—August 26, 1968

Sour Milk Sea was written by George Harrison for Jackie Lomax, a fellow Liverpudlian who used to be lead singer with The Undertakers. The single was produced by George, and features Eric Clapton on guitar, and also appears on Lomax's excellent Apple album, *Is This What You Want*. The single did not feature in either the British Top 30 or the American Top 100.

23 BADGE (WHAT A BRINGDOWN)

Cream
2058-285 Polydor (UK)—April 3, 1969
6668 Atco (US)—March 17, 1969

George co-wrote this number with Eric Clapton, providing Cream with another hit. The single was in the British Top 30 for seven weeks, reaching No. 19, but in America only reached the lower regions of the Top 100 for five weeks, its

highest position being No. 60.

Before *Badge*, Cream had six chart entries: *Wrapping Paper*, *I Feel Free*, *Strange Brew*, *Anyone For Tennis*, *Sunshine Of Your Love* and *White Room*.

THE "PAUL IS DEAD" STORY

In October 1969, a rumour spread across America, and eventually around the world, that Paul McCartney was dead. The story had started as "a rather capricious term paper" by a college student, and after being picked up by the college paper, it was eventually broadcast on Radio WKNR, Detroit, Michigan, by Russ Gibb, their Programme Co-ordinator.

The story, based on "clues" on Beatle records and album sleeves, was that Paul had actually been killed in a car accident in November, 1966. Researchers discovered a car accident, which happened around that time, involving two passengers, whose driver, a young dark haired male, was disfigured beyond recognition. Then, in the winter of 1966, a "Paul look-a-like" contest was held by the group, and although thousands entered, no winner was ever announced. But a winner did emerge in William Campbell, a Scot, who was paid a lot of money to play along as Paul, rather than bask in the obvious glory of being announced as the winner. Nothing was ever heard from or about Campbell again, And so the story went that the "stand-in" had been playing Paul since 1966, and that since then the other Beatles had been putting various clues onto Beatles records and sleeves, to break the news gently to their fans.

The "clues" are of two kinds; those actually recorded on records and those on the album sleeves, as follows:

ON RECORD

YELLOW SUBMARINE
During the middle section where various submarine noises are heard and various naval orders are shouted out by John, there is a line that sounds like "Paul's a queer". (Exactly what John says here is almost impossible to decipher.) This, says the story, was to try to turn Paul's fans against him, so that his death wouldn't affect them so much.

A DAY IN THE LIFE
In the first verse there is a reference to a car accident: "He blew his mind out in a car". Supposedly, the car accident which claimed Paul.

STRAWBERRY FIELDS FOREVER
At the end of the last few seconds of the fade out, a voice says "I buried Paul". (This is slightly distorted, but is definitely on the record although it is supposedly John saying "cranberry sauce".)

REVOLUTION 9
A certain part of the song, when played backwards, reveals the words "Turn me on, dead man, turn me on, dead man". (Attempts to verify this "clue" have been hindered by an understandable reluctance to play expensive LP records backwards.)

RECORD SLEEVES

SGT. PEPPER
The front cover shows The Beatles and other "mourners" gathered around a symbolic grave, with the words "Beatles" written out in flowers, below which is a bass guitar also made up of flowers. A close inspection of the flowers forming the guitar reveals, roughly spelt, the word "PAUL?". The story suggests that this means that Paul's existence is in doubt. There is a raised hand above Paul's head, supposedly an Indian sign of death. It was also suggested that the four-armed Shiva (the small statuette at the bottom of the picture) was a symbol of death — if so, its left back hand is pointing at Paul.

On the back cover group photo, Paul has his back to the camera. Why? (See British *Sgt. Pepper* entry, page 47, for explanation.)

On the centre spread, Paul is wearing a badge on his left sleeve which reads "O.P.D." — "Officially Pronounced Dead"!! (In fact, Paul acquired the badge in Canada, and the letters stand for "Ontario Police Department".)

MAGICAL MYSTERY TOUR
On the front cover, Paul is dressed as a walrus, which in Lewis Carroll's *Alice In Wonderland* devoured oysters, thus, according to the story, becoming a symbol of death.

On page three of the enclosed booklet, Paul is sitting at a desk, on which there is a large sign reading "I WAS"! On pages 12/13, the centre spread, Paul is not wearing shoes — in some parts of the world, people are buried without their shoes on. Page 18 shows Paul with a raised hand above his head — an Indian symbol of death? On page 23, The Beatles are seen dressed in pure white suits, with a carnation in the button hole; why is Paul wearing a black carnation and the others red? And on page 24, Paul appears with a hand raised above his head, again!

YELLOW SUBMARINE
Here again Paul appears with a raised hand above his head.

ABBEY ROAD
It was the many "clues" on this sleeve that

sparked off the original story. The Beatles are walking across the road in line — or is it the funeral procession, with John as the preacher, Ringo the grave digger, Paul the deceased and George the mourner? Paul is barefoot again, and out of step — thus showing a separation from the others. In the background the number plate of a parked VW reads "281F". At first this was taken to mean that Paul would have been 28 if he had lived, but as he was born in 1942, that would have made him 27 in 1969. But delving deeper, one realises that the Beatles were interested in Eastern mysticism at the time, and such followers believe that we are all a year old at birth, thus the clue stands up. On the back cover, the picture shows a wall with the Abbey Road street sign and above it the word "Beatles", which is cracked, again suggesting a break in the group.

There could be several other "clues" which might support this theory, although those listed are the main ones. At the time the rumours were spreading around the world, Paul had gone into a semi-retirement on his farm in Scotland, and as nothing had been heard or seen of him for several months, many people thought that there might be some truth in the rumours.

===

UNRELEASED STUDIO RECORDINGS

THE EMI RECORDINGS

The following is a list of titles of songs known to have been recorded by The Beatles (tapes of which must exist somewhere at EMI), but that have still not been officially released. (Some of them are available on various bootleg albums, but the quality of the recordings and pressings are not up to the standard one would expect from an official LP.) The list is of EMI studio recordings only (in chronological order) and does not include any illegal live/radio/television or film recordings.

JUNE 6, 1962
This was the date of The Beatles' audition with George Martin, after which he signed them up to the Parlophone label. The Beatles played early versions of *Love Me Do, P.S. I Love You, Ask Me Why, Hello Little Girl, Besame Mucho* and *Your Feet's Too Big*.

SEPTEMBER 11, 1962
The date of the *Love Me Do* recording session, at which The Beatles also recorded *Please Please Me* for the first time. It was later re-recorded on November 20 and the first version was never used.

NOVEMBER 26, 1962
George Martin saw Mitch Murray's *How Do You Do It* as a potential follow up single to *Love Me Do*, so the group recorded the song, but they did not like the number and deliberately performed badly in order that George Martin would agree to one of their own compositions, *Please Please Me*, as their next single. The Beatles' version of *How Do You Do It* was never released in Britain but the song was given to Gerry and The Pacemakers, who took it to No. 1 in Britain.

LATE 1962
Three tracks, *I Forgot To Remember To Forget* and *Lucille*, both sung by Paul, and John singing an early version of *Dizzy Miss Lizzy* — remain unreleased.

FEBRUARY 11, 1963
During the recording of their first album, *Please Please Me*, The Beatles recorded *Hold Me Tight* for the first time, and John sang *Keep Your Hands Off My Baby*.

MARCH 1963
Tip Of My Tongue recorded at Abbey Road Studios.

MID-1963
I Got A Woman, sung by John, and an Arthur Alexander number, *Soldiers Of Love*, were recorded.

AUGUST 14, 1964
Leave My Kitten Alone was recorded during sessions for the *Beatles For Sale* album.

SEPTEMBER/OCTOBER, 1964
During the *Beatles For Sale* sessions, George sang *You'll Know What To Do* and Paul *Always And Only*.

MAY/JUNE 1965
During the recording of some of the *Help!* songs, John re-recorded *Keep Your Hands Off My Baby*.

OCTOBER/NOVEMBER 1965
The *Rubber Soul* sessions produced one extra song; *If You've Got Troubles* by Paul.

MID-1966
Pink Litmus Paper Shirt, by George, and *Colliding Circles*, by John, were probably recorded during the *Revolver* sessions.

SPRING/1967
The *Sgt. Pepper* sessions produced six extra recordings: *Not Unknown, Anything, India* (George), *Annie* (Paul), *What's The New Mary Jane* (John) and *Peace Of Mind*.

SUMMER, 1968
The recording sessions for *The Beatles* (white double album) produced several unreleased tracks; *Not Guilty* by George (featuring Eric Clapton), *Junk* by Paul (this later appeared on Paul's solo album *McCartney*), *What's The New Mary Jane*, by John (see *Let It Be* single), a full twenty-four minute version of *Helter Skelter*, the full ten minute version of *Revolution No. 9* and the fourth version of the vocal *Revolution*. A rehearsal — with Donovan — of Paul's song, *Heather* (inspired by his stepdaughter), was also recorded.

JANUARY/FEBRUARY 1969
During the filming and recording for *Let It Be* many songs were put down on tape including: *Love Me Do, All Things Must Pass, Don't Let Me Down* (another version to that on the "B" side of *Get Back*), *Jazz Piano Song, Suzy Parker, Besame Mucho, You Really Got A Hold On Me, Shake Rattle And Roll, Kansas City, Lawdy Miss Clawdy, Dig It* (full version), *The Long And Winding Road* (without orchestration), *Let It Be* (without orchestration and with different guitar break by George), *Save The Last Dance For Me, Teddy Boy* (later recorded by Paul for his *McCartney* solo album), and many others. (See *Let It Be* LP in British section.)

EARLY MARCH 1969

Early versions of *Maxwell's Silver Hammer, Polythene Pam* and *Octopus's Garden* were recorded along with re-takes of John's *What's The New Mary Jane*, Paul's *Junk* and George's *Not Guilty*. Ringo's song, *I Should Like To Live Up A Tree*, was also recorded. John recorded *Watching Rainbows* in the Apple basement studio.

MID-1969

During the *Abbey Road* sessions, *When I Come To Town* and *Four Nights In Moscow* were recorded.

THE BBC RADIO RECORDINGS

Between March 7, 1962 and June 7, 1965, The Beatles recorded a total of fifty-two radio shows for the BBC, at nine different venues in either London or Manchester. The total number of performances that The Beatles made was 286, of a total of ninety-four songs, fifty-two of which were officially recorded and released for EMI, with the remaining forty-two either never officially recorded for EMI, or recorded but never officially released.

It can be seen from the two BBC song lists below, that the most performed officially recorded song was *From Me To You* (fifteen times) followed by *Please Please Me* (twelve times), *I Saw Her Standing There* (twelve times) and *She Loves You* (eleven times), while the most performed unrecorded songs were *Memphis Tennessee* and *Hippy Hippy Shake* (five times each). Evidently The Beatles preferred to sing American songs, rather than perform "hits" of the time; of the forty-two "unrecorded" songs, only eight were actually hits in Britain.

Looking at the two lists of songs that The Beatles performed for the BBC, one would think that somewhere in the BBC archives lies a veritable goldmine of unreleased Beatles material, but unfortunately, the majority of the tapes were destroyed, due to a severe shortage of storage space. The BBC cannot hope to preserve every minute of broadcasting time since it began in 1922, and therefore certain tapes are destroyed after a time, if they are not considered to be of historical interest or value.

The number of programmes that the BBC actually kept "in the can" is debatable; moreover, the number of Beatles songs they have preserved in their archives is also difficult to establish. 1982 saw the twentieth anniversary of The Beatles first appearance (March 7, 1962) in a BBC radio studio, the Playhouse Theatre, Manchester. To celebrate this event the BBC broadcast a special programme called "The Beatles At The Beeb" on March 7, 1982. The programme was made up of various interviews with people associated with The

Beatles' appearance on the BBC, along with some studio chat between The Beatles and early programme presenters — Brian Matthews and Alan Freeman — taken from the original radio programmes. Most importantly, the narrative, by Andy Peebles, was augmented with musical examples of The Beatles' BBC recordings. In all, a total of thirty-eight Beatles songs were broadcast in the programme, but whether these recordings are from the BBC's own archives or from private collections is difficult to establish.

The programme included the following songs: *From Us To You, The Hippy Hippy Shake, Memphis Tennessee, Please Mr. Postman, Too Much Monkey Business, Do You Want To Know A Secret, I'll Be On My Way, Crying, Waiting, Hoping, Pop Go The Beatles, To Know Her Is To Love Her, Don't Ever Change, Carol, Soldier Of Love (Lay Down Your Arms), Lend Me Your Comb, Clarabella, A Shot Of Rhythm And Blues, Matchbox, Sure To Fall (In Love With You), Lonesome Tears In My Eyes, I Got A Woman, The Honeymoon Song, All My Loving, Roll Over Beethoven, Till There Was You, I Wanna Be Your Man, Can't Buy Me Love, This Boy, Long Tall Sally, And I Love Her, A Hard Day's Night, Things We Said Today, I'm A Loser, She's A Woman, I Feel Fine, Kansas City/Hey Hey Hey Hey, Everybody's Trying To Be My Baby, Dizzy Miss Lizzy* and *Ticket To Ride.*

On December 27, 1982, the BBC broadcast a revised edition of "The Beatles At The Beeb", replacing certain numbers with a further selection of Beatles' BBC recordings. The new songs included were: *Dream Baby, Happy Birthday, I Got To Find My Baby, Nothin' Shakin' (But The Leaves On The Trees), So How Come (No One Loves Me)* and *Some Other Guy* — an extra six songs. Thus a total of forty-four Beatles songs recorded by the BBC are in existence in one form or another, but still remain officially unreleased.

A possible release of the BBC recordings has been under negotiation between the BBC and EMI since 1980. The October 1980 issue of *The Beatles Monthly* first reported that secret negotiations were taking place between the two parties, but no further news was forthcoming until June 1982. Obviously, for the recordings to be released, the individual members of The Beatles had to give their approval. In June 1982 *The Beatles Monthly* reported that three of the four parties (Paul, George, Ringo and Yoko — who was in charge of John's estate) had agreed to the release; and in August 1982 came a report that a double album of the BBC songs would be released. At the time of writing it seems that further problems have arisen — legal difficulties are apparently preventing the release of the recordings.

THE SONGS PERFORMED BY THE BEATLES ON BBC RADIO

The following two lists detail the songs The Beatles performed on BBC radio and the number of times each song was recorded.

Songs officially recorded by The Beatles:
All My Loving (4)
And I Love Her
Anna (Go To Him) (2)
Ask Me Why (5)
Baby It's You (3)
Boys (7)
Can't Buy Me Love (3)
Chains (4)
Devil In Her Heart (2)
Dizzy Miss Lizzy
Do You Want To Know A Secret (6)
Everybody's Trying To Be My Baby (5)
From Me To You (15)
A Hard Day's Night (2)
Honey Don't (4)
I Call Your Name
I Feel Fine (2)
I Saw Her Standing There (12)
I Should Have Known Better (2)
I Wanna Be Your Man (2)
I Want To Hold Your Hand (3)
If I Fell (2)
I'll Follow The Sun
I'll Get You (5)
I'm A Loser (3)
I'm Happy Just To Dance With You
Kansas City/Hey Hey Hey Hey(3)
Long Tall Sally (7)
Love Me Do (9)
Matchbox(2)
Misery (7)
Money (That's What I Want) (6)
The Night Before
P.S. I Love You (3)
Please Mr. Postman (3)
Please Please Me (12)
Rock And Roll Music
Roll Over Beethoven (7)
She Loves You (11)
She's A Woman (3)
Slow Down
A Taste Of Honey (9)
Thank You Girl (3)
There's A Place (3)
Things We Said Today (2)
This Boy (2)
Ticket To Ride (2)
Till There Was You (7)
Twist And Shout (10)
Words Of Love
You Can't Do That (4)
You Really Got A Hold On Me (4)

Songs which did not appear on official Beatle releases
This list gives composer(s) in brackets followed by the original recording artist for each particular song.

Beautiful Dreamer
(Stephen Foster) Slim Whitman
Besame Mucho
(Valasquez/Skylar) The Coasters
Carol
(Berry) Chuck Berry
Clarabella
(Pingatore) The Jodimars
Crying, Waiting, Hoping
(Holly) Buddy Holly
Don't Ever Change
(Goffin/King) The Crickets/1962 British hit
Dream Baby
(C. Walker) Roy Orbison/1962 British hit
From Us To You
(Lennon/McCartney) *From Me To You* with words changed
Glad All Over (2)
(Schroeder/Tepper/Bennett) Carl Perkins
Happy Birthday
(Trad. arranged Lennon)
The Hippy Hippy Shake (5)
(Chan Romero) Chan Romero
The Honeymoon Song
(Theodorakis) Manuel and His Music Of The Mountains
I Forgot To Remember To Forget
(Kesler/Feathers) Elvis Presley
I Got A Woman (2)
(Charles/Richards) Ray Charles
I Got To Find My Baby (2)
(Berry) Chuck Berry
I Just Don't Understand
(Wilkin/Westberry) Ann Margret
I'll Be On My Way
(Lennon/McCartney) Billy J. Kramer
I'm Gonna Sit Right Down and Cry (Over You)
(Thomas/Biggs) Roy Hamilton & Elvis Presley
Johnny B. Goode
(Berry) Chuck Berry
Keep Your Hands Off My Baby
(Goffin/King) Little Eva
Lend Me Your Comb
(Twomey/Wise/Weissman) Carl Perkins
Lonesome Tears In My Eyes
(Burnette/Burnette/Burlison/Mortimer) Johnny Burnette
Lucille (3)
(Penniman/Collins) Little Richard/1957 British hit
Memphis Tennessee (5)
(Berry) Chuck Berry/1963 British hit
Nothin' Shakin' (But The Leaves On The Trees)
(Colacrai/Gluck/Fontaine/Lampot) Eddie Fontaine

Ooh! My Soul
(Penniman) Little Richard
A Picture Of You
(Beveridge/Oakman) Joe Brown/1962 British
hit
Pop Go The Beatles
(Trad. arranged Patrick)
Sheila
(Roe) Tommy Roe/originally recorded by
Tommy Roe and The Satins in 1960, but re-
recording by Tommy Roe.1962 British hit.
A Shot Of Rhythm And Blues (3)
(Thompson) Arthur Alexander
Side By Side
(Sung with the Karl Denver Trio)
(Wood) Paul Whiteman Orchestra
So How Come (No One Loves Me)
(Bryant) Everly Brothers
Soldier Of Love (Lay Down Your Arms)
(Cason/Moon) Arthur Alexander
Some Other Guy (3)
(Leiber/Stoller/Barrett) Ritchie Barrett
Sure To Fall (In Love With You) (4)
(Perkins/Claunch/Cantrell) Carl Perkins
Sweet Little Sixteen (2)
(Berry) Chuck Berry/1958 British hit
(I'm) Talking About You
(Berry) Chuck Berry
That's Alright Mama
(Crudup) Arthur 'Big Boy' Crudup & Elvis
Presley
Three Cool Cats (2)
(Leiber/Stoller) The Coasters
To Know Her Is To Love Her
(Spector) The Teddy Bears/1958 British hit
Too Much Monkey Business (4)
(Berry) Chuck Berry
Youngblood
(Leiber/Stoller/Pomus) The Coasters

THE DECCA AUDITION RECORDINGS

With the Audiofidelity release *The
Complete Silver Beatles* in 1982, only three
recordings remain unreleased from the
Decca session: the Lennon and McCartney
originals *Love Of The Loved, Hello Little
Girl* and *Like Dreamers Do*. (See *The
Complete Silver Beatles* album in Appendix
4.)

THE HAMBURG RECORDINGS (and other non-EMI recordings)

All the songs recorded by Tony Sheridan and The Beatles in Hamburg, Germany, were cut in May, 1961, in the hall of an infants' school, with Bert Kaempfert producing. The Beatles were on their third trip to Hamburg, and received 300 marks (£26) for the sessions, which produced eight songs. At the time of the recording there were five Beatles: John, Paul and George plus Pete Best on drums and Stu Sutcliffe on bass. Bert Kaempfert re-named The Beatles "The Beat Brothers" for the German release of *My Bonnie*, as he thought that the word "Beatles" would mean nothing to the German public.

Tony Sheridan was born Anthony Esmond Sheridan McGuinnity in Norwich in 1941. An ex-art student, Sheridan played in many German clubs in the early Sixties, becoming a famous recording artist there, but was never able to emulate this success outside Germany.

In Britain the eight Kaempfert-produced Hamburg tracks were used by Polydor Records on four singles, one EP and six albums, with Charly Records releasing a special ten-inch album in 1982. After the initial release of the live Hamburg tapes in 1977, these recordings have now appeared on seven albums (and one single) issued by three labels. Polydor issued the first Beatle interview album in 1976, with a total of four issued to the end of 1982. The first official appearance of the Decca audition tapes was also at the end of 1982.

MY BONNIE *(2.06)*
THE SAINTS *(2.17)*

NH 66-833 January 5, 1962
May 24, 1963, February 21, 1964

Raymond Jones entered the NEMS Record Store in Whitechapel, Liverpool, on Saturday, October 28, 1961, and asked Brian Epstein for *My Bonnie* by The Beatles. Epstein had never heard of the song or the group, but told Mr Jones that he would look into it. The rest is history. The record was released in Britain by Polydor, who originally released the record in Germany in June 1961. The single, although selling well in Liverpool and very well in Germany (100,000), had only a small sale in Britain, and only managed to enter the Top 50 chart for one week at No. 48 on July 6, 1963, after its first re-issue of May 24, 1963. It was again re-issued on February 21, 1964, and with American sales of 300,000, the single is reputed to have sold a million globally.

My Bonnie

On *My Bonnie*, Tony Sheridan sings lead vocal, with John and Paul supplying harmony. The single version of the song includes a slow tempo introduction by Sheridan before the opening guitar riff. This is missing on the later album version. *My Bonnie* first appeared in 1881 in a songbook, "Student Songs Of 1881", and was first published in 1882 by Charles Pratt, credited jointly to J.T. Woods and H.J. Fuller. It was given its first rock treatment by Ray Charles on his single released on August 6, 1958, on the Atlantic label.

The Saints

Again Tony Sheridan sings lead, singing very much like Elvis Presley. This is a traditional American song, and Bill Haley and The Comets recorded a hit version released on March 21, 1956, on the Brunswick label in Britain, re-titled *The Saints Rock 'n' Roll*, which reached No. 5, and was in the chart for twenty-four weeks. The correct title of the song is *When The Saints Go Marching In*.

MY BONNIE

H 21-610—July 12, 1963

This EP was released by Polydor in the wake of The Beatles hits on Parlophone, but with no chart success.

A SIDE

My Bonnie *(2.06)*
(See above.)

Why (Can't You Love Me Again) *(2.56)*
Tony Sheridan sings lead, with The Beatles providing harmony. The song was written by Tony Sheridan and Bill Crompton in 1958.

B SIDE

Cry For A Shadow *(2.22)*
This is the first Beatles instrumental, written by John and George as a parody of The Shadows.

The Saints *(2.17)*
(See above.)

SWEET GEORGIA BROWN *(2.02)*
NOBODY'S CHILD *(3.52)*

NH 52-906—January 31, 1964

The third Polydor release, which again met with no chart success.

Sweet Georgia Brown

This song features Tony Sheridan as lead vocalist, with The Beatles supplying backing, and possibly Paul on the piano. The original song was recorded in May, 1961 in Hamburg, with Tony's vocal re-recorded in 1963.

Sweet Georgia Brown was written by Ben Bernie, Maceo Pinkard and Kenneth Casey, and first performed in Spring 1925 by Ben Bernie and his Orchestra. The Coasters released their single version on November 13, 1957 on the Atco label in America, but it did not enter the Top 20.

Nobody's Child

Sheridan adopts his Presley style vocal for this song, with support from The Beatles instrumentally only.

Nobody's Child was written by Cohen and Foree and was a hit for Karen Young in Britain in 1969, when it peaked at No. 6, staying in the charts for twenty-one weeks.

WHY (CAN'T YOU LOVE ME AGAIN) *(2.56)*
CRY FOR A SHADOW *(2.22)*

NH 52-275—February 28, 1964

Polydor were still unable to get a record in the Top 30 using the two tracks off the earlier EP which had not previously appeared in single form.

LET'S DO THE TWIST, HULLY GULLY, SLOP, LOCOMOTION, MONKEY

SLPHM 237-622—May 8, 1964

A Polydor compilation album featuring the four tracks from the *My Bonnie* EP. Tracks and artists are as follows: (Please note The Beat Brothers featured on this album are not The Beatles who were given the name for their first Hamburg release by Bert Kaempfert.)

A SIDE
Lantern Hully Gully
The Beat Brothers

Nick Nack Hully Gully
The Beat Brothers

Cry For A Shadow
The Beatles

My Bonnie
Tony Sheridan & The Beatles

The Saints
Tony Sheridan & The Beatles

Why (Can't You Love Me Again)
Tony Sheridan & The Beatles

Be My Baby
The Jacques Denjean Orchestra

The Touch Touch
The Jacques Denjean Orchestra

B SIDE
Ginchy
Flashes

Twistarella
Flashes

Sheba
The Players

America
The Gerard Poncert Orchestra

If I Had A Hammer
The Gerard Poncert Orchestra

Maria
The Gerard Poncert Orchestra

Surf And Surf
The Gerard Poncert Orchestra

Let's Slop
Tony Sheridan & The Beat Brothers

AIN'T SHE SWEET *(2.08)*
IF YOU LOVE ME, BABY *(2.50)*

NH 52-317 — May 29, 1964

At last Polydor scored a hit with an old Beatles recording, probably due to the fact that the vocals are handled by a Beatle instead of Tony Sheridan. *Ain't She Sweet* **entered the** *NME* **Top 30 on June 3 at No. 27, going to No. 24 the following week, but then dropping out. It returned for one week at No. 29 on June 24.**

Ain't She Sweet

This is the only Hamburg recording to feature a Beatle, John, as lead vocalist.

Ain't She Sweet was written by Jack Yellen and Milton Ager and was first performed by Paul Ash and his Orchestra in 1927. Eddie Cantor had a vaudeville hit with the song, and Gene Vincent recorded a rock version for his album *Bluejean Bop*, released on Capitol on August 30, 1956.

If You Love Me Baby (also called Take Out Some Insurance On Me, Baby)

Sheridan sings lead in his Elvis style. The song was written by Charles Shingleton and Waldenese Hall, and released as a single by Jimmy Reed on the Vee Jay label in the US on April 13, 1959.

THE BEATLES' FIRST

236-201—June 19, 1964
Re-issued August 4, 1967

This album features all eight songs recorded by Tony Sheridan and The Beatles in Hamburg in 1961. The other tracks were recorded by Tony Sheridan with a backing group using the name The Beat Brothers, the name Bert Kaempfert gave the Beatles for the original German Polydor release of *My Bonnie*.

A SIDE
Ain't She Sweet

Cry For A Shadow

Let's Dance
Tony Sheridan & The Beat Brothers

My Bonnie

If You Love Me, Baby

What'd I Say
Tony Sheridan & The Beat Brothers

B SIDE
Sweet Georgia Brown

The Saints

Ruby Baby
Tony Sheridan & The Beat Brothers

Why (Can't You Love Me Again)

Nobody's Child

Ya Ya
Tony Sheridan & The Beat Brothers

POP PARTY

236 517-8-9—1968

This three album various artists boxed set released by Polydor included two of The Beatles Hamburg songs. Other artists on the albums included The Bee Gees, Cream, Jimi Hendrix Experience, The Who, The Crazy World Of Arthur Brown, and Julie Driscoll with The Brian Auger Trinity.

Record Two
B SIDE

Ain't She Sweet *(Cut 6)*

Record Three
B SIDE

Cry For A Shadow *(Cut 6)*

THE EARLY YEARS

Contour 287011—June 18, 1971

A re-release and re-package of *The Beatles First* LP on Polydor. The track listing is exactly the same, but the album is presented in a new sleeve.

THE STORY OF POP VOLUME 1

K Tel TE 295—January, 1974

This compilation album was one of two
companion records, to the *Story Of Pop*
weekly magazine, which built up into a four
volume work. It was available by mail order
as two single albums through the magazine,
and later as a double album on general
release. The album entered the *NME* Top 30
Album Chart on March 19 at No. 27 for one
week, falling out the following week and re-
entering again at No. 28, rising to No. 16. It
dropped out again the following week, but
entered again for a final week at No. 20 on
April 23, 1974.

B SIDE
MY BONNIE *(Cut 1)*

THE BEATLES FEATURING TONY SHERIDAN

Contour CN 2007—June 4, 1976

Another re-release of *The Beatles' First* **LP**,
again with new packaging and with the same
track listing.

THE BEATLES TAPES FROM THE DAVID WIGG INTERVIEWS

2683 068 Polydor—July 30, 1976

Between 1968 and 1973 David Wigg, a Fleet
Street writer for the *Daily Express*,
interviewed the individual Beatles on seven
occasions. Wigg came into contact with The
Beatles during the Sixties, when he wrote his
own column in the *Evening News*, called
"Young London". This album contains each
interview edited by David Wigg, and
interspersed with musical interludes
arranged by Martyn Ford and John Bell,
conducted and produced by Martyn Ford
and recorded at Ramport Studios (*Hey Jude*
and *Give Peace A Chance*) and Polydor
Studios, London (others). The songs chosen to
separate the dialogue are supposedly
appropriate choices for each Beatle being
interviewed, but the McCartney side
includes *Because* (from *Abbey Road*), which
was written by John!

The gatefold sleeve contains an eight page
black and white booklet of thirty-one
interesting photographs of The Beatles
(taken by Dezo Hoffmann, David Nutter,
Michael Putland and Larry Ellis) including
pictures taken of the group with Ken Dodd,
Marlene Dietrich, David Jacobs and a series
of Paul and Linda and John and Yoko with
David Wigg.

George and Ringo tried unsuccessfully to
prevent the record being released in Britain,
but it never appeared in the U.S.A.

A SIDE
**JOHN LENNON WITH YOKO ONO
INTERVIEW**
(June 1969 at Apple Offices, 3 Savile Row,
London)
Part 1
GIVE PEACE A CHANCE
Part 2
IMAGINE
Part 3
COME TOGETHER

INTERVIEW
(October 1971 at San Regis Hotel, New York)

B SIDE
PAUL McCARTNEY INTERVIEW
(March 1970 at Apple Offices)
Part 1
BECAUSE
Part 2
YESTERDAY
Part 3
HEY JUDE

C SIDE
GEORGE HARRISON INTERVIEW
(March 1969 at Apple Offices)
Part 1
HERE COMES THE SUN
Part 2
SOMETHING

D SIDE
RINGO STARR INTERVIEW
(December 1968 in Mercedes en route to London)
INTERVIEW
(July 1970 at Apple Offices)
INTERVIEW
(December 1973 at Apple Offices)
Part 1
OCTOPUS'S GARDEN
Part 2
YELLOW SUBMARINE

THE BEATLES LIVE! AT THE STAR CLUB IN HAMBURG, GERMANY, 1962.

LNL 1—May 25, 1977

Originally issued in Germany on the Bellaphon label on April 8, 1977, this double LP was officially released in Britain after The Beatles had failed to prevent its release with a court injunction.

The tapes were recorded at the request of Liverpool singer Ted "Kingsize" Taylor, who asked a friend, Adrian Barber, to record some shows on a mono Grundig tape recorder, using a hand held microphone. The tapes, as well as The Beatles performance, included Taylor's own group, The Dominos, and Cliff Bennett and The Rebel Rousers. Taylor offered the tapes to Brian Epstein, who would only offer him £20 for them, as he felt they had no commercial value. Taylor gave the tapes to a recording engineer in the hope that they might eventually be released. The engineer later moved from his premises in Hackins Hey, Liverpool, leaving the tapes behind in the derelict offices for many years. Allan Williams, who managed The Beatles for several months before Brian Epstein, had a chance meeting with the engineer in 1972, and was told that the tapes might still be in the old house. The engineer and Kingsize Taylor

went to the old offices and found the tapes under a pile of rubbish, and Williams then set about trying to get the tapes released, starting by having talks with George Harrison and Ringo Starr. Williams tried to do a deal with the two Beatles, but neither George nor Ringo were willing to hand over the required five thousand pounds to Williams, as this was the time when Apple and The Beatles were experiencing financial difficulties.

After being turned down by Apple and EMI, Williams eventually sold the tapes to Paul Murphy, Head of BUK Records (who once worked for Polydor as a producer). Murphy later gave distribution rights to New York based Double H Licensing Corp. £50,000 was spent cleaning up the tapes, using various recording techniques, and transferring the original mono recordings to sixteen track tape. Double H licensed the authorized Bellaphon Records to release the records in Germany; German copyright laws are different from those in Britain, and it was anticipated that lawsuits might follow. When the package was later released in Britain on the Lingasong label — via RCA — The Beatles did file an injunction to stop the records being sold. However, because the courts ruled that the tapes were of historical interest, and that the records were being sold for what they were — old recordings (which was plainly stated on the sleeve) — the injunction was overruled on April 5, 1977. Therefore no lawsuit followed. The courts also ruled that The Beatles should have sued at an earlier date instead of waiting until the records had been released.

In the Castleman/Podrazik book, *The Beatles Again*, the authors enter into a lengthy "Perry Mason" style investigation concerning the exact date of the recording of the Hamburg tapes, as on the record sleeve it is only stated as "sometime" in 1962. The date is correctly stated in *The Beatles Again* as December, 1962, which is deduced after four pages of investigation, but one only has to listen to the album to confirm the time of year — between the two songs *Sweet Little Sixteen* and *Lend Me Your Comb*, John shouts "Christmas comes but once a year, when it does it brings good cheer", which certainly seems to indicate December. Had Brian Epstein but realised in 1963, when he was offered the tapes, The Beatles were already under contract to EMI in December 1962, and therefore the tapes legally belonged to Parlophone anyway. At the time of the recording, the line-up of The Beatles was George on lead guitar, John on rhythm guitar, Paul on bass and Ringo on drums. Ringo by this time had officially joined the group, and was not, as stated on the record sleeve, "sitting in" for Pete Best. Ringo had joined The Beatles by the time they recorded *Love Me Do*, which was September 11, 1962, and thus would have been the group's permanent and official drummer in December, 1962.

The "Star Club" album entered the NME Top 30 Album Chart on June 4, 1977 at No. 29, rising to No. 27 the following week, and then dropping out, thus staying in the chart for only two weeks.

Record One
A SIDE
I SAW HER STANDING THERE *(2.23)*
First of the Lennon and McCartney originals featured on the album. Paul sings lead on this song, which appeared on their first album, *Please Please Me*.

ROLL OVER BEETHOVEN *(2.14)*
As on their later EMI recording (*With The Beatles*), George handles the lead vocal on this Chuck Berry classic.

HIPPY HIPPY SHAKE *(1.51)*
Paul sings. *Hippy Hippy Shake* was written and recorded by Chan Romero, and released as a single on July 6, 1959 in America. It was a hit in 1964 for the Swinging Blue Jeans, reaching No. 2 in Britain and No. 24 in America.

SWEET LITTLE SIXTEEN *(2.46)*
John sings this Chuck Berry original. Berry had a Top 20 hit with the song in 1958, when it reached No. 16 in Britain and No. 2 in America. It was a million seller for Berry.

LEND ME YOUR COMB *(1.45)*
George sings lead vocal. *Lend Me Your Comb* was written by Kay Twomey, Fred Wise and Ben Weisman, and released by Carl Perkins on the Sun label on December 30, 1957.

YOUR FEET'S TOO BIG *(2.23)*
Paul sings this old Fats Waller song, written by Ada Benson and Fred Fisher.

B SIDE
TWIST AND SHOUT *(2.05)*
John sings this early rendition of what eventually became a Beatles "rock and roll" standard, to be featured on their *Please Please Me* album.

MR. MOONLIGHT *(2.08)*
John sings this Roy Lee Johnson number, which he later recorded for the *Beatles For Sale* album.

A TASTE OF HONEY *(1.45)*
Paul handles the vocals on this ballad, as he later did on the *Please Please Me* album.

BESAME MUCHO *(2.37)*
Paul sings this song, which he later sang in the *Let It Be* film. The song was written in 1941 by Mexican lady composer Consuelo Velazquez, with English words by Sunny Skylar. It was originally recorded by Jimmy Dorsey and his Orchestra, with vocals by Bob Eberle and Kitty Kallen, on December 17, 1943. It was a million seller for Dorsey, spending seven weeks at No. 1 and sixteen weeks in the USA charts. The Coasters recorded the first rock version, released by Atco on April 16, 1960.

REMINISCING *(1.40)*
George sings this King Curtis composition, which was a hit for Buddy Holly in September, 1962. It was released on the Coral label, and reached No. 17 in the British charts, and No. 2 in the American charts.

KANSAS CITY/HEY HEY HEY HEY *(2.10)*
Paul sings this medley of songs which later appeared on their *Beatles For Sale* album.

Record Two
A SIDE
NOTHIN' SHAKIN' (BUT THE LEAVES ON THE TREES) *(1.17)*
George sings lead vocal on a song written by Cirino Colacrai, Eddie Fontaine, Dianne Lampert and Jack Cleveland. The song was a minor hit for Eddie Fontaine when released in America during 1958.

TO KNOW HER IS TO LOVE HER *(3.03)*
John sings this classic Phil Spector song, which was a No. 1 single in the US and No. 2 in Britain for The Teddy Bears, a vocal trio led by Phil Spector. The record was released in America on September 15, 1958 and sold 1,200,000 there alone, and eventually sold 2.5 million globally.

LITTLE QUEENIE *(3.55)*
Another Chuck Berry number, this time sung by Paul. Chuck Berry released his version on March 9, 1959, on the Chess label.

FALLING IN LOVE AGAIN *(1.59)*
Paul sings this Marlene Dietrich classic. The song was written by Sammy Lerner and Frederick Hollander for the 1930 film *The Blue Angel*, in which Marlene Dietrich sings it in German. She later recorded it in English accompanied by Frederick Hollander and Sein Jazzsymphonicker, released on December 30, 1930, on the Victor label.

ASK ME WHY *(2.26)*
The second Lennon and McCartney original, sung by John.

BE-BOP-A-LULA *(2.27)*
This song was sung by the German waiter Horst Obber. *Be-Bop-A-Lula* was written by Gene Vincent and Tex Davis, and was a hit for Gene Vincent when released on May 28, 1956 in America, reaching No. 9. In Britain it reached No. 16. The record was Gene Vincent's first million seller, and he was featured singing it in the classic rock'n'roll film *The Girl Can't Help It* (1957).

HALLELUJAH, I LOVE HER SO *(2.14)*
Again sung by Horst Obber, this Ray Charles song was released on May 14, 1956, on the Atlantic label in America, but was not a Top 20 hit.

B SIDE
RED SAILS IN THE SUNSET *(2.01)*
Paul sings this song written by Jimmy Kennedy and Will Grosz, which was first performed in the US by Ray Noble and his Orchestra. It was released by Joe Turner on March 19, 1957, on the Atlantic label in America, but was not a hit, and was also recorded by Tab Hunter and Fats Domino, who scored a minor British hit with his 1963 version.

EVERYBODY'S TRYING TO BE MY BABY *(2.24)*
George handles this Carl Perkins song, later to appear on the *Beatles For Sale* album.

MATCHBOX (2.33)
John sings this second Carl Perkins song, which Ringo later sang on the *Long Tall Sally* EP.

I'M TALKING ABOUT YOU *(1.47)*
John sings the fourth Chuck Berry number featured in this live set. Berry released his single on February 6, 1961, on the Chess label in America. (The song is listed incorrectly on the record sleeve as *Talking 'Bout You*, a different song written by Ray Charles.)

SHIMMY SHAKE *(2.16)*
Paul sings this Joe South/Billy Land original. Billy Land released his version on May 13, 1959, in America.

LONG TALL SALLY *(1.48)*
Paul sings this Little Richard rocker, later to become the title track on an EP.

I REMEMBER YOU *(1.56)*
Paul sings this song made famous by Frank Ifield, who took the song to No. 1 for seven weeks in Britain. *I Remember You* was written by Johnny Mercer and Victor Schertzinger for the 1942 film *The Fleet's In* and was sung by Dorothy Lamour with Jimmy Dorsey and his band. Frank Ifield released his version in 1962, when it stayed in the British charts for twenty-eight weeks, selling 102,000 in one day, and 367,000 in five days. In America it reached No. 5 and eventually sold two million globally after being released on the Vee Jay label.

TWIST AND SHOUT *(2.03)*
FALLING IN LOVE AGAIN *(1.59)*

NBI—June 24, 1977

A single taken from the *Star Club* album. It did not make the charts.

HEAR THE BEATLES TELL ALL

CRV 202 Charly Records—March, 1981

This identical record was originally released in America by Vee Jay Records in September 1964, at the height of Beatlemania, and as with that release made no impression on the charts. (See American release.)

THE BEATLES/EARLY YEARS (1)

PHX 1004 Phoenix—July 17, 1981

The Beatles Early Years (1) & (2) are two very deceptive re-releases of the original Hamburg Tapes (*The Beatles Live At The Star Club In Hamburg, Germany, 1962* released by Lingasong Ltd in 1977). Firstly, there is no mention on either album that the recordings are the live Hamburg tapes, and secondly both albums wrongly title one song, thus giving the impression that each contains a completely new Beatles recording. (See track listings below for details.) The original "Hamburg Tapes" were purchased by Audiofidelity Enterprises (UK) Ltd who released these two albums on the Phoenix label (distributed by President Records) in Great Britain on July 17, 1981. The cover pictures of The Beatles were taken by Dezo Hoffman, one of the first professional photographers employed to work with The Beatles. The record labels title the two albums as *Early Beatles — Volume One* and *Early Beatles — Volume Two.*

The "Title and Composer" credits listed below are as stated on the record sleeves and labels — where these are incorrect the correct credits are given.

A SIDE
I SAW HER STANDING THERE
Lennon/McCartney (2.23)

ROLL OVER BEETHOVEN
Chuck Berry (2.14)

HIPPY HIPPY SHAKE
Chan Romeo (1.51)
(Credited as Chan Romeo but should read Chan Romero.)

SWEET LITTLE SIXTEEN
Chuck Berry (2.46)

GOTTA GO HOME
Unknown (1.45)
(Incorrect song title — this should read *Lend Me Your Comb* a song originally recorded by Carl Perkins. Label gives no composer credit — it was written by Kay Twomey/Fred Wise/Ben Weisman.)

B SIDE
TWIST AND SHOUT
Medley/Russell (2.05)

MR. MOONLIGHT
Ray Lee Johnson (2.08)
(Composer credit should read Roy Lee Johnson.)

A TASTE OF HONEY
Bobby Scott/Rick Marlow (1.45)
(Composer credit should read Ric and not Rick.)

BESAME MUCHO
Velasquez/Skylar (2.37)
(Composer credit should read Velazquez/Skylar.)

REMINISCING
Curtis (1.40)

THE BEATLES/EARLY YEARS (2)

PHX 1005 Phoenix—July 17, 1981

Released simultaneously with *The Beatles/ Early Years (1)* (see above).

A SIDE
AIN'T NOTHIN SHAKIN' (BUT THE LEAVES ON THE TREES)
Dallas/Frazier/Owen (1.17)
(Both title and composer credits are incorrect — title should read *Nothin' Shakin' (But The Leaves On The Trees)* and the composer credits should be Colacrai/Fontaine/Lampert/Cleveland.)

TO KNOW HER IS TO LOVE HER
Phil Spector (3.03)

LITTLE QUEENIE
Chuck Berry (3.55)

FALLING IN LOVE AGAIN
Lerner/Hollander (1.59)

ASK ME WHY
Lennon/McCartney (2.26)

B SIDE
RED SAILS IN THE SUNSET
Kennedy/Williams (2.01)
(Composer credits should read Kennedy/

Grosz.)

EVERYBODY'S TRYING TO BE MY BABY
Carl Perkins (2.24)

YOU AIN'T NO FRIEND
Andy Fairweather-Lowe (2.33)
(Not only titled incorrectly, but the composer credit is also wrong. The song is actually *Matchbox* written by Carl Perkins, and not by Andy Fairweather-Low — which is also incorrectly spelt as "Lowe".)

TALKIN' 'BOUT YOU
Ray Charles (1.47)
(This song is not *Talking' 'Bout You* by Ray Charles as stated on the label, but is *I'm Talking About You* by Chuck Berry. This same error appeared on the original double album containing the Hamburg Tapes.)

SHIMMY SHAKE
Joe South/Billy Land (2.16)

THE BEATLES HISTORIC SESSIONS

AFELD 1018 Audiofidelity Enterprises (UK) Ltd—September, 1981

The third appearance of the Hamburg Tapes. This double album features the entire recording made by Ted "Kingsize" Taylor in December, 1962 at the Star Club in Hamburg, Germany. The original double album, released in 1977, omitted four songs, which were of even poorer sound quality than the rest of the recordings, and they appear on this release for the first time in Britain.

The front cover of the album, as well as crediting John, Paul, George and Ringo as performers, also lists Stuart Sutcliffe — whether the album compilers are trying to imply that Sutcliffe actually performed at the "Historic Session" in Hamburg is not known, but as he died of a brain haemorrhage on April 10, 1962, he could not have been present at the performance.

The album cover includes the sleeve notes by Chris White, as they appeared on the original double in 1977, plus a 1963 period photograph of The Beatles, taken by Dezo Hoffman. The album package was designed by Robin Nicol of Design Machine, London.

As with their earlier single album releases of the Hamburg Tapes, Audiofidelity Enterprises again made several title and composing credit errors (see below). The "Title and Composer" credits listed below are as stated on the record sleeve and labels — where these are incorrect, the correct credits are given.

Record One
A SIDE
I'M GONNA SIT RIGHT DOWN AND CRY OVER YOU
Thomas/Biggs (2.41)
(Title incorrect — it should read *I'm Gonna Sit Right Down And Cry (Over You).)*

I SAW HER STANDING THERE
McCartney/Lennon (2.23)

ROLL OVER BEETHOVEN
Chuck Berry (2.14)

HIPPY HIPPY SHAKE
Chan Romero (1.51)

SWEET LITTLE SIXTEEN
Chuck Berry (2.46)

LEND ME YOUR COMB
Fred Wise/B. Weisman (1.45)
(Written by Kay Twomey/Fred Wise/Ben Weisman.)

YOUR FEETS TOO BIG
Benson/Fisher (2.23)

B SIDE
TWIST AND SHOUT
Medley/Russell (2.05)

MR. MOONLIGHT
Johnson (2.08)

A TASTE OF HONEY
Bobby Scott/Rick Marlow (1.45)
(Composer credit should read Bobby Scott/ Ric Marlow.)

BESAME MUCHO
Velasquez/Skyla (2.37)
(Composer credit should read Velazquez/ Skylar.)

CAN'T HELP IT/BLUE ANGEL
Roger Cook (1.40)
(The title and composer credits are completely wrong. The song is *Reminiscing* written by King Curtis, and originally sung by Buddy Holly. Although Roger Cook wrote many songs (with Roger Greenaway and others) in the late Sixties and through the Seventies, he did not write *Reminiscing*.)

KANSAS CITY/HEY, HEY, HEY, HEY
Leiber/Stoller (2.10)
Kansas City was written by Leiber/Stoller, but the second song, *Hey Hey Hey Hey*, was written by Richard Penniman (Little Richard).

WHERE HAVE YOU BEEN ALL MY LIFE
Cynthia Weil/Barry Mann

Record Two
A SIDE
TILL THERE WAS YOU
Meredith Wilson (1.58)

AIN'T NOTHIN' SHAKIN' LIKE THE LEAVES ON THE TREES
Dallas/Frazier/Owen
(Title and composers are again incorrectly credited as on the earlier *Early Years* release. Correct credits are *Nothin' Shakin' (But The Leaves On The Trees)* by Cirino Colacrai, Eddie Fontaine, Dianne Lampert and Jack Cleveland.)

TO KNOW HER IS TO LOVE HER
P. Spector (3.03)

LITTLE QUEENIE
Chuck Berry (3.55)

FALLING IN LOVE AGAIN
Hollander/Connally (1.59)
(Written by Sammy Lerner and Frederick Hollander.)

ASK ME WHY
Lennon/McCartney (2.26)

BE-BOP-A-LULA
Gene Vincent/Sheriff/Tex/Davis (2.27)
(Should be Sheriff Tex Davis.)

HALLELUJAH I LOVE HER SO
Ray Charles (2.14)

B SIDE
SHEILA
Tommy Roe (1.59)

RED SAILS IN THE SUNSET
Kennedy/Williams (2.01)
(Written by Jimmy Kennedy and Will Grosz.)

EVERYBODY'S TRYING TO BE MY BABY
Carl Perkins (2.24)

MATCHBOX
Carl Perkins (2.33)

TALKIN' 'BOUT YOU
Ray Charles (1.47)
(This title and composer credit have never been corrected from the first time the song erroneously appeared on the original Lingasong double album. The song is Chuck Berry's *I'm Talking About You*.)

SHIMMY SHAKE
Joe South/Billy Land (2.16)

LONG TALL SALLY
Johnson/Penniman/Blackwell (1.48)

I REMEMBER YOU
Schertzinger/Metter (1.56)
(Written by Johnny Mercer and Victor Schertzinger.)

RARE BEATLES

PHX 1011 Phoenix Records — January 22, 1982

The third release from Phoenix Records (a division of Audiofidelity Enterprises (UK) Ltd) containing material from the live Hamburg tapes. The cover features the same Dezo Hoffman picture used on Audiofidelity's *Historic Sessions* release; but here it is colour tinted, and also reproduces part of the original sleeve notes from *The Beatles Live! At The Star Club* album of 1977.

As with their earlier releases, a few errors have been made concerning the composer credits to each song, but the song titles are correct.

A SIDE

BE-BOP-A-LULA *(2.27)*

LONG TALL SALLY *(1.48)*

YOUR FEET'S TOO BIG *(2.23)*

I'M GONNA SIT RIGHT DOWN AND CRY (OVER YOU) *(2.41)*

WHERE HAVE YOU BEEN ALL MY LIFE *(1.56)*

B SIDE

SHEILA *(1.59)*

HALLELUJAH I LOVE HER SO *(2.14)*

TILL THERE WAS YOU *(1.58)*

KANSAS CITY/HEY HEY HEY HEY *(2.10)*

I REMEMBER YOU *(1.56)*

THE BEATLES/EARLY YEARS (1) & (2)

PHX 1004 & PHX 1005 Phoenix Records — 1982

A re-release and re-package of the two albums issued by Phoenix Records in July 1981, which received heavy criticism from *Beatles Monthly* at the time (due to the misleading packaging and incorrect titles for two songs). The new covers credit the correct titles for *Lend Me Your Comb* and *Matchbox* (originally titled *Gotta Go Home* and *You Ain't No Friend* respectively), and also include a sleeve note stating that the recordings are from the Star Club tapes.

Although the song titles were corrected, the other errors on the original releases have been continued into these reissues. (See original releases page 000 for track listings.)

THE BEATLES TALK DOWNUNDER

GP 5001—Goughsound Ltd.—May 1, 1982

The third Beatles interview album to be released in Britain, it was originally

released by Raven Records in Australia (where it was compiled by Glenn A. Baker and Warren Barnett). The record features over an hour of interviews with The Beatles, recorded during their June 1964 tour of Australia and New Zealand. The album cover features photographs included in the companion paperback book, *The Beatles Downunder*, by Glenn A. Baker, and published by Wild & Woolley.

A SIDE

MESSAGE FROM ENGLAND (0.55)
This is comprised of a studio tape sent to DJ Barry Ferber in March 1964, and features The Beatles singing a short rendition of *Waltzing Matilda*.

HONG KONG (2.18)
Interviews at the President Hotel on June 10, by Bob Rogers, also featuring The Beatles singing *Waltzing Matilda* and the title line of *Tie Me Kangaroo Down Sport*.

DARWIN (1.12)
On June 11 The Beatles landed at Darwin Airport, where John Edwards conducted the first Beatles' interview on Australian soil.

SYDNEY (7.00)
As The Beatles flew into Mascot Airport, Kevin O'Donohue described their arrival; this is followed by their first Sydney press conference at the Sheraton Hotel, on June 11, when Jimmy Nicol — Ringo's stand-in — answered questions.

ADELAIDE (10.00)
On the plane between Sydney and Adelaide on June 12, The Beatles were interviewed by Bob Rogers. They later appeared on the balcony of the South Australia Hotel, and this balcony appearance — described by Bob Francis — is followed by an interview conducted by Bob Rogers in The Beatles' hotel room.

SYDNEY (3.30)
Ringo was interviewed by Garvin Rutherford during his trip to Melbourne to join the rest of the group on June 14.

MELBOURNE (5.52)
The Beatles were in Melbourne from June 15 to 17, during which time they appeared on the balcony of the Southern Cross Hotel and were interviewed by Allan Lappin and Bob Rogers. Also included here are concert recordings of The Beatles' announcements at the Melbourne Festival Hall.

SYDNEY (5.06)
The Beatles returned to Sydney on June 18 to celebrate Paul's birthday at the Sheraton

Hotel. During one interview, Mike Walsh gives Ringo a kazoo lesson. Then on June 21 The Beatles flew to Wellington, New Zealand, and were interviewed *en route* by Bob Rogers.

B SIDE

WELLINGTON (5.30)
The Beatles were in Wellington from June 21 to 23, and Bob Rogers conducted interviews at the St. George Hotel.

AUCKLAND/DUNEDIN (14.55)
The Beatles stayed in Auckland on June 24 and 25, and in Dunedin on June 26, and interviews were conducted by Bob Rogers at the Royal International Hotel and the New City Hotel. During the interviews, Bob Rogers asked George and Ringo about their song writing, and Paul is heard singing Ringo's song *Don't Pass Me By*.

BRISBANE (2.48)
During their stay in Brisbane, on June 29 and 30, The Beatles were interviewed by Tony McArthur at Lennon's Hotel.

SYDNEY (9.52)
The Beatles flew home to London on July 1, but not before a farewell interview conducted by Bob Rogers and Garvin Rutherford at the airport.

THE BEATLE INTERVIEWS

CBR 1008 Everest Records — June 25, 1982

The fourth Beatles' interview record to appear in Britain, this time featuring recordings of press conferences and interviews from 1964 and 1966 in America and Canada (originally released on disc in America in November 1978 as *Beatle Talk — The Way They Were With Red Robinson*). The front cover features a four colour photograph, probably taken by Dezo Hoffman. However, he is not credited either for this or for the back cover photo —

the same as that used on the *Rare Beatles* album, which does credit Hoffman. The album was compiled and edited by Ron Winter, with sleeve design by Jo Mirowski.

A SIDE

NEWSCAST AND INTERVIEW: FEBRUARY 1966 REGARDING JOHN LENNON'S STATEMENT IN DATEBOOK MAGAZINE THAT THE BEATLES WERE MORE POPULAR THAN CHRIST (1.00)

PRESS CONFERENCE: RECORDED AT THE ASTOR HOTEL, CHICAGO, ILLINOIS, 12th AUGUST 1966 (17.07)

B SIDE

NEWSCAST (CONCERNING JOHN LENNON) INCLUDING INTERVIEWS WITH: JOHN LENNON, TOMMY JAMES (not the notable sixties' rock star, but the American disc jockey who first publicised the "Beatles bigger than Jesus" story), **MAUREEN CLEAVE, LES PERRIN AND BRIAN EPSTEIN** (7.12)

RED ROBINSON TALKS ABOUT THE EFFECTS OF THE BEATLES' MUSIC ON AMERICAN AND CANADIAN AUDIENCES AND THEIR APPEARANCE AT THE EMPIRE STADIUM IN VANCOUVER IN 1964 / PRESS CONFERENCE WITH THE BEATLES RECORDED AT THE EMPIRE STADIUM IN VANCOUVER, CANADA, 26th AUGUST 1964 (13.13)
The Beatles did not perform at the Empire Stadium in Vancouver on August 26, 1964, but on August 22. By August 26 they were in Denver, Colorado, performing at the Red Rock Stadium.

THE SAVAGE YOUNG BEATLES

CFM 701 Charly Records — July 31, 1982

This is the first Beatles ten-inch record, a facsimile of an illegal record that appeared in America in the summer of 1964 on Savage Records, called *This Is The Savage Young Beatles*. The album (catalogue number BM 69) contained eight tracks: four were by Sheridan and The Beatles, the other four were album fillers by Sheridan and The Beat Brothers. This release was a standard sized album, and was re-released in 1966.
Although both albums have a similar sleeve design — using the same photograph with Pete Best on drums — the Charly Records release features very interesting sleeve notes by Tony Barrow, the Beatles and NEMS early press officer. The cover photograph was taken by Albert Marrion, and originally appeared on the front page

of the January 4-18, 1962, issue of *Mersey Beat*, the local Liverpool music paper founded by Bill Harry.

A SIDE

WHY *(2.56)*

CRY FOR A SHADOW *(2.22)*

LET'S DANCE *(2.27)*
Tony Sheridan & The Beat Brothers

YA YA *(2.24)*
Tony Sheridan & The Beat Brothers

B SIDE

WHAT'D I SAY *(2.35)*
Tony Sheridan & The Beat Brothers

RUBY BABY *(2.47)*
Tony Sheridan & The Beat Brothers

TAKE OUT SOME INSURANCE ON ME BABY *(2.50)*

SWEET GEORGIA BROWN *(2.02)*

THE COMPLETE SILVER BEATLES

AFELP 1047 Audiofidelity Enterprises (UK) Ltd. — September 10, 1982

Twenty years after The Beatles entered their first British recording studio, these historic tapes were officially made available to the public by Audiofidelity, who had previously released six packages containing the live Hamburg tapes.

This album contains twelve of the fifteen songs that The Beatles performed at this audition at the West Hampstead Studios of Decca Records on January 1, 1962. Previously these recordings had only been available on a selection of bootleg albums (notably *The Decca Tapes, The Beatles Decca Auditions Tapes* and *The Decca Gone Sessions)* containing all fifteen songs. The three missing songs on the official

release are the three original Lennon & McCartney numbers: *Love Of The Loved, Hello Little Girl* and *Like Dreamers Do*. These were omitted from the album either to save them for a possible later release, or because of legal difficulties in obtaining the publishers' permission to use the songs.

The album title, *The Complete Silver Beatles*, is very misleading and also incorrect; at the time of the Decca audition The Beatles were known simply as "The Beatles". They first used "The Silver Beatles" towards the end of 1959, and were billed as "The Silver Beatles" for their tour of Scotland in the spring of 1960 (when they lacked Johnny Gentle); however, by the summer of 1961 the "Silver" had been dropped.

The front cover shot of George, Pete Best, John and Paul, taken in The Cavern in 1961 by Dick Matthews, is laterally reversed — unlike original appearances of the photograph in such publications as *Shout! The True Story Of The Beatles* by Philip Norman, and *The Beatles* by Geoffrey Stokes. The picture is made more ghastly by its colouring of green and gold. Dick Matthews, who is not credited on the sleeve, helped launch *Mersey Beat* in 1961 when he took many photographs of The Beatles performing at The Cavern. The album sleeve notes were supplied by Walter Podrazik who co-authored — with Harry Castleman — the trilogy of Beatles discographies *All Together Now, The Beatles Again* and *The End Of The Beatles.*

On December 13, 1961, Brian Epstein signed The Beatles to a formal managerial contract, and immediately began the task of acquiring a recording contract for them. One of his first approaches was to the A&R Department of Decca Records, headed by Dick Rowe, who delegated the task to a new assistant, Mike Smith. Smith wanted to see The Beatles perform on their home ground, so he travelled up to Liverpool towards the end of December 1961. He was very impressed with their performance at The Cavern and arranged for an audition at Decca's West Hampstead Studios in London, on January 1, 1962. Epstein travelled to London by train, while John, Paul, George and Pete Best (Ringo had not yet joined) travelled down on New Year's Eve in a specially rented van — driven by Neil Aspinall, their Road Manager. During the morning audition, The Beatles performed about fifteen songs; these included several standards that Brian Epstein had insisted they play to impress Mike Smith, as well as three of their own compositions.

On the same day, Mike Smith auditioned another group, Brian Poole and The Tremeloes. Smith had been given a directive from his boss, Dick Rowe, that he could only sign one new group; since Brian Poole and The Tremeloes were a local band — from Dagenham in Essex — it was decided to record them rather than The Beatles. Epstein was told of the decision in March 1962. He was given the tape of the Decca audition, however, and used this to approach other record companies; these included Pye, Phillips, Columbia and HMV (the latter two being subsidiaries of EMI, who also owned Parlophone, the label which eventually signed them).

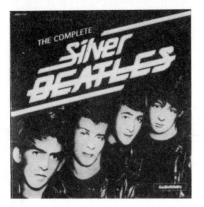

A SIDE

THREE COOL CATS *(2.17)*
George sings this Jerry Leiber/Mike Stoller composition, with John and Paul harmonising, and John assisting with certain vocal refrains. The song was originally recorded by an American group, The Coasters, who released their version on January 23, 1959, on Atco.

CRYING, WAITING, HOPING *(1.56)*
George again takes the vocal spotlight on this Buddy Holly song; it was originally recorded by the composer and was released in America on July 27, 1959, on Coral, as the flip-side to *Peggy Sue Got Married*. Holly's single reached No. 13 in the UK, staying in the charts for ten weeks after entering in September 1959. John and Paul supply backing vocals on The Beatles' version of this song.

SEARCHIN' *(2.53)*
Paul takes the lead vocal parts (although the record sleeve notes credit John) with John and George helping on backing. It was another Jerry Leiber and Mike Stoller composition, recorded by The Coasters on Atco and giving the group their first million seller in 1957. The record reached No. 5 in the US charts, where it stayed for a total of twenty-six weeks. It was a double "A"-sided hit with *Young Blood* — also featuring in the

US charts where it reached No. 18. The Coasters had three further million-selling singles with *Yakety Yak* (1958), *Charlie Brown* (1959) and *Poison Ivy* (1959).

SHEIK OF ARABY *(1.34)*
George handles lead vocal on this standard written by Harry Smith, Francis Wheeler and Ed Snyder; John and Paul provide vocal support. The song was originally recorded by Jay Wilbur and His Band; it has also been released by a host of well known artists including Duke Ellington, The Quintet Du Hot Club De France, Fats Domino, Louis Armstrong and Joe Brown And The Bruvvers.

MONEY *(2.18)*
John sings lead vocal on this early Motown classic that he later handled on *With The Beatles* album, with Paul and George helping out on backing vocals.

B SIDE

TO KNOW HER IS TO LOVE HER *(2.25)*
Incorrectly titled on the album as *To Know Him Is To Love Him*, John sings "To know her is to love her", with Paul and George backing. The Beatles also sang this number at the Star Club in Hamburg, and it appears on the live double album *The Beatles Live! At the Star Club*.

TAKE GOOD CARE OF MY BABY *(2.16)*
George handles lead vocals with John and Paul assisting. The song was written by Gerry Goffin and Carole King, and was recorded by Bobby Vee in 1961, giving him his third million seller and reaching No. 1 in the US for three weeks and in the UK for one week. Bobby Vee achieved a pair of million sellers in 1960 with *Devil Or Angel* and *Rubber Ball*, and followed *Take Good Care Of My Baby* with a fourth in 1961, *Run To Him*.

MEMPHIS *(2.12)*
John takes solo vocal on this Chuck Berry classic, which has entered the British charts on three separate occasions, and the US charts twice. Chuck Berry originally recorded the song in 1959, but didn't have a hit until October 1963, when it reached No. 6 in the British charts (as a double "A"-sided single with *Let It Rock*), staying thirteen weeks in the chart. Lennie Mack's instrumental version reached No. 5 in America in 1963, selling a million, as did Johnny Rivers' version in 1964, when it peaked at No. 2 in the US charts. In Britain, Dave Berry secured a No. 19 hit with the song, and Lonnie Mack's reissued version crept up to No. 47 in 1979.

SURE TO FALL (IN LOVE WITH YOU)
(1.55)
The album sleeve notes state that John sings lead on this Carl Perkins number; however, although both John and Paul can be heard singing, Paul appears to sing the lead lines, with John and George helping. Carl Perkins originally recorded the song as a single — released on January 23, 1956, on Sun.

TILL THERE WAS YOU *(2.53)*
Paul sings solo on this standard, which he later recorded for the *With The Beatles* album.

SEPTEMBER IN THE RAIN *(1.48)*
Paul sings solo. The song was written in 1937 by Al Dubin and Harry Warren for the film *Melody For Two*, when it was sung by James Melton. The George Shearing Quintet had a million-selling hit with the number in 1949, and Dinah Washington took it to No. 35 in the UK charts in November 1961; at the same time, Washington's version peaked in the United States at No. 23.

SEARCHIN' *(2.53)*
MONEY *(2.18)*/TILL THERE WAS YOU *(2.53)*

AFE AFS1 — October 29, 1982

Audiofidelity Enterprises released this three track single, from *The Complete Silver Beatles* album, in a picture sleeve using the same Dick Matthews photograph of The Beatles at The Cavern. The "A" side, *Searchin'*, is one of the songs that Paul picked for his "Desert Island Disc" selection, when he appeared on that radio programme on January 30, 1982. As with the album, the single did not enter the charts.

U.S.A. RELEASES

By April 1982, the eight Hamburg studio tracks recorded by Tony Sheridan and The Beatles were used in America on five singles and thirteen albums — issued by eight record labels. The first American Beatle interview album appeared in June 1964, with a further six following to April 1982.

MY BONNIE/THE SAINTS

Decca 31382—April 23, 1962

MY BONNIE/THE SAINTS

MGM K13213—January 27, 1964

Only two weeks after *I Want To Hold Your Hand* had stormed up the American charts, this single was re-released on MGM to cash in on the Capitol hit. It entered the Top 100 charts on February 15 at No. 67 and reached No. 26 on March 14. It stayed in the Top 100 for six weeks, selling 300,000 copies in America.

THE BEATLES WITH TONY SHERIDAN AND THEIR GUESTS

MGM SE 4215—February 3, 1964

The first of many albums featuring the Hamburg songs. The album entered the Top 200 chart at No. 147 and bubbled under the Top 100 for six weeks, entering at No. 87 on March 28, peaking at No. 68 and staying in the Top 100 for six weeks, and the Top 200 for a total of fourteen weeks.

A SIDE
MY BONNIE

CRY FOR A SHADOW

JOHNSON RAG
The Titans

SWANEE RIVER
Tony Sheridan & The Beat Brothers

FLYING BEAT
The Titans

THE DARKTOWN STRUTTER'S BALL
The Titans

B SIDE
THE SAINTS

RYE BEAT
The Titans

YOU ARE MY SUNSHINE
Tony Sheridan & The Beat Brothers

SUMMERTIME BEAT
The Titans

WHY

HAPPY NEW YEAR BEAT
The Titans

WHY/CRY FOR A SHADOW

MGM K13227—March 27, 1964

This single entered the Top 100 for one week at No. 88 on April 18.

SWEET GEORGIA BROWN/TAKE OUT SOME INSURANCE ON ME BABY

Atco 6302—June 1, 1964

Atco owned four of the eight 1961 Hamburg recordings (the remaining four belonged to MGM) and two singles resulted from these recordings. This one — the first release — did not enter the charts, but the following single, made up of the two remaining tracks owned by Atco, did break into the Top 100.

THE AMERICAN TOUR WITH ED RUDY
Radio Pulsebeat News Documentary No. 2 — June 9, 1964

News reporter Ed Rudy followed The Beatles throughout their 1964 American Tour, taping most of their press conferences. Using these recordings, he re-recorded himself asking the questions that other reporters had asked, then dubbed in the appropriate answers from his collection of conference recordings. This album entered Billboard's Hot Hundred for thirteen weeks.

AIN'T SHE SWEET/NOBODY'S CHILD

Atco 6301—July 6, 1964

This entered the Top 100 on July 18 at No. 90, rising to No. 19 and staying in the Top 100 for nine weeks, and in the Top 30 for five.

HEAR THE BEATLES TELL ALL

PRO 202 Vee Jay—September, 1964

During The Beatles second American tour, John gave an interview to John Steck, and all four Beatles were recorded in snatches of conversation with Dave Hull during their departure at the Los Angeles airport in August 1964. The Lennon interview contains background percussion, scored by Lou Adler and played by Hal Blaine. The album was released by Vee Jay in September 1964, but did not make any impression on the charts, and was soon deleted, becoming a collector's item. Most Vee Jay copies of the album available today are probably pirated albums, and not originals. The album is probably of interest more for the sleeve than the contents of the record, as the back cover shows three original Vee Jay Beatles' albums and three picture sleeve singles.

A SIDE
JOHN STECK INTERVIEWS JOHN LENNON

B SIDE
DAVE HULL INTERVIEWS JOHN, PAUL, GEORGE, RINGO

AIN'T SHE SWEET

Atco SD 33-169—October 5, 1964

The first album on Atco features the four songs released as singles, along with eight other Mersey-connected tracks performed by the virtually unknown Swallows.

A SIDE
AIN'T SHE SWEET

SWEET GEORGIA BROWN

TAKE OUT SOME INSURANCE ON ME BABY

NOBODY'S CHILD

I WANNA BE YOUR MAN
The Swallows

SHE LOVES YOU
The Swallows

B SIDE
HOW DO YOU DO IT

PLEASE PLEASE ME

I'LL KEEP YOU SATISFIED

I'M TELLING YOU NOW

I WANT TO HOLD YOUR HAND

FROM ME TO YOU
All by The Swallows

ED RUDY WITH NEW US TOUR (THE BEATLES GREAT AMERICAN TOUR)
Radio Pulsebeat News 2 — 1001/1002 (News Documentary No. 3) — 1965

As with Rudy's previous album, this was comprised of recordings taken from The Beatles press conferences, and over-dubbed with Rudy's own questions. This album did not enter the charts.

THE GREAT AMERICAN TOUR — 1965 LIVE BEATLEMANIA CONCERT
Lloyds E.R.M.C. Ltd. Records — 1965

The third Ed Rudy album consisted of concert recordings of The Beatles, over-dubbed with the performances of a group called The Liverpool Lads. This obliterated The Beatles singing, but allowed the in-between numbers chat to be heard. Rudy recorded The Beatles during their second US Tour of 1964. The album did not gain any chart success.

THIS IS WHERE IT STARTED

Metro MS 563—August 15, 1966

A re-release of *The Beatles With Tony Sheridan And Their Guests*.

A SIDE
MY BONNIE

CRY FOR A SHADOW

JOHNSON RAG
The Titans

SWANEE RIVER
Tony Sheridan & The Beat Brothers

THE DARKTOWN STRUTTER'S BALL
The Titans

B SIDE
THE SAINTS

RYE BEAT
The Titans

YOU ARE MY SUNSHINE
Tony Sheridan & The Beat Brothers

SUMMERTIME BEAT
The Titans

WHY

THE AMAZING BEATLES AND OTHER GREAT ENGLISH GROUP SOUNDS

Clarion 601—October 17, 1966

A re-release of the *Ain't She Sweet* album on Atco.

A SIDE
AIN'T SHE SWEET

PLEASE PLEASE ME
The Swallows

FROM ME TO YOU
The Swallows

TAKE OUT SOME INSURANCE ON ME BABY

NOBODY'S CHILD

B SIDE
SHE LOVES YOU
The Swallows

I'M TELLING YOU NOW
The Swallows

SWEET GEORGIA BROWN

I WANT TO HOLD YOUR HAND
The Swallows

I WANNA BE YOUR MAN
The Swallows

THE ORIGINAL DISCOTHEQUE HITS

Clarion 609—November 28, 1966

A various artists compilation album.

A SIDE (cut 3)
TAKE OUT SOME INSURANCE ON ME BABY

THE BEATLES — CIRCA 1960 — IN THE BEGINNING

Polydor 24-4504—May 4, 1970

This album is the same as the British release *The Early Years*, having a similar cover; it rose to No. 117 in the Billboard album chart.

A SIDE
AIN'T SHE SWEET

CRY FOR A SHADOW

LET'S DANCE
Tony Sheridan & The Beat Brothers

MY BONNIE

TAKE OUT SOME INSURANCE ON ME BABY

WHAT'D I SAY
Tony Sheridan & The Beat Brothers

B SIDE
SWEET GEORGIA BROWN

THE SAINTS

RUBY BABY
Tony Sheridan & The Beat Brothers

WHY

NOBODY'S CHILD

YA YA
Tony Sheridan & The Beat Brothers

THE FLASHBACK GREATS OF THE 60'S

K-Tel TU 229—October, 1973

A US mail-order album on K-Tel.

A SIDE (cut 2)
MY BONNIE

HISTORY OF BRITISH ROCK VOLUME 2

Sire SASH 3705—December 2, 1974

A various artists compilation double album.

RECORD 1 A SIDE (cut 1)
AIN'T SHE SWEET

THE HISTORY OF BRITISH ROCK VOLUME 3
Sire SASH-3712 — October 27, 1975

Another various artists compilation album from Sire, featuring one Beatles/Tony Sheridan track, *My Bonnie.*

THE BEATLES LIVE! AT THE STAR CLUB IN HAMBURG, GERMANY, 1962

Lingasong LS 2 7001—June 13, 1977

The American release of this album differs from the British release in that four numbers on the British album are replaced on the American version: *I Saw Her Standing There* is replaced by *I'm Gonna Sit Right Down And Cry (Over You). Twist And Shout* is replaced by *Where Have You Been All My Life. Reminiscing* is replaced by *Till There Was You* and *Ask Me Why* is replaced by *Sheila.*
    The album rose to No. 111 in the Billboard chart.

Record One
A SIDE
**I'M GONNA SIT RIGHT DOWN AND CRY
(OVER YOU)**
(See below.)

ROLL OVER BEETHOVEN

HIPPY HIPPY SHAKE

SWEET LITTLE SIXTEEN

LEND ME YOUR COMB

YOUR FEET'S TOO BIG

B SIDE
WHERE HAVE YOU BEEN ALL MY LIFE
(See below.)

MR. MOONLIGHT

A TASTE OF HONEY

BESAME MUCHO

TILL THERE WAS YOU
(See below.)

KANSAS CITY/HEY HEY HEY HEY

Record Two
A SIDE
**NOTHIN' SHAKIN' (BUT THE LEAVES ON
THE TREES)**

TO KNOW HER IS TO LOVE HER

LITTLE QUEENIE

FALLING IN LOVE AGAIN

SHEILA
(See below.)

BE-BOP-A-LULA

HALLELUJAH, I LOVE HER SO

B SIDE
RED SAILS IN THE SUNSET

EVERYBODY'S TRYING TO BE MY BABY

MATCHBOX

I'M TALKING ABOUT YOU

SHIMMY SHAKE

LONG TALL SALLY

I REMEMBER YOU

**I'M GONNA SIT RIGHT DOWN AND CRY
(OVER YOU)**
John sings this song written by Joe Thomas
and Howard Biggs. It was released as a single
by Roy Hamilton on January 25, 1954 on the
Epic label in America, and was covered
unsuccessfully by Elvis Presley on September
10, 1956 on RCA.

WHERE HAVE YOU BEEN ALL MY LIFE
John sings this Barry Mann/Cynthia Weil
song, originally recorded by Arthur
Alexander on Dot, and released on May 7,
1962.

SHEILA
George handles the vocals on this Tommy
Roe million seller. Written by Tommy Roe, the
song was released on May 28, 1962 on ABC,
and went to No. 1 in America for two weeks,
staying in the charts for fourteen weeks. In
Britain it reached No. 3 after release on HMV,
and remained in the charts for fourteen
weeks.

TILL THERE WAS YOU
Paul sings this ballad from the 1957 play, *The
Music Man*. It later appeared on the *With The
Beatles* album in Britain.

THE BEATLES TAPES

P.B.R. International 7005/7006—1978

**This double album had been released in
Great Britain in 1976; however, it did not at
that time get an American release, and was
imported into the country from Britain.
Released two years after its original British
release, the American double album
features a different cover design, and was
pressed on blue vinyl. (See British release
for tracks.)**

BRITISH GOLD

Sire R-224095—1978

**The third compilation from Sire to feature a
Beatles Hamburg track: *Ain't She Sweet*.**

**BEATLE TALK — THE WAY THEY WERE
WITH RED ROBINSON**

*Great North West Music Co. GWC-4007—
November 15, 1978*

**The interviews contained on this album are
from the private collection of Red Robinson, who recorded the Beatles' press conferences in Vancouver, Canada, in 1964
and Seattle, US, in 1966.**

FIRST LIVE RECORDINGS VOLUME ONE

Pickwick SPC-3361—January 24, 1979

Pickwick Records acquired the rights to the original Hamburg 1962 tapes, re-arranged the tracks and released them as two separate volumes.

A SIDE

WHERE HAVE YOU BEEN ALL MY LIFE

A TASTE OF HONEY

YOUR FEET'S TOO BIG

MR. MOONLIGHT

BESAME MUCHO

I'M GONNA SIT RIGHT DOWN AND CRY (OVER YOU)

BE-BOP-A-LULA

B SIDE

HALLELUJAH I LOVE HER SO

TILL THERE WAS YOU

SWEET LITTLE SIXTEEN

LITTLE QUEENIE

KANSAS CITY/HEY HEY HEY HEY

HULLY GULLY

(This last track, although from the Star Club tapes (several groups were recorded) is not by The Beatles.)

FIRST LIVE RECORDINGS VOLUME TWO

Pickwick SPC-3362—January 24, 1979

Released simultaneously with Volume One.

A SIDE

NOTHIN' SHAKIN' (BUT THE LEAVES ON THE TREES)

EVERYBODY'S TRYING TO BE MY BABY

MATCHBOX

I'M TALKIN' ABOUT YOU

LONG TALL SALLY

ROLL OVER BEETHOVEN

HIPPY HIPPY SHAKE

B SIDE

FALLING IN LOVE AGAIN

LEND ME YOUR COMB

SHEILA

RED SAILS IN THE SUNSET

TO KNOW HER IS TO LOVE HER

SHIMMY SHAKE

I REMEMBER YOU

BRITISH ROCK CLASSICS

Sire R-234021—1979

The fourth compilation from Sire to feature a Beatles' Hamburg cut: *My Bonnie.*

THE HISTORIC FIRST LIVE RECORDINGS

Pickwick PTP-2098—May 16, 1980

As in Britain, a second double album of the live Hamburg recordings appeared in America, Pickwick combining their two 1979 single albums and repackaging them as a double, with a new sleeve and sleeve notes by Howard Brindman.

RECORD ONE
A SIDE
WHERE HAVE YOU BEEN ALL MY LIFE

A TASTE OF HONEY

YOUR FEET'S TOO BIG

MR. MOONLIGHT

BESAME MUCHO

I'M GONNA SIT RIGHT DOWN AND CRY (OVER YOU)

BE-BOP-A-LULA

B SIDE

AIN'T NOTHIN' SHAKIN' (BUT THE LEAVES ON THE TREES)

EVERYBODY'S TRYING TO BE MY BABY

MATCHBOX

I'M TALKING ABOUT YOU

LONG TALL SALLY

ROLL OVER BEETHOVEN

HIPPY HIPPY SHAKE

RECORD TWO
A SIDE
HALLELUJAH I LOVE HER SO

TILL THERE WAS YOU

SWEET LITTLE SIXTEEN

LITTLE QUEENIE

KANSAS CITY/HEY HEY HEY HEY

HULLY GULLY

B SIDE

FALLING IN LOVE AGAIN

LEND ME YOUR COMB

SHEILA

RED SAILS IN THE SUNSET

TO KNOW HER IS TO LOVE HER

SHIMMY SHAKE

I REMEMBER YOU

TIMELESS

Silhouette music SM-10004—March 1, 1981

The two press conferences contained on this "limited edition picture disc" were originally released on disc in 1978, as *Beatle Talk — The Way They Were With Red Robinson* by the Great North West Music Co. The rest of the album is made up of session musicians playing poor versions

of *Imagine* and *Let It Be*, and renditions of two Beatles' fans' songs *We Love You Beatles* and *We Love The Beatles*, performed by six "starlets" dubbed "The Beatlettes".

The picture disc features four pictures of John on the "A" side, with a picture of all four Beatles wearing matadors' costumes on the "B" side.

A SIDE

IMAGINE (EXTRACT, BUT DESCRIBED AS "OUT-TAKE")

NEWSCAST (CONCERNING JOHN LENNON)

IMAGINE (COMPLETE)

PRESS CONFERENCE (WITH JOHN LENNON)
Recorded at the Astor Tower Hotel, Chicago, Illinois, August 12, 1966.

LET IT BE

B SIDE

WE LOVE YOU BEATLES
Sung by The Beatlettes

PRESS CONFERENCE (WITH THE BEATLES)
Recorded at the Empire Stadium in Vancouver, Canada, August 26, 1964. As with the British release, the date for this conference is incorrect, as it should be August 22, 1964.

WE LOVE THE BEATLES
Sung by The Beatlettes

MAGICAL MYSTERY MESSAGE
This is a short piece of gibberish, which when played backwards reveals the message "We'll miss you John".

DAWN OF THE SILVER BEATLES

PAC Records UDL 2333—April 16, 1981

PAC Records were a mail order company operating from Phoenix, Arizona. This album had a limited run of 153,000 and featured tracks from the Decca auditions.

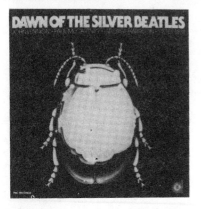

A SIDE

LOVE OF THE LOVED

MONEY

SURE TO FALL (IN LOVE WITH YOU)

TAKE GOOD CARE OF MY BABY

THREE COOL CATS

B SIDE

LIKE DREAMERS DO

**CRYING, WAITING, HOPING
SEARCHIN'**

TILL THERE WAS YOU

MEMPHIS

LIGHTNIN' STRIKES TWICE

PAC Records UDL 2382—1981

This record, of dubious origin and legality, featured a side of Beatles material from the Decca auditions — the remaining tracks not used on the *Dawn Of The Silver Beatles* album, plus a side of Elvis Presley tracks (which were almost certainly owned by RCA). By the end of 1981, PAC Records had deserted their Phoenix, Arizona, address and the album was no longer available. Beatles' tracks on the album were: *Sheik Of Araby, To Know Her Is To Love Her, Hello Little Girl, September In The Rain* and

Besame Mucho.

THE AMERICAN TOUR WITH ED RUDY

INS Radio News Documentary No. 2—1981

A reissue of the album originally released in June 1964, it reappeared in 1981 to cash in on Lennon's death.

IN THE BEGINNING (CIRCA 1960)

Polydor 24-4504—October, 1981

A re-release of the May 1970 album, except that the gatefold sleeve was dropped. (Tracks same as original.)

LIVE AT THE STAR CLUB, 1962, HAMBURG, GERMANY

Hall Of Music HMI 2200—1981

Another reissue of the live Hamburg tapes. (Tracks as original release.)

FIRST MOVEMENT

Phoenix PHX 339—April 1982

Re-release of the Polydor tracks.

A SIDE

CRY FOR A SHADOW

LET'S DANCE

IF YOU LOVE ME BABY .

WHAT'D I SAY

B SIDE

SWEET GEORGIA BROWN

RUBY BABY

YA YA

WHY

Beatles' bootlegs

THE BEATLES' BOOTLEGS

Along with Bob Dylan, The Rolling Stones and Pink Floyd, The Beatles are one of the main targets for "bootleggers". Up to 1976, there were between 160 and 170 Beatle bootlegs, and this figure will have inevitably increased greatly up to the present time. Most of The Beatles' bootlegs available are of extremely poor quality, and are very often tapes of tapes, but because they contain some officially unreleased material, are very much sought after by collectors.

Before looking at a selection of Beatles' bootlegs, one must understand exactly what a bootleg is, other than being an illegal record. There are three types of illegal records; a bootleg, a pirated album and a counterfeit album. Firstly a bootleg (or "underground record" as they were at one time called) consists of material recorded at concerts, from radio, television or film appearances, or from tapes illegally acquired from a recording studio. A pirated album consists of officially released material sleeved in a different cover from the original, such as the four album sets *The Beatles Alpha Omega*, distributed in America by Audio Tape Inc., which included over one hundred songs originally released by Capitol. A counterfeit record is an exact duplicate of an officially released album, with label and cover copying the original. Several of The Beatles' American albums have been counterfeited, including *Introducing The Beatles, Jolly What, Songs And Pictures Of The Fabulous Beatles* and *Hear The Beatles Tell All* on Vee Jay Records, as well as the Capitol albums *Sgt. Pepper* and *Let It Be*.

The Beatles' bootlegs can be separated into four recording categories: live concert recordings, radio and television appearances, film soundtrack recordings and studio material. In some cases, a certain bootleg may fall into two or more categories, i.e. a live radio recording, or may contain material from different categories. Many bootlegs contain songs from different sources, and such records are very often bootlegs of bootlegs, made up of a selection of tracks from various other bootlegs, which are invariably of appalling quality.

The following selection of Beatles' bootlegs refers only to those that fall mainly into one particular category. Although it is not a complete listing of every Beatle bootleg released (this would probably take up another book), it is intended to be a cross-section of those available.

THE CONCERT RECORDINGS
The concert recordings are very often duplicates of other live bootlegs, and although there are probably well over fifty live bootlegs, these seem to consist of only a dozen actual recordings, which have been duplicated over and over again, sometimes crediting the recording to another concert. For example, the Hollywood Bowl recording of August 23, 1964, has been bootlegged under the following titles: *Live At Shea* (double EP), *Live At Shea Stadium, 1964* and *Shea The Good Old Days*. The *Live At Shea* double EP also wrongly states the date of the concert as March, 1964, when in fact The Beatles never appeared at Shea in that month, or even in that year — their first appearance at Shea Stadium took place on August 15, 1965.

As there are so many live bootleg albums, they have been separated into the major concerts, listing the main titles bootlegged at each particular concert. Some of the albums do not contain the same tracks or the tracks in the same order as listed. Some of the dates for particular concerts are incorrectly listed on the albums, but the correct concert dates are given below.

THE ROYAL VARIETY PERFORMANCE AT THE PRINCE OF WALES THEATRE, LONDON, NOVEMBER 11, 1963.

APPEARS ON: *Cavern Club*

TRACKS: *Medley: Love Me Do; Please Please Me; From Me To You/I Want To Hold Your Hand/Can't Buy Me Love/Long Tall Sally/She Loves You.*

This album features a medley of The Beatles first three hits on the "A" side, with the "B" side containing recordings of the Shea Stadium concert of August 8, 1965.

EMPIRE THEATRE, LIVERPOOL, DECEMBER 1963

APPEARS ON: *Tour Years: Sixty Three-Sixty Six (1st side)*

TRACKS: *From Me To You/I Saw Her Standing There/Roll Over Beethoven/Boys/Till There Was You/This Boy/I Want To Hold Your Hand/Money (That's What I Want).*

This recording of The Beatles in their home town of Liverpool, could have been recorded on either December 7 or December 22, 1963, as they appeared at the Empire on both dates — the album sleeve notes do not give an exact date. (The third side of the *Tour Years* double album features a recording supposedly from Red Rock Stadium, Boulder, Colorado, in 1965, but The Beatles did not play at this venue in 1965, although they did appear there on August 26, 1964. However, this recording could not have been from 1964 as it includes such songs as *Day Tripper, Yesterday* and *Nowhere Man*, which did not appear until 1965.)

THE COLISEUM, WASHINGTON D.C., USA, FEBRUARY 11, 1964

APPEARS ON: *First United States Performance; First US Concert.*

The Beatles first concert appearance in the US at the Washington Coliseum was recorded by CBS TV.

TRACKS 1) *Roll Over Beethoven/From Me To You/I Saw Her Standing There/This Boy/All My Loving.*
TRACKS 2) *I Wanna Be Your Man/Please Please Me/Till There Was You/She Loves You/I Want To Hold Your Hand/Twist And Shout.*

CARNEGIE HALL, NEW YORK, USA, FEBRUARY 12, 1964

APPEARS ON: *Renaissance Minstrels 1*

TRACKS 1) *From Me To You/Twist And Shout/This Boy/I Saw Her Standing There/She Loves You*
TRACKS 2) *I Want To Hold Your Hand/Please Please Me/All My Loving/She Loves You.*

KB HALL, COPENHAGEN, DENMARK, JUNE 4, 1964

APPEARS ON: *John, Paul, George And Jimmy*

TRACKS: *I Want To Hold Your Hand/All My Loving/She Loves You/Till There Was You/Roll Over Beethoven/Can't Buy Me Love/This Boy/Twist And Shout.*

This concert features Jimmy Nicol deputising for Ringo, who was in hospital. The first side of the album features the Copenhagen recording, while the second contains BBC recordings.

FESTIVAL HALL, MELBOURNE, AUSTRALIA, JUNE 16, 1964

APPEARS ON: *Melbourne And Washington (1st side); Melbourne And Vancouver (1st side); Live in Melbourne; Buried Treasure; Tour Years: Sixty Three-Sixty Six (2nd side).*
TRACKS: *I Saw Her Standing There/You Can't Do That/All My Loving/She Loves You/Till There Was You/Roll Over Beethoven/Can't Buy Me Love/This Boy/Twist And Shout/Long Tall Sally.*

This live concert recording was made from a TV show sponsored by Shell (who are mentioned several times during the introductions and announcements that can be heard throughout the recording). The recording is also notable as it features Ringo's first appearance on the tour — he had been in hospital having his tonsils removed.

EMPIRE STADIUM, VANCOUVER, CANADA, AUGUST 22, 1964.

APPEARS ON: *Live In Vancouver (1st side); Vancouver 1964; Melbourne And Vancouver (2nd side)*

TRACKS: *Twist And Shout/You Can't Do That/All My Loving/She Loves You/Things We Said Today/Roll Over Beethoven/Can't Buy Me Love/If I Fell/Boys/A Hard Day's Night/Long Tall Sally.*

THE HOLLYWOOD BOWL, LOS ANGELES, USA, AUGUST 23, 1964.

APPEARS ON: *Back In 1964 At The Hollywood Bowl; The Beatles Hollywood Bowl 1964; Live At Shea 1 & 2 (2 EP's); Live At The Shea Stadium; Live In Vancouver (2nd side); Second To None; Get Yer Yeah Yeahs Out.*

TRACKS 1) *Twist And Shout/You Can't Do That/All My Loving/She Loves You/Things We Said Today/Roll Over Beethoven.*
TRACKS 2) *Can't Buy Me Love/If I Fell/I Want To Hold Your Hand/Boys/A Hard Day's Night/Long Tall Sally.*

Supposedly this original tape was officially recorded by Capitol Records for live release, but The Beatles would not allow its use. This is possibly the most used Beatles bootleg tape of all.

THE CONVENTION HALL, ATLANTA CITY, USA, AUGUST 30, 1964 and THE CONVENTION HALL, PHILADELPHIA, USA, SEPTEMBER 2, 1964.

APPEARS ON: *The Beatles In Atlanta Whiskey Flats; Alive At Last In Atlanta; Live Concert Atlanta, GA; Live Concert At Whiskey Flats.*

TRACKS: *as per Hollywood Bowl.*

It is debatable which concert was used for these particular bootlegs — some sources give Philadelphia and some Atlanta, but either way, it is an exact duplication in terms of songs of the *Hollywood Bowl* concert, as it was recorded from the same American Tour.

PALAIS DES SPORTS, PARIS, FRANCE, JUNE 20, 1965 (two shows)

APPEARS ON: *Live At The Paris Olympia (1st show); Paris Again (1st show); Paris '65 (both shows); Paris Sports Palais (1st show); Paris Sports Palais 1965 (2nd show); Sports Palais France (2nd show).*

TRACKS 1)*I Feel Fine/Twist And Shout/She's A Woman/Ticket To Ride/Can't Buy Me Love/I'm A Loser.*
TRACKS 2) *I Wanna Be Your Man/A Hard Day's Night/Baby's In Black/Rock 'N' Roll Music/Everybody's Trying To Be My Baby/Long Tall Sally.*

SHEA STADIUM, NEW YORK, USA, AUGUST 15, 1965.

APPEARS ON: *Last Live Show; Shea Stadium; Live Performance Shea 15-8-1965; Cavern Club (2nd side).*

TRACKS 1)*Twist And Shout/I Feel Fine/Dizzy Miss Lizzy/Ticket To Ride.*
TRACKS 2) *Act Naturally/Can't Buy Me Love/Baby's In Black/A Hard Day's Night/Help/I'm Down.*

Although one of the albums is titled *Last Live Show*, their Shea Stadium concert of August 15, 1965, was not their last performance. The record also features an interview with The Beatles, Ed Sullivan and Brian Epstein and an introduction by Murray The K. This recording was taken from a TV broadcast of the Shea Stadium concert.

SAM HOUSTON COLISEUM, HOUSTON, TEXAS, USA, AUGUST 19, 1965 (two shows)

APPEARS ON: *Live From Sam Houston Coliseum; Texan Troubadours*

TRACKS: *Twist And Shout/She's A Woman/I Feel Fine/Dizzy Miss Lizzy/Ticket To Ride/Everybody's Trying To Be My Baby/Can't Buy Me Love/Baby's In Black/I Wanna Be Your Man/A Hard Day's Night/Help!/I'm Down.*

These recordings — made at both afternoon and evening concerts at the Sam Houston Coliseum, on the Beatles Second American Tour in 1965 — include various introductions, announcements and instructions made from the stage to the audience by the concert organisers. The Beatles performed the same numbers for both the afternoon and evening performances: both shows are included on the two double albums that feature the recordings.

CIRCUS KRONE, MUNICH, WEST GERMANY, JUNE 24, 1966

APPEARS ON: *Live In Germany EP*

TRACKS 1) *Rock and Roll Music/I Feel Fine/Yesterday*
TRACKS 2) *Nowhere Man/I'm Down*

This EP demonstrates that The Beatles were no strangers to Germany and its language, as they introduce the songs in German as well as English.

BUDOKAN HALL, TOKYO, JAPAN, JULY 1/2, 1966

APPEARS ON: *The Beatles Tour The Great Take-Over (July 1); Five Nights In A Judo Arena (July 2); Second To None (July 2); Tokyo '66 (July 1); On Stage In Japan, 1966 (July 2); Tour Years: Sixty Three-Sixty Six (4th side).*

TRACKS 1) *Rock'n'Roll Music/She's A Woman/If I Needed Someone/Day Tripper/Baby's In Black/I Feel Fine*
Tracks 2) *Yesterday/I Wanna Be Your Man/Nowhere Man/Paperback Writer/I'm Down*

There were two concerts at the Budokan Hall, the earlier performance supposedly being used on *The Beatles Tour The Great Take-Over*, which also includes a press conference, and the July 2 concert recordings being used for the other albums.

CANDLESTICK PARK, SAN FRANCISCO, CALIFORNIA, USA, AUGUST 29, 1966

APPEARS ON: *Live At San Francisco's Candlestick Park*

TRACKS 1) *Rock'n'Roll Music/She's A Woman/If I Needed Someone/Day Tripper/ Baby's In Black*
TRACKS 2) *I Feel Fine/Yesterday/I Wanna Be Your Man/Nowhere Man/Paperback Writer/ I'm Down*

This was The Beatles' very last public performance, and the song selection is the same as for the Budokan Hall concert, which was part of the tour of Germany and the Far East undertaken a month before their last American Tour.

The above is only a selection of the main live bootlegs. There are many other live songs included on many other different bootlegs, which are made up of songs from a variety of sources.

All live Beatles recordings are from the period 1963-1966, during the peak of Beatlemania, and as most were recorded using a single microphone within the audience, the sound quality is appalling, and all suffer from the continual screaming of thousands of fans. The total number of different songs performed by The Beatles during the above fifteen concerts was thirty-five, which is a small number when one considers that they had released over 110 songs between 1962 and 1966. These thirty-five songs are duplicated on over forty bootleg albums.

RADIO AND TELEVISION APPEARANCES
The bootlegged radio and television appearances originated from concerts or live performances taped specifically for broadcasting. A bootleg taped directly from radio or television gives poor recording

quality, with the possibility of the usual interference associated with these media. The majority of these tapes feature the same songs as the "live" bootlegs and are thus not dissimilar to those albums. However, the most interesting recordings in this section must be the BBC appearances, as they feature songs officially never released by The Beatles (see *Unreleased Recordings* appendix for BBC recordings information).

As with the "live" recordings, this bootleg category lists original appearances, but it is probably safe to say that many of the bootlegs containing the BBC recordings have been made directly from misappropriated original BBC tapes, and thus the quality of these bootlegs is generally superior to the others in this section.

BBC RADIO APPEARANCES 1962—1965
There are many bootlegs with selected BBC radio recordings, but those listed below are comprised entirely (or one whole side) of BBC recordings:

YELLOW MATTER CUSTARD
(also available as *As Sweet As You Are*.)

TRACKS 1) *I Got A Woman/Glad All Over/I Just Don't Understand/Slow Down/Don't Ever Change/A Shot Of Rhythm And Blues/ Sure To Fall (In Love With You).*
TRACKS 2) *Nothing Shakin' (But The Leaves On The Trees)/Lonesome Tears In My Eyes/ So How Come (No One Loves Me)/I'm Gonna Sit Right Down And Cry (Over You)/Crying, Waiting, Hoping/To Know Her Is To Love Her/The Honeymoon Song.*

This is probably the best known of the "BBC" albums. Many of the songs are titled incorrectly on the album; the correct titles are given above.

REUNION NONSENSE — NINTH AMENDMENT

TRACKS 2nd side only: *Soldier Of Love (Lay Down Your Arms)/I Got A Woman/Kansas City/Some Other Guy/Lend Me Your Comb/ Carol/Lucille/The Hippy Hippy Shake/ Shout/Memphis Tennessee.*

STUDIO SESSIONS 1
(also called *Outtakes 1*)

TRACKS 1) *You Really Got A Hold On Me/The Hippy Hippy Shake/Misery/Money (That's What I Want)/Till There Was You/Do You Want To Know A Secret.*
TRACKS 2) *From Me To You/Roll Over Beethoven/Love Me Do/Kansas City/Long Tall Sally/Please Please Me.*

STUDIO SESSIONS 2
(also called *Outtakes 2*)

TRACKS 1) *Honey Don't/Chains/I Saw Her Standing There/Sure To Fall (In Love With You)/Lucille/Boys.*
TRACKS 2) *She Loves You/Words Of Love/Devil In Her Heart/Anna (Go To Him)/Money (That's What I Want)/There's A Place.*

BEATLES' BROADCASTS

TRACKS 1) *Pop Go The Beatles/Long Tall Sally/Carol/Soldier Of Love (Lay Down Your Arms)/Lend Me Your Comb/Clarabella/Memphis/I Got A Woman/Sure To Fall (In Love With You)/Do You Want To Know A Secret.*
TRACKS 2) *The Hippy Hippy Shake/Till There Was You/Matchbox/I'm A Loser/She's A Woman/I Feel Fine/Everybody's Trying To Be My Baby/I'll Follow The Sun*

THE BEATLES AT THE BEEB

TRACKS: *From Us To You/The Hippy Hippy Shake/Memphis Tennessee/Please Mr. Postman/Too Much Monkey Business/Do You Want To Know A Secret/I'll Be On My Way/Crying, Waiting, Hoping/Pop Go The Beatles/To Know Her Is To Love Her/Don't Ever Change/Carol/Soldier Of Love (Lay Down Your Arms)/Lend Me Your Comb/Clarabella/S Shot Of Rhythm And Blues/Matchbox/Sure To Fall (In Love With You)/Lonesome Tears In My Eyes/I Got A Woman/The Honeymoon Song/From Us To You/All My Loving/Roll Over Beethoven/Till There Was You/I Wanna Be Your Man/Can't Buy Me Love/This Boy/Long Tall Sally/And I Love Her/A Hard Day's Night/Things We Said Today/I'm A Loser/She's A Woman/I Feel Fine/Kansas City — Hey Hey Hey Hey/Everybody's Trying To Be My Baby/Dizzy Miss Lizzy/Ticket To Ride.*

On March 7, 1982, the BBC celebrated the twentieth anniversary of The Beatles first appearance in a BBC studio by broadcasting a two hour special called "The Beatles At The Beeb" on Radio 1. In the July issue of *Record Collector* it was reported that a double album of the radio show, released by BBC Transcription Services, was available on BBC CN 3970, containing thirty-six Beatle songs. During the summer of 1982 a bootleg double album, titled *The Beatles At The Beeb*, was available, and this probably originated from the official BBC record.

SWEDISH RADIO BROADCAST (1963)

APPEARS ON: *Sweden 1963.*

TRACKS 1st side only: *I Saw Her Standing There/From Me To You/Money (That's What I Want)/Roll Over Beethoven/You Really Got A Hold On Me/She Loves You/Twist And Shout.*

These songs were recorded at a Beatles' concert at Karlaplan, Stockholm, during their Swedish Tour of 1963, on October 24, and were broadcast on Swedish radio. Some sources incorrectly credit this recording to the Swedish television programme *Drop In*, which was recorded on October 30, and broadcast on November 3, 1963; this recording did not include *Roll Over Beethoven.*

"AROUND THE BEATLES" TV PROGRAMME, MAY 6, 1964

APPEARS ON: *Around The Beatles (1st side); EMI Outtakes (2nd side).*

TRACKS: *Twist And Shout/Roll Over Beethoven/I Wanna Be Your Man/Long Tall Sally/Medley — Love Me Do; Please Please Me; From Me To You; She Loves You/I Want To Hold Your Hand/Can't Buy Me Love/Shout*

"SHINDIG" CBS TV 1964

APPEARS ON: *Live In Europe And US TV Casts (2nd side); Live In Washington D.C. (2nd side).*

TRACKS: *Kansas City/Boys/I'm A Loser.*

This recording was made at the Granville Theatre, London on October 9, 1964, for the American CBS TV programme *Shindig* and broadcast later that month.

ED SULLIVAN SHOWS, FEBRUARY 9th AND 23rd, 1964

APPEARS ON: *Ed Sullivan Show CBS TV Studio*

TRACKS: *All My Loving/She Loves You/This Boy (from 9th) and I Saw Her Standing There/I Want To Hold Your Hand/From Me To You/Twist And Shout/Please Please Me/She Loves You (from 23rd).*

The very first Beatles' appearance on the Ed Sullivan Show was recorded on February 7, 1964, in New York and broadcast two days later. The second show was recorded at the Beauville Hotel, Miami Beach, on February 16, and broadcast on February 23.

ED SULLIVAN SHOW, SEPTEMBER 12, 1965

APPEARS ON: *Peace Of Mind (2nd side)*

TRACKS: *I Feel Fine/I'm Down/Act Naturally/Ticket To Ride/Yesterday/Help!*

The Beatles' third "live" appearance on the Ed Sullivan Show was recorded in New York on August 14, 1965, and broadcast on September 12, 1965, on CBS TV.

FILM SOUNDTRACKS

There are several methods of recording this type of bootleg: 1) at the cinema, which would probably result in very poor quality; 2) from a television playback, giving better quality than the previous method, but still being possibly impaired by interference and 3) the latest form, that of recording from video cassette, which would be far superior in sound quality to the first two methods.

Most of the soundtrack recordings are of terrible sound quality, and without the visual element of the film, the soundtrack very often means nothing. With the advent of the video cassette, this type of bootleg will probably disappear, as no one will be prepared to buy sound only recordings when they can acquire the sound and vision in excellent quality — both *Magical Mystery Tour* and *Let It Be* were made available on video cassette in America during 1981.

The Beatles made five major films between 1964 and 1970, which are listed below along with the main bootlegs containing each.

A HARD DAY'S NIGHT

APPEARS ON: *A Hard Day's Night and Cinelogue 3 (both double albums)*

SONGS PERFORMED IN THE FILM ARE: *A Hard Day's Night/I Should Have Known Better/I Wanna Be Your Man/Don't Bother Me/All My Loving/If I Fell/Can't Buy Me Love/And I Love Her/I'm Happy Just To Dance With You/Ringo's Theme (This Boy) (instrumental)/A Hard Day's Night (instrumental)/Can't Buy Me Love/Tell Me Why/If I Fell/I Should Have Known Better (instrumental)/She Loves You/A Hard Day's Night.*

HELP!

APPEARS ON: *Cinelogue 4 (double album)*

SONGS PERFORMED IN THE FILM ARE:

Help!/You're Going To Lose That Girl/You've Got To Hide Your Love Away/Ticket To Ride/I Need You/The Night Before/Another Girl/Help and the following instrumentals: The Bitter End (including You Can't Do That)/From Me To You Fantasy/In

The Tyrol (including Wagner's Overture to Act III Of "Lohengrin")/Another Hard Day's Night and The Chase. All were performed by Ken Thorne and his Orchestra.

MAGICAL MYSTERY TOUR

APPEARS ON: *Cinelogue 5 (double album)*

SONGS PERFORMED BY THE BEATLES ARE: *Magical Mystery Tour/The Fool On The Hill/Flying/I Am The Walrus/Blue Jay Way/Your Mother Should Know/Hello Goodbye (part)/and Magical Mystery Tour (again).* Also included are instrumental versions of *All My Loving* and *Yesterday, The Bonzo Dog Band* performing *Death Cab For Cutie* and Shirley Collins, an accordionist, performing two Beatles originals, *Shirley's Wild Accordion* and *Jessie's Dream.* Also included are a medley of *Toot Toot Tootsie Goodbye/The Happy Wanderer/When Irish Eyes Are Smiling* and *Never On Sunday.*

YELLOW SUBMARINE

APPEARS ON: *Cinelogue 2 (double album)*

SONGS INCLUDED ARE: *Yellow Submarine/Eleanor Rigby/Within You Without You (part)/A Day In The Life (orchestral build-up only)/All Together Now/When I'm Sixty Four/Only A Northern Song/Nowhere Man/Lucy In The Sky With Diamonds/Sgt. Pepper's Lonely Hearts Club Band/With A Little Help From My Friends (part)/All You Need Is Love/Baby You're A Rich Man (part)/Hey Bulldog/It's All Too Much (including extra verse not on album version)/All Together Now.*

Hey Bulldog was cut from American prints of the film when initally released, and therefore does not appear on the bootleg albums.

LET IT BE

APPEARS IN ITS ENTIRETY ON: *Cinelogue 1 (double album)*
APPEARS IN PART ON: *Get Back Sessions 2; Virgin Plus Three; More Get Back Sessions; Some Like It Hot.*

The Beatles performed the following numbers in the film: Piano solo (by Paul)/*Don't Let Me Down/Maxwell's Silver Hammer/Two Of Us/I Got A Feeling/Oh Darling/One After 909/Jazz Piano Song/Two Of Us (No. 2)/Across The Universe/Dig A Pony/Suzy Parker/I Me Mine/For You Blue/Besame Mucho/Octopus's Garden/You Really Got A Hold On Me/The Long And Winding Road* (reggae version)/*The Long And Winding Road* (short version)/*Shake Rattle And Roll/Kansas City/Lawdy*

Miss Clawdy/Dig It (full version)/*Two Of Us (No. 3)/Let It Be/The Long And Winding Road* (full version)/*(Get Back/Don't Let Me Down (No. 2)* and *The "Laughing" Get Back,* which is played over the credits.

Of all The Beatles films, *Let It Be* has the most interesting soundtrack, as it gives an insight into how The Beatles recorded and developed their songs in the studio.

THE STUDIO OUTTAKES

Probably the most interesting of the four bootleg categories, as these sometimes contain material not officially released. Normally the source by which these recordings are acquired is illegal, i.e. stolen tapes from the recording studio. They can often be of very good quality compared to other types of bootlegs, as they are invariably taken directly from a studio tape.

There are many bootlegs in this category which contain alternative versions of officially released recordings. The list below gives those songs which have never been released officially, plus the *Get Back* sessions.

THE GET BACK SESSIONS

The *Get Back* sessions have found their way on to bootlegs via two sources: the promotional copies of the original *Get Back* album distributed to disc jockeys in America before the whole album was shelved, and tapes acquired from Twickenham Film Studios.

THE PROMOTIONAL ALBUM

There are about ten bootlegs containing the songs from this album, which consisted of: *Get Back/When You Walk/Let It Be/One After 909/Teddy Boy/Two Of Us/Don't Let Me Down/I've Got A Feeling/The Long And Winding Road/Dig It/For You Blue/Dig A Pony/Get Back.*

Although not always in the same order, and sometimes titled incorrectly, these songs appear on the following bootlegs: *A Studio Recording* (also includes *Across The Universe*), *Fab Four, Get Back Sessions* (includes *Across The Universe*), *Get Back To Toronto* (included Christmas Message/ Peace Message), *Kum Back, Let It Be Live* (includes *Across The Universe*), *The Let It Be Performance* (includes *Save The Last Dance For Me/Maggie Mae* — double album with live second LP), *Next To The Last Recording Session — Fifth Amendment* (Same as first album of *The 'Let It Be' Performance*), *Renaissance Minstrels 2* (includes *Across The Universe/I'm Down/Instant Karma*), *The Very Best Of The Beatles Rarest Vol. 6* (same as *The 'Let It Be' Performance*).

TWICKENHAM FILM STUDIOS

These tapes, recorded during the rehearsals for the *Let It Be* album (see *Let It Be* album in British section), contain several versions of many of the songs performed in the film along with a few other gems, including many early versions of *Get Back*. The recordings appear on the following bootlegs: *Sweet Apple Trax* (a double album), *Sweet Apple Trax Vols One & Two* (two double albums), *Hahst Az Son, Hi Ho Silver, Hot As Sun* and *The Very Best Of The Beatles Rarest Vol 1.*

The songs included on the above albums are: *Two Of Us/Don't Let Me Down/When You Get To Suzy Parker Everybody Gets Well Done/I've Got A Feeling/No Pakistanis* (early version of *Get Back*)/*Get Back/Don't Let Me Down (2)/Be Bop A Lula/She Came In Through The Bathroom Window/High Heeled Sneakers/I Me Mine/I've Got A Feeling (2)/One After 909/Norwegian Wood/She Came In Through The Bathroom Window (2)/Let It Be/Shakin' In The Sixties/Good Rockin' Tonight/Across The Universe/Two Of Us (2)/Momma You've Been On My Mind/Tennessee/House Of The Rising Sun/Back To The Commonwealth/White Power; Promenade/Hi Ho Silver/For You Blue/Let It Be (2).*

OTHER UNRELEASED EMI RECORDINGS

Of the twenty-five to thirty known unreleased Beatles songs recorded by EMI (other than those from the so-called *Get Back* sessions) only three have appeared on bootlegs to date. These are *How Do You Do It* (from 1962), *Peace Of Mind* (1967) and John's *What's The New Mary Jane* (from 1967 and 1969). Each song has appeared many times on various bootlegs, which include a variety of songs from radio, television, film soundtrack, live and studio sources. The three songs can be found on the following albums:
How Do You Do It — How Do You Do It.
Peace Of Mind — Dr. Robert, Peace Of Mind, 20 x 4, Strawberry Fields.

What's The New Mary Jane — Dr. Robert, Spicy Beatles Songs, Super Tracks 1, Bye Bye Bye, EMI Outtakes, The Very Best Of The Beatles Rarest Vol. 4 and *What's The New Mary Jane.*

THE DECCA RECORDS AUDITION TAPE

These recordings appear on several bootleg albums — the main titles being *The Decca Tapes, The Beatles Decca Audition Tapes* and *The Decca Gone Sessions* — as well as on a series of singles pressed on coloured vinyl, all in individual picture sleeves. *The Decca Tapes* album has a bogus Decca Records catalogue number, LK 4438-1, and also credits Mike Smith as producer. (See *Complete Silver Beatles* album in Appendix 00.) The album contains the following numbers: *Like Dreamers Do/Money (That's What I Want)/Till There Was You/Shiek of Araby/To Know Her Is To Love Her/Take Good Care Of My Baby/ Memphis/Sure To Fall (In Love With You)/Hello Little Girl/Three Cool Cats/ Crying, Waiting, Hoping/Love Of The Loved/September In The Rain/Besame Mucho/Searchin'.*

One bootleg called *Decca Audition Outtakes — Super Studio Series 2*, a double album containing twenty-four songs, is not the Decca recordings, as the title suggests, because the track listing includes *She Loves You* and *From Me To You*, which hadn't been written at the time of the audition. Of the twenty-four songs on the album only one, *Money (That's What I Want)* was performed by The Beatles at the Decca auditions.

THE BEATLES IN THE BMRB CHART 1962 — 1982

The British Market Research Bureau Chart, which is compiled for the BBC and *Music Week*, has over the past few years, since the publication of the excellent *Guinness Book Of British Hit Singles*, become the "Chart Bible". *Record Retailer* which later became *Music Week*, first published a Top 50 singles chart on March 10, 1960, by basing their figures on the average from *NME, Melody Maker, Disc* and *Record Mirror*. In 1969 the British Phonographic Industry engaged the BMRB (British Market Research Bureau) to compile a weekly singles chart, which is broadcast by the BBC and published by *Music Week* and *Record Mirror*. On May 13, 1978, the Top 50 was extended to a Top 75. *The Guinness Book Of British Hit Singles* first appeared in 1977,

and instantly become one of the top selling books in the country. As it is updated every two years, 1981 saw the appearance of the third edition.

The Beatles hits in the BMRB Chart amount to twenty-eight, with ten re-entries listed. The hit songs written by The Beatles (up to 1970) and recorded by other artists amount to sixty-one, making a grand total of eighty-nine song hits on the BMRB Chart. The list below includes those songs written by Lennon, McCartney and Harrison up to 1970, but does not include those written during the "solo years" e.g. *Come And Get It*, recorded by Apple group Badfinger, was written solely by Paul McCartney, and is therefore not included.

ARTIST	SONG TITLE	ENTRY DATE	HIGHEST POSITION WEEKS AT NO. 1	WEEKS IN CHART
APPLEJACKS	Like Dreamers Do	11/6/64	20	11
KENNY BALL & HIS JAZZMEN	When I'm 64	19/7/67	43	2
BARRON KNIGHTS	Call Up The Groups (includes I Wanna Be Your Man)	9/7/64	3	13
SHIRLEY BASSEY	Something	20/6/70	4	21
	Something (re-entry)	23/1/71	50	1
	The Fool On The Hill	2/1/71	48	1
BEATLES	Love Me Do	11/10/62	17	18
	Please Please Me	17/1/63	2	18
	From Me To You	18/4/63	1/7	21
	She Loves You	29/8/63	1/6	31
	I Want To Hold Your Hand	5/12/63	1/5	21
	Can't Buy Me Love	26/3/64	1/3	14
	She Loves You (re-entry)	9/4/64	42	2
	I Want To Hold Your Hand (re-entry)	14/5/64	48	1
	Ain't She Sweet	11/6/64	29	6
	Can't Buy Me Love (re-entry)	9/7/64	47	1
	A Hard Day's Night	16/7/64	1/3	13
	I Feel Fine	3/12/64	1/5	14
	Ticket To Ride	15/4/65	1/3	12
	Help!	29/7/65	1/3	14
	Day Tripper/We Can Work It Out	9/12/65	1/5	12
	Paperback Writer	16/6/66	1/2	11
	Yellow Submarine/ Eleanor Rigby	11/8/66	1/4	13
	Penny Lane/Strawberry Fields Forever	23/2/67	2	11

	All You Need Is Love	12/7/67	1/3	13
	Hello Goodbye	29/11/67	1/7	12
	Magical Mystery Tour (double EP)	13/12/67	2	12
	Lady Madonna	20/3/68	1/2	8
	Hey Jude	4/9/68	1/2	16
	Get Back	23/4/69	1/6	17
	Ballad Of John And Yoko	4/6/69	1/3	14
	Something/Come Together	8/11/69	4	12
	Let It Be	14/3/70	2	9
	Let It Be (re-entry)	24/10/70	43	1
	Yesterday	13/3/76	8	7
	Hey Jude (re-entry)	27/3/76	12	7
	Paperback Writer (re-entry)	27/3/76	23	5
	Strawberry Fields Forever (re-entry)	3/4/76	32	3
	Get Back (re-entry)	3/4/76	28	5
	Help! (re-entry)	10/4/76	37	3
	Back In The USSR	10/7/76	19	6
	Sgt. Pepper's Lonely Hearts Club Band — With A Little Help From My Friends	7/10/78	63	3
	The Beatles Movie Medley	5/6/82	10	9
	Love Me Do (re-entry)	16/10/82	4	7
BEDROCKS	Ob-La-Di Ob-La-Da	18/12/68	20	7
CLIFF BENNETT AND THE REBEL ROUSERS	Got To Get You Into My Life	11/8/66	6	11
CILLA BLACK	Love Of The Loved	17/10/63	35	6
	It's For You	6/8/64	7	10
	Step Inside Love	13/3/68	8	9
JOE BROWN	With A Little Help From My Friends	29/6/67	32	4
DAVID CASSIDY	Please Please Me	27/7/74	16	6
RAY CHARLES	Yesterday	20/12/67	44	4
	Eleanor Rigby	31/7/68	36	9
JOE COCKER	With A Little Help From My Friends	2/10/68	1/1	13
CREAM	Badge	9/4/69	18	10
	Badge (re-entry)	28/10/72	42	4
DAVID AND JONATHAN	Michelle	13/1/66	11	6
D.B.M.	Disco Beatlemania	12/11/77	45	3
DOLLAR	I Wanna Hold Your Hand	24/11/79	9	14
DOWLANDS	All My Loving	9/1/64	33	7
EARTH, WIND AND FIRE	Got To Get You Into My Life	7/10/78	33	7
MARIANNE FAITHFULL	Yesterday	4/11/65	36	4
BRYAN FERRY	"Extended Play" EP includes It's Only Love	7/8/76	7	9
ELLA FITZGERALD	Can't Buy Me Love	30/4/64	34	5
FOURMOST	Hello Little Girl	12/9/63	9	17
	I'm In Love	26/12/63	17	12
FOUR SEASONS	We Can Work It Out	27/11/76	34	4
STEVE HARLEY & COCKNEY REBEL	Here Comes The Sun	31/7/76	10	7
EMMYLOU HARRIS	Here There And Everywhere	6/3/76	30	6

HOLLIES	If I Needed Someone	9/12/65	20	9
MARY HOPKIN	Goodbye	2/4/69	2	14
ELTON JOHN	Lucy In The Sky With Diamonds	23/11/74	10	10
ELTON JOHN & JOHN LENNON	I Saw Her Standing There	21/3/81	40	4
BILLY J. KRAMER AND THE DAKOTAS	Do You Want To Know A Secret	2/5/63	2	15
	Bad To Me	1/8/63	1/3	14
	I'll Keep You Satisfied	7/11/63	4	13
	From A Window	23/7/64	10	8
MARMALADE	Ob-La-Di Ob-La-Da	4/12/68	1/3	20
SIMON MAY	We'll Gather Lilacs/All My Loving (medley)	21/5/77	49	2
MATT MONRO	Yesterday	21/10/65	8	12
RAY MORGAN	The Long And Winding Road	25/7/70	32	6
NATURALS	I Should Have Known Better	20/8/64	24	9
OVERLANDERS	Michelle	13/1/66	1/3	10
PETER AND GORDON	A World Without Love	12/4/64	1/2	14
	Nobody I Know	4/6/64	10	11
	Woman	24/2/66	28	7
WILSON PICKETT	Hey Jude	8/1/69	16	9
PLASTIC ONO BAND	Give Peace A Chance	9/7/69	2	13
	Give Peace A Chance (re-entry)	24/1/81	33	5
P.J. PROBY	That Means A Lot	30/9/65	30	6
OTIS REDDING	Day Tripper	23/3/67	43	6
REZILLOS	I Wanna Be Your Man	18/8/79	71	1
ROLLING STONES	I Wanna Be Your Man	14/11/63	12	16
ST. LOUIS UNION	Girl	13/1/66	11	10
PETER SELLERS	A Hard Day's Night	23/12/65	14	7
TONY SHERIDAN AND THE BEATLES	My Bonnie	6/7/63	48	1
SILKIE	You've Got To Hide Your Love Away	23/9/65	28	6
STAR SOUND	Stars On 45 (including Beatles medley)	18/4/81	2	14
ROD STEWART	Get Back	20/11/76	11	9
THREE GOOD REASONS	Nowhere Man	10/3/66	47	3
TRASH	Golden Slumbers/Carry That Weight	25/10/69	35	3
TRUTH	Girl	3/2/66	27	6
STEVIE WONDER	We Can Work It Out	15/5/71	27	7
YOUNG IDEA	With A Little Help From My Friends	29/6/67	10	6

SONG RECORDING DATES

The following is an alphabetical listing of The Beatles songs giving the recording dates for each. It is not possible to give the exact date of each recording, as not all are known, and the recording of some songs, especially in the later years, was spread over several days, weeks or even months — in these cases, the date listed reflects when recording began on a particular song. With some songs only an approximation can be given.

Also included in the list are the "other" recording studios used on certain songs.

Nearly all The Beatles' songs were recorded at EMI's St. John's Wood Studios in Abbey Road. There are four of these studios, numbered 1, 2, 3 and 4. The largest is No. 1, which is used mainly for orchestral and operatic recordings. The Beatles used No. 2 studio most often, but they did use No.'s 3 and 4 from time to time, and even the largest studio, No. 1, was used for a few songs. Where no studio is listed, it is assumed that studio No. 2 was used. An overall recording "period" is given for each of the original albums.

TITLE	STUDIO (OR RECORDING VENUE) where known	TIME OF RECORDING (Std = STARTED RECORDING) or extent of recording
ABBEY ROAD (LP)	Mainly No. 2	April — August, 1969
Across The Universe (version 1)		February 1968
Across The Universe (version 2)	Apple	Late January 1969
Act Naturally		Late May — Early June '65
All I've Got To Do		July 15, 1963
All My Loving		July 15, 1963
All My Loving — Live	Hollywood Bowl	August 23, 1964
All Together Now		Mid June, 1967
All You Need Is Love	Olympic	June 14, 1967
And I Love Her		March — April 1964
And Your Bird Can Sing		Std April, 1966
Anna (Go To Him)		February 11, 1963
Another Girl		Early February — Early March, '65
Any Time At All		June 1-3, 1964
Ask Me Why		November 26, 1962
Baby It's You		February 11, 1963
Baby You're A Rich Man	Olympic	May 11, 1967
Baby's In Black		Late September — Mid October, 1964
Back In The USSR		Std August 22, 1968
Bad Boy		May 10-11, 1965
Ballad Of John And Yoko, The	Apple	April 22, 1969
BEATLES, THE (LP)	EMI & Trident	May 30 - October 17, 1968
BEATLES FOR SALE (LP)		Late September — Mid October, 1964
Because		Early September — Mid August, 1969
Being For The Benefit Of Mr. Kite		Std February 17, 1967
Birthday		September 18, 1968
Blackbird		Std June 11, 1968
Blue Jay Way		Std September 6, 1967
Boys		February 11, 1963
Boys — Live	Hollywood Bowl	August 23, 1964
Can't Buy Me Love	Pathé Marconi, Paris	January 29, 1964 and
	Abbey Road	February 25, 1964
Can't Buy Me Love — Live	Hollywood Bowl	August 30, 1965
Carry That Weight		April — August, 1969

Chains		February 11, 1963
Come Together		Std July 21, 1969
The Continuing Story Of		
Bungalow Bill		October 9-10, 1968
Cry Baby Cry		Std July 15, 1968
Day In The Life, A	(Studio No. 1)	Std January 19, 1967, Orch — February 10, 1967
Day Tripper		Early November, 1965
Dear Prudence	Trident	Std August 28, 1968
Devil In Her Heart		July 15, 1963
Dig A Pony	Apple	Std January 20, 1969
Dig It	Apple	January, 1969
Dizzy Miss Lizzy		May 10-11, 1965
Dizzy Miss Lizzy — Live	Hollywood Bowl	August 30, 1965
Dr. Robert		April, 1966
Don't Bother Me		July 15, 1963
Don't Let Me Down	Apple	Late January, 1969
Don't Pass Me By		Std July 12, 1968
Do You Want To Know A Secret		February 11, 1963
Drive My Car		Mid October — Early November, 1965
Eight Days A Week		Late September — Mid October, 1964
Eleanor Rigby — vocal		April 20, 1966
— backing		April 20 & 28, 1966
The End		April — August 1969
Everybody's Got Something To Hide Except Me And My Monkey		Std July 31, 1968
Everybody's Trying To Be My Baby		Late September — Mid October, 1964
Every Little Thing		Late September — Mid October, 1964
Fixing A Hole		Std February 21, 1967
Flying		Std September 8, 1967
Fool On The Hill, The		Std September 25, 1967
For No One		April, 1966
For You Blue	Apple	Late January, 1969
From Me To You		March 4, 1963
Get Back (both versions)	Apple	Late January, 1969
Getting Better		Std March 9, 1967
Girl		Mid October — Early November, 1965
Glass Onion		May 30 — October 14, 1968
Golden Slumbers		Std July 31, 1968
Good Day Sunshine		April, 1966
Good Morning, Good Morning		Std February 16, 1967
Goodnight		Std June 11, 1968
Got To Get You Into My Life		April, 1966
Happiness Is A Warm Gun		Std September 23, 1968
A Hard Day's Night		April 16, 1964
A Hard Day's Night — Live	Hollywood Bowl	August 30, 1965
A HARD DAY'S NIGHT (LP)		March — June, 1964
Hello Goodbye		Std October 2, 1967
Help!		April 13, 1965
Help! — Live	Hollywood Bowl	August 30, 1965
HELP! (LP)		Early February — Early June, 1965
Helter Skelter		Std September, 1968
Her Majesty		April — August, 1969

Here Comes The Sun		Std Early July, 1969
Here, There And Everywhere		April, 1966
Hey Bulldog		Mid February, 1968
Hey Jude — group	Trident	July 31, 1968
—orchestra	Trident	August 1, 1968
Hold Me Tight		July 15, 1963
Honey Don't		Late September — Mid October, 1964
Honey Pie	Trident	Std October 1, 1968
I Am The Walrus		September, 1967
I Call Your Name		Late February, 1964
I Don't Want To Spoil The Party		Late September — Mid October, 1964
I Feel Fine		Early October, 1964
I Me Mine		January 3, 1970
I Need You		Early February — Early March, 1965
I Saw Her Standing There		February 11, 1963
I Should Have Known Better		March — April, 1964
I Wanna Be Your Man		July 15, 1963
I Want To Hold Your Hand		October 19, 1963
I Want To Tell You		April, 1966
I Want You (She's So Heavy)		April — August, 1969
I Will		Std September 16, 1969
If I Fell		March — April, 1964
If I Needed Someone		Mid October — Early November, 1965
I'll Be Back		June 1-3, 1964
I'll Cry Instead		June 1-3, 1964
I'll Follow The Sun		Late September — Mid October, 1964
I'll Get You		July 7, 1963
I'm A Loser		Late September — Mid October, 1964
I'm Down		Late May, 1965
I'm Happy Just To Dance With You		March — April, 1964
I'm Looking Through You		Mid October — Early November, 1965
I'm Only Sleeping		April, 1966
I'm So Tired	Trident	October 9, 1968
In My Life		Mid October — Early November, 1965
The Inner Light — backing	EMI, Bombay, India	January, 1968
— vocal		February 6, 1968
It Won't Be Long		July 15, 1963
It's All Too Much		Mid June, 1967
It's Only Love		Late May — Early June, 1965
I've Got A Feeling	Apple	Late January, 1969
I've Just Seen A Face		Late May — Early June, 1965
Julia		October 13, 1968
Kansas City/Hey Hey Hey Hey		Late September — Mid October, 1964
Komm, Gib Mir Deine Hand	Pathé Marconi, Paris	January 29, 1964
Lady Madonna		February 3-4, 1968
Let It Be (both versions)	Apple	Late January, 1969
LET IT BE (LP)	Apple	January, 1969 — January, 1970
Little Child		July 15, 1963
Long And Winding Road, The	Apple	Late January, 1969

Long, Long, Long		Std October 8, 1968
Long Tall Sally		Late February, 1964
Long Tall Sally — Live	Hollywood Bowl	August 23, 1964
LONG TALL SALLY (EP)		Late February, 1964
Love Me Do (both versions)		September 11, 1962
Love You Too		April, 1966
Lovely Rita		Std February 22, 1967
Lucy In The Sky With Diamonds		Std May 2, 1967
Maggie Mae	Apple	Late January, 1969
Magical Mystery Tour		April 25 — May 5, 1967
MAGICAL MYSTERY TOUR (EP)		End of April to End of September, 1967
Martha My Dear	Trident	Std October 4, 1968
Matchbox		Late February, 1964
Maxwell's Silver Hammer		Std July 9, 1969
Mean Mr. Mustard		Std July 24, 1969
Michelle		Mid October — Early November, 1965
Misery		February 11, 1963
Mr. Moonlight		Late September — Mid October, 1964
Money (That's What I Want)		July 15, 1963
Mother Nature's Son		August 9, 1968
Night Before, The		Early February — Early March, 1965
No Reply		Late September — Mid October, 1964
Norwegian Wood (This Bird Has Flown)		Mid October — Early November, 1965
Not A Second Time		July 15, 1963
Nowhere Man		Mid October — Early November, 1965
Ob-La-Di Ob-La-Da		Std July 2, 1968
Octopus's Garden		Std April 26, 1969
Oh! Darling		July, 1969
Old Brown Shoe		April, 1969
One After 909	Apple roof	January 30, 1969
Only A Northern Song		Mid February, 1968
P.S. I Love You		September 11, 1962
Paperback Writer	EMI Studio 3	April 16, 1966
Penny Lane		1st 2 weeks in January, 1967
Piggies		Std September 19, 1968
Please Mr. Postman		July 15, 1963
Please Please Me		November 26, 1962
PLEASE PLEASE ME (LP) (new titles)		February 11, 1963
Polythene Pam		Std July 28, 1969
Rain		Late April, 1966
Revolution		End of July, 1968
Revolution 1		June — July, 1968
Revolution 9		Std May 30, 1968
REVOLVER (LP)	EMI — Mainly No. 2 sometimes No. 3	Early April — Mid June, 1966
Rock And Roll Music		Late September — Mid October, 1964
Rocky Racoon		August 15, 1968
Roll Over Beethoven		July 15, 1963
Roll Over Beethoven — live	Hollywood Bowl	August 23, 1964

RUBBER SOUL		Mid October — Early November, 1965
Run For Your Life		Mid October — Early November, 1965
Sgt. Pepper's Lonely Hearts Club Band		Std February 1, 1967
Sgt. Pepper's Lonely Hearts Club Band (reprise)		Std March 17, 1967
SGT. PEPPER'S LONELY HEARTS CLUB BAND (LP)		December 10, 1966 — April 2, 1967
Savoy Truffle	Trident	Std October 3, 1968
Sexy Sadie		Std July 19, 1968
She Came In Through The Bathroom Window		Std July 25, 1969
She Loves You		July 1, 1963
She Loves You — Live	Hollywood Bowl	August 23, 1964
She Said She Said		April, 1966
She's A Woman		Early October, 1964
She's A Woman — live	Hollywood Bowl	August 30, 1965
She's Leaving Home		Std March 17, 1967
Sie Liebt Dich	Pathé Marconi, Paris	January 29, 1964
Slow Down		Late February, 1964
Something — backing	No. 1	May 2, 1969
— vocal		July 12, 1969
Strawberry Fields Forever		December, 1966
Sun King		Std July 24, 1969
Taste Of Honey, A		February 11, 1963
Taxman		April, 1966
Tell Me What You See		May 10-11, 1965
Tell Me Why		March — April, 1964
Thank You Girl		March 4, 1963
There's A Place		February 11, 1963
Things We Said Today		June 1-3, 1964
Things We Said Today — live	Hollywood Bowl	August 23, 1964
Think For Yourself		Mid October — Early November, 1965
This Boy		October 19, 1963
Ticket To Ride		February, 1965
Ticket To Ride — live	Hollywood Bowl	August 30, 1965
Till There Was You		July 15, 1963
Tomorrow Never Knows		Std April 6, 1966
Twist And Shout		February 11, 1963
Twist And Shout — live 1	Hollywood Bowl	August 23, 1964
Twist And Shout — live 2	Hollywood Bowl	August 30, 1965
Two Of Us	Apple	Late January, 1969
Wait		Mid October — Early November, 1965
We Can Work It Out		Early November, 1965
What Goes On		Mid October — Early November, 1965
What You're Doing		Late September — Mid October, 1964
When I Get Home		June 1-3, 1964
When I'm Sixty Four		Std December 10, 1966
While My Guitar Gently Weeps		Std July 25, 1968
Why Don't We Do It In The Road		October 10, 1968
Wild Honey Pie		Std August 20, 1968
With A Little Help From My Friends		Std March 30, 1967
Within You, Without You		Std March 15, 1967
WITH THE BEATLES (LP)		July 15, 1963

Word, The		Mid October — Mid November, 1965
Words Of Love		Late September — Mid October, 1964
Yellow Submarine		June, 1966
YELLOW SUBMARINE (LP)		Mid June, 1967 and Mid February,
(new titles)		1968
Yer Blues		Std August 13, 1968
Yes It Is		February, 1965
Yesterday		Late May — Early June, 1965
You Can't Do That — backing	Pathé Marconi, Paris	January 29, 1964
— vocal	EMI	February 25, 1964
You Know My Name (Look Up		
The Number)		Early 1967
You Like Me Too Much		May 10-11, 1965
You Never Give Me Your		
Money		Std July 15, 1969
You Really Got A Hold On Me		July 15, 1963
You Won't See Me		Mid October — Early November, 1965
Your Mother Should Know	Chappell Studios, New Bond Street	Std August 22, 1967
You're Going To Lose That Girl		Early February — Early March, 1965
You've Got To Hide Your Love Away		Early February — Early March, 1965

THE BEATLES' CHRISTMAS RECORDS

By the Summer of 1963, The Beatles had sold over two million records in Britain and their fan club membership had reached 25,000. As a "thank you" to their British fans, The Beatles wanted to give them something special for the Christmas of 1963, and it was decided to make a special record with a Christmas message for all the fan club members. By 1964, the fan club membership had reached 65,000, the largest for any fan club, and the Christmas message was continued for this year and every year up to 1970. From 1963 to 1967 The Beatles recorded the Christmas message together, but in 1968 and 1969 each Beatle recorded his segment separately, and they were edited together by Kenny Everett. In 1970, The Beatles, as a group, had virtually split up, and no Christmas message was recorded, so all seven previous messages were put together on one hard vinyl twelve inch disc, as opposed to the seven inch flexidiscs of the previous issues, for distribution to the fan club members for the last time. By Christmas 1971, The Beatles Fan Club had folded, along with *The Beatles Monthly* magazine which had included the Fan Club newsletter.

THE BEATLES CHRISTMAS RECORD *(5.00)*

LYN 492—December 6, 1963

The first Christmas message was recorded by The Beatles in EMI Studio No. 2 at Abbey Road, on October 17, 1963, and was produced by George Martin. As with all the seven inch records, it was a flexidisc made by Lyntone Recordings.

Good King Wenceslas	0.32
John Talking	1.14
Paul talking	1.24
Good King Wenceslas (John)	0.19
Ringo talking	0.25
Good King Wenceslas (Ringo)	0.14
George talking	0.32
Good King Wenceslas (George)	0.11
Rudolph The Red Nosed Ringo	0.19

ANOTHER BEATLES CHRISTMAS RECORD *(3.58)*

LYN 757—December 18, 1964

The second Christmas record was recorded between October 26-28, 1964, at EMI No. 2 Studios, with George Martin producing.

Jingle Bells	0.28
Paul talking	0.43
John talking	0.51
George talking	0.46
Ringo talking	1.04
Can You Wash Your Father's Shirts	0.12
Happy Christmas	0.14

THE BEATLES THIRD CHRISTMAS RECORD *(6.22)*

LYN 948—December 17, 1965

The third message was recorded on October 19, 1965, just after the group had completed work on the *Rubber Soul* album recordings, again with George Martin producing at EMI No. 2 studio. The front cover picture was taken by Robert Whitaker in the Manchester Studios of Granada Television, during the filming of The Beatles spectacular *The Music Of Lennon And McCartney*. Just after the photograph was taken, The Beatles performed *Day Tripper*.

Yesterday (all singing out of tune)	0.12
All talking	1.04
Happy Christmas (John)	0.30
Auld Lang Syne (all)	0.15
All talking	0.15
Same Old Song (John)	0.07
All talking	0.45
Auld Lang Syne (all)	0.20
All talking	0.35

Christmas Comes But Once A Year (all)	0.30
Yesterday/Happy Christmas (all)	1.59

THE BEATLES FOURTH CHRISTMAS RECORD — PANTOMIME: EVERYWHERE IT'S CHRISTMAS (6.38)

LYN 1145—December 16, 1966

This year, instead of the usual "thank you's" that The Beatles put into the Christmas messages, they changed the format and presented a rather "Goonish" pantomime. A special recording session was arranged for the record at Dick James Music headquarters in New Oxford Street, London, on November 25, 1966, with George Martin producing. This was the first double sided Beatles Xmas record.

A SIDE	(3.05)
Everywhere It's Christmas (all)	0.32
Orowanyna (Intro/Paul, all singing)	0.48
A Rare Cheese (Intro/Ringo, George & John)	0.28
The Feast (all)	0.49
The Loyal Toast (Intro/George, Toast/Ringo)	0.28

B SIDE	(3.33)
Podgy The Bear & Jasper (Intro/Paul, Podgy/John, Jasper/George)	0.51
Felpin Mansions (The Count/John, Butler/Ringo)	1.06
Please Don't Bring Your Banjo Back (Paul, all)	0.42
Everywhere It's Christmas (all)	0.54

THE BEATLES FIFTH CHRISTMAS RECORD — CHRISTMAS TIME (IS HERE AGAIN) (6.09)

LYN 1360—December 15, 1967

For the fifth Beatles Christmas record, the boys continued with their "Goonish" pantomime formula of the previous year. They recorded the record on Tuesday, November 28, 1967, at EMI Studio No. 2, with George Martin producing for the last time, and with The Beatles recording the "Christmas Message" together for the last time. The applause used on the record was recorded on location in Dublin. The front cover design was by John and Ringo, with the back cover painting by Julian Lennon, John's son. This was a single sided flexidisc.

Christmas Time (Is Here Again) (Intro/John, all singing)	0.40
The boys arrive at BBC House (BBC Wise One/Victor Spinetti)	0.18
An Audition (John)	0.13
Tap Dancing (Ringo & Victor Spinetti)	0.16
Are You 13 Amp (Mal Evans)	0.06
Get One Of Those For Your Trousers (John)	0.15
Sir Gerald (Michael/Paul, Sir Gerald/John)	0.19
Christmas Time (Is Here Again)	0.12
Onto The Next Round & Introduction (George)	0.10
Plenty Of Jam Jars	0.36
Quiz Show (Quizmaster/John, Prizewinner/George)	0.30
Get One Of Those For Your Trousers	0.06
Theatre Hour (Ringo)	0.30
Christmas Time (Is Here Again)	0.49
They'd Like To Thank You... (George Martin & all)	0.14
When Christmas Time Is O'er (Organ/George Martin, Scottish Poet/John, Piano/John & Paul)	0.44

THE BEATLES SIXTH CHRISTMAS RECORD — CHRISTMAS 1968 (7.50)

LYN 1743/4—December 20, 1968

The Beatles recorded their individual pieces separately in November 1968 — John and Paul at their London homes, Ringo in Surrey and George in America, with Mal Evans and Tiny Tim. Some of the musical links were recorded during rehearsals for the *White Album* in George's Esher home. Kenny Everett edited the various tapes together, and is credited as producer on the sleeve. Kenny Everett started his musical career as a disc jockey on the pirate ship, Radio London, after which he joined the BBC Radio One team in 1967, achieving fame with his Saturday programme. He was sacked from the BBC, and joined London's Capitol Radio and eventually branched out into television, with his incredible *Kenny Everett Video Show* and later *The Kenny Everett Video Cassette Show*.

In 1981, he returned to BBC radio and BBC television.

A SIDE *(3.33)*
Ringo/Ob-La-Di 0.28
Happy Christmas, Happy New
Year (Paul) 1.01
link Helter Skelter 0.21
Yok And Jono (John — poem) 0.48
link 0.07
George from America (with
Mal Evans) 0.48

B SIDE *(4.17)*
Ringo Starr 0.37
Introduction/Ringo 0.15
Happy Christmas, Happy New
Year (Paul) 0.11
Once Upon A Pool Table (John
— poem) 0.43
George & Tiny Tim 0.54
Nowhere Man (Tiny Tim) 1.16
Ending 0.21

**THE BEATLES SEVENTH CHRISTMAS
RECORD — HAPPY CHRISTMAS 1969 *(7.40)***

LYN 1970/1—December 19, 1969

The final flexidisc Christmas record was again recorded separately by The Beatles: John and Yoko at Ascot in Berkshire, Ringo from Weybridge in Surrey, Paul from St. John's Wood in London, and George from Apple in the West End of London, all during the Autumn of 1969. The tapes were again put together by Kenny Everett, who is credited on the sleeve under his real name of Maurice Cole. The front cover sleeve photograph was taken by Ringo, with the back cover drawing by Ringo's son Zak.

A SIDE *(3.33)*
Happy Christmas (Ringo) 0.12
John & Yoko talking 0.37
Wonderful Christmas (George) 0.20
Ringo talking 0.19
link: The End 0.11
John & Yoko talking 0.33
This Is To Wish All A Merry
Merry Christmas (Paul) 0.44
Paul talking 0.14
This Is To Wish You Reprise 0.26

B SIDE *(4;.07)*
John & Yoko talking (including
John singing) 1.14
Happy Christmas (John & Yoko
à la Two Virgins) 1.25
Happy Christmas/Magic Christian
(Ringo) 0.12
Ringo talking 0.07
John & Yoko talking 1.09

**FROM THEN TO YOU — THE BEATLES
CHRISTMAS RECORD 1970**

*Apple LYN 2154—December 18, 1970
(UK release)*

THE BEATLES CHRISTMAS ALBUM

*Apple SBC 100—December 18, 1970
(US release)*

Wth no fresh recordings from The Beatles, the Fan Club in Britain put together a twelve inch album of all seven previous Christmas messages, with a sleeve showing the front covers of all the original sleeves of the seven inch flexidiscs. In America, where the flexidiscs had never been issued, the album was put out in a completely different, but far better sleeve.

A SIDE
The Beatles Christmas Record (1963) 5.00

Another Beatles Christmas Record
(1964)   3.58
The Beatles Third Christmas Record
(1965)   6.22
The Beatles Fourth Christmas Record
(1966)   6.38

B SIDE
Christmas Time (Is Here Again) (1967)   6.09
The Beatles Sixth Christmas Record
(1968)   7.50
The Beatles Seventh Christmas Record
(1969)   7.40

BIBLIOGRAPHY

This book could not have been compiled without researching other books for facts and information. The following is a bibliography of the books used for research, along with other Beatles books, which together constitute a definitive library for any Beatle fanatic.

Abbey Road Brian Southall (Patrick Stephens 1982)
The Album Cover Album Storm Thorgerson (Hipgnosis)/Roger Dean/Dominy Hamilton (Dragon's World Books 1977)
All Together Now Harry Castleman/Walter Podrazik (Pierian Press 1976)
All You Needed Was Love John Blake (Hamlyn 1981)
All You Need Is Ears George Martin/Jerome Hernsby (Macmillan London Ltd. 1979)
Apple To The Core Peter McCabe/Robert D. Schonfeld (Martin Brian & O'Keefe Ltd. 1972/Sphere Books Ltd. 1973)
As Time Goes By Derek Taylor (Davis-Poynter Ltd. 1973/Sphere Books Ltd. 1974)
The Beatles Geoffrey Stokes (W.H. Allen & Co. Ltd. 1980)
The Beatles: A Collection Robert & Cindy DelBuono (RobCin Associates 1982)
The Beatles Again Harry Castleman/Walter Podrazik (Pierian Press 1977)
The Beatles Album File And Complete Discography Jeff Russell (Blandford Press 1982)
Beatles Anniversary Bill Harry (Colourgold Ltd. 1982)
The Beatles: An Illustrated Record Roy Carr/Tony Tyler (New English Library 1975/1978/1980)
The Beatles Apart Bob Woffinden (Proteus Books 1981)
The Beatles At The Beeb Kevin Howlett (British Broadcasting Corporation 1982)
The Beatles: A To Z Goldie Friede/Robin Titone/Sue Weiner (Methuen 1980)
The Beatles: The Authorized Biography Hunter Davis (William Heineman Ltd. 1968)
The Beatles Concerted Efforts Jan Van De Bunt (Beatles Unlimited 1979)
The Beatles Discography Mitchell McGreary (Ticket To Ryde Ltd. 1975)
The Beatles Down Under Glenn A. Baker, with Roger Delernia (Wild & Wooley 1982)
The Beatles' England David Bacon/Norman Maslov (Columbus Books 1982)
The Beatles Forever Nicholas Schaffner (McGraw-Hill Book Co. 1977)
The Beatles Forever Helen Spence (Colour Library International Ltd. 1981)
The Beatles For The Record No author (Stafford Pemberton Publishing 1981)
The Beatles In Help! Al Hine (Mayflower Books Ltd. 1965)
The Beatles Monthly Books Various — edited by Johnny Dean (Beat Publications Ltd. 1963-9/Re-published from 1976)
The Beatles Illustrated Lyrics edited by Alan Aldridge (MacDonald Unit 75 1969)
The Beatles Illustrated Lyrics Volume 2 edited by Alan Aldridge (BPC Publishing Ltd. 1971)
The Beatles In Their Own Words Miles (Omnibus Press 1978)
The Beatles Complete Lyrics (Futura Publications 1974)
The Beatles On Record Mark Wallgren (Simon & Schuster 1982)
The Beatles' Who's Who Bill Harry (Aurum Press 1982)
The Beatles: Yesterday And Today Rochelle Larkin (Scholastic Book Services 1974)
Behind The Beatles Songs Philip Cowan (Polytantric Press 1978)
The Book Of Golden Discs Joseph Murrells (Barrie & Jenkins Ltd. 1974/1978)
The Book Of Rock Lists Dave Marsh/Kevin Stein (Sidgwick & Jackson 1981)
The Bootleg Bible (Hot Wacks Book IX) (Babylon Books 1981)
British Beat Chris May/Tim Philips (Sociopack Pub. 1974)
British Record Charts 1955-1979 Tony Jasper (Futura Publications 1979)
A Cellarful Of Noise Brian Epstein (Souvenir Press 1964/New English Library 1965/1981)
Chart File 1982 Barry Lazell/Dafydd Rees/Alan Jones (Virgin Books 1982)
A Day In The Life Tom Schultheiss (Pierian Press 1980)
Dig It: The Beatles Bootleg Book Volume One Koos Janssen/Erik M. Bakker (Rock Book Centre Publications 1974)
Encyclopedia Of Rock Volumes 1-3 edited by Phil Hardy/Dave Laing (Panthar Books Ltd.1976)
Facts About A Pop Group (Wings) David Gelly (G. Whizzard Pub. Ltd. 1976)
George Harrison Yesterday And Today Ross Michaels (Flash Books 1977)
The Gimmix Book Of Records Frank Goldman/Klaus Hiltscher (Virgin Books 1981)
Grapefruit Yoko Ono (Peter Owen Ltd. 1964/Sphere Books 1971)
Growing Up With The Beatles Ron Schaumberg (Pyramid Books 1976/G.P. Putnam's Sons 1980)
The Guinness Book Of British Hit Singles Jo & Tim Rice/Paul Gambaccini/Mike Read (Guinness Superlatives Ltd. 1977/1979/1981)

The Guinness Book Of Records Norris McWhirter (Guinness Superlatives Ltd. yearly)

'Hands Across The Water' Wings Tour USA Hipgnosis (Paper Tiger 1978)

A Hard Day's Night John Burke (Pan Books Ltd. 1964)

The Illustrated Book Of Rock Records Barry Lazell/Dafydd Rees (Virgin Books 1982)

The Illustrated History Of The Rock Album Cover Angie Errigo (Octopus Books Ltd. 1979)

The Illustrated NME Encyclopedia of Rock Nick Logan/Bob Woffinden (Hamlyn Publishing Ltd. 1976)

I Me Mine George Harrison (Genesis Publications 1980/W.H. Allen 1982)

In The Footsteps Of The Beatles Mike Evans/Ron Jones (Merseyside County Council 1982)

The Joel Whitburn Record Research Series Joel Whitburn (Record Research Inc. yearly)

John Lennon In His Own Words Miles (Omnibus Press 1980)

John Lennon In His Own Write John Lennon (Jonathan Cape 1964)

John Lennon 1940-1980 A Biography Ray Connolly (Fontana Books 1981)

John Lennon: One Day At A Time, A Personal Biography Of The Seventies Anthony Fawcett (New English Library 1976)

The John Lennon Story George Tremlett (Futura Pub. Ltd. 1976)

Lennon And McCartney Malcolm Doney (Midas Books 1981)

Lennon Remembers edited by Jann Wenner (Talmy, Franklin Ltd. 1972)

The Lennon Tapes Andy Peebles (BBC Publications 1981)

Linda's Pictures: A Collection Of Photographs Linda McCartney (Jonathan Cape 1976)

The Longest Cocktail Party Richard DiLello (Charisma Books 1973)

Love Me Do — The Beatles Progress Michael Braun (Penguin Books Ltd. 1964)

The Man Who Gave The Beatles Away Allan Williams/William Marshall (Elm Tree Books Ltd. 1975)

Mersey Beat: The Beginning Of The Beatles edited by Bill Harry (Omnibus Press 1977)

The NME Book Of Rock edited by Nick Logan/Rob Finnis (W.H. Allen Ltd. 1975)

New Rock Record Terry Hounsome/Tim Chambre (Blandford Press 1981)

Nothing To Get Hung About Mike Evans (City Of Liverpool Public Relations Office 1974)

Paul McCartney And Wings Tony Jasper (Octopus Books Ltd. 1977)

Paul McCartney And Wings Jeremy Pascall (Phoebus Publishing Co. 1977)

Paul McCartney In His Own Words Paul Gambaccini (Omnibus Press Ltd. 1976)

The Paul McCartney Story George Tremlett (Futura Pub. Ltd. 1975)

The Penguin John Lennon John Lennon (Penguin Books Ltd. 1966)

The Playboy Interviews With John Lennon And Yoko Ono conducted by David Sheff (New English Library 1981)

P.S. We Love You: The Beatles Story 1962-3 Tony Barrow (Mirror Books Ltd. 1982)

Record Collector various authors/editor — Johnny Dean (Diamond Publishing Group Ltd. 1979 to the present)

Rock Family Trees Pete Frame (Omnibus Press 1979)

Rock File Pete & Annie Fowler/editor — Charlie Gillett (Pictorial Presentations Ltd. 1972)

Rock File 2 as above with various other authors (Panther Books Ltd. 1974)

Rock File 3 as above with various other authors (Panther Books Ltd. 1975)

Rock File 4 as above with various other authors (Panther Books Ltd. 1976)

Rock File 5 as above with various other authors (Panther Books Ltd. 1978)

Rock Legends: Beatles Mike Davies/John Tobler (SB Publishing & Promotions Ltd. 1982)

Rock'n'Roll Times Jurgen Vollmer (Google Plex Books 1981)

The Rolling Stones: An Illustrated Record Roy Carr (New English Library 1976)

Shout: The True Story Of The Beatles Philip Norman (Hamish Hamilton Ltd. 1981)

A Spaniard In The Works John Lennon (Jonathan Cape Ltd. 1965)

The Story of Pop various/editor — Jeremy Pascall (Phoebus Publishing Co./BBC 1973/4/5)

Strawberry Fields Forever: John Lennon Revisited Vic Garbarini/Brian Cullman/Barbara Graustark (Bantam Books Inc. 1980)

Thank U Very Much: Mike McCartney's Family Album Mike McCartney (Granada Publishing Ltd. 1982)

A Twist Of Lennon Cynthia Lennon (W.H. Allen & Co. Ltd. 1978)

With The Beatles: The Historic Photographs Of Dezo Hoffman Dezo Hoffman (Omnibus Press 1982)

Who's Who In Rock William York (Omnibus Press 1982)

Yellow Submarine Lee Minoff/Al Brodax/Jack Mendelsohn/Erich Segal (New English Library 1968)

Index

This index refers only to the Beatles' official releases, and therefore does not include bootleg album titles or unreleased song titles. Albums and EPs are listed in UPPER CASE, with reference to the first page of entry, while page references to song titles (in the main section of the book) may be repeated, where songs appear on a page more than once.